MFA HIGHLIGHTS arts of japan

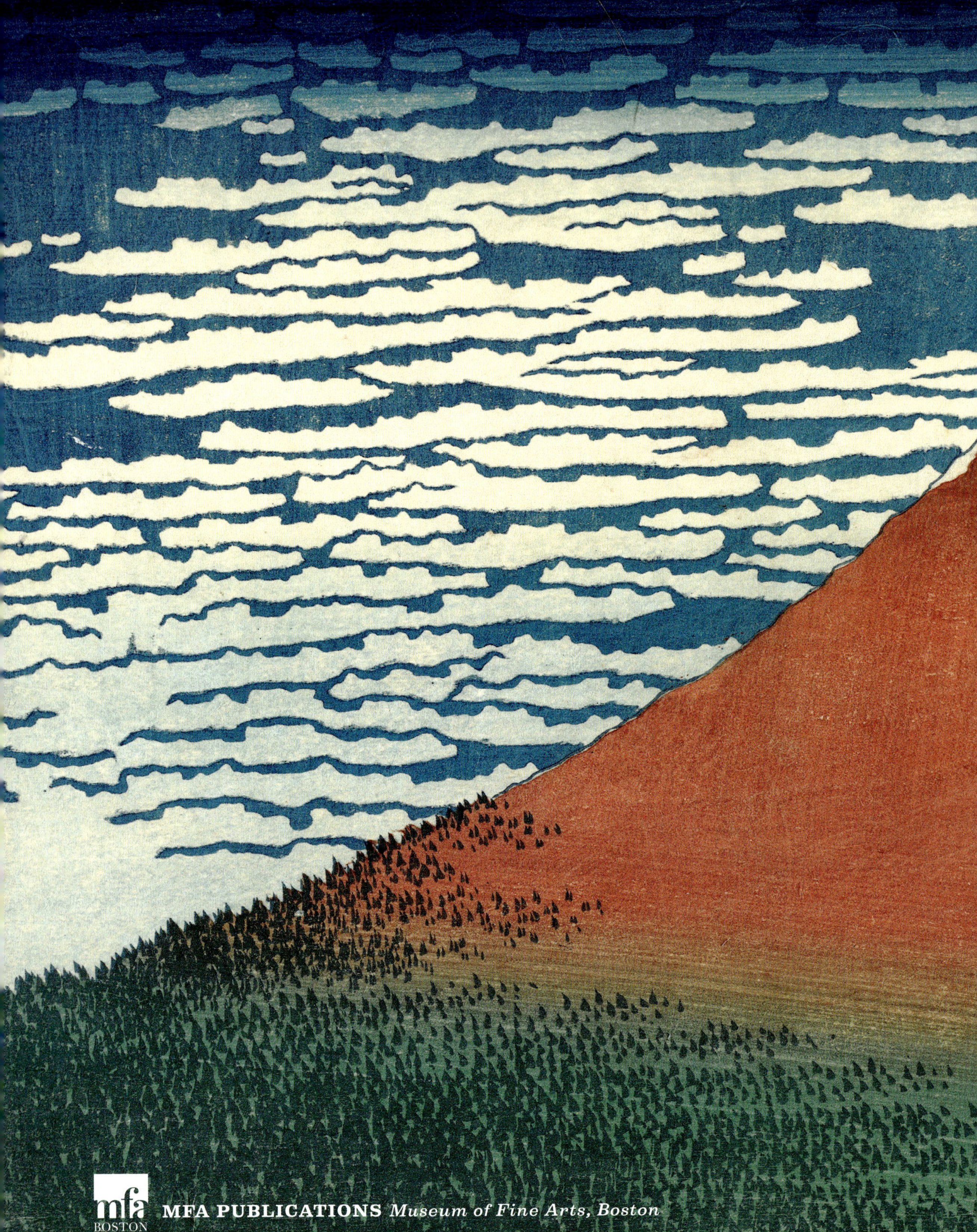

mfa BOSTON **MFA PUBLICATIONS** *Museum of Fine Arts, Boston*

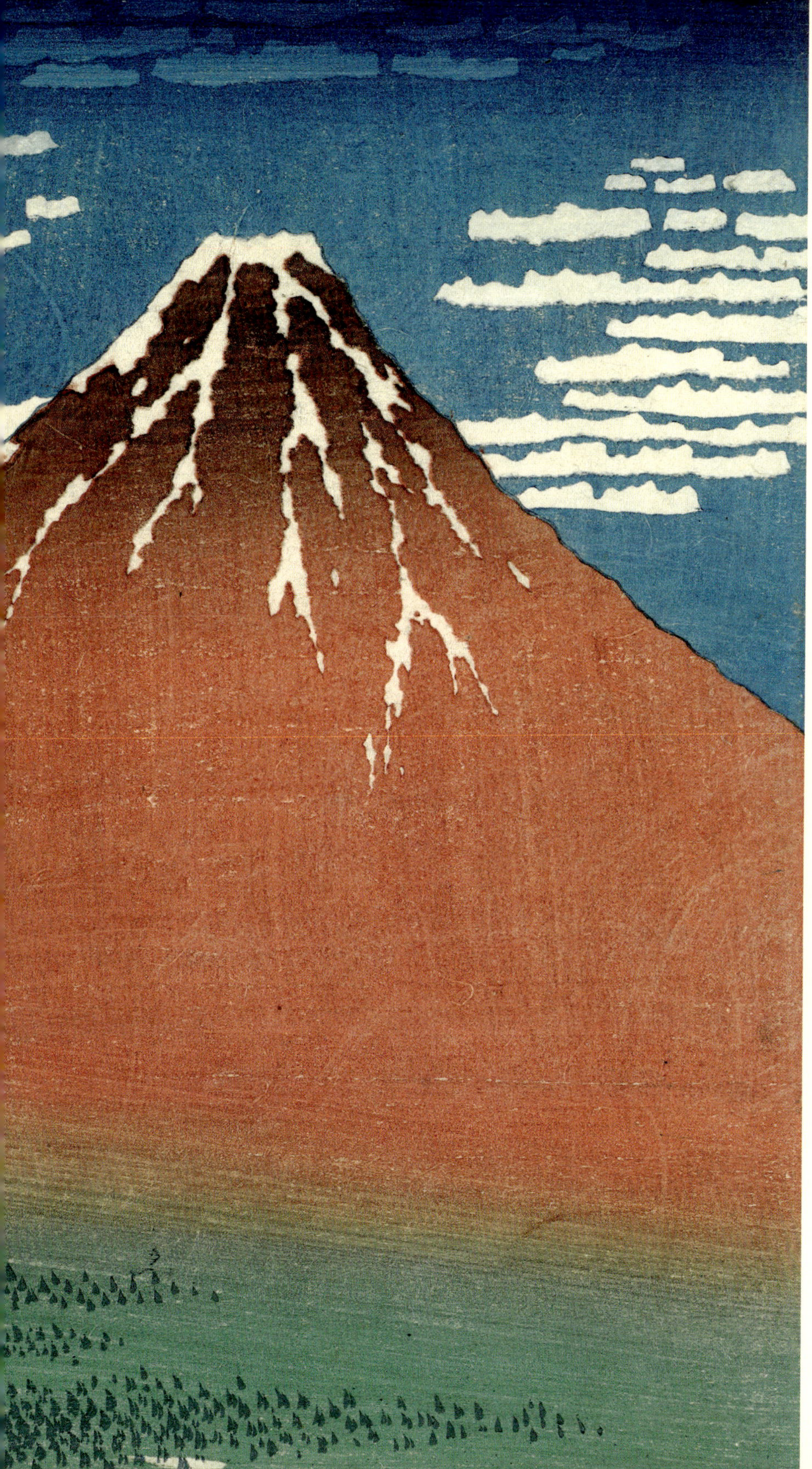

MFA HIGHLIGHTS arts of japan

Anne Nishimura Morse, Sarah E. Thompson, Joe Earle, and Rachel Saunders

Frontispiece: Detail from Katsushika Hokusai, *Fine Wind, Clear Weather*, about 1830–31 (p. 173)

MFA Publications
Museum of Fine Arts, Boston
465 Huntington Avenue
Boston, Massachusetts 02115
www.mfa.org/publications

Library of Congress Control Number: 2008932606
ISBN 978-0-87846-714-3

While the objects in this publication necessarily represent only a small portion of the MFA's holdings, the Museum is proud to be a leader within the American museum community in sharing the objects in its collection via its Web site. Currently, information about more than 330,000 objects is available to the public worldwide. To learn more about the MFA's collections, including provenance, publication, and exhibition history, kindly visit *www.mfa.org/collections*.

For a complete listing of MFA publications, please contact the publisher at the address at left, or call 617 369 3438.

All photographs are by the Imaging Studios, Museum of Fine Arts, Boston, unless otherwise noted.

Grateful acknowledgment is made to the copyright holders for permission to reproduce the following works:

Akiyama, *Metavoid 4*, © Akiyama Yō

Moriyama, *Store Opening Flowers*, © Daidō Moriyama

Murakami, *If the Double Helix Wakes Up . . .*, Courtesy of Marianne Boesky Gallery, New York, © 2002 Takashi Murakami / Kaikai Kiki Co., Ltd. All Rights Reserved

Sugimoto, *Radio City Music Hall, New York*, © Hiroshi Sugimoto

The poems translated by Edwin A. Cranston (on pp. 93 and 115) will appear in vol. 3 of *A Waka Anthology*, forthcoming from Stanford University Press, and are reprinted here by permission.

Manuscript edited by Sarah McGaughey Tremblay and Melanie B. D. Klein
Designed and produced by Terry McAweeney
Series design by Lucinda Hitchcock
Printed and bound at CS Graphics PTE LTD, Singapore

Trade distribution:
D.A.P. / Distributed Art Publishers
155 Sixth Avenue, 2nd floor
New York, New York 10013
Tel. 212 627 1999 Fax 212 627 9484

FIRST EDITION
Printed in Singapore
This book was printed on acid-free paper.

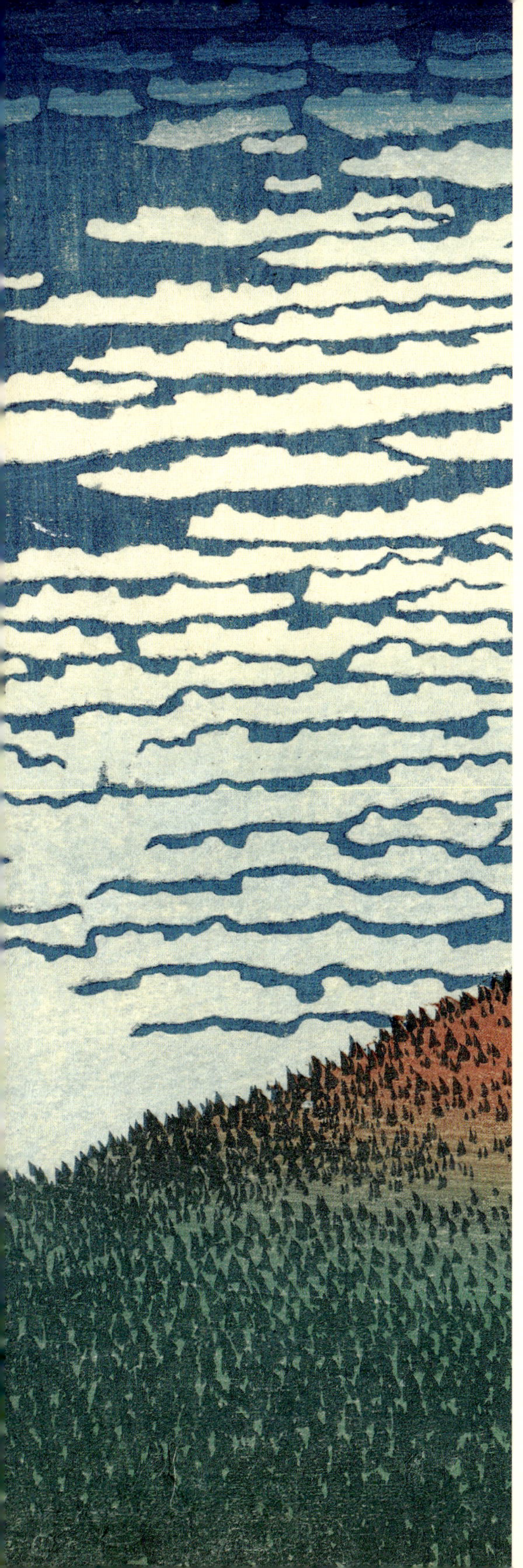

Contents

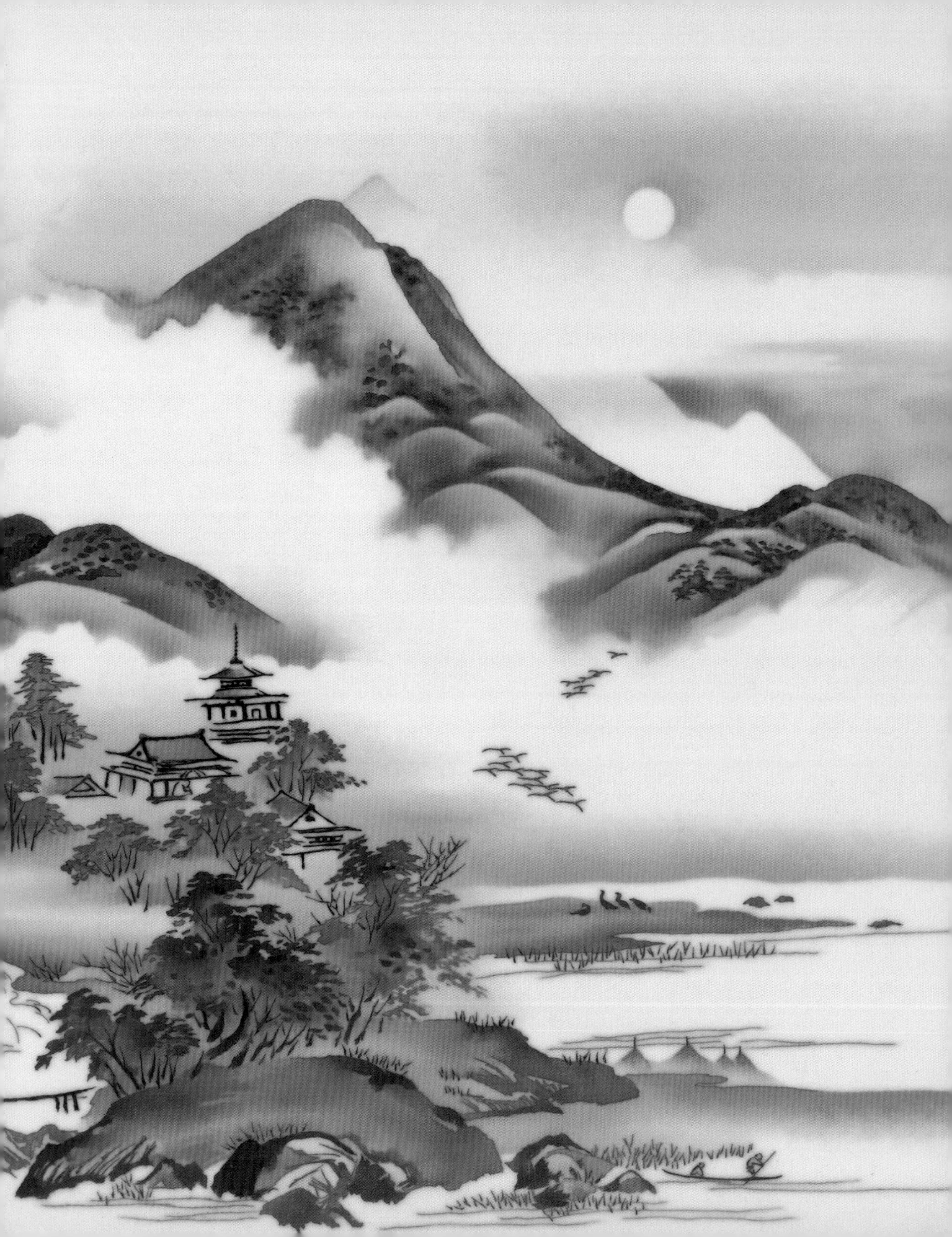

Director's Foreword

Art is for everyone, and it is in this spirit that the MFA Highlights series was conceived. The series introduces some of the greatest works of art in a manner that is both approachable and stimulating. Each volume focuses on an individual collection, allowing fascinating themes — both visual and textual — to emerge. We aim, over time, to represent every one of the Museum's major collections in the Highlights series, thus forming a library that will be a wonderful resource for the understanding and enjoyment of world art.

It is our goal to make the Museum's artworks accessible by every means possible. We hope that each volume of MFA Highlights will help you to know and understand our encyclopedic collections and to make your own discoveries among their riches.

Malcolm Rogers
Ann and Graham Gund Director
Museum of Fine Arts, Boston

Acknowledgments

In the late nineteenth century, supporters of the Museum of Fine Arts, Boston, had the foresight and passion to develop the finest holdings of Japanese art in the West. Although the collection is by no means comprehensive, new generations of donors have ensured that it continues to reflect the diversity of Japan's art and the dynamism of its culture. Not surprisingly, narrowing down the selection for this Highlights book was a challenge, but our goal was to present the breadth of the Museum's Japanese collection and to introduce some of our recent acquisitions. We hope that readers who are interested in learning more will consult the many other MFA publications that explore particular genres of Japanese art.

We would like to express our appreciation to Malcolm Rogers, Ann and Graham Gund Director, and Katherine Getchell, Deputy Director, for their commitment to making the Museum's collections accessible through exhibitions and publications. Many individuals collaborated in the development and production of this book. The curatorial team of Joe Earle, formerly Matsutarō Shōriki Chair of the Art of Asia, Oceania, and Africa; Sarah E. Thompson, Assistant Curator for Japanese Prints; and Rachel Saunders, Research Associate, Japanese Art; and I wrote the section introductions. The individual entries were completed by the members of this team according to our areas of specialty and interest.

Japanese art has been acquired by several other departments at the MFA, and we thank our colleagues Cheryl Brutvan, former Robert L. Beal and Enid L. and Bruce A. Beal Curator of Contemporary Art; Anne E. Havinga, Estrellita and Yousuf Karsh Senior Curator of Photographs; and Pamela Parmal, David and Roberta Logie Curator of Textile and Fashion Arts, for making their objects available for this publication. We would also like to thank the many scholars who have shared their expertise with us, in particular those who, under the leadership of Professor Tsuji Nobuo, participated in the collaborative project to recatalogue the MFA's collections of Japanese paintings, sculpture, and decorative arts with the support of the Kajima Foundation of the Arts. The Museum would like to acknowledge the support of the donors who have funded the ongoing cataloguing of the Japanese prints and illustrated books, including State Street Corporation. In addition we are grateful to Nagasaki Iwao, Kadowaki Yukie, Izumi Mari, Meghan Melvin, and Richard Newman for their insights pertaining to particular objects.

In the Art of Asia, Oceania, and Africa, we were given great assistance by Angie Simonds, who helped manage the project, and Nozomi Naoi and Miki Morita, who helped develop the object files. Over the years, our colleagues in Asian Conservation have played important roles in conserving and preserving the collection; we appreciate the specialized knowledge that they bring to our understanding of the artworks. Thank you also to the members of the Imaging Studios—Michael Gould, Greg Heins, David Mathews, Jared Medeiros, and Jennifer Riley—who so ably provided the photography for this publication.

In MFA Publications and beyond, we extend our gratitude to Mark Polizzotti for his oversight of the project, Sarah McGaughey Tremblay for her thorough and patient editing, Melanie B. D. Klein for her help with the manuscript editing, Julia Gaviria for her careful proofreading, Terry McAweeney for her beautiful design for the book, and Jodi Simpson and Sheila Gafvert for their production assistance.

We would also like to acknowledge the support of the Toshiba International Foundation, which made possible the photography and research assistance for this project.

Anne Nishimura Morse
William and Helen Pounds Senior Curator of Japanese Art
Art of Asia, Oceania, and Africa

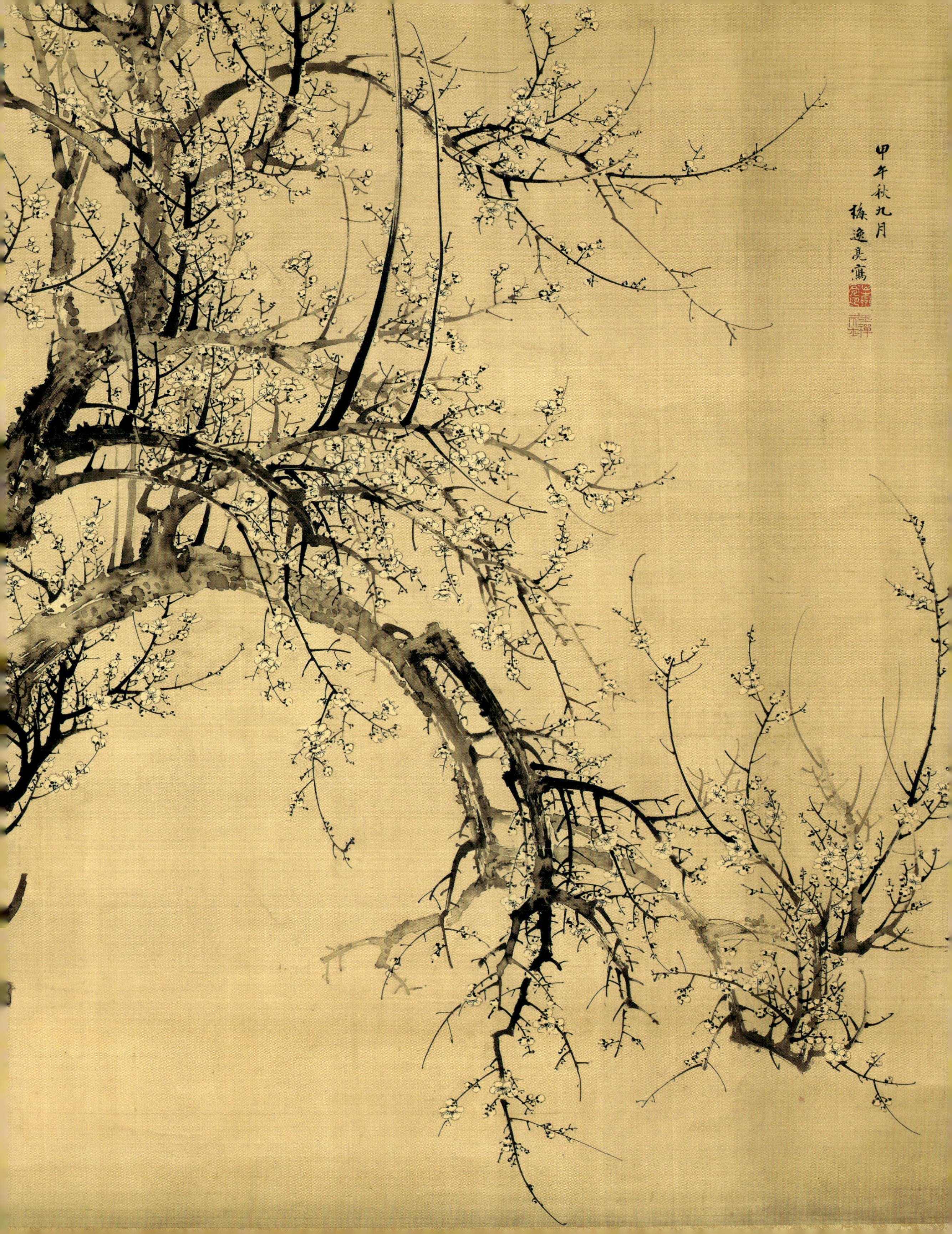
甲午秋九月
梅逸亮寫

Note to the Reader

Names

All Japanese and Chinese names appear in traditional style, with surnames preceding personal names (or in some cases, artistic names). For Japanese individuals active prior to the Meiji era (1868–1912), subsequent mentions use the personal or artistic name. For artists and individuals active in the Meiji era and later, the surname or the personal (or artistic) name may be used, depending on the convention that has developed in each case.

Periods and Eras

The Japanese followed a lunar calendar until 1873. Therefore, period and era years may overlap according to the Gregorian calendar.

late Asuka period	662–710 C.E.
Nara period	710–794
Heian period	794–1185
Kamakura period	1185–1333
Nanbokuchō period	1333–1392
Muromachi period	1392–1568
Momoyama period	1568–1615
Edo period	1615–1868
Meiji era	1868–1912
Taishō era	1912–1926
Shōwa era	1926–1989
Heisei era	1989–

Painting Formats

Japanese handscrolls, which often include written narratives explaining the illustrations, are read from right to left. Pairs of screens are also meant to be viewed in this order. In this book, when the design has necessitated that a pair of screens be illustrated one above the other, the right one is shown on top.

Figure Illustrations

Many of the figure illustrations in the chapter introductions are details of artworks that appear later in the chapter. The pages on which the full images and identifying information can be found are noted in the Figure Illustrations list.

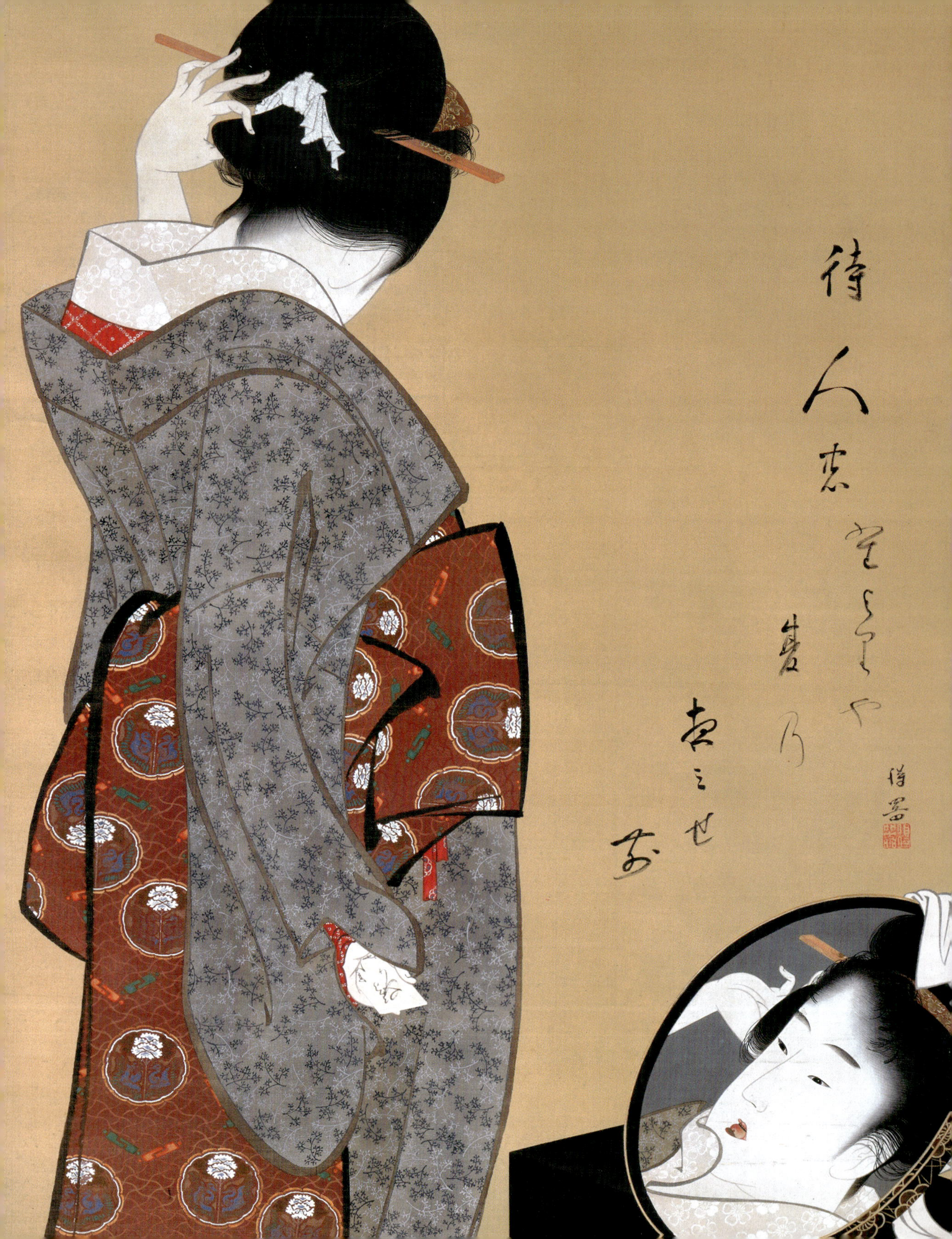

Japanese Art: Evolving Definitions

Anne Nishimura Morse

> Let us conclude more specifically with Japanese art, recalling that its essential characteristics are asymmetry, style, and color—as well as inventiveness and imagination in transforming nature (of which their knowledge is deep and scholarly) and bending it to the expressive imperatives of art. Let us recall the sense of perfectly balanced color contrasts, which allow Japanese artists to explore the most intense effects. Let us recall the dazzling richness of their painted compositions, their search for harmony in form and ornamentation. . . .
>
> –Ernest Chesneau, "L'Art Japonais"

Until 1873, when the Japanese government presented exhibits of ceramics, lacquer, and textiles at the International Exposition in Vienna, the Japanese had no words in their language to express the concepts of "fine arts" or "decorative arts," and certainly not of a national art, of "Japanese art." The country had enjoyed a history of more than fifteen hundred years of creating remarkable images—painted, printed, and sculpted—and producing exquisite utilitarian objects. Yet only painters and calligraphers were accorded a status comparable to that of artists in the West. The individuals who produced the monumental Buddhist images enshrined in temples throughout the land were not thought of as "sculptors"; they were *busshi*, or Buddhist masters. Artists who captured the pleasures of urban life, such as the celebrated Katsushika Hokusai, were considered "skilled craftsmen." They might have created inventive hanging scrolls for viewers' delight, but they had also painted everyday objects, including lanterns, banners, and textile gift covers. Furthermore, Japan boasted a long tradition of schools of connoisseurs who had pronounced on the authenticity of individual works, and tea masters who had articulated their own preferences in the modes of display for objects. These men had long discriminated between paintings of Chinese and Japanese origin, elevating objects that had been imported from the

fig. 1 **Katsushika Hokusai was heralded as a "genius" in the West for his inventive designs. In this painting, the artist reveals the face of the standing woman in the surface of the mirror.**

continent. But it was not until Japan was forced to abandon its three-hundred-year policy of seclusion and confront the West, after the opening of its ports in 1854, that the Japanese felt a need to develop a history of Japanese art that would systematically examine the achievements of a particular artist in the context of his or her own time, or ascribe stylistic and cultural characterizations to a particular era.[1] The creation of this history was the result of a dynamic dialogue between Japan and the West that occurred during the period of Japan's rapid modernization in the second half of the nineteenth century—and in fact, the Museum of Fine Arts, Boston, and its curators were central players in this process.

Japan and the West: A Dialogue Shaping the Concept of Art

The earliest attempts to produce a systematic history of Japanese art took place in Europe. By the late eighteenth century, the French had been able to procure only a limited number of woodblock prints and highly coveted lacquers and porcelains through the Dutch trading post on the island of Deshima in Nagasaki harbor. But following the conclusion of a trade treaty between Japan and France in 1858, works of Japanese art quickly became more available. By the mid-1860s, shops in the fashionable Paris neighborhood around rue de Rivoli offered prints and decorative objects for sale, and members of the intelligentsia became enamored of the images of urban pleasures and famous scenic places from the cluster of "mysterious islands, thrown by violent volcanic eruptions to the edge of the Far Eastern seas."[2] Among the early enthusiasts for the "new Japanese aesthetic" were the nineteenth-century writers Charles Baudelaire and Emile Zola, and the painters Edouard Manet and James Abbott McNeill Whistler.

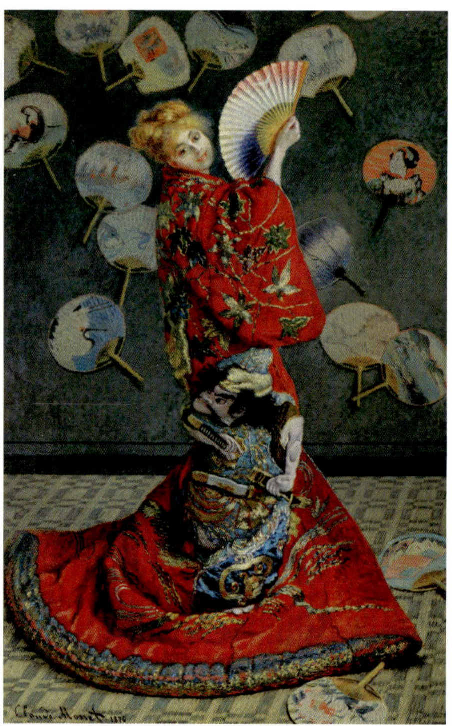

fig. 2 Like many Impressionists, Claude Monet was enthralled by "things Japanese." He depicted his wife dressed in a Kabuki costume and surrounded by fans decorated with Japanese woodblock prints.

The critic Ernest Chesneau described the new visual modes presented by the works that so

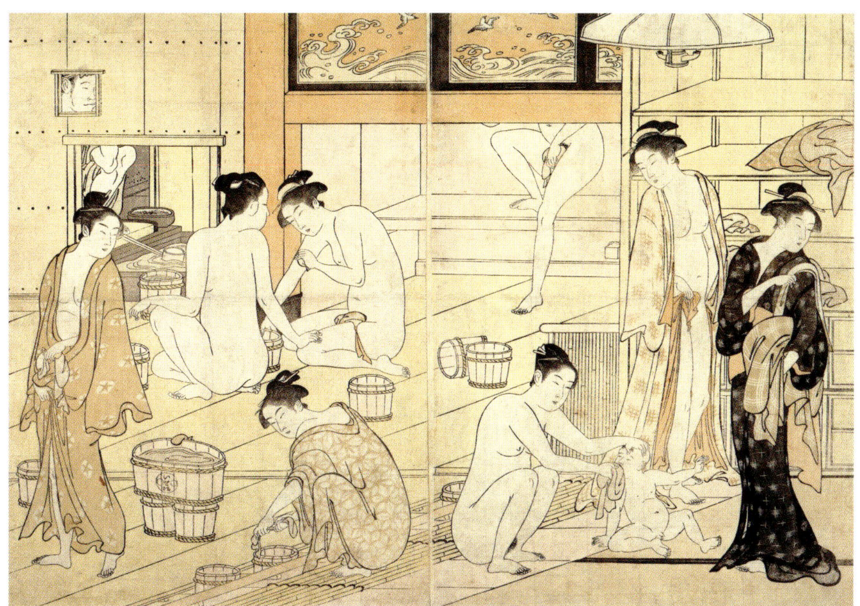

fig. 3 **Edgar Degas received inspiration for his own paintings of bathers from Japanese woodblock prints. This diptych by the eighteenth-century artist Torii Kiyonaga once hung over his bed.**

enthralled the French in an address to the Union des Beaux-Arts Appliqués á l'Industrie in 1869. As quoted at the beginning of this essay, Chesneau remarked on the bold asymmetry of forms and the contrasts of bright colors found in Japanese art. Later, others would go so far as to proclaim that the Japanese possessed a particular genius for design, as if this were something inborn. Painters such as Claude Monet and Edgar Degas investigated the oblique angles and cropped compositions presented by woodblock prints. In Degas' numerous paintings of female nudes, there are strong resonances with the rare diptych entitled *Interior of a Bathhouse*, by Torii Kiyonaga, which once hung above the painter's bed. Indeed, for many nineteenth-century French artists, Japanese images provided affirmation for their decision to break from the traditions of classical art.

In 1882, responding to the enthusiasm for Japanese art in France, the critic Louis Gonse ventured to write a historical survey of Japanese art—one of the first of its kind in the world. Separate chapters were devoted to painting, architecture, sculpture, metalwork, lacquer, textiles, ceramics, and prints; much of the discussion centered around biographical details of individual artists. Gonse had no opportunity to travel to Japan, however, and was thus compelled to rely on notes provided by Japanese residents in Paris, men such as the dealer Wakai Kenzaburō. His direct experience with works of Japanese art was similarly limited. That same year, Gonse organized an exhibition of Japanese objects from Parisian collections. Featured were an eighteenth-century wooden statue of a tiger

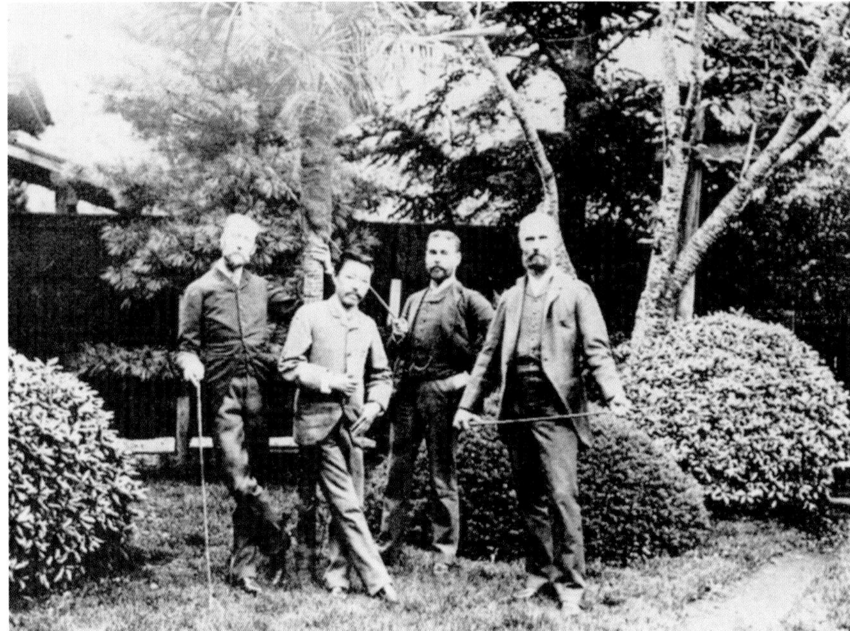

fig. 4 **The Bostonians Morse, Fenollosa, and Bigelow traveled throughout Japan with their translator and fellow connoisseur Okakura, searching out works of art.**

belonging to the actress Sarah Bernhardt and decorative objects offered by the dealer Siegfried Bing. Only a small number of paintings (said to be from the seventeenth century and later) were included. As early as 1867, the critic Zacharie Astruc had already questioned whether the French had been able to procure the best works, or whether they actually had acquired only those that the Japanese did not want. "Were there still masterpieces to be found in inland towns, far from the prying eyes of Europeans?"[3] Four men from Boston proved him to be correct.

Edward Sylvester Morse, Ernest Francisco Fenollosa, William Sturgis Bigelow, and Okakura Kakuzō were critical to the formation of the collections of Japanese art at the Museum of Fine Arts and were engaged in the discussions that led to the creation of a more systematic investigation of the arts of Japan. Invited to assume a position of zoology at Tokyo Imperial University by the Westward-looking Japanese government in 1877, Morse soon developed a passionate interest in ceramics. He collected more than five thousand examples from all over the country, in an attempt to chronicle all of the kilns that were in operation at that time; these works were later acquired by the Museum through subscription in 1892. Fenollosa also accepted a contract at Tokyo University, to lecture on Hegelian philosophy, in 1878, and later became a member of the Imperial Art Commission, charged with cataloging Japan's artistic heritage and reporting on art education abroad. His collection of over one thousand paint-

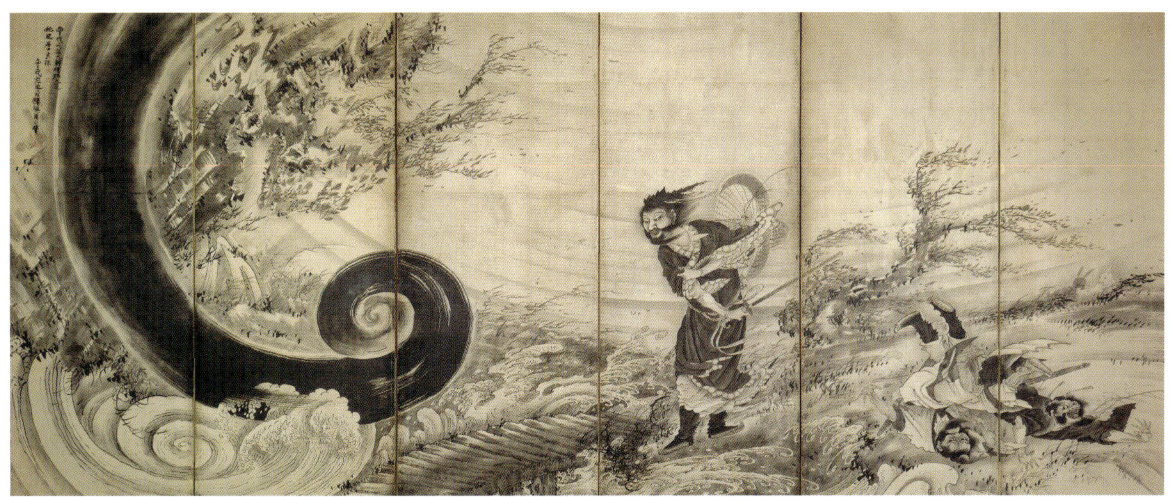

fig. 5 **Fenollosa and Bigelow were among the first to collect paintings by the eccentric eighteenth-century artist Soga Shōhaku. Today, Shōhaku is widely acclaimed for his humor and expressive brushwork.**

ings, which included such well-known masterpieces as the thirteenth-century *Illustrated Scrolls of the Events of the Heiji Era*, and *The Four Sages of Mount Shang* by the eighteenth-century eccentric painter Soga Shōhaku, was purchased by the Boston physician Charles Goddard Weld, who bequeathed it to the Museum in 1911.

William Sturgis Bigelow, a wealthy Bostonian who counted Henry Adams, Edith Wharton, and Theodore Roosevelt among his friends, abruptly forsook a career in medicine and took up residence in Japan from 1882 to 1889. Although he received some guidance from Fenollosa in his acquisition of screens and scrolls, Bigelow's interests were wide ranging (extending not only to painting but also to sculpture, swords, textiles, lacquer, and prints), and his pockets were deep. Over a forty-year period, he gave the Museum approximately four thousand paintings, countless objects, and more than thirty thousand woodblock prints. Okakura, one of Fenollosa's university students, came to Boston to serve as advisor and later curator in what was then the Department of Chinese and Japanese Art. During his tenure from 1904 to his death in 1913, he catalogued the holdings of the Museum and sought to strengthen areas that were underrepresented until then. Furthermore, Okakura was an eloquent spokesperson who wrote *The Book of Tea* for his Boston friends and "arouse[d] this community to a realizing since of what a wonderful treasure it possesses in the Japanese and Chinese collections."[4]

Unlike most nineteenth- and early-twentieth-century Europeans, Morse, Fenollosa, and Bigelow not only resided in Japan for extended periods but gained entrée to Japanese intellectual and cultural circles. Although Morse delivered lectures on evolution at Tokyo Imperial University—lectures that were attended by members of the imperial family, the prime minister, and other luminaries—he assumed the role of student in the field of ceramics. The respected antiquarian Ninagawa Noritane was generous with his expertise and gave Morse a foundation in identifying and dating pottery. Similarly, Fenollosa was able to develop his own eye for painting under the tutelage of some of the most celebrated Japanese artist-connoisseurs of the day—men such as Kano Eitoku Tatsunobu and Sumiyoshi Hirokata. From these members of the Kano and Tosa schools, the official painters to the ruling military and aristocratic classes, respectively, he inherited an appreciation for lineages of artists and a definite predilection for the art of the elite. (Today the Museum is particularly well known for its holdings of Kano-school painting.) Bigelow, for his part, became a leading supporter of the arts in Japan, providing financial assistance to impoverished contemporary artists and underwriting conservation work for treasures in some of the temples in the Nara region.

This group of Bostonians firmly believed in the importance of understanding Japanese art from what they supposed to be a traditional Japanese point of view. Fenollosa exasperatedly complained that in the West there had been no awareness of the Japanese pictorial tradition: "To [Westerners] paintings have been only a single species of curio, to be ranked under the name of kakemono, side by side with porcelain, tea-sets, lacquer. . . . An American, to whom I was once speaking of Japanese pictorial beauties, gave voice to the prevalent perplexity by exclaiming: 'But *do* the Japanese have pictures, *real pictures, you know, in gold frames?*'"[5] To address this misperception Fenollosa drafted *Epochs of Chinese and Japanese Art*, which was published in 1910 after his death.

In the introduction to his two-volume book, Fenollosa stated that his purpose was to "contribute first-hand material toward a real history of East Asiatic Art" by classifying works according to successive "creative periods" rather than by materials.[6] Thus, the chapters of his book bear titles such as "Graeco-Buddhist Art in Japan," "Mystical Buddhist Art in Japan," "Feudal Art in Japan," and "Idealistic Art in Japan." Despite Fenollosa's apparent pride in being able to transmit information about specific artists that was clearly provided by Japanese connoisseurs, the organization of the book emphasized Western notions of history and aesthetics, particularly the ideas of the German philosopher Georg Hegel. Mixed with his personal responses to individual objects and stylistic analogies to Western works of art—such as the "Parthenon torsos and the Venus of Milo"—Fenollosa attempted to craft a lofty, coherent narrative of the history of Japan and its art that would demonstrate to Europe and the United States the universality of human aspirations, in the East and West. Later, Okakura, in his

Ideals of the East, adopted a similar historical model but placed particular emphasis on Buddhist paintings and sculptures. He believed that these works possessed a spirituality that not only transcended time but embodied a sensibility unique to the Japanese. Many of these characterizations by Fenollosa and Okakura came to be widely accepted by the Japanese themselves.

Writing in the late nineteenth and early twentieth centuries, when Japan was resolute in assuming its place among the modernized countries of the world, Fenollosa and Okakura were likewise determined to give Japan an identity through a history of its art—a history that would parallel those of Western cultures. Similarly, the collections that they developed for the Museum of Fine Arts were meant to illustrate the entire evolution of Japanese art (as they perceived it, of course) for the West. Although by no means complete, the collection of paintings they assembled does provide an excellent overview, with examples dating from the eighth century to the Meiji era.

Which Japanese Art: Art of "Old Japan" or "New Japan"?

Morse and Fenollosa had been invited to teach by the government of Japan as part of its campaign to rapidly modernize and Westernize its political and cultural institutions. In its headlong drive to industrialization, the Meiji government sent delegations abroad to learn from the West, and sought out foreign scholars to provide instruction for a new generation of Japanese. While the Medical College at Tokyo Imperial University was staffed by Germans and the School of Language by French, German, English, and Chinese teachers, art was taught at the Technical Fine Arts School by the Italian painter Antonio Fontanesi. Under his guidance, men such as Asai Chū took up charcoal and oils to capture scenes of contemporary Japan in the style of the Barbizon school. Concerned that Japan—in its wholesale support for instruction in these Western painting methods—would undervalue its rich artistic past, the Bostonians became powerful advocates for traditional Japanese culture and "urged the importance and necessity of the Japanese adhering to their own methods of drawing and painting."[7] In 1882, at a gathering of the Ryūchikai, an organization dedicated to promoting Japan's arts, Fenollosa declared,

> Despite such superiority the Japanese despise their classical paintings, and with adoration for western civilization admire its artistically worthless modern paintings and imitate them for nothing. . . . The Japanese should return to their nature and its old racial traditions; and then take, if there are any, the good points of Western painting.[8]

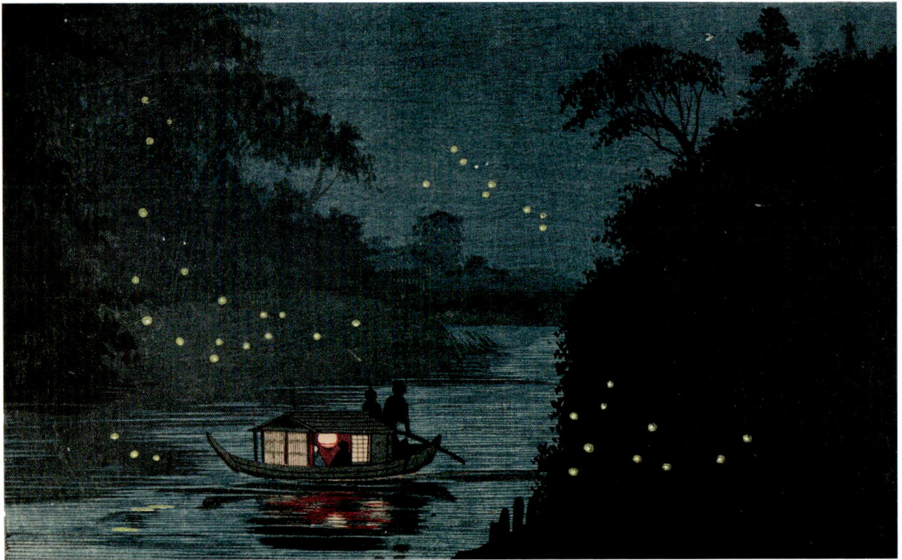

fig. 6 **Although nineteenth-century Bostonians collected contemporary prints, they favored images that presented a pre-industrial Japan.**

While many Japanese artists would continue to study oil painting and even enjoyed success in the academic salons of Paris, Fenollosa's arguments had a profound effect upon the collecting and study of Japanese art, in both Japan and the West. Until about thirty years ago, Japanese art was generally defined in the West as works that had been made before the Meiji Restoration of 1868 and art produced using traditional Japanese methods. Even today the Museum of Fine Arts, like many other Western institutions, does not own a single Japanese painting created in oils, and photographs, lithographs, and acrylic paintings are most often catalogued by media and housed with Western art. Similarly, the Nara and Kyoto National Museums, which place emphasis on archaeological material, religious art, and historical painting schools, for the most part have not displayed Western-influenced works.

Despite the evidence of Japan's modernization—its train lines, factories, and Western-style brick architecture—most European and American collectors until recently tried to preserve an image of the country unsullied by industrialization and Westernization. Although they might acquire woodblock prints by the late-nineteenth-century artist Kobayashi Kiyochika, who chronicled and commented on the transformation of the country, the works they selected were by-and-large prosaic images of traditional scenic spots. They frequently eschewed paintings, prints, and even photographs that illustrated Japan's modernization. Fortunately, once again Boston has been at the forefront of a reassessment of the arts of Japan. In the last decade, the Museum of Fine Arts has benefited from a new

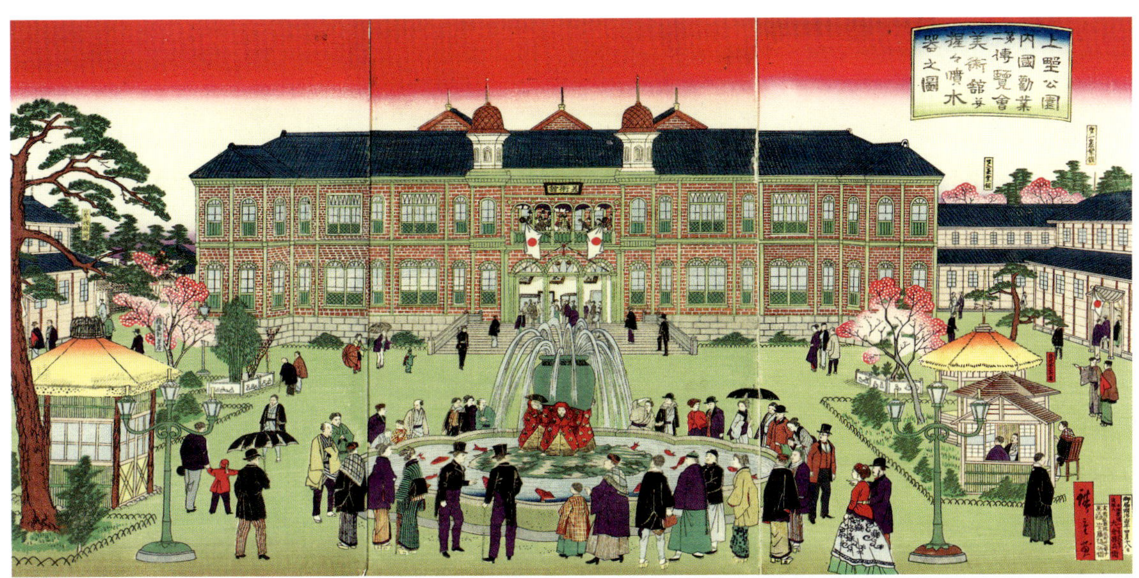

fig. 7 **In the twenty-first century, the MFA's collection has grown to include images of Japan's modernization and Westernization.**

generation of farsighted collectors. The gift of over 650 woodblock prints that celebrate Japan's engagement with the West by Jean S. and Frederic A. Sharf in 2000 and the subsequent donation of twenty thousand postcards by Leonard A. Lauder in 2002 dramatically transformed the definition of Japanese art at the MFA.[9] Furthermore, the Museum's exhibition of the postcards in Japan has established a new presence for this material. Japanese art as presented in this volume embraces all works of art that were created in Japan or produced by Japanese nationals, irrespective of period, subject matter, or technique.

The Japanese Aesthetic: *Wabi-Sabi*, *Kazari*, *Kawaii*, or All of the Above?

Since the early twentieth century, Japanese and Western writers alike have repeatedly tried to define the essence of the Japanese aesthetic as they have formulated histories of Japanese art. These commentators have often been at the very center of Japanese artistic production and cultural studies; one of the best known of these attempts is *The Book of Tea*, published by Okakura Kakuzō in 1906. The circumstances under which the book was written have never been clear, but it is believed that the text was based on informal talks that Okakura had given in Boston at Fenway Court, the museum-home of his soulmate Isabella Stewart Gardner. In the volume,

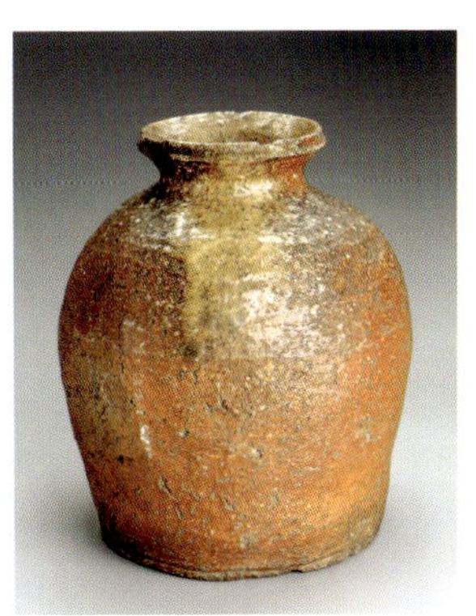

fig. 8 **The rough surface and accidental nature of the ash glaze on this jar are prized in the *wabi* aesthetic.**

Okakura describes an aesthetic of simplicity, a beauty that "could be discovered only by one who mentally completed the incomplete."[10] For him, the tearoom, where tea masters and guests had engaged in the drinking of tea and the contemplation of works of art since the fifteenth century, embodied the vitality of art. He admired the ephemeral nature of the wooden and papered structure, the sparseness of its decoration with its rough walls, and the imperfection of its sense of beauty.

Since its publication, *The Book of Tea* has been revered by a wide range of intellectuals—among them the poet Wallace Stevens and the architects Frank Lloyd Wright and Bruno Taut. And the interest in the spare and simple exalted in its pages has continued to this day. Popular books have transformed the tea aesthetics of *wabi* (humility) and *sabi* (rusticity) and combined them into the catch-all compound noun *wabi-sabi*. The *wabi* aesthetic that originated in the practices of the fifteenth-century tea master Murata Jukō, who not only utilized celebrated Chinese ceramics but also introduced everyday Japanese objects into the tearoom, has been romanticized by those who continue to seek an idealized alternative to modern industrialized life.

Contemporary critics have explored other Japanese terms that have enjoyed historical usage in discussing the Japanese aesthetic. Many of these are seemingly at odds with simplicity. For example, the art historian Tsuji Nobuo has proposed *kazari*, a term associated with decoration or ornamentation, as embodying the enduring Japanese approach to the arts.[11] In addition to the formal qualities of asymmetry and stylization that nineteenth-century French writers (such as Ernest Chesneau) noted in their descriptions of the decorative in Japanese art, *kazari* is said to be characterized by improvisation, playfulness, and eccentricity. Among the works that Tsuji cites are the elegant pages of the twelfth-century *Anthology of Thirty-six Poets* (p. 93), with their torn and textured papers and refined calligraphy, and paper lanterns emblazoned with images of a tiger and dragon by Hokusai (fig. 9).

The most recent Japanese term to dominate discourse on contemporary Japanese aesthetics is *kawaii*, or cute. Popularized by the artist Murakami Takashi, *kawaii* has been used to describe the preoccupation in Japanese society since the 1980s with the consumer culture centered around adolescent girls—the saccharine culture that idolizes Hello Kitty and wide-eyed cartoon figures.[12] Murakami correlates the pervasiveness of this aesthetic with the subservient position that Japan has assumed in its own governmental affairs since the conclusion of World War II and the Occupation by the United States.

Can we then define a "Japanese" aesthetic that existed over time? In surveying the objects that are included in this Highlights volume, we truly find that Japan-

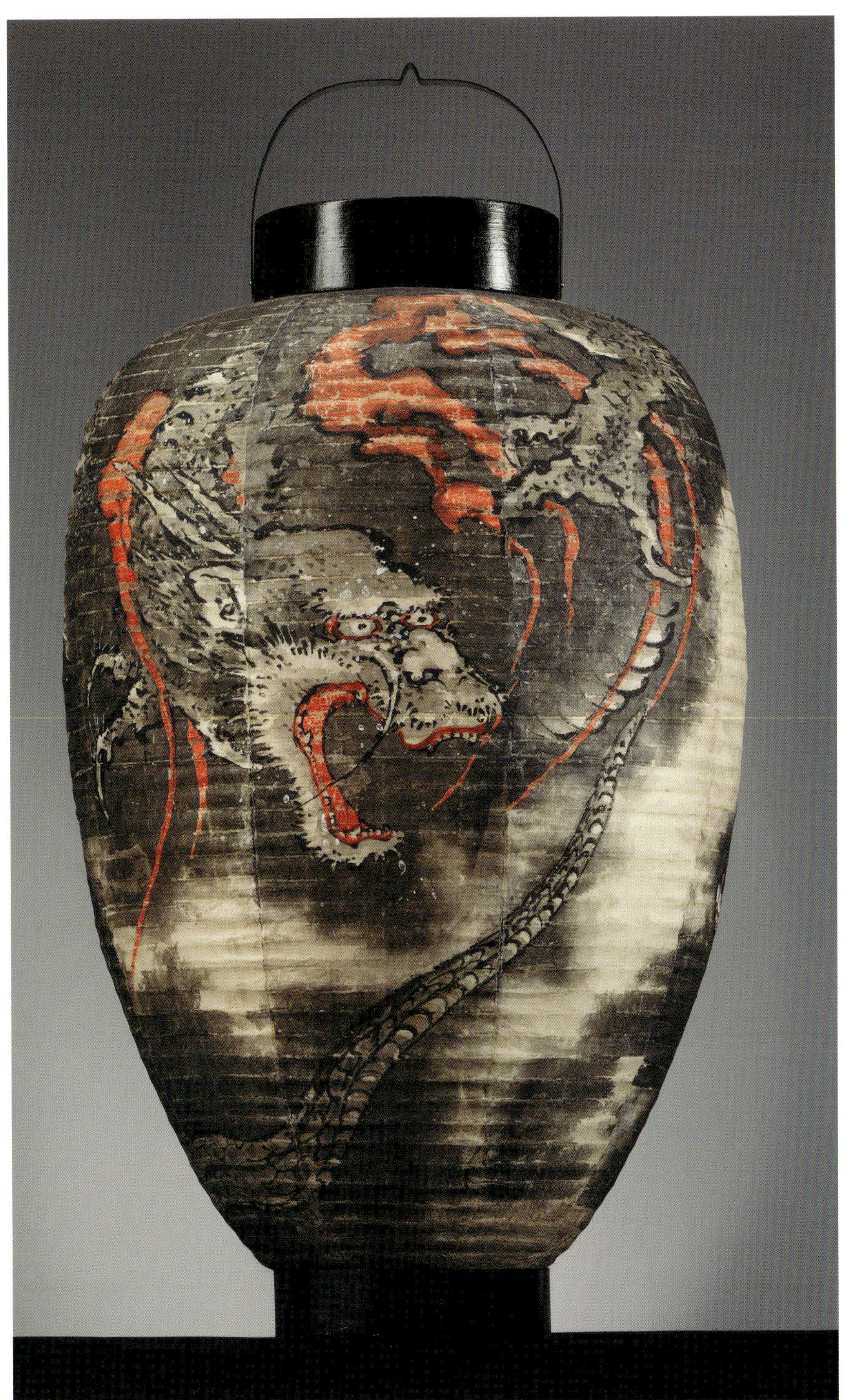

fig. 9 **Although the Japanese are said to value simplicity, many of their artworks are also known for their bold, playful designs.**

ese art astonishes in its variety. For every composition in muted shades of ink, there is one resplendent in color and gold leaf; for every meticulously crafted lacquer box, there is a tea ceramic glorious in its imperfections. Instead of suggesting an overarching conception of beauty invested in the individual works of art, the scholar Takashina Shūji has argued that Japanese aesthetics are best understood as being "situational."[13] Using the tearoom as his example, Takashina writes that the impact of Japanese art is realized only when different elements—the architectural setting, the hanging scroll, the tea bowl, and the other implements—are brought together. Unlike in the West, where art is on semi-permanent view (whether on the walls or shelves of a grand house or in a museum), displays in Japan are always changing. Indeed, the formats of Japanese painting—the screen, hanging scroll, handscroll, and album—permit only temporary viewing. Whether in a temple, palace, tearoom, or private dwelling, works of art are brought out for particular occasions, and their selection is often influenced by the season. Thus, while a situational aesthetic defies easy characterization, it ensures that the art of Japan is able to constantly reinvent itself and actively engage its audiences.

The present book does not attempt to provide a chronological survey of its subject. Rather, it explores the range of artworks in the Museum's collection—paintings, sculptures, prints, photographs, and decorative arts—in the historical context of the important social groups that commissioned them. The chapter "Art of the Temple" looks at the icons and texts that were the focus of rituals in Buddhist establishments and the ritual implements that adorned the compound halls. "Art of the Ruling Classes" is devoted to the works created at the behest of two elite groups: the court and the samurai. (For much of Japan's history, the members of the imperial court ruled in name only, but provided legitimacy for the members of the military class who held the actual political power.) In "Art of the Town," we present the objects that were made for Japan's major urban centers—Kyoto, Osaka, and Edo (present-day Tokyo)—and the trend-setting merchant class that arose in the seventeenth century. The last chapter of the book, "Japan and the Outside World," discusses works that were informed by the rich cultural exchanges that Japan enjoyed with the Asian continent throughout its history and with the West from the late sixteenth century onward. Of course, many of the individual works do not fit neatly into only one category, but the authors have tried to create a "situational aesthetic" that we hope our readers will find insightful and visually appealing.

1 The British scholar Craig Clunas has made similar observations about the art of China: "'Chinese art' is quite a recent invention, not much more than a hundred years old. . . . Rather it was by nineteenth-century Europe and North America that 'Chinese art' was created." Craig Clunas, *Art in China* (Oxford and New York: Oxford University Press, 1997), 9.

2 Ernest Chesneau, "L'Art Japonais: Conférence Faite á l'Union des Beaux-Arts Appliqués á l'Industrie," delivered on February 19, 1869, and quoted in http://geographis.ch/~podouphis/chesneau-japon_2.htm (accessed January 25, 2008). Translation from the French by Mark Polizzotti.

3 Zacharie Astruc, "L'Empire du Soleil Levant," *L'Etendard*, February 27, 1867, cited by Sharon Flescher, *Zacharie Astruc: Critic, Artist, and Japoniste* (New York and London: Garland Publishing, 1978), 356–57. Translation by Mark Polizzotti.

4 William Sturgis Bigelow and John Ellerton Lodge, "Okakura Kakuzō, 1862–1913," *Museum of Fine Arts Bulletin*, December 1913, 75.

5 Ernest Francisco Fenollosa, "Review of the Chapter on Painting, in *L'Art Japonais*, by L. Gonse," *Japan Weekly Mail* 2, no. 2 (July 12, 1884): 38.

6 Ernest Francisco Fenollosa, *Epochs of Chinese and Japanese Art*, vol. 1 (1913; repr., New York: Dover Publications, 1963), xxvii.

7 Edward Sylvester Morse, *Japan Day by Day 1877, 1878–79, 1882–83*, vol. 2 (Boston and New York: Houghton Mifflin, 1917), 216.

8 Ernest Francisco Fenollosa, "Truth of Fine Arts" (*Bijutsu shinsetsu*), delivered on May 14, 1882, quoted in Lawrence W. Chisolm, *Fenollosa: The Far East and American Culture* (New Haven and London: Yale University Press, 1963), 50–51.

9 See *Japan at the Dawn of the Modern Age: Woodblock Prints from the Meiji Era, 1868–1912* (Boston: MFA Publications, 2001), and *Art of the Japanese Postcard* (Boston: MFA Publications, 2003).

10 Okakura Kakuzō, *The Book of Tea* (1906; repr., Rutland, VT, and Tokyo: Charles E. Tuttle Company, 1956), 70.

11 Tsuji Nobuo, "On Kazari," in *Kazari: Decoration and Display in Japan, 15th–19th Centuries*, ed. Nicole Coolidge Rousmaniere (New York: Japan Society, 2002), 14–19.

12 Matsui Midori, "Beyond the Pleasure Room to a Chaotic Street: Transformations of Cute Subculture in the Art of the Japanese Nineties," in *Little Boy: The Arts of Japan's Exploding Subculture*, ed. Murakami Takashi (New York: Japan Society, 2005), 209–39.

13 Takashina Shūji, "Beauty in Japan and in the West," in *Face to Face: Shiseido and the Manufacture of Beauty, 1900–2000*, ed. Lynn Gumpert (New York: Grey Art Gallery, 2000), 60.

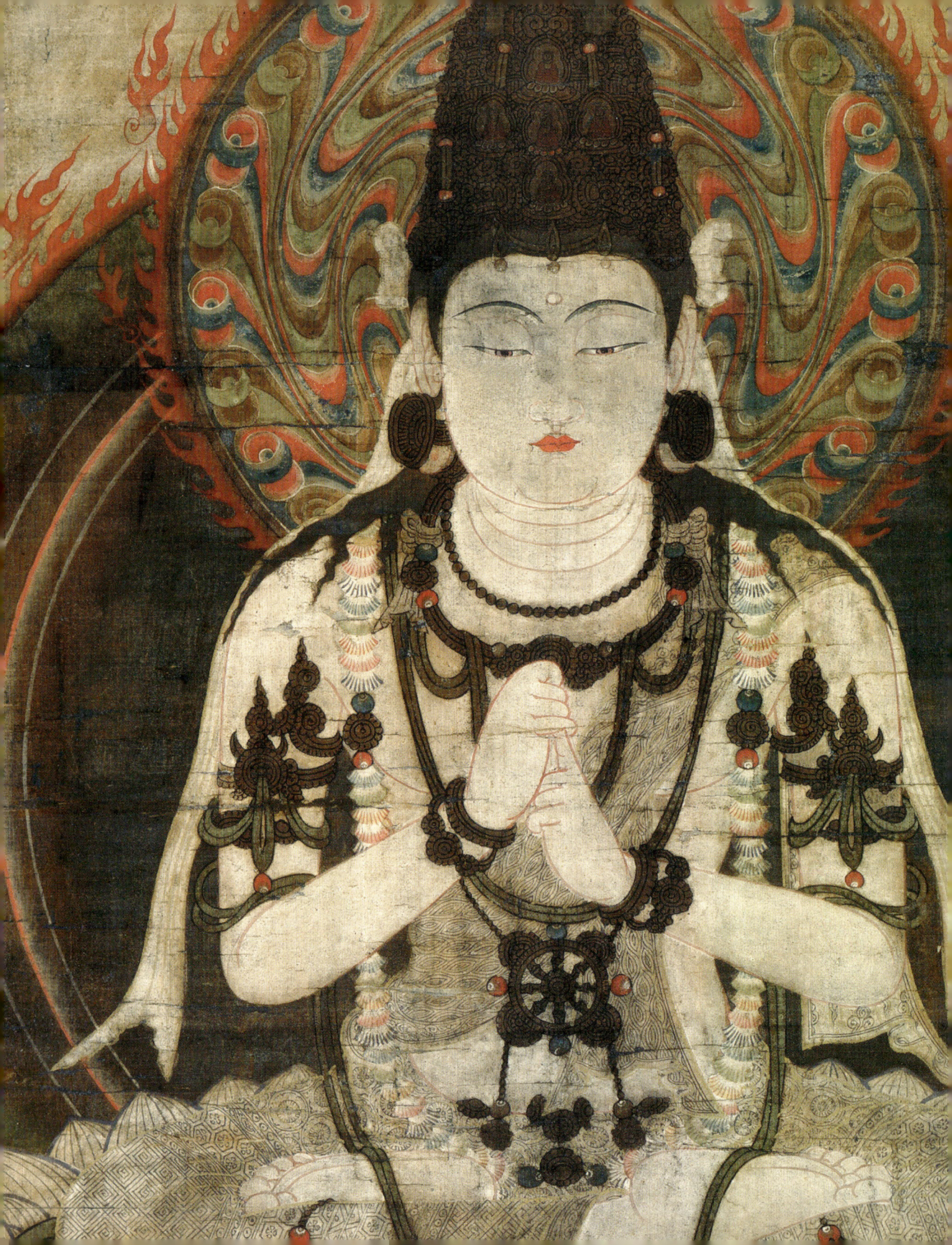

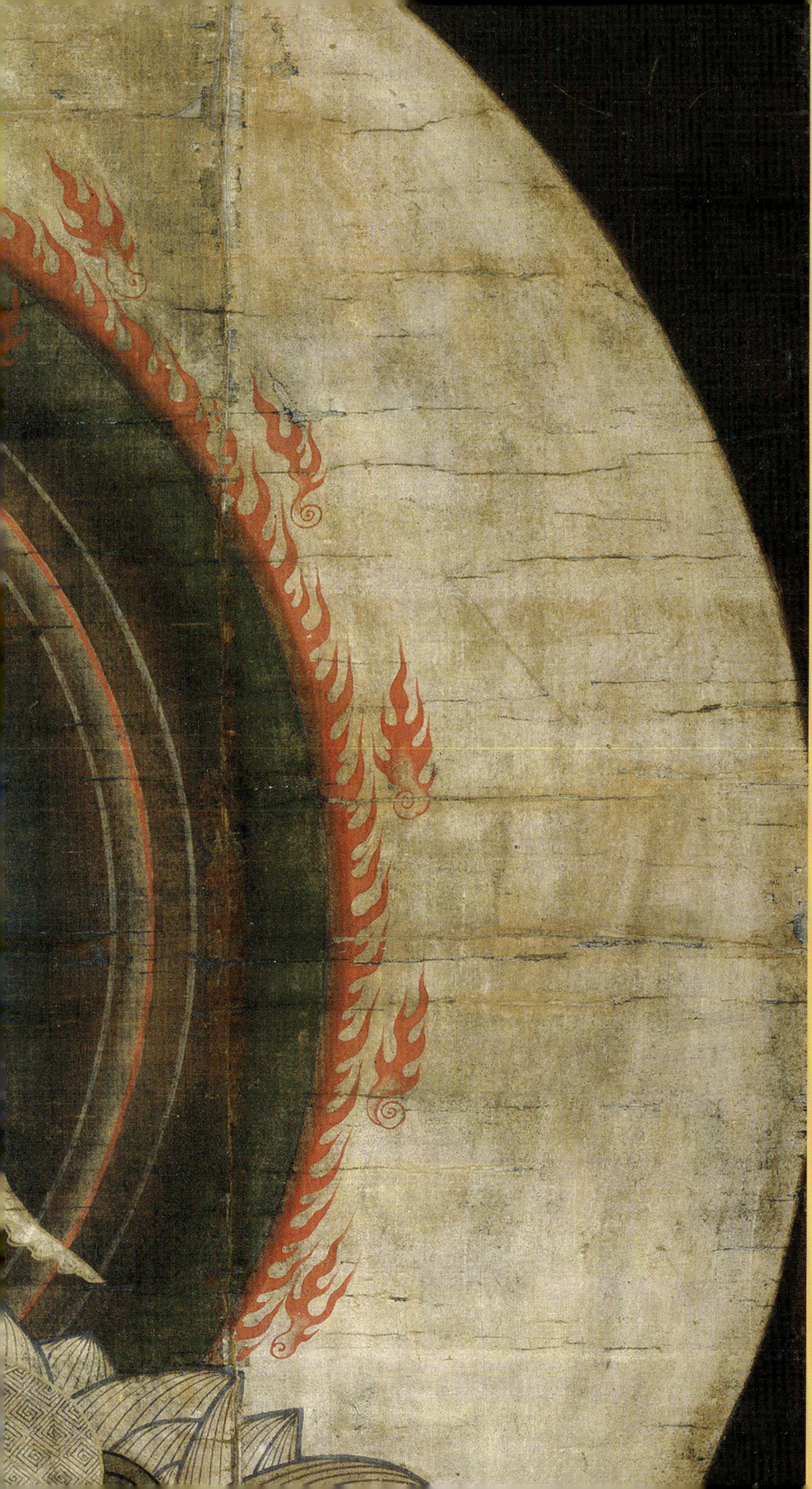

1 art of the TEMPLE

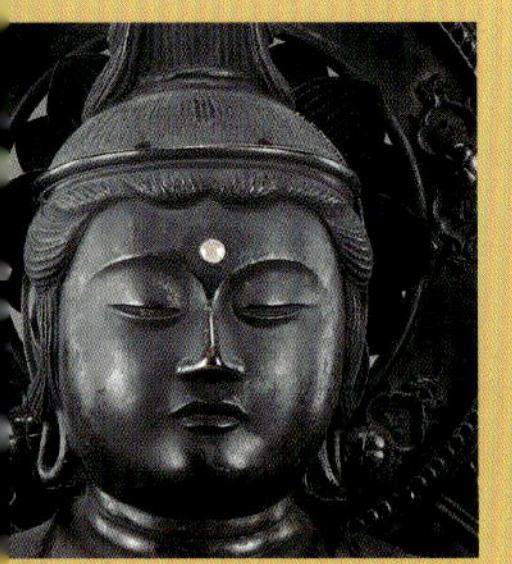
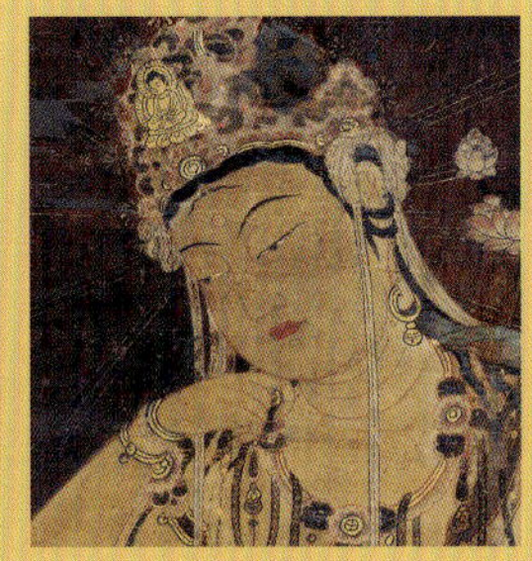
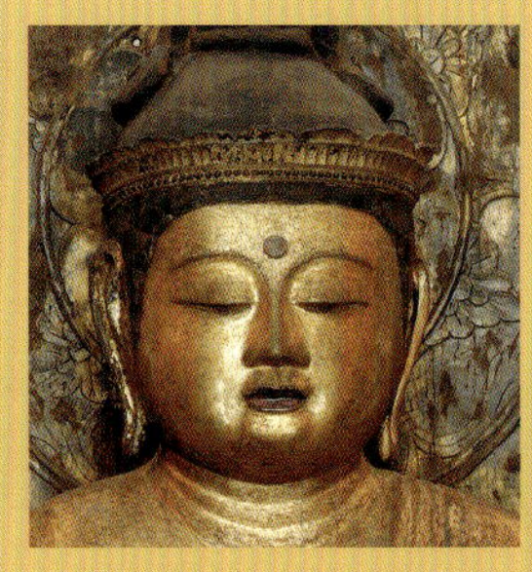
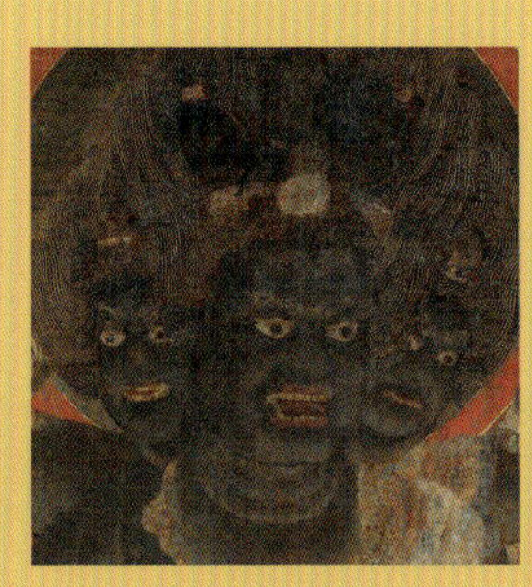
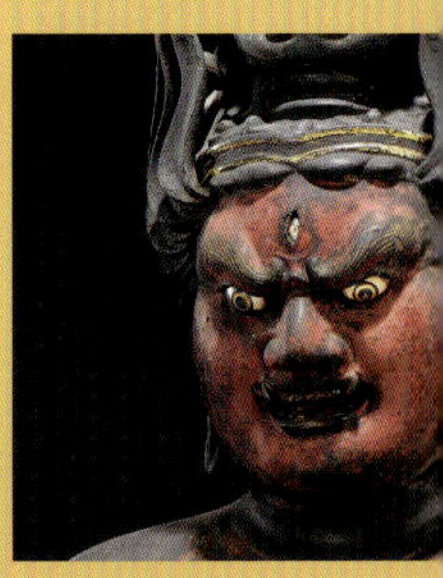

Art of the Temple

Anne Nishimura Morse

> In front of the Buddha there stood a flower stand and pedestal tray, both inlaid with mother-of-pearl, as well as sacred vessels of gold. The flowers were made of the seven treasures; the oblatory vessels were decorated with the same rare substances. The air was fragrant with the scent of precious incenses, burning in the censers, and everywhere there were rows of pennants and banners; all compounded of the seven treasures.
>
> –**A Tale of Flowering Fortunes** (trans. William H. and Helen Craig McCullough)

Beginning in the sixth century, when Buddhism was introduced to Japan from the Korean peninsula, the Japanese established vast temple complexes as expressions of their faith. These compounds featured halls housing sculpted images of individual deities, which today remain the focus of elaborate rituals conducted for the protection of the nation or for more immediate personal concerns. The passage quoted above from the eleventh-century history *A Tale of Flowering Fortunes* (*Eiga monogatari*) emphasizes the predilection for particularly luxurious ornamentation that characterized the Heian period (794–1185), but the Japanese people have always associated the efficacy of religious rituals with aesthetic experience. Thus, the images, texts, and ritual implements they have commissioned for their temples comprise some of the most visually compelling works in the history of Japanese art.

Buddhism in Japan

The Buddhist faith had its origins in India. The Historical Buddha, Śākyamuni, is generally thought to have been a prince of the Śākya clan, members of the warrior caste who lived near the foothills of the Himalayas, and to have died sometime around 480 B.C.E. He abandoned his aristocratic heritage and assumed the life of an ascetic, but came to realize instead that a course of moderation—a Middle Way—would lead to understanding, awakening, and ultimately enlighten-

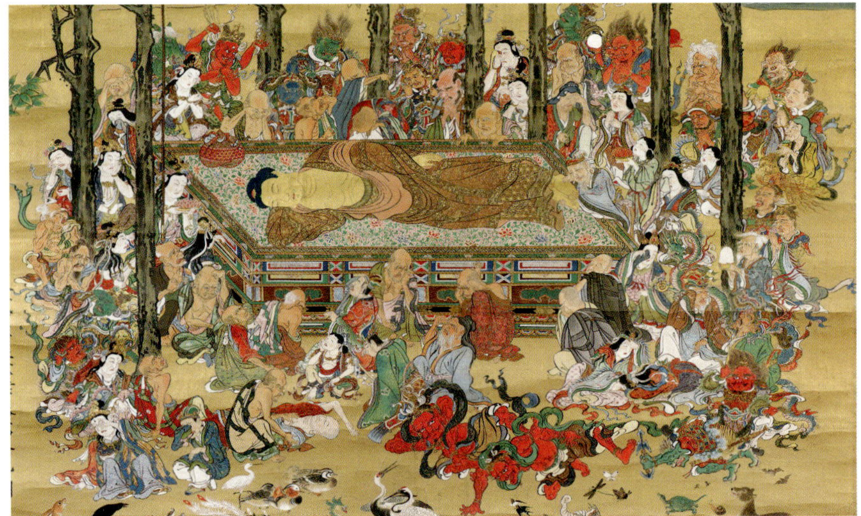

fig. 10 **The Historical Buddha achieved his final enlightenment when he passed from earthly life. Those who did not understand the significance of this event were prostrate with grief.**

ment. Śākyamuni described this way as the Noble Eight-Fold Path, which is comprised of correct views, thoughts, speech, actions, modes of living, efforts, mindfulness, and meditation. He also identified Four Noble Truths: the first, that human existence is suffering; the second, that suffering is caused by human desires; the third, that liberation from suffering is enlightenment; and the fourth, that the way to achieve this liberation is to follow the Noble Eight-Fold Path.

Around the third century B.C.E., one group of Śākyamuni's followers came to view him as a transcendent being rather than a historical personage. This idea developed into the new doctrine of Mahāyāna Buddhism, which proclaimed the Historical Buddha to be just one of many Buddhas who exist simultaneously, each presiding over his own universe, which includes a paradise where believers can accumulate merit in their pursuit of enlightenment. These Buddhas intercede in different ways to aid all sentient beings in their quest for enlightenment. Equally important to the Mahāyāna tradition is the ideal of the bodhisattva—a being who postpones his own enlightenment until all are saved.

Missionaries from northwest India propagated Mahāyāna Buddhist doctrines across the Pamir Mountains into Turkestan, and by the early second century C.E. these doctrines had reached China. Mahāyāna beliefs were transmitted even farther eastward to the kingdoms of Goguryeo, Baekje, and Silla on the Korean peninsula during the late fourth and early fifth centuries, and then to Japan in the sixth century, when King Seong of the kingdom of Baekje presented Buddhist texts and images to the court.

Prior to the arrival of Buddhism, the Japanese held a loosely organized set of religious beliefs focusing on nature worship, fertility cults, and ancestor veneration. Many members of the court were eager to adopt the new religion, for not only did it provide a well-established pantheon and an extensive liturgy for the protection of the state, but it also offered entrée into the sophisticated culture of the Asian continent. Indeed, stylistic developments in Chinese and Korean art would greatly influence forms of Buddhist imagery in Japan throughout much of its history.

Over time, new types of Buddhism emerged. During the ninth century, the Japanese aristocracy embraced Esoteric Buddhism, which offered its adherents the possibility of enlightenment in this lifetime through the mastery of the Three Mysteries—the Mysteries of Word, Body, and Thought. The Mystery of the Word could be understood through the recitation of complicated magical chants known as *mantra*, and the Mystery of the Body through the memorization of *mudrā*, symbolic gestures that carry sacred meaning. The Mystery of Thought was best comprehended through meditation on diagrams known as *mandala*, which related the organization of the Buddhist cosmos and its hierarchy of deities. With the development of Esoteric Buddhism came the incorporation of numerous local deities into the rapidly expanding pantheon, many with wrathful guises and multiple appendages. Through the efforts of the monks Saichō, who established the Tendai sect on Mount Hiei northeast of Kyoto, and Kūkai, who introduced the Shingon sect—which had its centers on Mount Kōya south of Nara and the temple Tō-ji in Kyoto—Esoteric Buddhism was the dominant doctrine until the end of the Heian period.

By the twelfth century, Buddhism had all but disappeared from India, and only the Chan (Japanese: Zen) sect retained any vitality in China. As a consequence, Japanese Buddhism moved largely away from continental forms of the faith and doctrines and developed its own practices. Many of the ensuing changes were reactions to the domination of the faith by the aristocratic elite during the Heian period. For example, the Jōdō sect of Pure Land Buddhism founded by Hōnen and the Shin sect of Pure Land Buddhism founded by Shinran popularized a set of beliefs that promised rebirth in the Western Paradise of the Buddha Amida for all its adherents, no matter how humble. The charismatic thirteenth-century monk Nichiren preached exclusive devotion to the *Lotus Sutra*, which also promised salvation for all.

Images

When Buddhism was first introduced to Japan, Buddhist images were enshrined in small devotional halls, which were often renovated residential structures. In

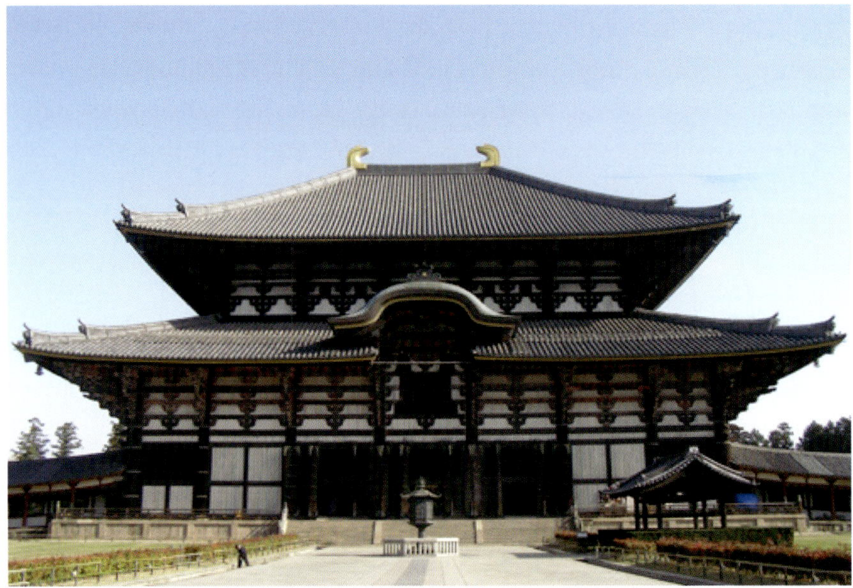

fig. 11 **The Main Image Hall of Tōdai-ji in Nara, which houses the Cosmic Buddha, is the largest wooden structure in the world.**

the organization of the first temple compounds, primacy was given to the pagoda, which functioned as a symbolic reliquary honoring the Historical Buddha. By the eighth century, however, the image hall had become the primary focus of the temple, and pagodas became subsidiary structures located outside the cloister. The monumental complex of Tōdai-ji, constructed in the newly established capital of Nara as a sanctuary for the protection of the state, exemplified this new arrangement by housing a colossal bronze statue of Rushana, the Cosmic Buddha (or Great Buddha), in its Main Image Hall.

The interior of an image hall has always been considered a consecrated space in which the faithful can realize the world of the Buddha in the present surroundings. A work of sculpture permanently located in the center of the altar is the focus of the temple's daily rituals, but paintings are also hung temporarily on the walls or on special stands for certain annual ceremonies or specific rituals.[1] Although the rituals vary from sect to sect, texts are read before the image and offerings of food and flowers are given in order to evoke the presence of the object of worship.

Most Japanese Buddhist images belong to one of two types: those that venerate a great teacher or devotee—such as the Historical Buddha or Prince Shōtoku, one of the earliest patrons of Buddhist art—or those that represent the transcendent Buddhas, bodhisattvas, and other deities in the extensive Buddhist pantheon. The iconography of the different deities was largely determined on

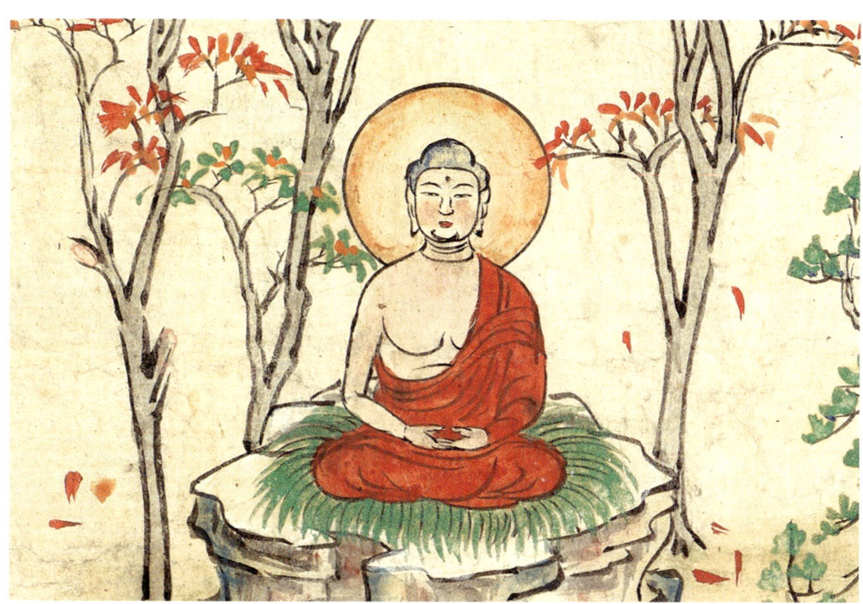

fig. 12 **The Buddha is depicted with an extracranial protrusion and a tuft of hair in the center of his forehead, two of the physical traits that symbolize his powers.**

the Asian continent. During the first and second centuries C.E., Indian sculptors produced images of the various Buddhas based on the model of the Historical Buddha. Because Śākyamuni had renounced the world to attain enlightenment, these figures are shown with their heads shorn and their idealized bodies garbed in monastic robes. Buddhas also bear thirty-two major and eighty minor signs that symbolize their transcendental powers. The most prominent of these are the *uṣṇīṣa*, an extracranial protrusion that signifies the wisdom of the Historical Buddha; the *ūrṇā*, a tuft of white hair between the eyebrows of the deity that emits a magical light; and the three rings of flesh around a Buddha's neck.

All Buddhas hold their hands in symbolic gestures, or *mudrā*, which generally recall important events in the legendary biography of the Historical Buddha. The *mudrā* of touching the ground (Japanese: *sokuchi-in*), in which the right hand is held in front of the knee, fingers pointing down, refers to the Buddha calling the earth to witness his merit at the moment he attained enlightenment. The *mudrā* of turning the wheel of the law (*tenpōrin-in*), in which the hands are held at chest-level with one finger of each hand touching the thumb, evokes the Buddha's first sermon. Other *mudrā* commonly found in Japanese Buddhist images include the gesture of concentration (*jō-in*), in which the extended fingers of the right hand rest on top of those of the left; and the gesture granting the absence of fear (*semui-in*), in which the right hand is raised with the palm to the viewer.

Bodhisattvas assume many guises but usually take the appearance of princely beings whose resplendent crowns and jewelry symbolize their transcendent powers. They are most easily identified by their attributes. In Japan the bodhisattvas most popularly worshipped are Kannon, the Bodhisattva of Compassion, who normally bears an image of the Buddha Amida in his crown; Monju, the Bodhisattva of Wisdom, who grasps a sword in his right hand and rides a lion; Fugen, the Bodhisattva of Universal Virtue, who holds his hands in prayer and rides an elephant; and Jizō, the Bodhisattva of the Earth Matrix, who assumes the guise of a young priest and holds a pilgrim's staff.

On the Asian continent, the favored medium for Buddhist sculptures was stone, although finely worked images for private devotion were also created in bronze. During the seventh and eighth centuries in Japan, sculptors made bronze, clay, and dry-lacquer statues, first in private workshops and then in government-sponsored ateliers. By the early ninth century, however, wood had become the preferred material of Japanese sculptors. Artists initially used solid blocks of Japanese cypress or other native woods; but finding themselves constrained by the natural size of individual trees and by the warping of the wood as it dried, they developed a system of joined woodblock construction, assembling multiple blocks of wood to form the rough shape of the desired image and then hollowing them out. This system allowed artists to make works of varying sizes and to produce images quickly in highly organized workshops. Although most statues were covered with lacquer and then painted or gilded, sculptors paid close attention to the surface effects of the grain of the wood on unpainted works. During the late twelfth century, artists added rock crystal to represent the figures' eyes, imbuing their statues with a new naturalism that became a characteristic feature of sculpture of the Kamakura period (1185–1333).

fig. 13 **Bodhisattvas are shown in princely form with upswept hairdos and elaborate jewelry.**

Because Buddhist iconography was so regimented, sculptors and painters had to observe strict rules when fashioning their images. Frequently they received instruction from drawings generated by scholar-monks that detailed the attributes of specific deities and provided color notations (see p. 57). Despite these apparent constraints, artists in different periods were able to incorporate their own unique interpretations of the divine, leading to changes in style. During the Nara period (710–794), many worked in the international style of the Chinese Tang dynasty (618–907), a style characterized by full proportions and a naturalistic treatment of drapery. By the eleventh and twelfth centuries, images were distinguished by an extreme idealization of the facial features and a particular elegance of the ornamentation. The image of Amida, the Buddha of Infinite Light, produced in 1053 by the sculptor Jōchō for the Phoenix Hall at the temple Byōdō-in in Uji, near Kyoto, served as an inspiration for sculptors throughout Japan during the late Heian period. Under a group of artists known as the Kei school, led by Unkei and Kaikei, statues during the succeeding Kamakura period revealed a restored interest in naturalism and dynamic movement. Similar trends can be found in contemporary painted images.

Texts

To ensure that the teachings of the Historical Buddha were transmitted correctly, compiling them became an important activity of the early Buddhist community in India. The initial canon, the *tripiṭaka* or "Three Baskets," was comprised of collections of monastic regulations, known as the *vinaya*; the discourse of the Buddha, known as the *sūtras*; and commentaries, known as the *abhidharma*. With the rise of Mahāyāna Buddhism came a new sacred literature attributed to the Historical Buddha, which was said to have been kept hidden for five hundred years until the appropriate time for its appearance. Many of these texts—such as the *Lotus Sutra*, which preaches that enlightenment is available to women and describes the thirty-three manifestations of Kannon—are devoted to the deities of the expanded Mahāyāna pantheon.

The first Buddhist texts introduced to Japan came from the Korean peninsula. Subsequent contacts with China led to the importation of many new documents. Soon the Japanese began the practice of copying sutras, and by the late seventh century they had transcribed the *tripiṭaka*. During the Nara period, a large number of texts were copied at government-sanctioned scriptoria as part of the state's policy of providing protection for the Buddhist faith. Most of these sutras are written in a formal script made popular in Tang-dynasty China, characterized by well-balanced, regular characters.

Aristocrats of the Heian period believed that copying sutras was a pious act and frequently transcribed texts on lavishly decorated papers. The ornamentation was thought not only to increase the aesthetic impact of the scrolls but also to amplify the splendor of the Buddha's teachings. *A Tale of Flowering Fortunes*, which chronicles the life and times of the powerful regent Fujiwara no Michinaga, describes one transcription project of the *Lotus Sutra*:

> The sutra was indescribably magnificent. Some chapters were true chrysographed texts, inscribed in gold on lustrous cobalt blue paper. Others were written over pictures superimposed on damask, or contained pictures above and below the text. . . . Their splendor and sumptuousness made them resemble collections of elegant verses rather than sutras. Jeweled rollers had been used, and almost every scroll was embellished with the seven treasures.[2]

The exquisite twelfth-century copy of *Sutra of the Retribution for Good and Evil Deeds* featured in this book (see p. 75) was part of a five-thousand-scroll set of the Buddhist canon that was executed by professional scribes and artists and donated to the temple Chūson-ji in northern Japan. Texts were generally chanted during the performance of rituals. When the chosen text was particularly lengthy, however, the reading would be symbolic, and monks would pass around the volumes, which were housed in lacquer boxes.

Implements

Buddhist decorative arts include ornaments for adorning Buddhist statuary or increasing the majesty of temple structures; ceremonial objects for offering incense, flowers, or light to images; ritual implements such as Esoteric *vajras*, which take their form from ancient weapons, for activating the altar during ceremonies; objects such as ewers and rosaries used by monks in their daily lives; and musical instruments such as temple bells. The prototypes for these different implements were established during the seventh and eighth centuries, when Japanese Buddhist art was strongly influenced by Chinese and Korean examples.

All of these types are represented in the MFA's collection. Most were acquired in the late nineteenth century by the Bostonian William Sturgis Bigelow, an ordained Esoteric Buddhist, for his own practice of rituals rather than for aesthetic considerations. In more recent years the Museum has collected a few works, such as a fourteenth–fifteenth-century brocade banner (p. 79) and a contemporary gilt bronze box for a priest's ordination documents (p. 80), that testify to the devotion not only of patrons but also of artists, who strove to create works of art with a refined aesthetic sensibility in order to express the divine.

Although standard histories of Japanese art have privileged images and decorative arts from the seventh through the fourteenth centuries, this book includes later works in order to explain the vital role that Buddhism has continued to play. Today, Japanese temples remain vibrant centers of religious activity and serve as important guardians of the country's enduring artistic tradition.

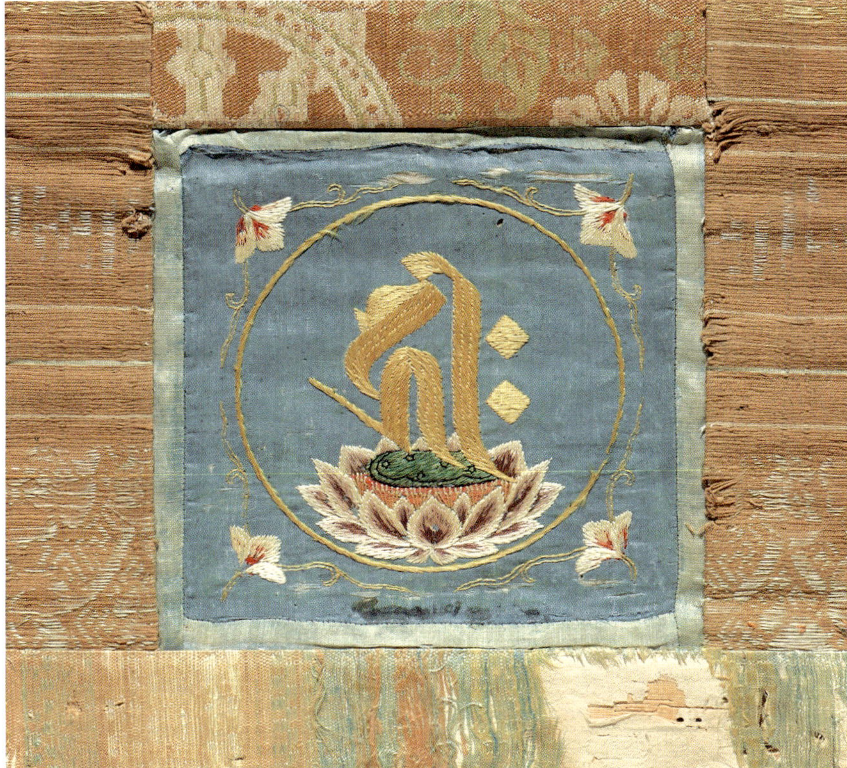

fig. 14 **The Sanskrit letter symbolizing the Buddha Amida and a richly colored lotus pedestal are embroidered on this banner for the ornamentation of image halls.**

1 This discussion about images draws upon Anne Nishimura Morse and Samuel Crowell Morse, "Introduction," *Object as Insight: Japanese Buddhist Art and Ritual* (Katonah, NY: Katonah Museum of Art), 7–11.

2 *A Tale of Flowering Fortunes*, trans. William H. and Helen Craig McCullough (Stanford, CA: Stanford University Press, 1980), 2:531–32.

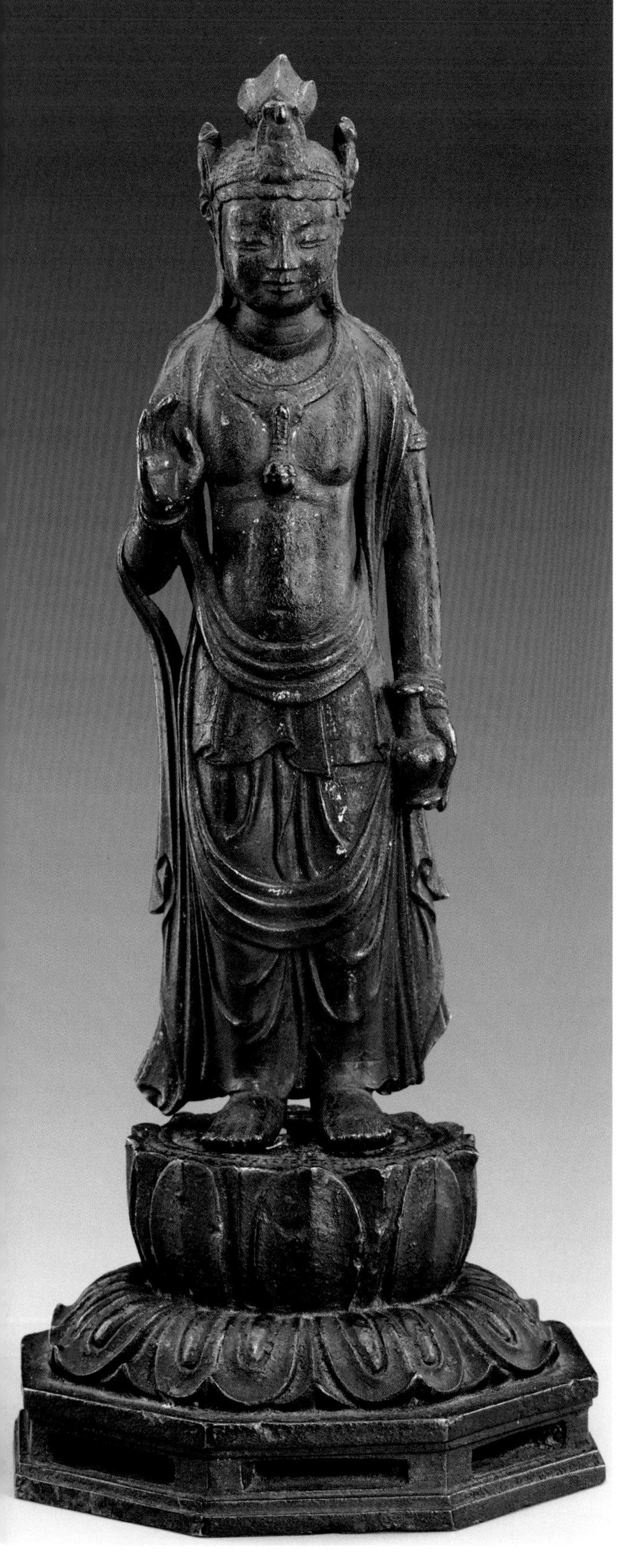

Kannon, the Bodhisattva of Compassion
Asuka period, late 7th–early 8th century

With the introduction of Buddhism to Japan in the early sixth century came the gift of small gilt images from the Korean kingdom of Baekje. Through the eighth century, bronze continued to be the preferred medium for Japanese sculptural production, and styles of Buddhist imagery from the Asian continent provided inspiration. This image of Kannon standing on a lotus pedestal, with his left hand holding a vase and his right raised in a gesture of reassurance, shares several formal qualities with Chinese statues of the Sui dynasty (581–618). Wearing the diaphanous robes, jewelry, and crown with an image of Amida, the Buddha of Infinite Illumination, that are standard to all images of Kannon, the figure has the slender proportions preferred by contemporary Chinese sculptors; the simplification of the drapery, though, is Japanese. The face, with its slightly downcast eyes and highly arched brows, appears mature, yet the expression retains a characteristic archaic smile.

At the end of the seventh century, a large number of gilt-bronze statues were produced in direct response to an edict issued by Emperor Tenmu (r. 672–686). Recorded in the *Chronicles of Japan* (*Nihon shoki*), the order states that every household in every province should construct a Buddhist shrine and equip it with images and texts. Prior to this time, the only people who worshipped Buddhist images in Japan had been naturalized Japanese from the continent or members of the aristocracy, but Tenmu's directive led Buddhism to gain wider acceptance among the populace.

Gilt bronze; lost-wax casting in one piece
H. of figure 22.5 cm (H. 8⅞ in.)
Special Chinese and Japanese Fund 05.229a–b

Bodhisattva

Heian period, late 8th–early 9th century

Carved primarily from one massive piece of wood that extends from the head to the tenons on the bottoms of the feet that hold the figure into the pedestal, this statue exemplifies the early-Heian-period style of sculpture in its sensuous physical features and stylized drapery. Prototypes for this type of imagery were costly bronze or dry-lacquer statues, inspired by works of the Chinese Tang dynasty (618–907), fashioned for the immense state-sponsored temples in Nara, Japan's capital at the time, during the mid-eighth century. By the third quarter of the century, Japanese artists took to producing works in wood. Not only could they readily find the material throughout the country, they also believed great trees to be of special sanctity. A recent examination of the back of this statue revealed several triangular indentations, which may indicate that the work was fashioned from a timber once used as an architectural support in a particularly revered temple structure.

The upswept coiffure, princely robes, jewelry, and graceful tilt of the hips of this image classify it as a bodhisattva; the arms, which could have held attributes providing a more specific identification of the deity represented, are later replacements. Although the grain of the wood now enhances the treatment of the drapery and the contoured planes of the body, the surface of the statue originally would have been covered with gesso and then painted with colors. Traces of azurite indicate that the long, flowing hair was once blue—a standard attribute of bodhisattvas.

Japanese cypress with polychrome;
single woodblock construction
H. of figure 176 cm (H. 69 5/16 in.)
Special Chinese and Japanese Fund 12.128

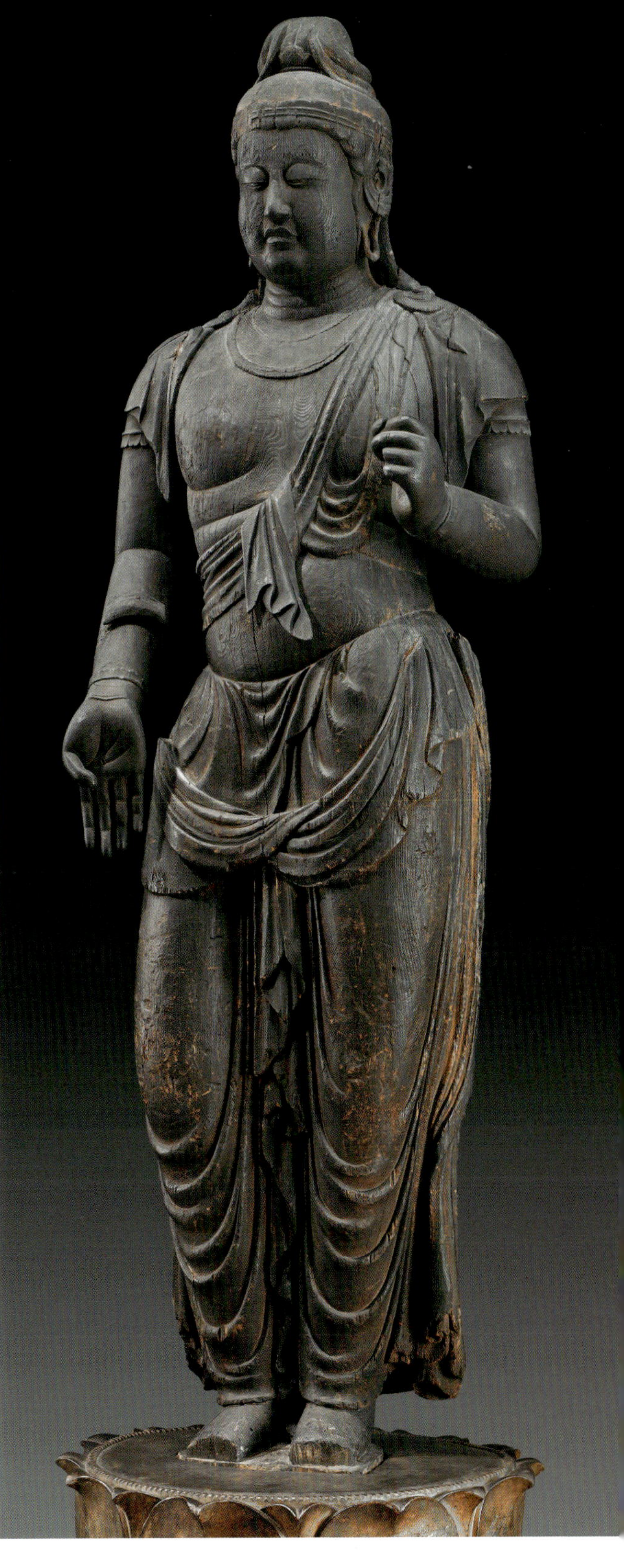

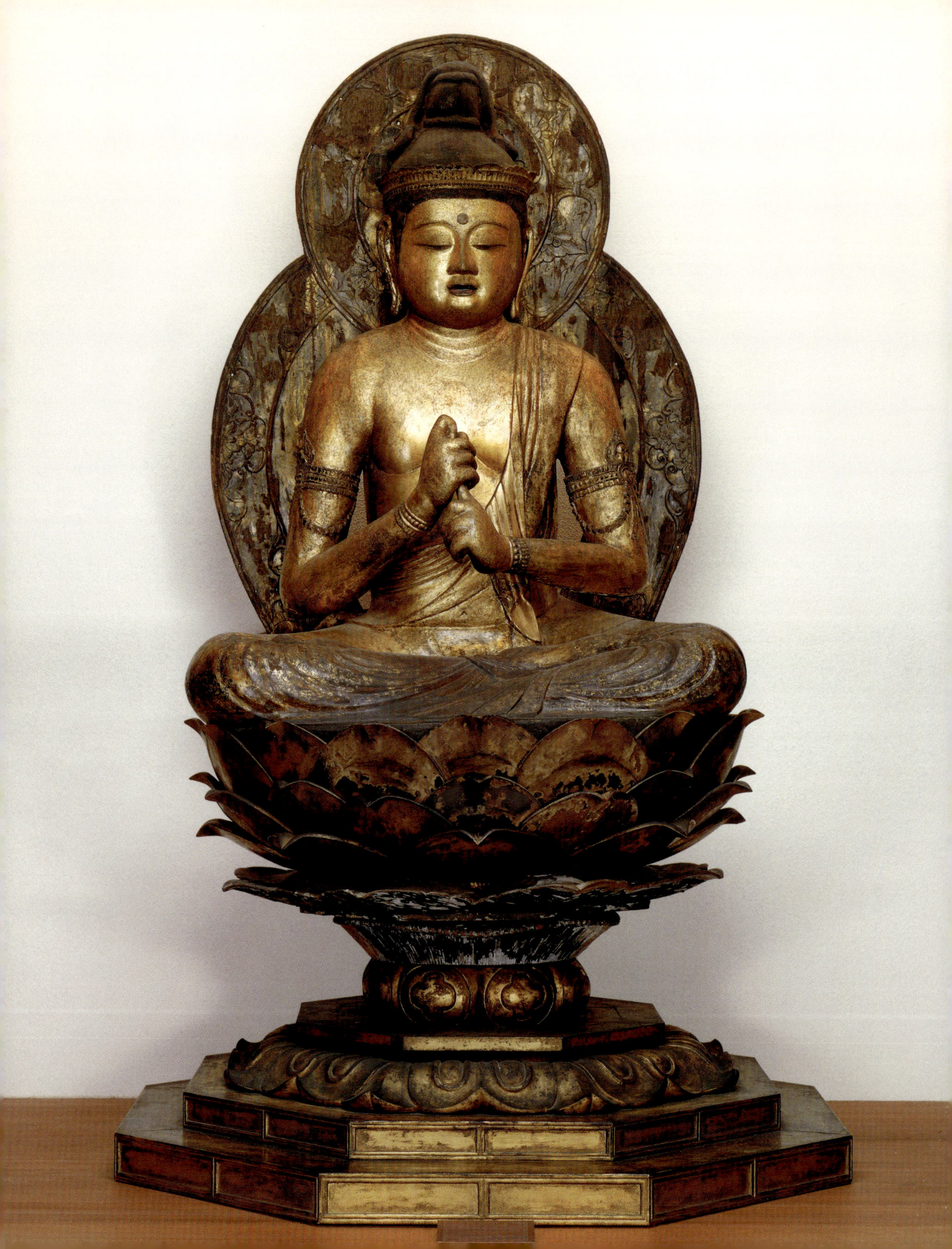

Dainichi, the Buddha of Infinite Illumination

Shin… (full name and dates unknown)

Keichi (dates unknown)

Jōryū (dates unknown)

Heian period, dated 1149

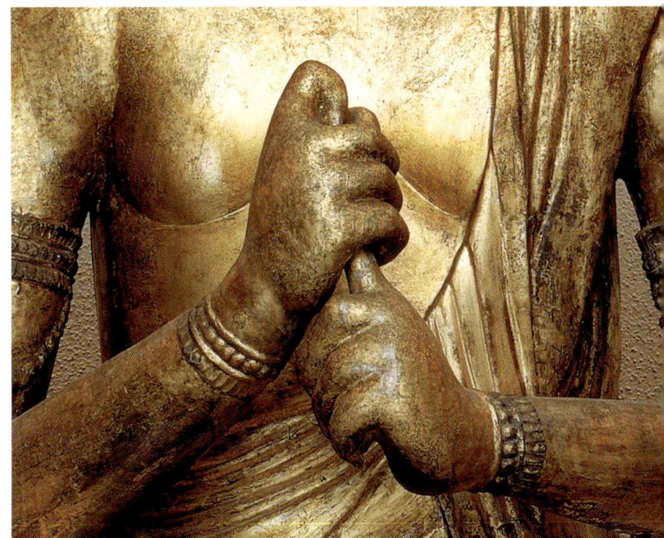

The central deity of Esoteric Buddhism and the generative principle of the universe, Dainichi sits here in a meditative posture. He holds his hands in the distinctive wisdom-fist gesture (*chiken-in*), symbolizing his infinite knowledge. Unlike other Buddhas, who have an extracranial protuberance and wear monastic garb, Dainichi wears a crown, an elaborate topknot, and princely robes—symbols of his dominion over all.

This image was created in the "true style," characterized by an extreme idealization of the face and body, an introspective expression, and a fluid yet linear treatment of the drapery. The style is associated with the eleventh-century master sculptor Jōchō, who provided statues for most of the important aristocratic temple commissions in and around Kyoto (then Japan's capital) during the eleventh century. His celebrated image of Amida at Byōdō-in, a temple just to the south of Kyoto, was widely copied for patrons throughout Japan who wished to emphasize their noble status.

Fashioned from camphor wood rather than the more typical cypress, this statue was definitely created for a provincial temple. An inscription on the interior of the image details the circumstances and date of its production; the sculptors required a little more than two months to complete the statue on the twenty-fourth day of the first month of Kyūan 5 (1149). Its place of origin, however, still remains a mystery.

Camphor wood with gold; joined woodblock construction
H. of figure 141.6 cm (H. 55¾ in.)
Denman Waldo Ross Collection 09.531a–c

Daiitoku myōō, the Wisdom King of Great Awe-Inspiring Power

Heian period, 12th century

Daiitoku myōō is one of the Five Wisdom Kings. These deities are worshiped in Esoteric Buddhism as manifestations of the wrath of the supreme deity Dainichi when confronted with ignorance and delusion. The first sculptural images of the group in Japan were commissioned by Kūkai, the ninth-century founder of the Shingon sect, for the altar in the lecture hall at Kyōōgokoku-ji (Tō-ji) in Kyoto. There they were the focus of rituals for the protection of the nation. Subsequently, many other Esoteric temples constructed halls dedicated to the deities and enshrined images that followed the iconography of these early-ninth-century icons.

Daiitoku is generally depicted with six heads, six arms, and six legs; many of these appendages have been lost from the MFA image. Each of the heads bears a ferocious countenance and hair that stands on end—expressions of the deity's righteous anger. Although today the image is seated on a lotus pedestal, originally he rode a water buffalo, symbolizing his subjugation of Enma, the King of Death, with whom the animal is generally associated.

The body of this remarkable statue was carved from a single piece of cypress, divided to form the front and back. The sapwood core was hollowed to prevent the statue from cracking, and additional pieces of wood were used for the lap and arms. The image was then ornamented with delicate motifs in mineral pigments and cut gold leaf.

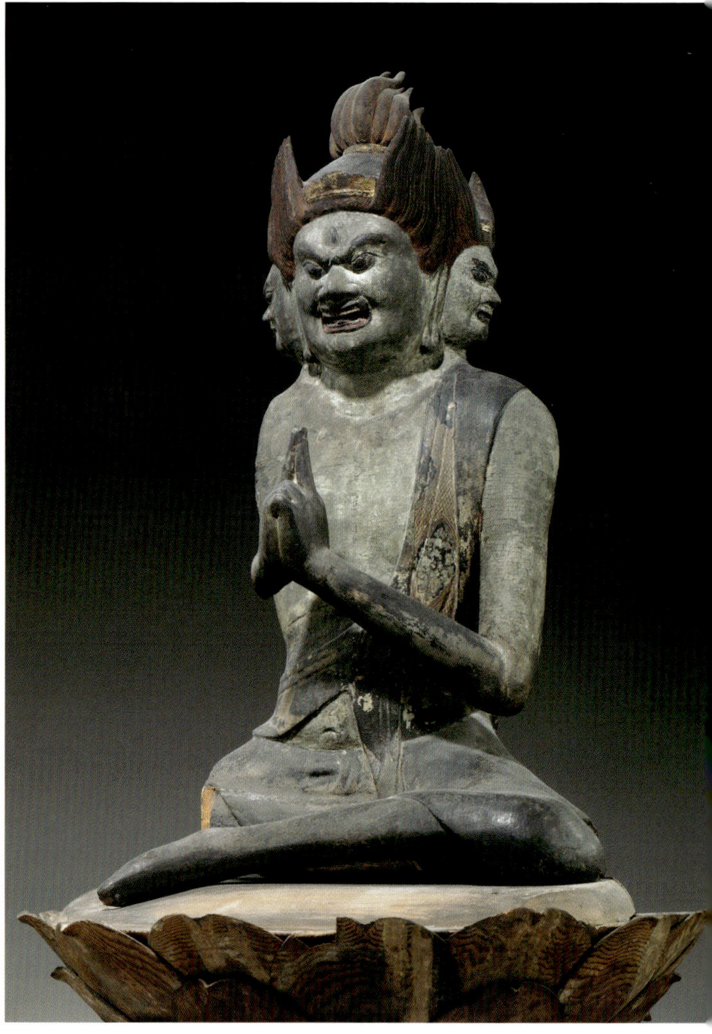

Japanese cypress with polychrome and gold; split-and-joined construction

H. of figure 87.9 cm (H. 34⅝ in.)

Special Chinese and Japanese Fund 05.228

Miroku, the Bodhisattva of the Future

Kaikei (active 1189–1223)

Kamakura period, 1189

This statue of Miroku is the earliest dated work by Kaikei, one of the master sculptors of the Kamakura period. He was part of a group of artists, known as the Kei school, centered in Nara who were chiefly responsible for refurbishing the damaged temples after the destruction of the ancient capital by battling warrior clans in 1180. The statues that these men created are noted for their new naturalism, evident here in the curve of the pose, the fullness of the body, and the use of inlaid crystal eyes. The understated refinement of the statue reflects Kaikei's personal interpretation of the emerging style, which tends to be more assertive in the works of other members of the school.

During the twelfth century, many Buddhists despaired that the ongoing civil wars and inauspicious fires marked the advent of the Period of the End of the Buddhist Law, an age when the teachings of the Historical Buddha would be lost. They turned to Miroku, the bodhisattva whom they believed would reestablish a perfect understanding of the law 584 million years after the death of the Buddha. Kaikei enclosed a copy of a Buddhist text describing Miroku's powers inside this statue, which was once housed at the Nara monastic center of Kōfuku-ji. A postscript states that he created the image for the repose of his deceased parents and teacher.

Japanese cypress with gold and inlaid crystal; split-and-joined construction
H. of figure 106.6 cm (H. 41 15/16 in.)
Chinese and Japanese Special Fund 20.723a–c

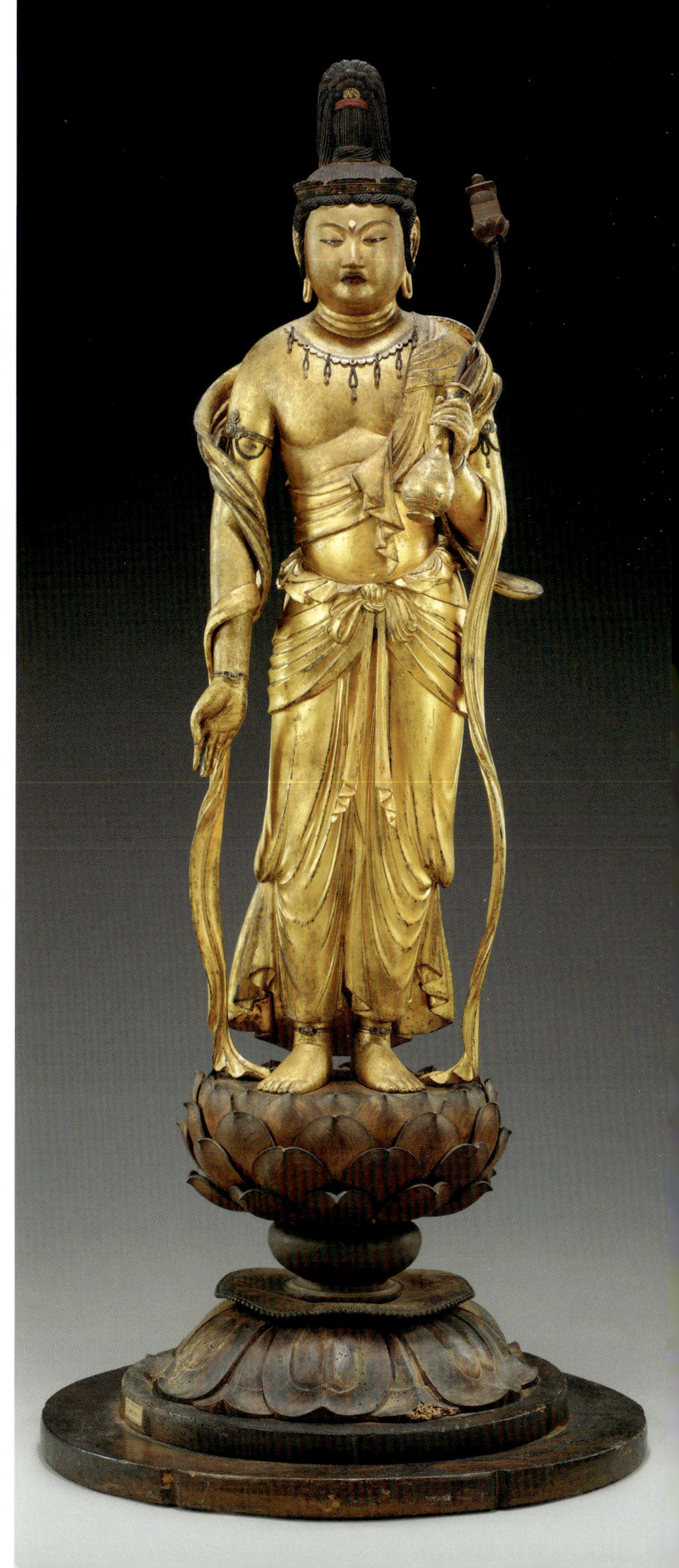

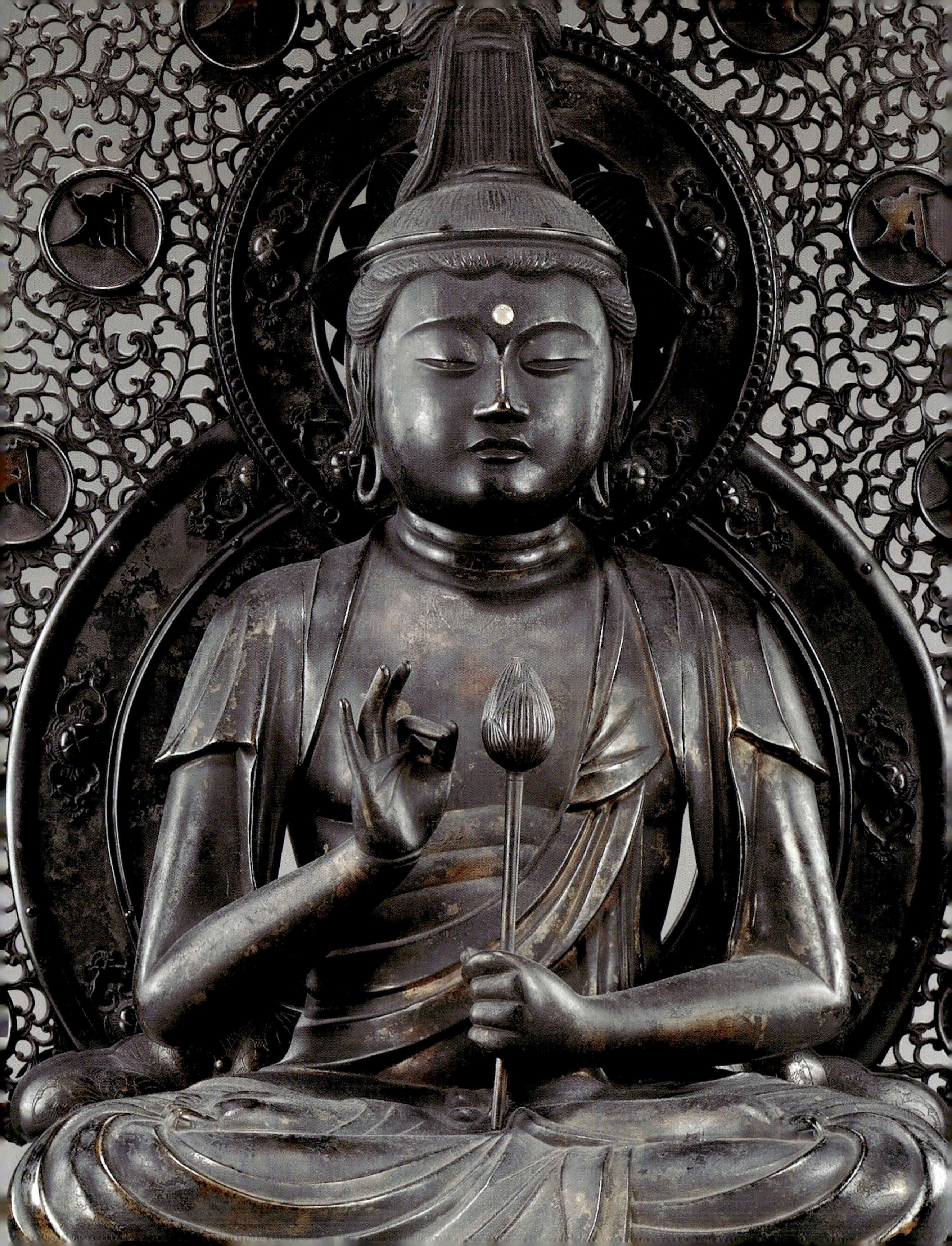

Shō Kannon, the Bodhisattva of Compassion

Saichi (dates unknown)

Kamakura period, 1269

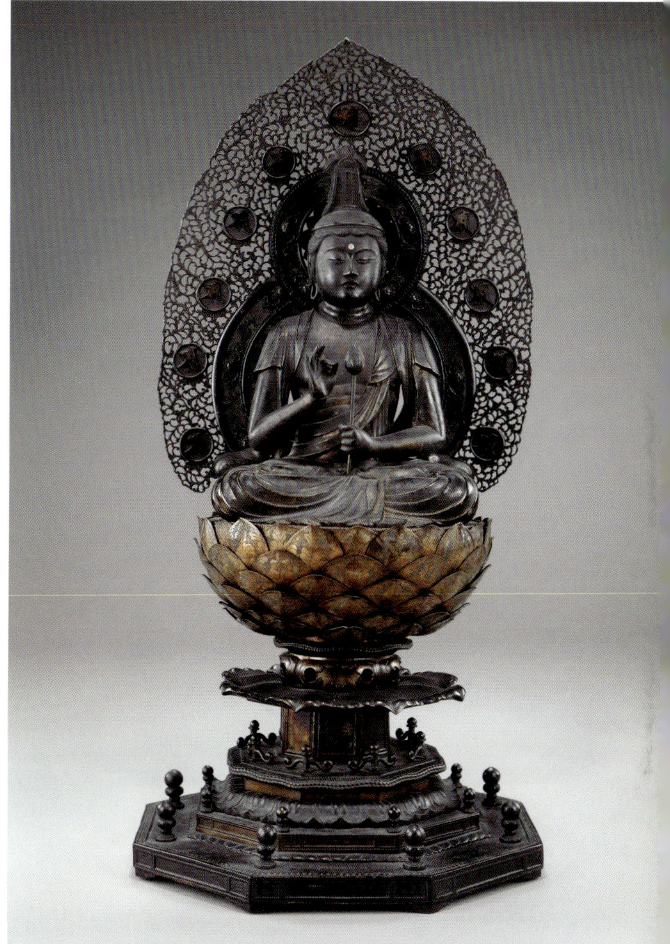

Kannon has always been one of the most popularly worshipped bodhisattvas in Japan. Images of the deity vary greatly, for texts describe many different manifestations of the bodhisattva, each with specific powers. Some have numerous heads or ferocious guises, but Shō Kannon, the most frequently encountered form of the deity, is identified by his benevolent expression and lotus attribute.

Considered one of the largest and finest examples of bronze sculpture dating to the Kamakura period, this image of Shō Kannon is seated upon an elaborate lotus pedestal with individually cast petals that once would have been further embellished with strands of colored glass beads. The deity holds a lotus in his left hand and positions the fingers of his right in a gesture of argumentation. Behind him is an intricate mandorla with an openwork floral arabesque pattern. Disks with the Sanskrit syllable that represents Kannon are arranged to the left and right; one with the syllable representing Dainichi, the supreme deity, is placed above the head.

An inscription engraved on the lowest section of the pedestal indicates that the statue was originally enshrined in the main hall of Matsuo-dera, a temple in Shiga Prefecture now known as Kongōrin-ji. The sculptor, Saichi, cast accompanying images of Fudō myōō and Bishamonten, which unfortunately no longer exist. Like many donors of the time, Inukami Toshiyoshi commissioned the statues so that his relatives—members of the Ochi and Hata clans—would thrive and would, according to the inscription, "achieve peace in this life and attain good incarnations in the future."

Gilt bronze; cast from piece molds
H. of figure 50.3 cm (H. 19 13/16 in.)
William Sturgis Bigelow Collection 11.11447

Hachiman in the Guise of a Buddhist Monk

Kōshun (active 1315–1328)

Kamakura period, dated 1328

This statue of the Shinto god Hachiman assuming the appearance of a Buddhist monk reflects the integration of indigenous Japanese religious beliefs with Buddhism. Originally a rather obscure deity whose main shrine was located in northern Kyushu, Hachiman was thought to have great oracular powers. Among these was the ability to locate the gold necessary to gild the colossal statue of the Great Buddha erected at Tōdai-ji in Nara in the middle of the eighth century, as a symbol of state support for the Buddhist faith. As a result, Hachiman was made a protective deity of the Nara temple and thereafter served as a protective deity of subsequent capitals of Japan.

In this image, Hachiman is depicted with the shorn head and robes of a monk. Carved from fourteen different pieces of wood that were first joined and then hollowed, the figure bears an inscription on the interior of the head stating that it was produced by the Buddhist sculptor Kōshun in 1328. A member of the Kei school active in the Nara region, Kōshun adopted his school's naturalistic style, evident in the deep folds of the robes and the full forms of the body. Scholars have suggested that the statue was made for Saidai-ji, a temple in Nara that conducted rituals calling on Hachiman to protect the nation from the threat of invading Mongols during the late thirteenth and early fourteenth centuries.

Japanese cypress with polychrome and inlaid crystal; joined woodblock construction
H. of figure 82.3 cm (H. 32⅜ in.)
Maria Antoinette Evans Fund and Contributions 36.413

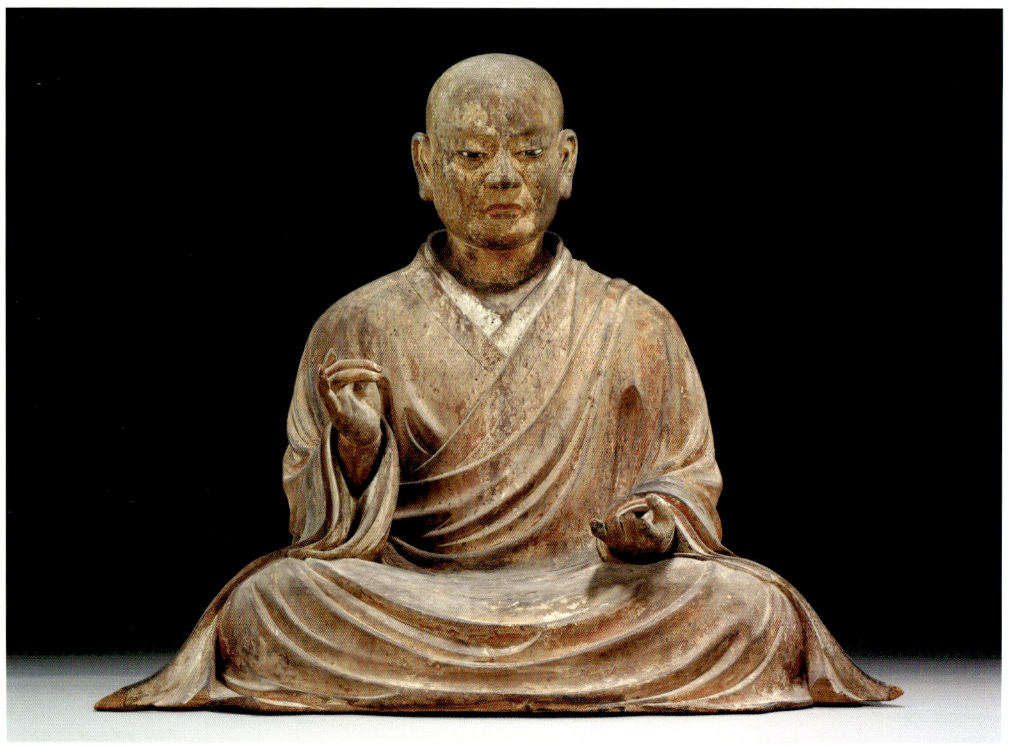

Aizen myōō, the Wisdom King of Passion

Nanbokuchō period, 14th century

Aizen myōō, a deity in the Esoteric Buddhist pantheon, is believed to transform the desire for worldly gain into the desire for enlightenment. The iconography of this wrathful Wisdom King was dictated by the *Yugi-kyō*, a Buddhist text brought to Japan from China in the ninth century. According to this text, Aizen should have skin the color of the rays of the sun, three eyes filled with rage, a crown with a lion head, and six arms. Also, he should bear implements that symbolize his resolve to conquer ignorance—the bow, arrow (now missing from this example), lotus flower, bell, and ritual thunderbolt. The volumetric treatment of the deity in this image and the use of cut gold leaf and floral arabesques to ornament the robes were artistic decisions made by the unknown sculptor and members of his atelier.

Worship of Aizen increased in popularity during the late thirteenth century, when Japan faced the threat of invasion by the Mongols. The deity was said to have the power to rally forces against the enemy, which eventually was repelled by storms off the coast of the southern island of Kyushu.

Cypress with polychrome, gold, and inlaid crystal; joined woodblock construction
H. of figure 91.7 cm (H. 36⅛ in.)
Gift of Francis G. Curtis 09.383

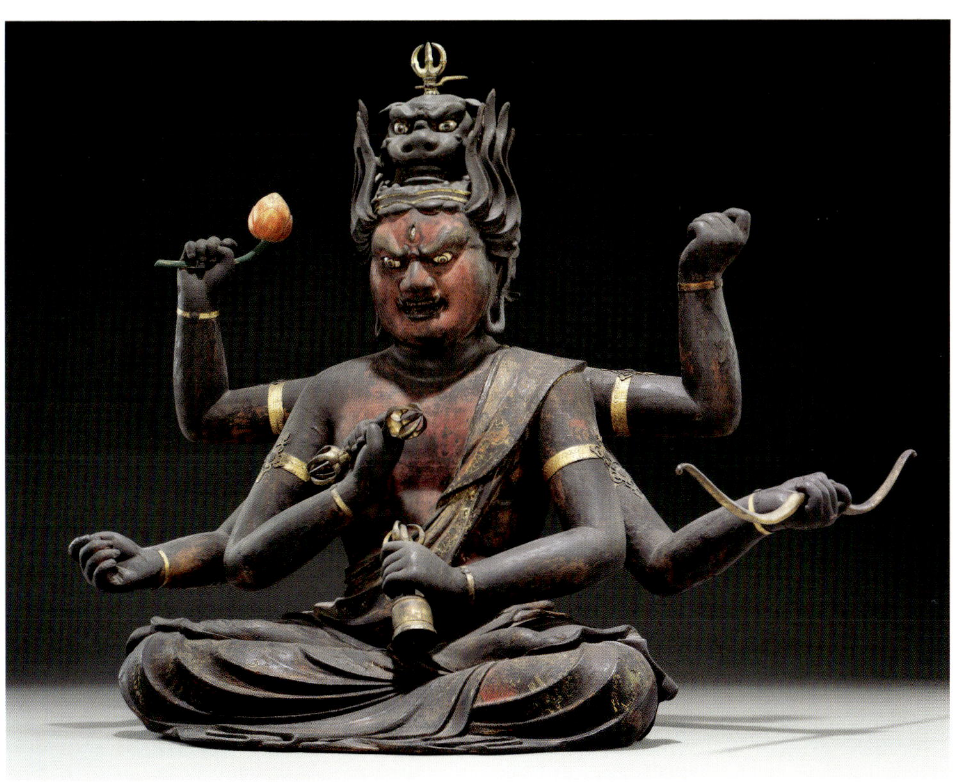

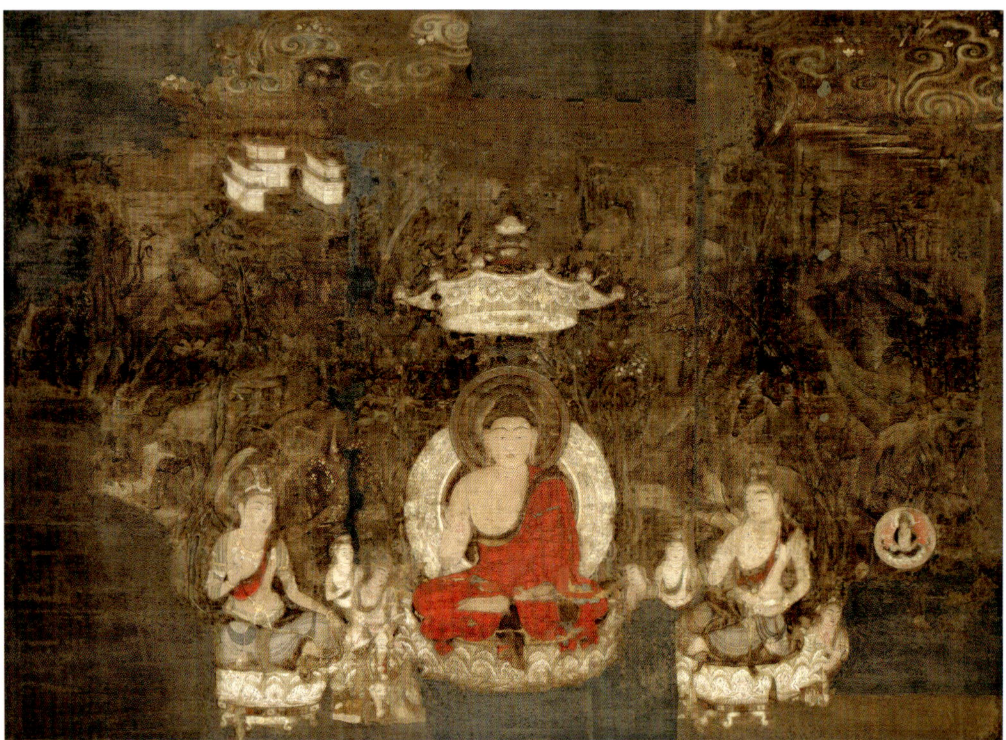

Shaka, the Historical Buddha, Preaching on Vulture Peak

Nara period, 8th century

Considered one of the most important landmarks in the history of East Asian art in a Western collection, *Shaka, the Historical Buddha, Preaching on Vulture Peak* is the earliest surviving monumental landscape composition on a woven support from anywhere in East Asia. In the foreground of this panel, the Historical Buddha preaches the *Lotus Sutra*, a text that promises salvation to both men and women, to his assembled followers and attendant bodhisattvas. Although difficult to discern, craggy mountain peaks and deep ravines extend across the background. The sixteenth chapter of the *Lotus Sutra* describes the setting for the sermon as a Pure Land in which there are lush gardens with jeweled trees and towers. The instruments of the heavenly musicians, who shower flowers down below, can be seen in the upper sections of the painting.

The work has suffered greatly over the centuries and has undergone several campaigns of restoration. An inscription dating to 1148 that was once affixed to its back described the work as the *Hokkedō konpon mandara*, the primary mandala of the Hokkedō (Lotus Hall), thereby associating it with the Lotus Hall (now popularly known as the Sangatsudō) at Tōdai-ji in Nara. The inscription went on to relate that by the twelfth century the sections below where the Historical Buddha is seated had already been entirely destroyed and required repair.

Panel; ink, color, and gold on ramie
107.1 x 143.5 cm (42 3/16 x 56 1/2 in.)
William Sturgis Bigelow Collection 11.6120

Daiitoku myōō, the Wisdom King of Great Awe-Inspiring Power

Heian period, 11th century

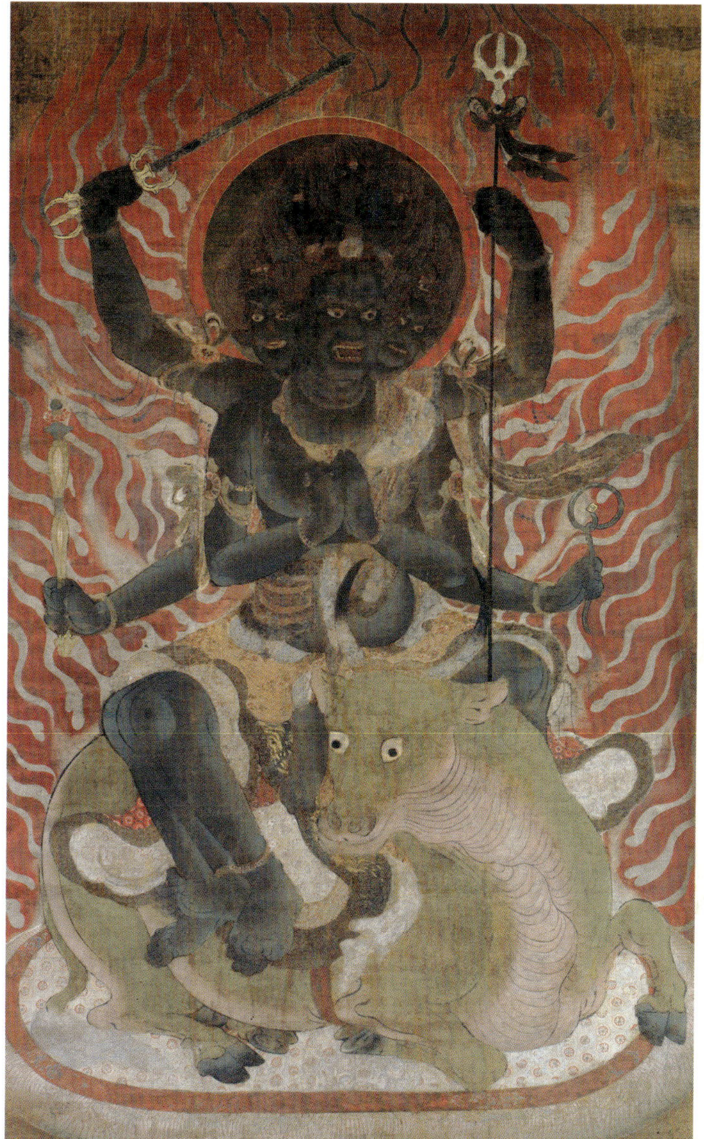

Believed by some to be one of the most important Japanese Buddhist paintings in a Western collection, this image depicts the six-headed, six-armed, six-legged Daiitoku myōō, who represents the ability of the enlightened believer to triumph over death. To symbolize this power, the deity sits on the back of a water buffalo, the animal traditionally associated with the King of Death. Daiitoku's multiple heads and limbs indicate that he is stronger than any human. The gesture made by his central hands symbolizes the ability of righteous wrath to pierce through ignorance, and the staff, sword, and club he holds are the weapons he uses to help a believer attain enlightenment. The noose is the noose of truth; once caught in its snare, the devotee cannot lie to himself or to others.

When worship of Daiitoku was first introduced to Japan, the deity was revered as one of the Five Wisdom Kings. By the late Heian period, rituals were often directed specifically to him, not only for the protection of the state but also for personal needs. The monumental scale of this painting suggests that the image was used for more public benefits. The vivid flames and bold forms of the deity and the bull increase the sense of the image's power, while the use of fine cut-gold-leaf patterns and floral motifs add to its elegance.

Panel; ink, color, gold, and silver on silk
194.3 x 118.8 cm (76½ x 46¾ in.)
Given in memory of Okakura-Kakuzō by William Sturgis Bigelow 20.750

Nyoirin Kannon, the Bodhisattva of Compassion, with the Wish-Granting Jewel and the Magic Wheel
Heian period, 12th century

Nyoirin Kannon is revered as one of the six forms of the Bodhisattva of Compassion, who appears in different guises to assist those trapped in the Six Realms of Existence. He is believed to preside over the realm of *devas*—the highest rank of beings, who dwell in the heavens but have yet to be released from the cycle of birth and rebirth. During the late Heian period, high-ranking monks performed rituals in front of Nyoirin's image to help others avert calamities, increase merit, and ensure affection. The deity's name stems from the magic jewel (*nyoi*), which fulfills all desires, and the wheel of the Buddhist law (*rin*), both of which he holds in his six arms.

Generally identified by his almost feminine appearance, Nyoirin is seated here in a pose of royal ease on an elaborate lotus pedestal in his mountain paradise of Potalaka, which rises from the roiling sea. Thin strips of cut gold leaf outline the folds of his luxurious multilayered robes, colored in silver and mineral pigments, and garlands of jewels and ribbons gracefully curve around his body. He wears an effigy of Amida, the Buddha of Infinite Light, in his elaborate floral crown. The painting is unusual in that Nyoirin is accompanied by Kichijōten, the goddess of wealth and beauty; her attendant Zennishi dōji; and Basu sennin, a mountain ascetic.

Panel; ink, color, gold, and silver on silk
98.8 x 44.7 cm (38⅞ x 17⅝ in.)
Fenollosa-Weld Collection 11.4032

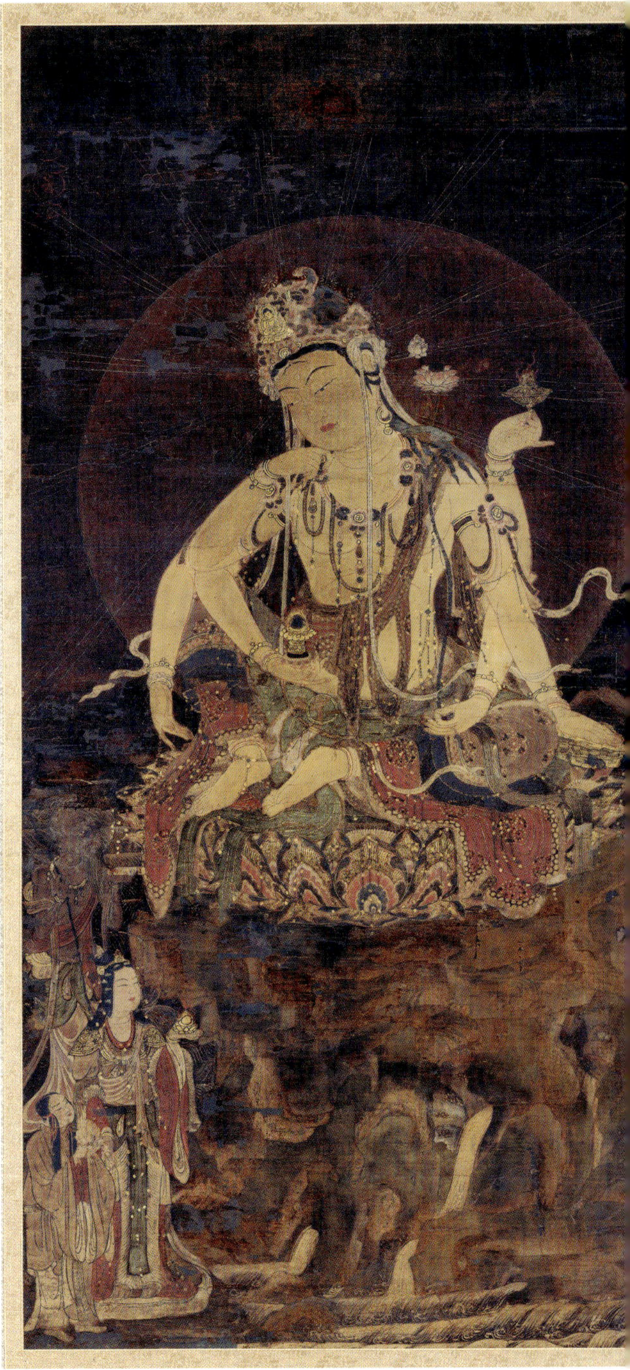

Batō Kannon, the Horse-Headed Bodhisattva of Compassion

Heian period, 12th century

With his three heads (each with three eyes and fanged teeth), eight arms, and intense red skin, Batō assumes a ferocious guise common to Wisdom Kings, but he is worshipped as one of the six forms of Kannon, the bodhisattva of compassion. Identified by the horse head in his crown and by his distinctive hand gesture with the palms pressed together, Batō is thought to preside over the fate of beings reborn in the form of animals because of their misdeeds. Furthermore, from the late eleventh century on, he became the focus of rituals to provide expiation for sins and power over enemies.

This painting is executed in the extremely sumptuous style that was dominant during the twelfth century, when aristocrats were the chief patrons of Esoteric Buddhism. Confronting the viewer, Batō sits under a floral canopy festooned with strands of jewels. His halo is decorated with intricate arabesques in gold leaf, and his robes and lotus pedestal are ornamented with thin lines of cut gold and silver and delicate floral patterns in polychrome. Three of his left hands hold an axe for protection against the enemies of the faith, a wheel of the law, and a fly whisk; on the right, he bears a monk's staff and a bird-headed ewer containing the nectar of life.

Panel; ink, color, gold, and silver on silk
166.1 x 82.7 cm (65 3/8 x 32 9/16 in.)
Fenollosa-Weld Collection 11.4035

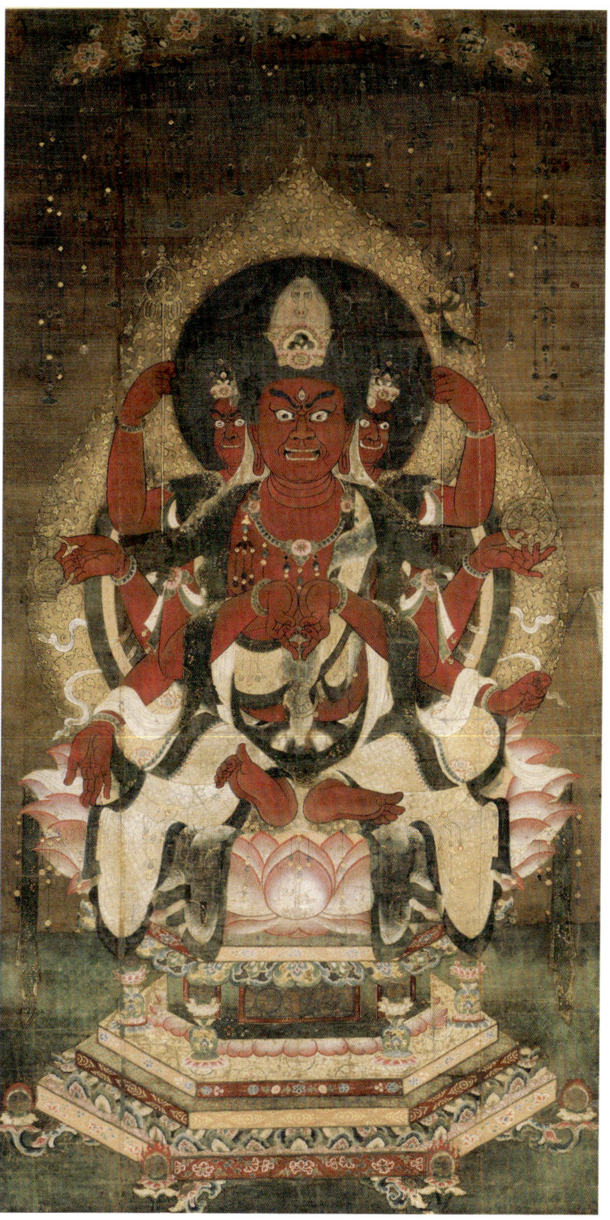

Fugen enmei, the Bodhisattva of Universal Virtue Who Prolongs Life
Heian period, 12th century

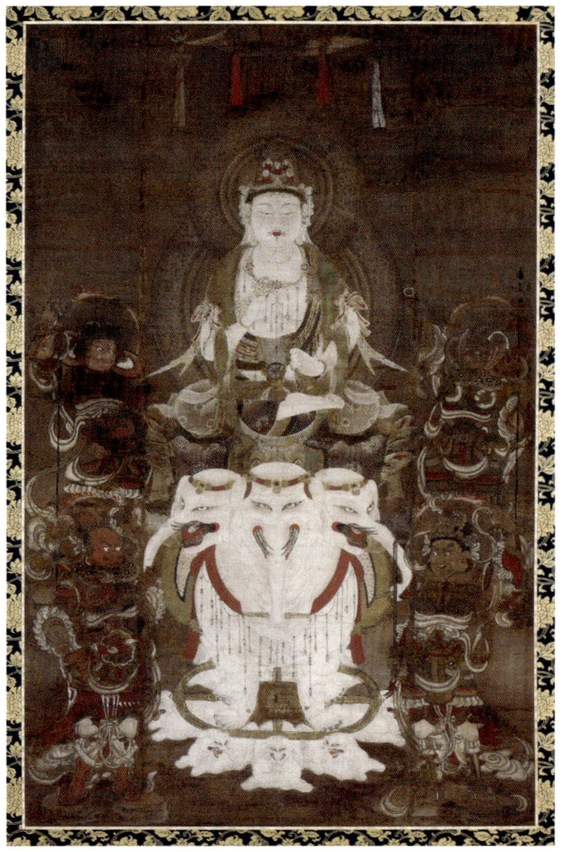

Fearing the possibility of premature death and believing that Fugen enmei had the ability to prolong life, members of the Heian aristocracy had rituals performed in front of a scroll of the deity. Each of these paintings featured Fugen facing forward, seated on a lotus pedestal. Yet within the two sects of Esoteric Buddhism—Tendai and Shingon—there were slight differences in the iconography: Shingon paintings depicted Fugen with twenty arms, whereas Tendai scrolls showed him with only two arms, as seen in this work. Here the deity is seated on the back of a three-headed elephant that stands on the Indestructible Wheel of the Cosmos, which in turn is supported by eight smaller elephants (not all of which are visible). Each of the primary elephant's heads has six tusks outlined in now-tarnished silver. Fugen holds a *vajra*, a ritual implement symbolizing a thunderbolt, in his right hand, and a bell in his left.

This image shares many of the compositional elements found in other twelfth-century paintings—the jeweled canopy, the elaborate mandorla, and the intricate floral and geometric patterns ornamenting the deity's robes in cut gold and polychrome. In contrast to the formal central deity, the Four Guardian Kings, who protect the cardinal directions, are rendered at his sides in fluid ink lines that display a sense of movement.

Panel; ink, color, gold, and silver on silk
141.7 x 88.3 cm (55 9/16 x 34 3/4 in.)
Fenollosa-Weld Collection 11.4036

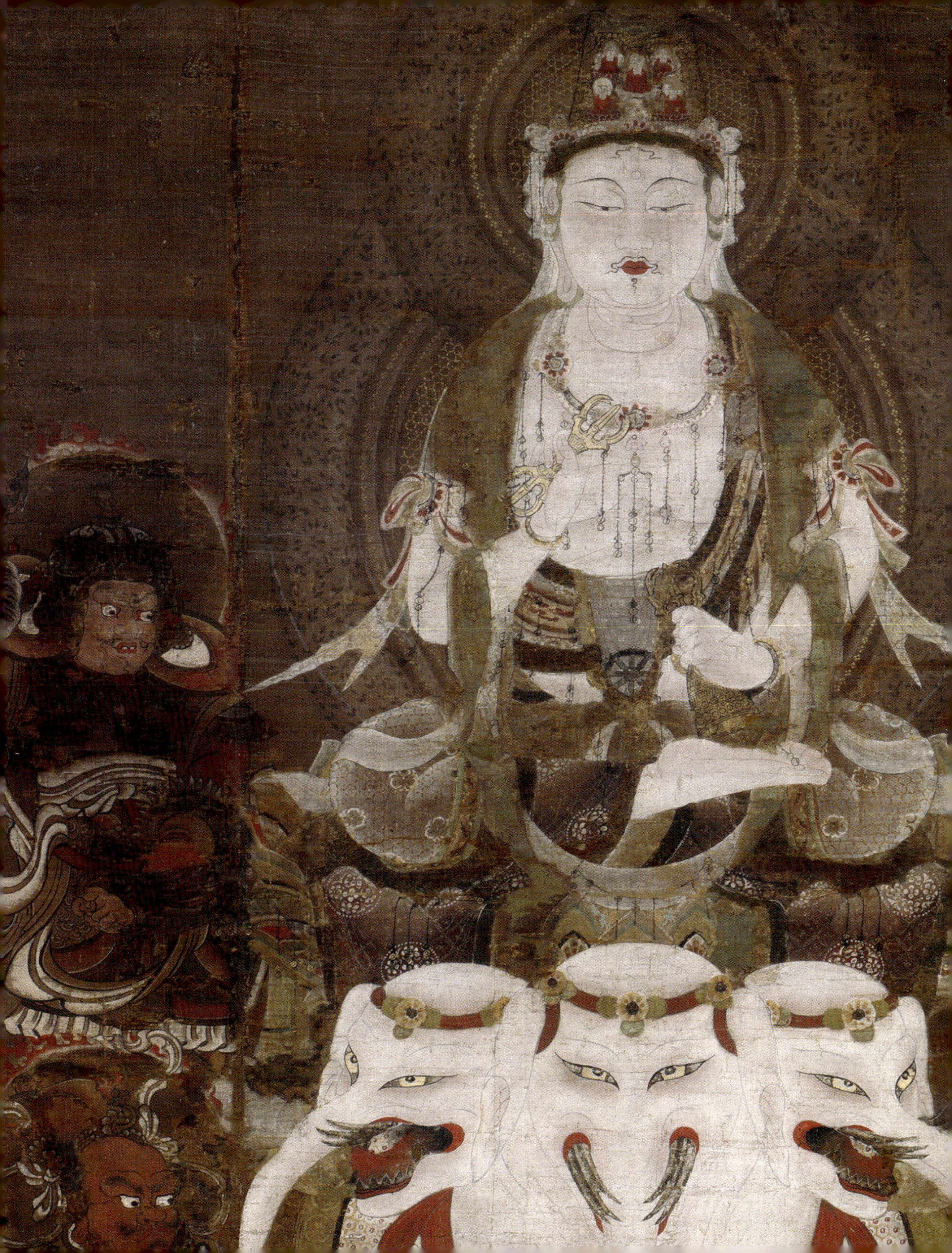

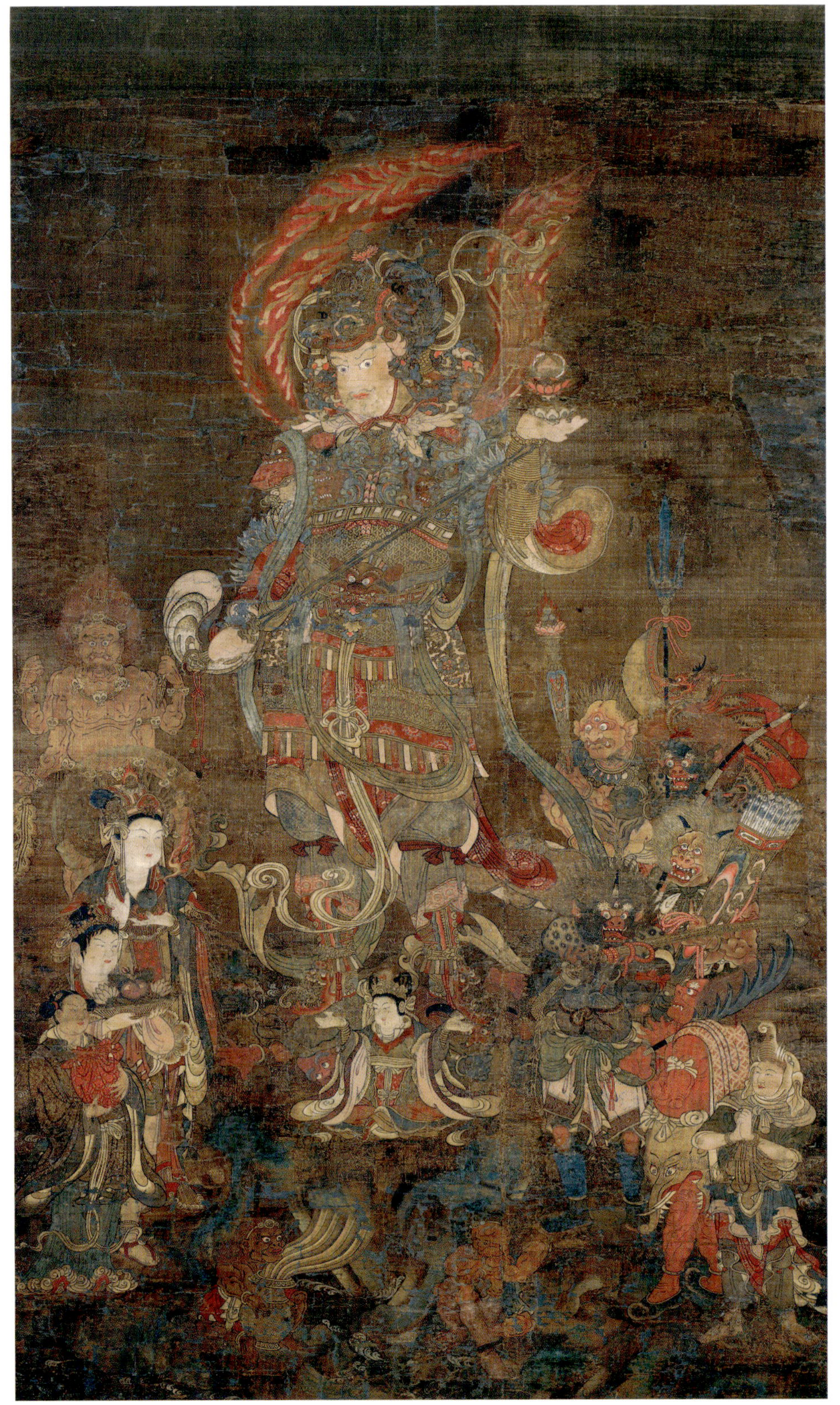

Bishamonten, the Guardian of the North, with His Retinue

Kamakura period, late 12th–early 13th century

This image of Bishamonten, the Guardian of the North, with his attendants is one of the most dramatic Buddhist paintings in the collection of the Museum of Fine Arts. Trampling two demons underfoot, Bishamonten wields a long, silver-edged sword in his right hand and holds a pagoda on a lotus pedestal in his left. Demonic heads embellish the breastplate, sleeves, and belt of his armor, and cinnabar and lead-red flames flash behind him. To Bishamonten's right stands his voluptuous consort, Kichijōten, the Goddess of Good Fortune, identifiable by her crown capped with a flaming jewel. She is accompanied by two other attendants—a young woman holding a basin of lotus blossoms and a young man, Zennishi dōji, clasping a bundle in both arms.

The special power of this painting lies in the detailing of the subsidiary deities. For example, through Kichijōten's silvery, semitransparent mandorla can be seen a four-armed, skull-ornamented demon. In one of his hands he clasps an animal skin, and in another he seizes a victim by the hair. To Bishamonten's left is a group of five monstrous figures, some sporting horns and others, extra eyes.

Bishamonten is one of the Four Guardian Kings who protect the cardinal directions. Since the north is thought to harbor particularly malevolent spirits, Bishamonten is accorded special reverence as the protector of towns and bearer of good fortune. When he is worshipped independently, he is often depicted as seen here, held aloft by Jiten, the Earth Deity.

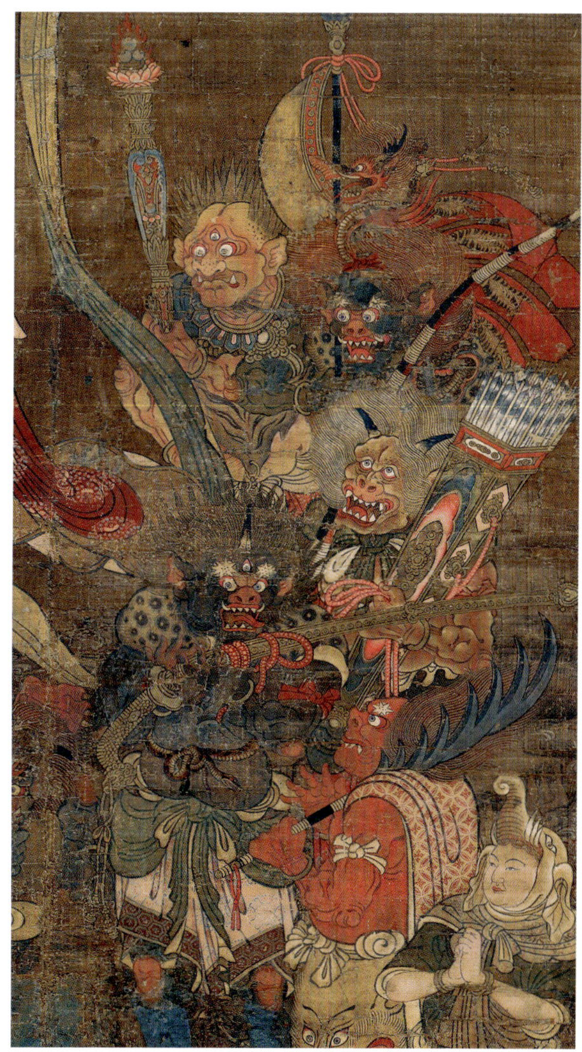

Panel; ink, color, gold, and silver on silk
119.1 x 68.1 cm (46 7/8 x 26 13/16 in.)
Special Chinese and Japanese Fund 05.202

Ichiji kinrin, the Cosmic Buddha of the Golden Wheel

Kamakura period, beginning of the 13th century

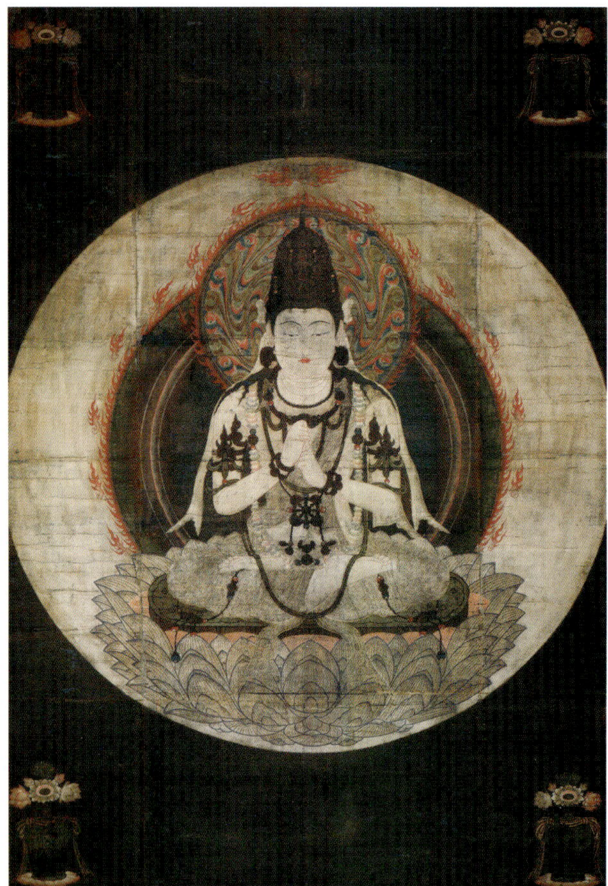

In the complex pantheon of Esoteric Buddhist deities, individual Buddhas and bodhisattvas may appear in different guises that embody specific powers. In this painting, Dainichi, the supreme deity of Esoteric Buddhism, is depicted in his manifestation of supernatural strength as the Buddha of the Golden Wheel. Seated on a white lotus pedestal, he is surrounded by a flaming halo suggesting mystical emanations of energy. Vases at the four corners of the painting represent the flowers of the four cardinal directions that are found on Esoteric Buddhist altars. On the deity's headdress are five small Buddhas that indicate his wisdom; around his neck is a pendant with a golden wheel that identifies him as the universal monarch. His hands are held in the *mudrā* called *chiken-in*, a ritual gesture that symbolizes his great knowledge.

During the twelfth and thirteenth centuries, rituals were conducted in front of images of Ichiji kinrin on behalf of those who wanted to ensure their safety; the ceremonies were believed to be effective at preventing floods and disease and prolonging life. The power of the rituals was thought to be so great that they could interfere with other ceremonies taking place within a five-mile radius. Thus, only the highest-ranking monks, who had mastered the complicated chants, memorized the intricate hand gestures, and achieved the necessary level of mental concentration, were permitted to officiate.

Panel; ink, color, gold, and silver on silk
117.9 x 78.5 cm (46 7/16 x 30 7/8 in.)
Fenollosa-Weld Collection 11.4039

Iconographic Drawing of Miroku, the Buddha of the Future

Kamakura period, 13th century

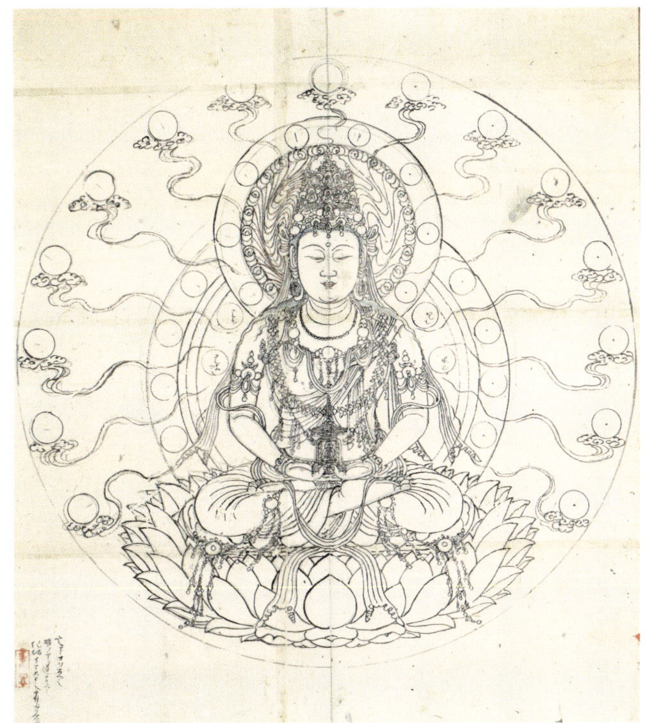

The bodhisattva Miroku is thought to be residing in his Tuṣita heaven until he eventually appears in the future as a Buddha. In East Asia, adherents of the Buddhist faith believe that there are three periods of the Buddhist law: the Period of the Perfect Law, which followed the death of the Historical Buddha, when his teachings were followed and enlightenment was possible; the Period of the Counterfeit Law, during which the Buddha's teachings were followed but enlightenment could no longer be achieved; and the present Period of the End of the Law, when the teachings cease to be practiced. Although Miroku will descend only after the conclusion of this latter period, he welcomes true believers upon death to his heaven, where they can strive to attain enlightenment.

In this drawing, Miroku wears elaborate jewelry and a crown adorned with the images of the Five Wisdom Buddhas, and holds his hands in the gesture of meditation, cradling a pagoda. Iconographic drawings, generally distinguished from other Buddhist paintings by their informality and free use of ink on paper, were often used in Esoteric temples to instruct monks in the mysteries of the teachings as conveyed by celebrated masters. Sometimes they were used as manuals with color notations for artists producing Buddhist images or as preparatory works. In the lower left corner of this drawing, the celebrated thirteenth-century monk Myōe added a three-line inscription suggesting that the artist change the position of the hands and the size of the Buddhas in the crown, and add a lotus base for the pagoda. The seal of Kōzan-ji, Myōe's monastery in northwest Kyoto, has been impressed on the reverse.

Panel; ink and color on paper
92.6 x 80 cm (36 7/16 x 31 1/2 in.)
William Sturgis Bigelow Collection 11.6237

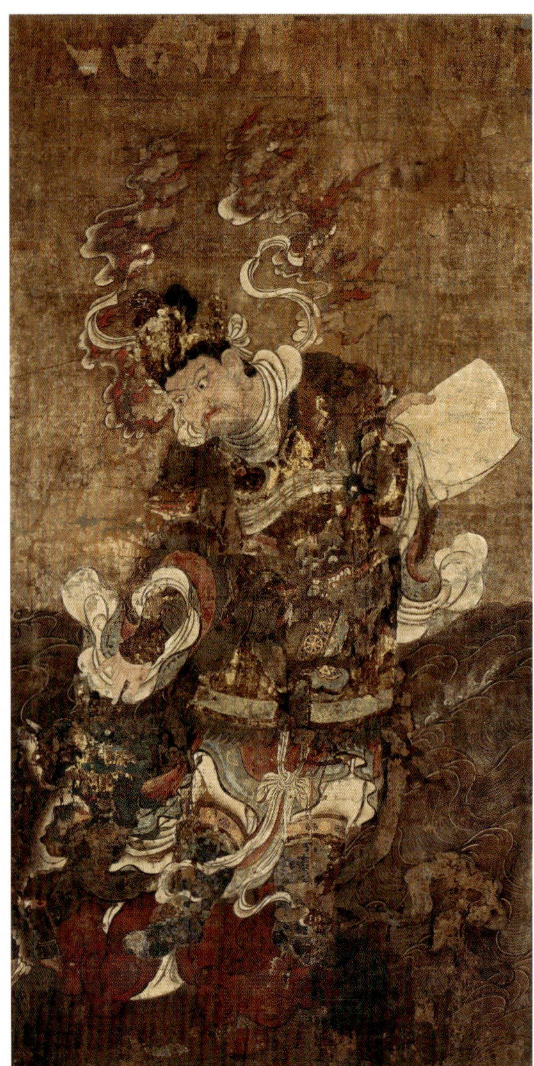

Four Guardian Kings (Kōmokuten, the Guardian of the West)

Chōmyō (active 1233–1295)

Kamakura period, about 1253

Until the fourteenth century, professional Buddhist painters rarely signed their works, so in most cases, authorship is unknown. This image of Kōmokuten is from a remarkable group of panels depicting the Four Guardian Kings, who protect the Buddhist law, trampling creatures symbolic of nonbelievers in the midst of a roiling sea. These paintings have been identified as the work of Chōmyō, one of the most well respected professional artists of his day. Active at an atelier associated with Kōfuku-ji, one of the great temples of Nara, Chōmyō not only executed paintings but also decorated a large number of Buddhist statues. The exacting detail found in the complicated floral, geometric, and Buddhist motifs on the deity's garments is characteristic of Chōmyō's works.

When the paintings were acquired by the MFA curator and supporter Ernest Fenollosa in the late nineteenth century, they were first thought to have come from the Nara temple Tōdai-ji. Scholars have since demonstrated, however, that they originally adorned a fixed partition behind the main deity of the Shingon hall at Eikyū-ji. Once a grand temple located southwest of Nara proper and associated with Isonokami Shrine, Eikyū-ji was dismantled during the nineteenth century following a government policy of banning integrated Shinto-Buddhist institutions. Its paintings and statues are now dispersed in museums throughout the world.

One of a set of four panels; ink, color, and gold on silk
148.7 x 72.3 cm (58 9/16 x 28 7/16 in.)
Fenollosa-Weld Collection 11.4064

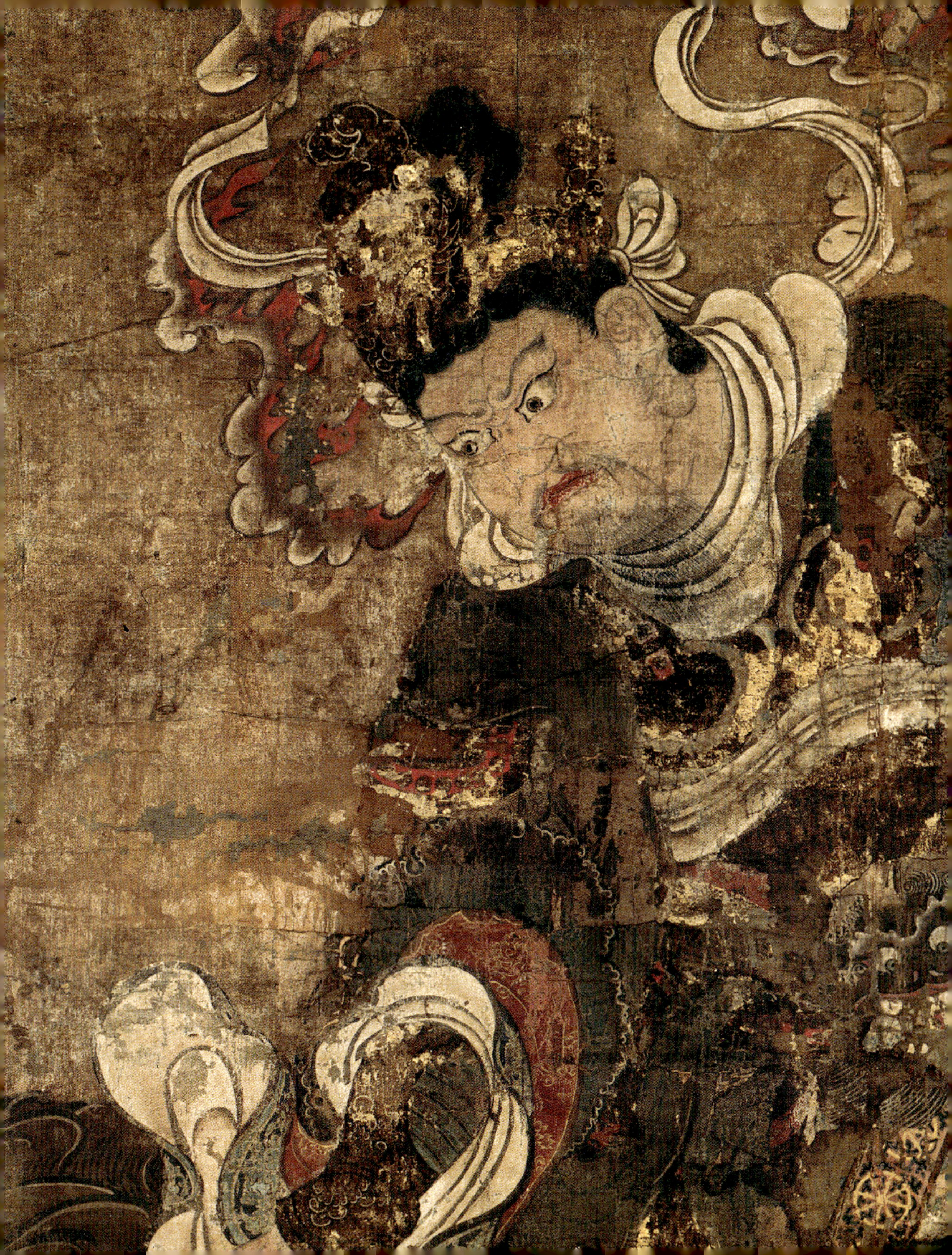

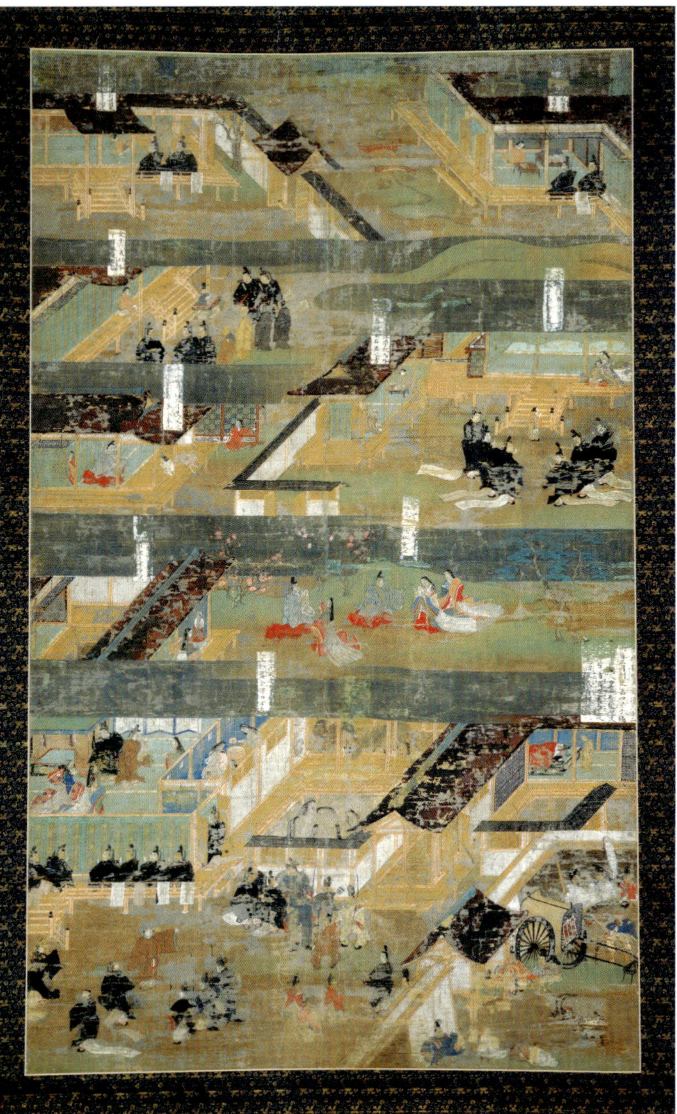

Pictorial Biography of Prince Shōtoku

Kamakura–Nanbokuchō periods, 14th century

Depictions of events from the life of the Historical Buddha set the prototype for pictorial biographies of eminent Buddhists throughout East Asia. Prince Shōtoku (574–622), who centralized the authority of the imperial court and authored Japan's first constitution, was also instrumental in disseminating Buddhism and founding some of the country's most important temples. Soon after the prince died, his biography became embroidered with legend, and over the centuries Buddhists of all sects worshipped him.

This monumental hanging scroll was once part of a set of ten that illustrated more than one hundred events in the prince's life; only five scrolls from the original group have survived. The works would have hung on either side of a central sculptural icon during the performance of important rituals. Monks would have pointed out the individual scenes, which are arranged in registers of architecture or landscape and separated by schematic bands of light blue clouds. White cartouches noting brief biographical details and the age of the prince provided guidance as to the sequence of the events.

One of the most celebrated stories is shown in the second register from the bottom. At the age of two, the prince stood on the verandah of his residence and clasped his hands in prayer. Turning to the east, he recited the name of the Buddha. This apocryphal event recalls the infant Buddha's proclamation of his future role as a religious leader when he took steps in the four directions and pointed to heaven and earth.

One from a set of ten hanging scrolls;
ink, color, and gold on silk
160.4 x 93.6 cm (63 1/8 x 36 7/8 in.)
Fenollosa-Weld Collection 11.4800

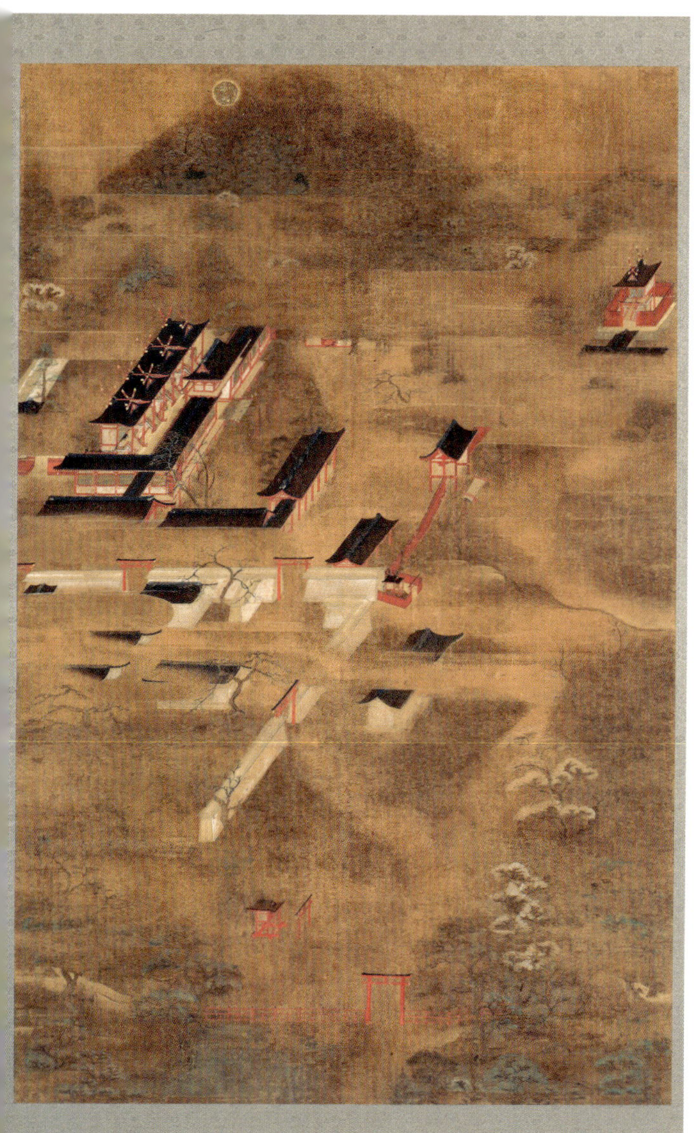

Mandala of Kasuga Shrine

Nanbokuchō period, 14th century

Established in the eighth century at the base of Mount Kasuga in Nara, then Japan's capital, Kasuga Shrine served as the tutelary shrine for the powerful Fujiwara family and was closely associated with their clan temple of Kōfuku-ji. Over time, the complex became the focus of a national cult. Even after the Fujiwara lost much of their political power in the twelfth century, the cult of Kasuga Shrine and its associated Buddhist and Shinto deities continued to flourish. During the fourteenth century, devotees of the shrine formed associations called Kasuga-kō to promote worship of the site and traveled from across Japan to worship there. Critical to their proselytizing efforts were devotional statues and depictions of the shrine precincts, known as mandalas.

Approaching Kasuga along a path through a red *torii* gate in the lower sections of this expansive composition, the viewer passes through groves of cedars and blossoming cherry trees. Deer, considered to be the messengers of the Kasuga gods, amble through the landscape. Extending across the center of the painting is a walled compound composed of the four shrines of the principal deities on the left and a subsidiary shrine, the *wakamiya*, devoted to a child-god on the right. In the upper registers rises the tree-covered form of Mount Kasuga, illuminated in the moonlight.

Panel; ink, color, and gold on silk
146.3 x 90.5 cm (57⅝ x 35⅝ in.)
William Sturgis Bigelow Collection 11.6261

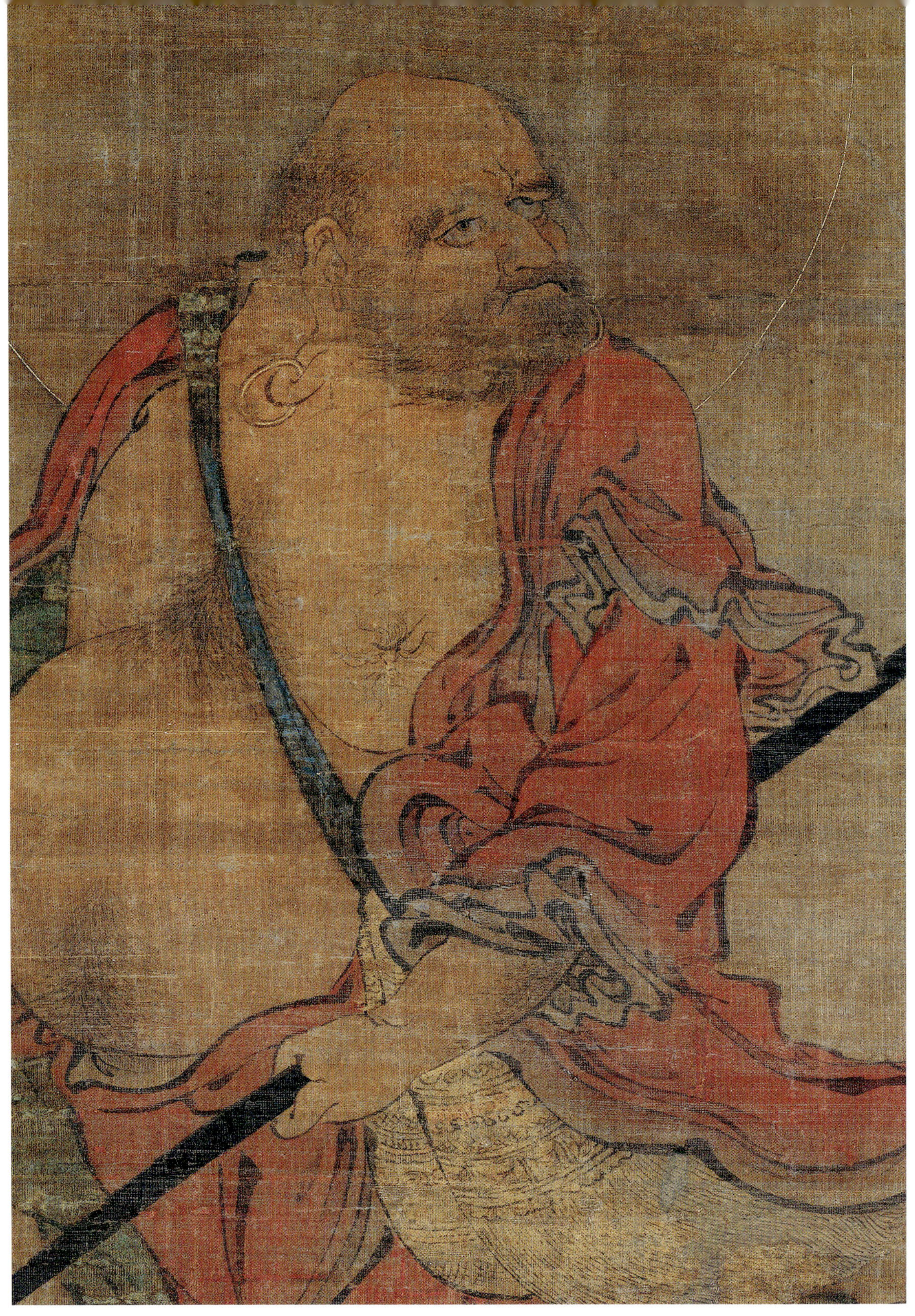

Bodhidharma (Daruma) on a Reed

Nambokuchō period, 14th century

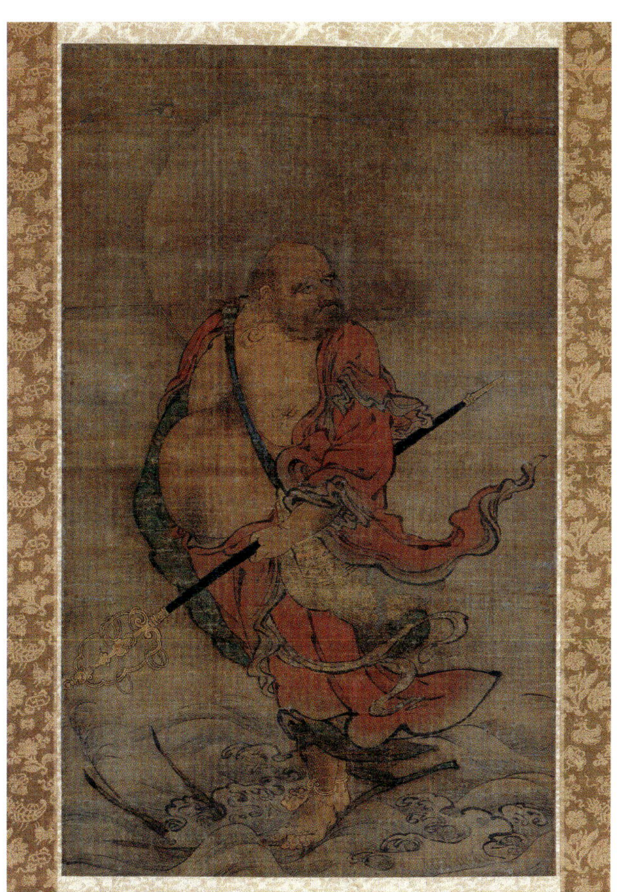

The Zen sect (called Chan in China) traces its legendary beginnings to the arrival in China of the Indian monk Bodhidharma in 520 C.E. Receiving an audience at the court of Emperor Wu of the Liang dynasty in the south, Bodhidharma tried to convince the ruler of the superiority of meditation over traditional devotional practices. The emperor was confounded, however, by the responses that Bodhidharma gave to his questions, phrases that defied conventional logic. Discouraged by this apparent lack of insight, Bodhidharma departed and miraculously rode a broken reed across the Yangzi River into northern China. He spent the next nine years at the Shaolin monastery, seated in meditation in front of a rock cave until acknowledging the Chinese monk Huike as his disciple.

When Zen first gained popularity in Japan, during the thirteenth and early fourteenth centuries, Bodhidharma and eccentric Zen masters were frequently the subjects of paintings produced for the monasteries by amateur as well as professional artists. In this scroll, the robust, red-robed sage rides across the Yangzi on a reed. He turns his head over his left shoulder; his bushy beard and gold earrings bespeak his Indian heritage. Over his right shoulder he wears a bag, and in his left hand he holds a pilgrim's staff. The stylized waves, indicated by ink lines and light blue wash, along with the billowing drapery suggest the velocity with which Bodhidharma was transported to the north.

Hanging scroll; ink, color, and gold on silk
69 x 40.6 cm ($27\frac{13}{16}$ x 16 in.)
William Sturgis Bigelow Collection 11.6312

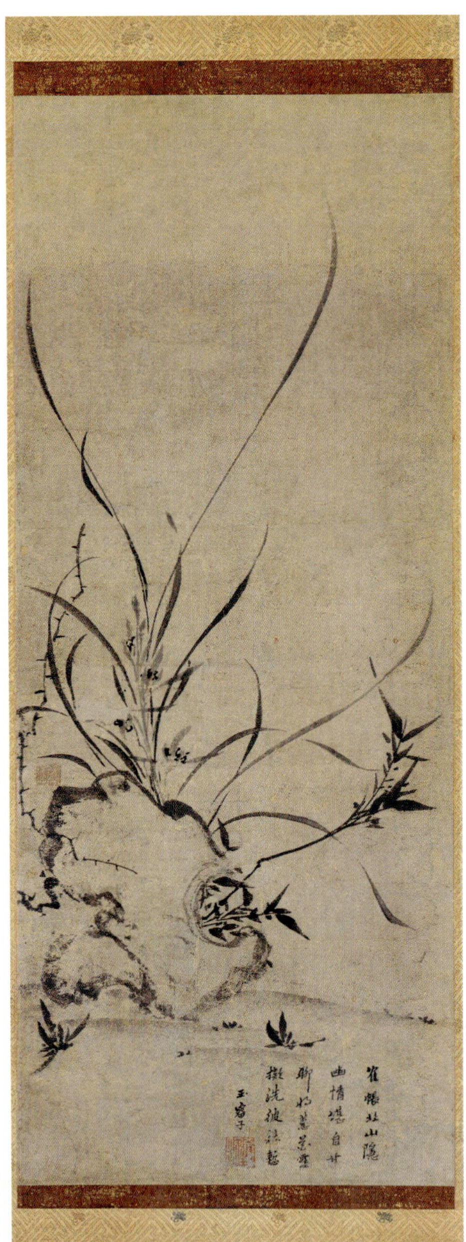

Orchids, Bamboo, and Rock

Gyokuen Bonpō (1349–after 1420)

Muromachi period, late 14th–early 15th century

In the early fourteenth century, with the arrival in Japan of prominent Chinese Chan prelates who were fleeing the invading Mongols, Zen monasteries became centers not only of religious practice but also of continental literati culture. Within the monastic complexes of both Kyoto (then the capital) and Kamakura (seat of the military government), Japanese monks became accomplished poets of Chinese-style verse as well as skilled amateur painters. Gyokuen Bonpō, who was the abbot of several leading temples, including Kennin-ji and Nanzen-ji in Kyoto, was an active member of these literary circles, and for a short period enjoyed the patronage of the military ruler Ashikaga Yoshimochi. His poetic inscriptions can be found on many well-known landscape paintings dating to the early fifteenth century.

Bonpō was also a talented painter. In this hanging scroll, he presents a weathered rock, branches of bamboo, and sprays of orchids with elegant, attenuated leaves, using a splayed brush in a traditional Chinese ink-painting technique known as "flying white," in which the surface of the paper can be seen through the brushwork. In China wild orchids symbolized the upstanding Chinese scholar who retreated to the mountains during periods of morally corrupt government. The subject became popular in Japan because of its strong Chinese associations. Bonpō explored the theme in more than twenty compositions, rearranging the floral motifs across the long, vertical expanse of the scroll format. Each painting became a meditative exercise that allowed him to go beyond the external appearance of the orchids to delve into deeper spiritual truths.

Hanging scroll; ink on paper
90.2 x 35.6 cm (35½ x 14 in.)
Gift of Sylvan Barnet and William Burto 2003.293

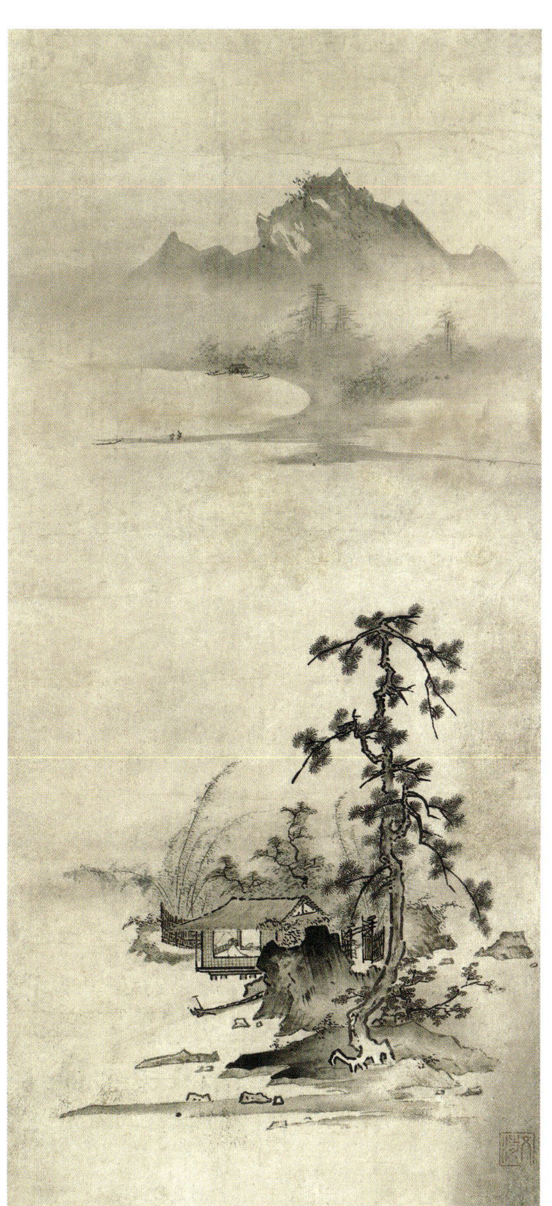

Landscape

Bunsei (active mid-15th century)

Muromachi period, second half of the 15th century

Attempting to find spiritual refuge from the bustle of metropolitan temple life, Zen monks commissioned paintings that depicted scholars' retreats and hermits' cottages. The foreground of this vertical hanging scroll is dominated by a rocky promontory and a towering pine tree, under which is nestled a thatched hut; its reclusive inhabitant can be seen through the open window. In the upper sections of the scroll, fishing skiffs rest along the shore and groves of trees give rise to distant mountains executed in washes of ink.

The juxtaposition of foreground and background elements across an expanse of unpainted paper suggesting misty waters is a spatial device that Japanese artists adopted from Chinese compositions of the Song (960–1279) and Yuan (1279–1368) dynasties. Little is known about the clearly accomplished painter Bunsei. Only six compositions can be attributed to him; four have figural subjects with Zen themes, and one depicts a scenic location in southern China. Bunsei's handling of the landscape forms in the Boston scroll, however, suggests that he was greatly influenced by the works of Shūbun, a celebrated fifteenth-century painter-monk at the Zen monastic complex Shōkoku-ji in Kyoto, who trained a generation of artists.

Hanging scroll; ink on paper
73.2 x 33 cm (28 13/16 x 13 in.)
Special Chinese and Japanese Fund 05.203

Three Sages and Lotuses

Sesshū Tōyō (1420–1506)

Muromachi period, 15th century

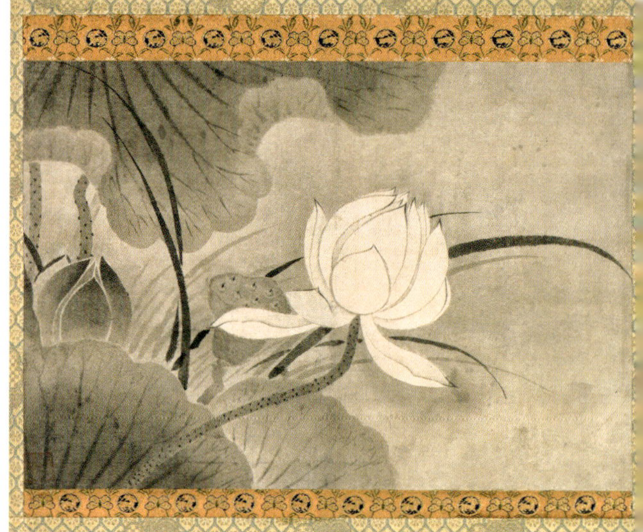

In the Zen sect, scrolls executed in ink on paper were used primarily for private contemplation, rather than for rituals involving members of the entire monastic complex. The theme of the central scroll in this triptych is based on a Chinese story that became popular in the Japanese Zen community. Huiyuan, a recluse, was visited by two friends. While seeing them off, he inadvertently crossed the Tiger Ravine, thus ending his self-imposed retirement from the world. The three men broke out into laughter when they realized the absurdity of Huiyuan's vow. The flanking scrolls depicting lotuses—Buddhist symbols of the faith gaining nourishment from the mundane world but transcending it—reinforce the message of the central painting.

Although he held only a minor monastic rank, Sesshū Tōyō is widely acclaimed as one of the true masters of Japanese ink painting. Trained under artist-monk Tenshō Shūbun at Shōkoku-ji in Kyoto, Sesshū left the monastic complex in the early 1460s after his teacher died. Like most artists of his day, he acquired his understanding of China and its art through books and paintings in Japanese temples and aristocratic collections. But in 1467, some time after executing these works, Sesshū went to China to gain firsthand experience of the landscape.

Set of three hanging scrolls; ink on paper
33.3 x 46.4 cm (13⅛ x 18¼ in.) each
Gift of Robert Treat Paine, Jr. 51.2490, 52.1544, 53.509

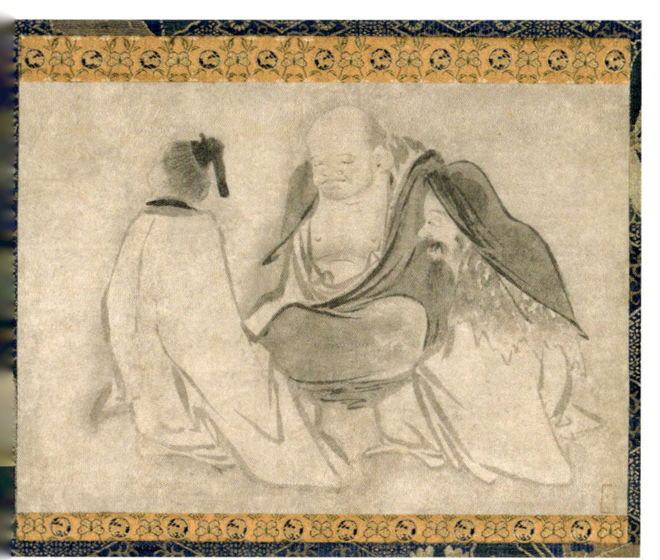

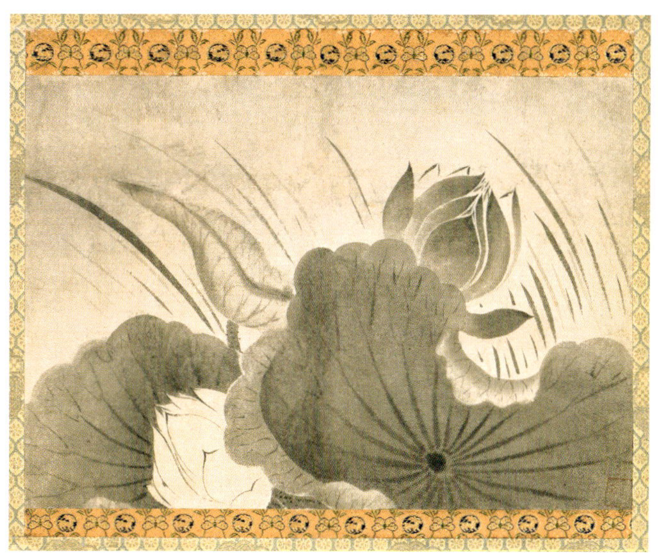

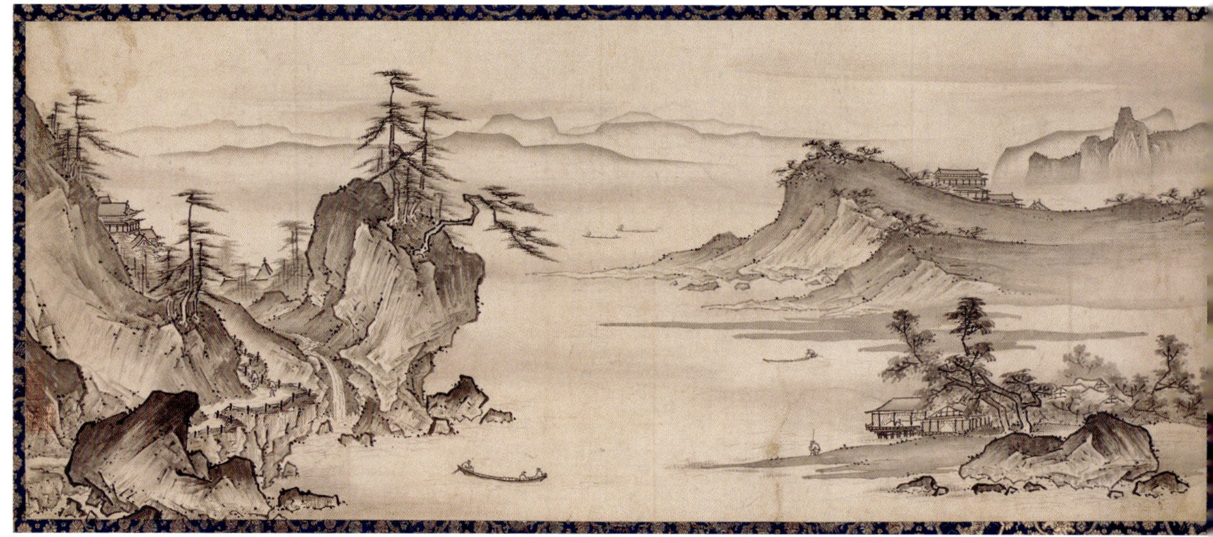

Landscape

Kenkō Shōkei (active late 15th–early 16th century)

Muromachi period, 15th–16th century

Beginning in 1467, the ten-year Ōnin civil wars laid waste to Kyoto, leading to the disintegration of the city's Zen monastic complexes as primary cultural centers. During the late fifteenth century, several artists, including Sesshū Tōyō, retreated to the provinces. In the eastern town of Kamakura, a new group under the tutelage of painter-monk Kenkō Shōkei developed its own style, informed by works of the Chinese Southern Song Academy.

In this hanging scroll, Shōkei presents a panoramic landscape with a fishing village looking out onto rocky promontories and distant mountains. He skillfully suggests recession into depth by staggering the topographical forms back and forth from the right and left across the vast body of water. In the right half of the composition, he adopts elements—the deciduous trees hovering over the low-lying buildings, and the shoreline executed only in bands of ink wash—from works attributed to the Chinese master Xia Gui (active late twelfth–early thirteenth century). Yet Shōkei also accepts the reinterpretations of Xia Gui's style by the fifteenth-century Japanese artist Geiami, with whom he studied for several years. In the towering cliffs on the left, Shōkei uses heavy lines to delineate rocks, "axe-cut" strokes to provide textures, and dark dots to represent foliage and enliven the composition—techniques that are commonly seen in Geiami's paintings.

Hanging scroll; ink on paper

39.2 x 91.4 cm (15 7/16 x 36 in.)

Fenollosa-Weld Collection 11.4127

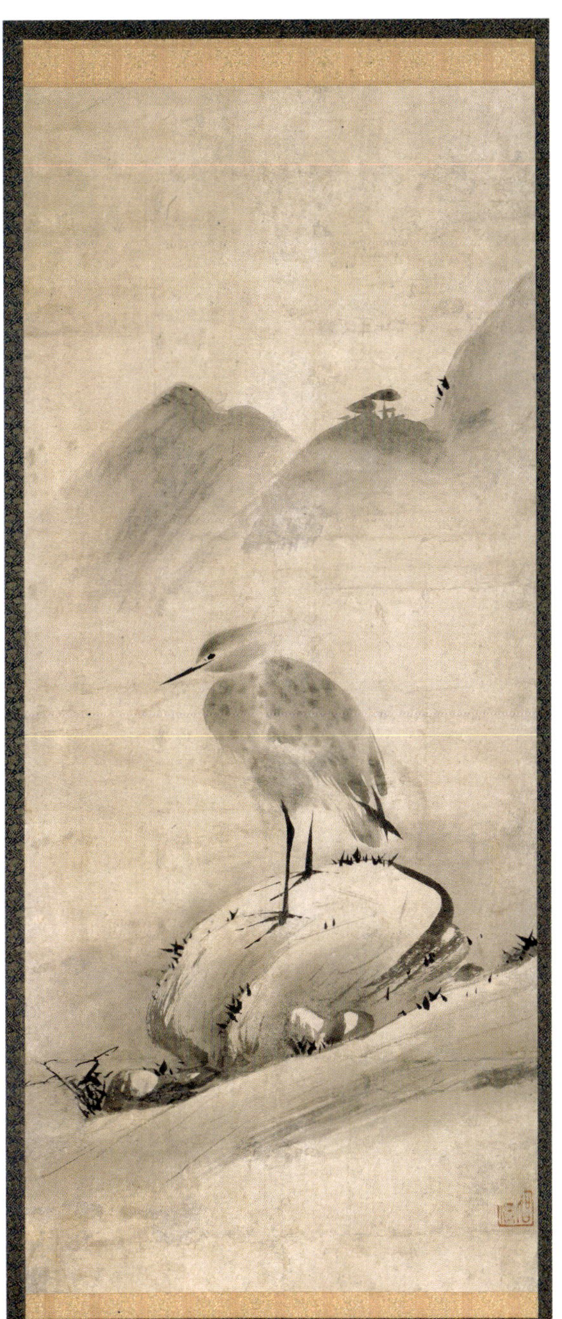

Heron

Tan'an Chiden (active 16th century)

Muromachi period, 16th century

During the early Muromachi period, Japanese artists of Chinese-style paintings were often affiliated with Zen Buddhist temples. Many of these monastic complexes had been founded by Chinese emigré prelates, who brought with them extensive collections of Chinese scrolls in the Chan tradition—works executed entirely in ink that emphasized values of spontaneity and spirituality. Some treated mundane subjects, but others, such as this scroll, may have contained embedded meanings for members of the Zen community. A fourteenth-century painting of a heron, similar to this one, was inscribed by a Chinese monk: "When the water becomes clear, fishes appear." Thus, to contemporary viewers, the clearing of muddy water may have suggested overcoming delusion, while the decisive movement of the heron catching a fish may have been comparable to the Zen Buddhist's experience of sudden enlightenment. Yet by the sixteenth century, when ink painting had become one of the primary modes of artistic expression in Japan, the avian subject may also have appealed primarily on aesthetic grounds.

The *Tōhaku gasetsu*, a late-sixteenth-century compilation of the views on painting held by the celebrated artist Hasegawa Tōhaku, provides limited biographical information about Tan'an Chiden. The treatise claims that Chiden was a disciple of Sōami, an ink painter and cultural advisor to the Ashigaka shogunate, who was a follower of the Pure Land rather than the Zen sect. Furthermore, Chiden is said to have enjoyed the patronage of Shōnyo, a prelate at Ishiyama Hongan-ji, a Pure Land temple in the Osaka region.

Hanging scroll; ink on paper
85.8 x 35.6 cm (33¾ x 14 in.)
William Sturgis Bigelow Collection 11.6335

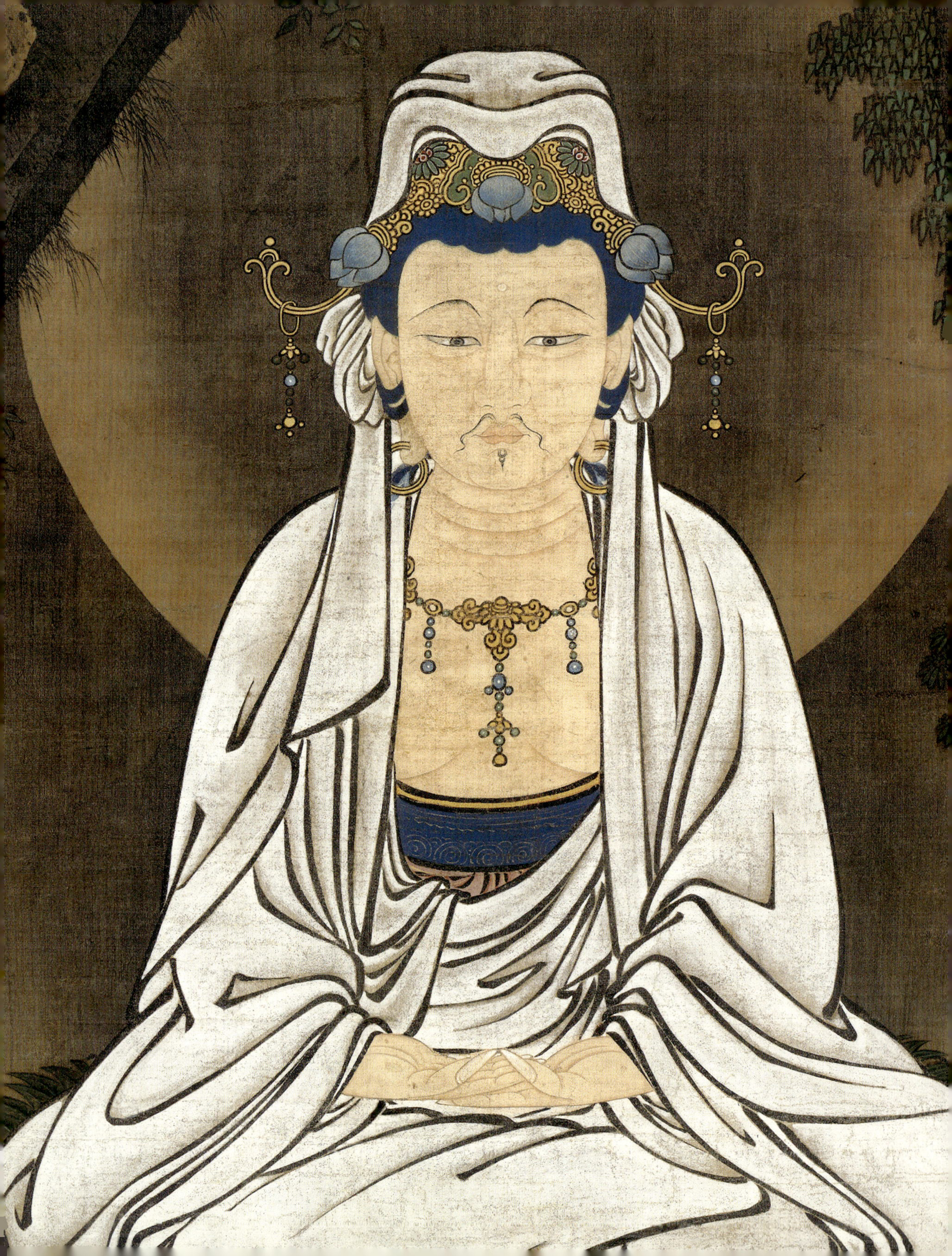

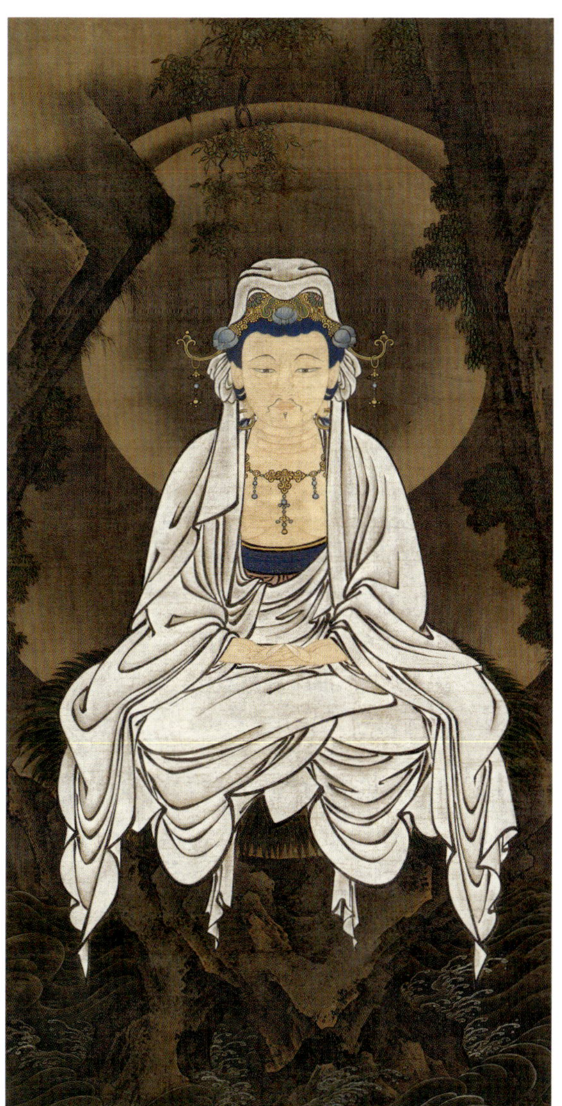

Byaku-e Kannon, the White-Robed Bodhisattva of Compassion

Kano Motonobu (1476–1559)

Muromachi period, first half of the 16th century

The White-Robed Bodhisattva of Compassion was the most popular subject of figure paintings commissioned by Zen Buddhist temples during the fourteenth through sixteenth centuries. As in many other contemporary works, the deity is shown here in deep contemplation, seated on a grass mat in a rocky grotto on his island paradise, Mount Potalaka, off the coast of southern China. For Zen Buddhists, this iconography resonated with their ideal of the scholar-monk, who was able to retreat from the concerns of everyday life. Several features, however, distinguish this depiction from the more informal images of the bodhisattva that were commonly produced in ink: the monumental scale of the scroll, the frontal posture of the deity, the pronounced use of thick mineral pigments for the clothing, and the inclusion of an elaborate headdress and jewelry.

The original provenance of this painting is not known, though it is thought to have been used for rituals in a monastic complex. According to Ernest Fenollosa, the MFA's first curator of Japanese art, the scroll later belonged to the Hachisuka family, the military governors of the Awa district (in present-day Aichi Prefecture) who had gained the favor of the sixteenth-century warlord Toyotomi Hideyoshi. By the early seventeenth century, the image was well known through numerous copies made by the descendants of Kano Motonobu for study in their workshops.

Hanging scroll; ink, color, and gold on silk
157.2 x 76.4 cm (61⅞ x 30¹⁄₁₆ in.)
Fenollosa-Weld Collection 11.4267

The Death of the Historical Buddha

Hanabusa Itchō (1652–1724)

Edo period, 1713

Every year, the Buddha's birth and death—upon which he attained final enlightenment and was released from the cycle of birth and rebirth—are celebrated in temple communities throughout Japan. Taking place on the fifteenth day of the second month, the rituals for the death of the Buddha are conducted in front of a monumental scroll depicting the event. The central elements of the iconography of paintings of this type were established in the Buddhist text *Dainehan-kyō*, which states that when the Historical Buddha took ill, he put down his pilgrim's staff and the cloth bundle containing his limited possessions, and reclined on a bier surrounded by a grove of sal trees at Kuśinagara in north-central India. Those who did not comprehend the significance of his final enlightenment were overcome by grief and fell to the ground. The Buddha's mother, Māyā, descended with her entourage from the heavens to witness the event.

The earliest extant Japanese painting of the death of the Buddha dates to the late eleventh century, and accomplished artists continued to provide for temple commissions in succeeding centuries. Hanabusa Itchō, best known for his satiric scenes of everyday life, enlivened the standard iconography for the composition through his masterful handling of the individual figures and his detailing of the grieving members of the animal kingdom. This scroll must have been treasured by the Zen temple to which it belonged, for when it was remounted in 1850, elaborate gilt fittings with mythical lions were specially ordered from the metalworker Yokoya Sōmin.

Hanging scroll; ink, color, and gold on paper
283 x 169 cm (111 7/16 x 66 9/16 in.)
Fenollosa-Weld Collection 11.4221

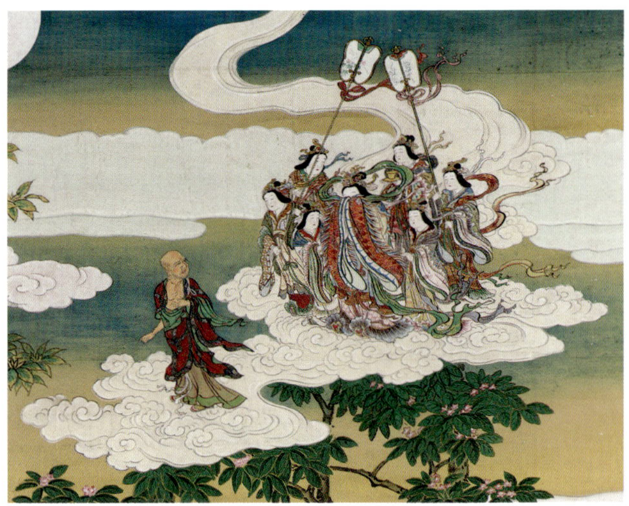

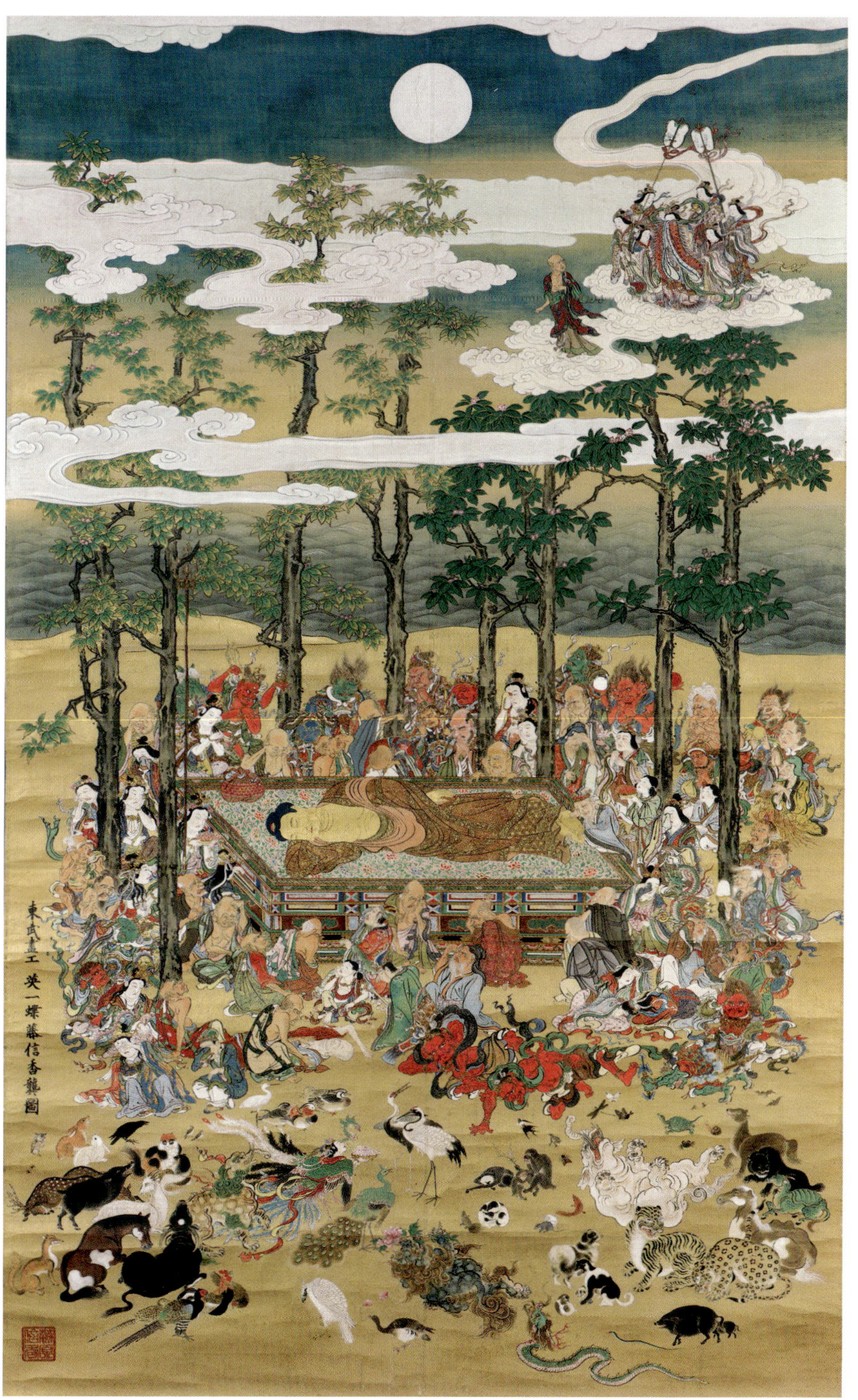
東武畫工 英一蝶藤信香謹圖

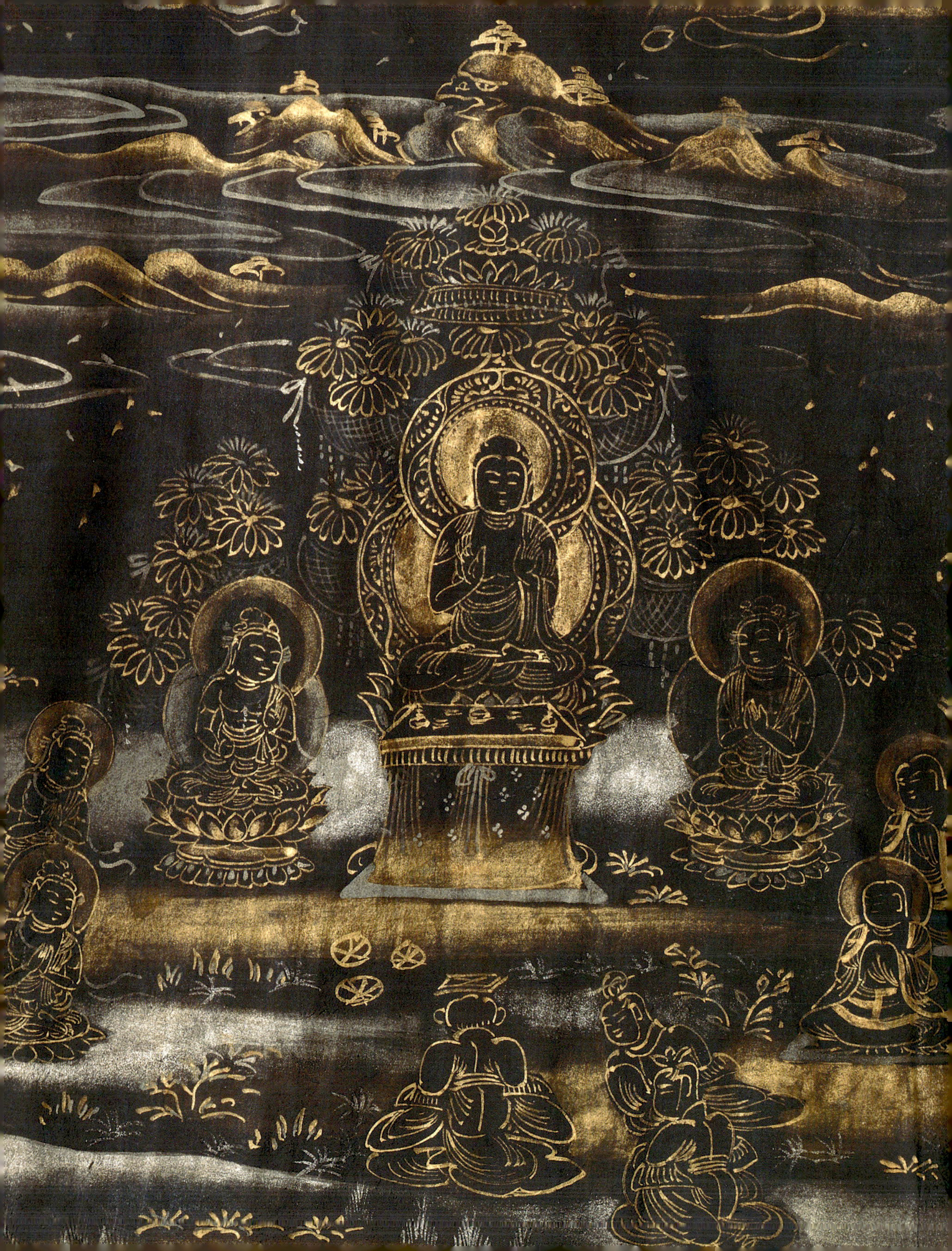

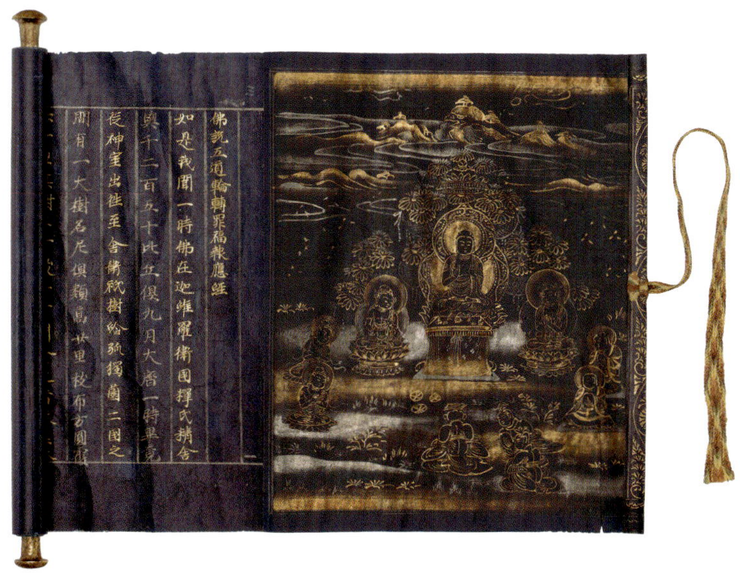

Sutra of the Retribution for Good and Evil Deeds (Zaifuku hōō-kyō)
Heian period, 12th century

In order to ensure an auspicious rebirth for themselves or for members of their families, twelfth-century aristocrats sponsored lavish transcriptions of the Buddhist canon. On occasion they even copied the texts themselves. This particular work was part of a five-thousand-scroll set of the Buddhist canon executed for Fujiwara no Kiyohira, the powerful ruler of northern Japan, by professional scribes and artists summoned from Kyoto. Following the completion of the ten-year project, the scrolls were donated to Chūson-ji, Kiyohira's tutelary temple in present-day Iwate Prefecture.

During the eighth century, the Japanese first copied Buddhist texts in gold or silver characters on purple or dark blue paper, in emulation of models from Tang-dynasty China. By the twelfth century, as can be seen in this scroll, the ornamentation became even more extravagant. This text is written in a formal script in alternating columns of silver and gold characters. Intricate patterns of luxuriant blossoms with twisting stems and delicate foliage decorate the outer cover, while a silver and gold painting depicting the Historical Buddha preaching on Vulture Peak embellishes the inside frontispiece. Gilt bronze rollers with "fish-roe" granulated metalwork and a multicolored securing braid complete the sumptuous production.

Handscroll; gold and silver on indigo paper
26.4 x 189.1 cm (10 3/8 x 74 7/16 in.)
Gift of Mrs. Albertine W. F. Valentine, residuary legatee under the will of Hervey E. Wetzel 19.688

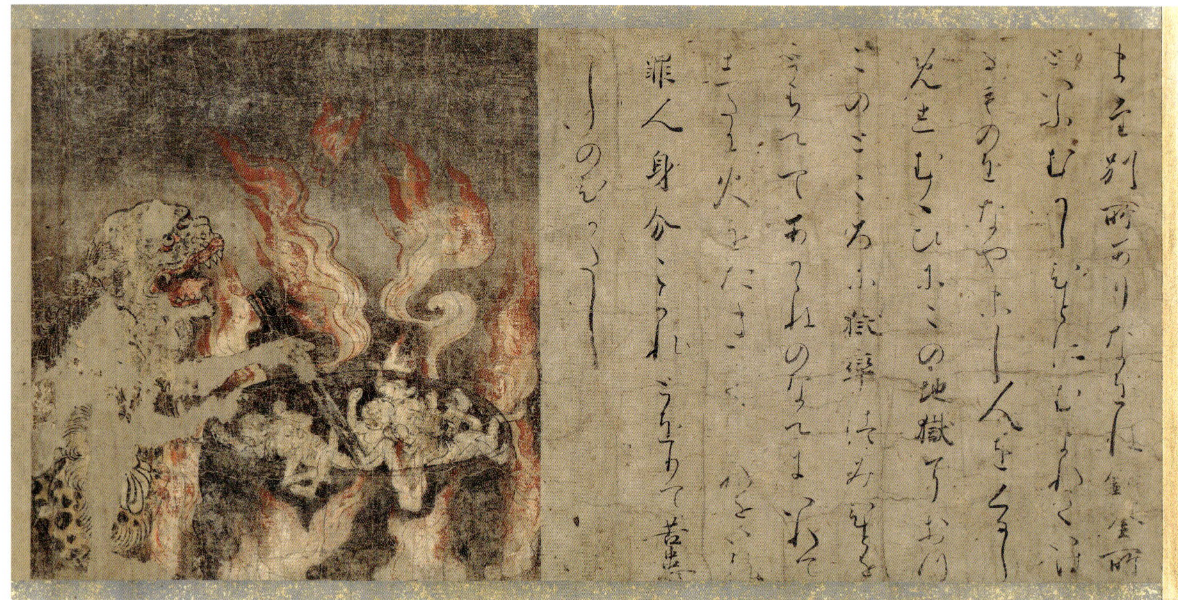

The Burning Cauldron, a section from the _Hell Scrolls_

Heian period, 12th century

Narrative handscrolls, in which sections of text alternate with images, were frequently employed by Buddhist priests for didactic purposes. Although the members of the court who would have viewed these works were highly literate, the vivid illustrations provided a sense of immediacy that words alone could not capture. Originally part of a longer scroll now in the Nara National Museum, this segment describes the horrible tortures awaiting those who transgress against the Buddhist law. The calligraphic text relates that those who torment human beings or animals will be consigned to the Hell of the Copper Cauldron.

In Buddhist cosmology, there are eight main hells, each subdivided into sixteen minor hells—one of which is the Hell of the Copper Cauldron. The painting makes effective use of strong color contrasts to suggest the terrors of this hell, with the murky darkness in black and the searing flames in red. The anguished sinners are left to boil under the supervision of a threatening demon, who prevents their escape with a pair of metal chopsticks.

During the twelfth and thirteenth centuries, Hell Scrolls were produced in response to the teachings of Genshin, who wrote the *Essentials of Salvation (Ōjō yōshū)* in the late tenth century. By contrasting the horrors of the hells with the Western Paradise of the Buddha Amida in this seminal text, Genshin sought to inspire individuals to follow the tenets of the Buddhist faith.

Section from a handscroll; ink and color on paper
25.6 x 52 cm (10 1/16 x 20 1/2 in.)
William Sturgis Bigelow Collection 11.6254

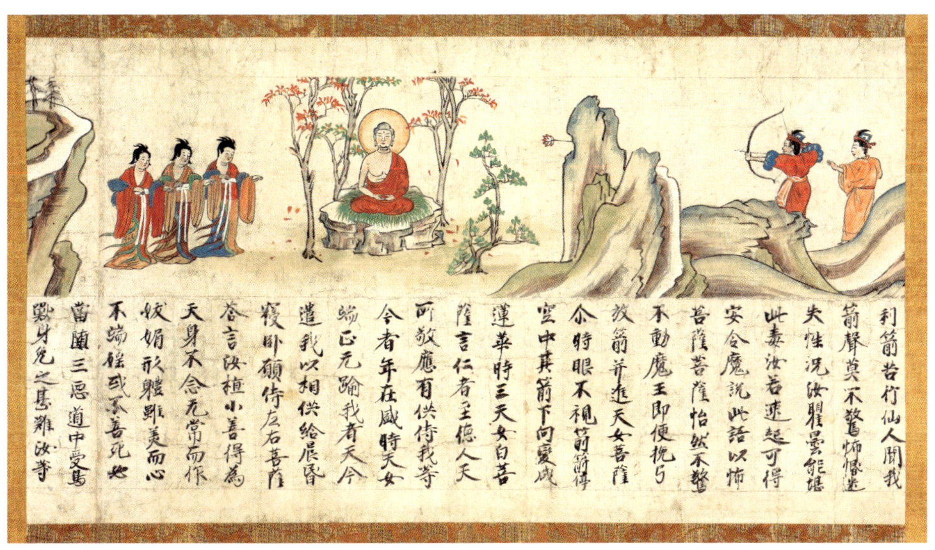

The Transformation of Māra's Arrows and the Temptation by Māra's Daughters*, a section from the *Sutra of Cause and Effect (Kako genzai inga-kyō)

Kamakura period, late 13th century

Three centuries after the death of the Historical Buddha, Indian adherents of the Buddhist faith compiled a text that described the exemplary life of their teacher. It narrated his previous incarnations, his renunciation of the princely life into which he was born, and his ultimate attainment of enlightenment. Thus, the text explained one of the Buddha's fundamental teachings—that the nature of one's life is determined by past and present actions until the cycle of reincarnation is broken when enlightenment is achieved.

During the first half of the fifth century, the Indian text was translated into Chinese by the monk Guṇabhadra. By the early Tang dynasty, illustrated versions of these stories of the Buddha's life had attained wide popularity—so much so that during the eighth century, the Japanese often copied the eight-volume Chinese sets. Five hundred years later, religious leaders in Japan, seeking stronger links to the past and to the Historical Buddha, commissioned more copies. This fragment comes from one such version.

A distinctive characteristic of this sutra is the placement of illustrations above the text, which is written in formal Chinese characters; the illustrations are composed of Chinese-style landscape elements and Chinese-garbed figures. The Buddha, seated in meditation on a rock dais beneath a grove of stylized trees, remains impervious to the malevolent forces that attempt to hinder his quest for the truth. To the right, the demon king Māra shoots an arrow at the Buddha, but it is transformed into a lotus. On the left, Māra's three daughters—Blissful to Behold, Pleasurable to Others, and Lust—unsuccessfully attempt to seduce the holy man.

Section of a handscroll mounted as a hanging scroll; ink and color on paper
27 x 48.1 cm (10 5/8 x 18 15/16 in.)
Promised gift of Sylvan Barnet and William Burto

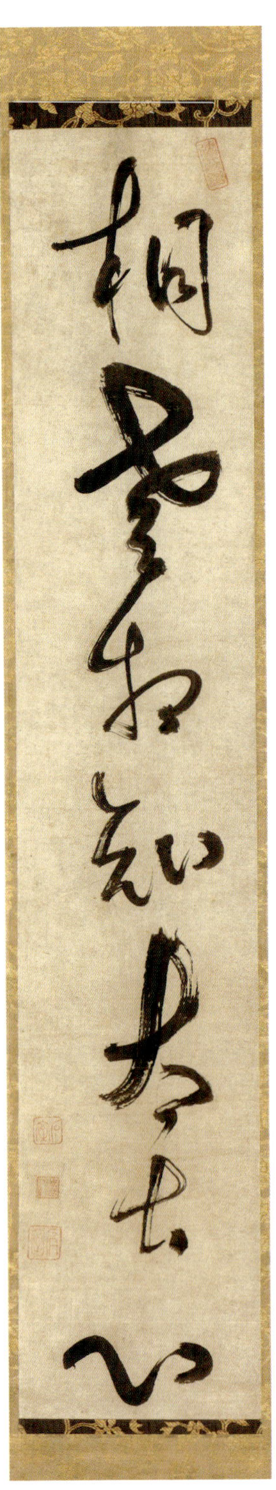

The Immortal Knows the Mind of Antiquity

Sekishitsu Zenkyū (1294–1389)

Nanbokuchō period, 14th century

Although the Zen sect professes the relative unimportance of texts in the attainment of enlightenment, members of the monastic community have always venerated the calligraphy of Zen prelates as the embodiment of the spirit of these masters. Not only is the content of such aphorisms considered meaningful, but the vigor and individuality of the brushstrokes are thought to reflect the personalities of their inscribers. Calligraphic hanging scrolls were frequently hung inside the meditation hall to engender in students the proper frame of mind for eventually attaining enlightenment. Beginning in the sixteenth century, these works were also treasured by masters of the ritual drinking of tea, who found their economy of expression to resonate with their preferred restrained aesthetic.

In this dynamic single line of characters, Sekishitsu Zenkyū rapidly moves his brush from top to bottom, circumscribing three-dimensional characters that both defy and assert the surface of the paper. The varying intensities of the ink and the splaying of the brush provide a vivid record of the Zen master's bold gestures. Celebrated for his distinctive style of cursive calligraphy, Zenkyū was an influential member of the Zen monastic hierarchy. He assumed the position of abbot at many important temples, including Tenryū-ji in western Kyoto and Engaku-ji and Kenchō-ji in Kamakura.

Hanging scroll; ink on paper
120.7 x 22.3 cm (47 1/2 x 8 13/16 in.)
Promised gift of Sylvan Barnet and William Burto

Ritual banner with decoration of Sanskrit characters

Nanbokuchō–Muromachi periods, 14th–15th century

Buddhist banners (*ban*) took their form from ancient Indian battle standards but eventually became insignia of religious communities. In Japan banners are some of the most important ornaments in the interior of image halls. Hung from the tops of pillars, they serve as symbols of the authority of the deity enshrined and increase the majesty of the ritual space. A number of Buddhist texts also indicate that particular benefits—including extending one's life or ensuring felicitous rebirth for the deceased—may be gained from presenting banners to temples, which may explain their great popularity in Japan.

Whether made from gilt bronze or cloth, like this example, banners always take a similar form, with a triangular top and three or four square sections below, from which are suspended long streamers. In this banner, each of the three cerulean squares is embroidered with the Sanskrit letter *kirīku*—a symbol of Amida, the Buddha of Infinite Light—resting on a lotus pedestal and surrounded by an orb. Stylized flowers and scrolling vines define the four corners. The outer brocade is figured with wheels of the Buddhist law, emblems signifying the teaching of the Historical Buddha. At the top of the banner, the gilt bronze fitting is finely worked with a lotus motif. Like all objects of adornment, which are actually often concealed from the laity's view, this banner is fashioned with meticulous craftsmanship.

Silk with gilt bronze fittings; brocade with embroidery
L. 86.8 cm (L. 34 3/16 in.)
Marshall H. Gould Fund 1972.857

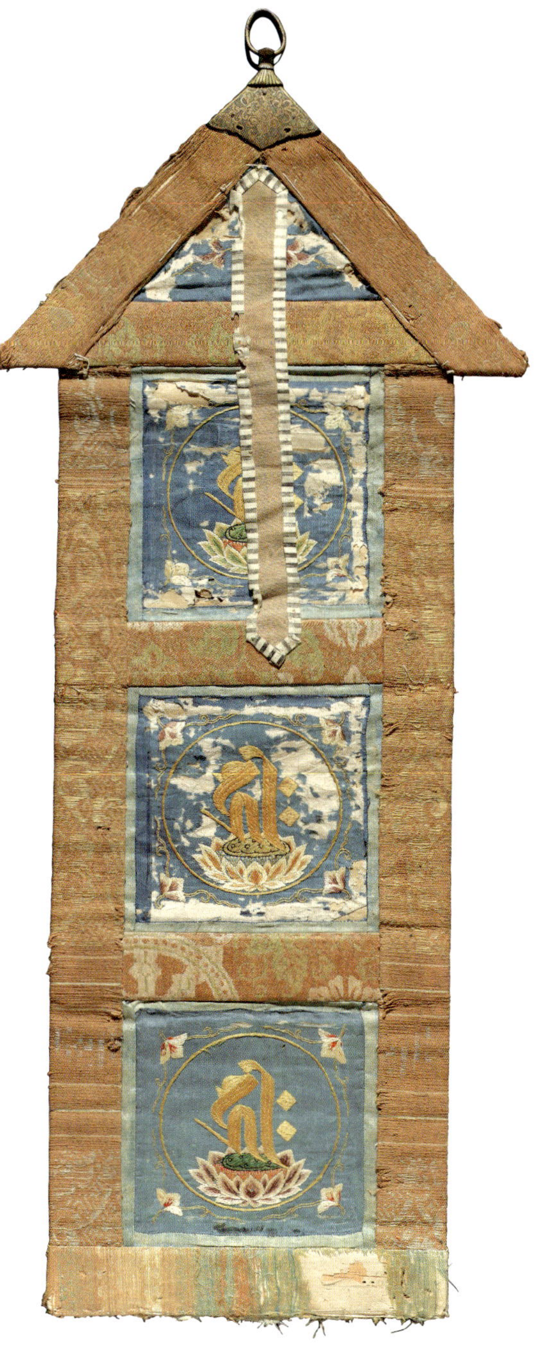

Box for ordination documents (*kaitaibako*)

Kamakura–Muromachi periods, 14th–15th century

This rectangular box ornamented with a design of lotus arabesques against a stippled background was used to house an ordination certificate and other scrolls that may have been important to a high-ranking priest. The center of the lid is embellished with a *rinpō*, the eight-spoked wheel used in the Esoteric tradition to symbolize the Buddha's teachings, and to either side a *katsuma*, the ritual implement that is placed at the four corners of the altar. Additional *rinpō* and *katsuma* adorn the sides of the box, and a securing cord originally would have been threaded through the stylized lotus-blossom fittings.

In ancient India, where Buddhism originated, aspirants to the priesthood were ordained once a community of monks agreed that they had undergone a sufficient period of training and were able to answer questions and recite the scriptures. During the Nara and Heian periods in Japan, however, ordination was regulated by the imperial court, and official certificates were often used as citation that monks had received the necessary religious education. Later, this government supervision became a formality, and by the time this box was created, the papers were more aesthetic objects than official documents.

Wood with lacquer and gilt bronze fittings
H. 12.6 cm, w. 35 cm, l. 11.9 cm
(H. 4 15/16 in., w. 13 3/4 in., l. 4 11/16 in.)
Keith McLeod Fund 1970.46

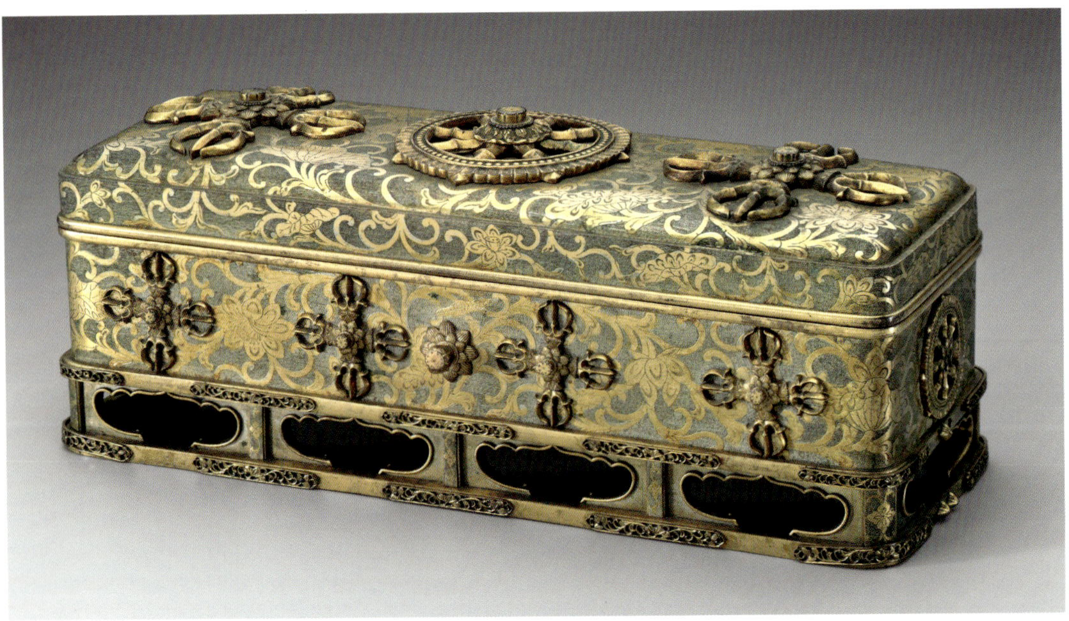

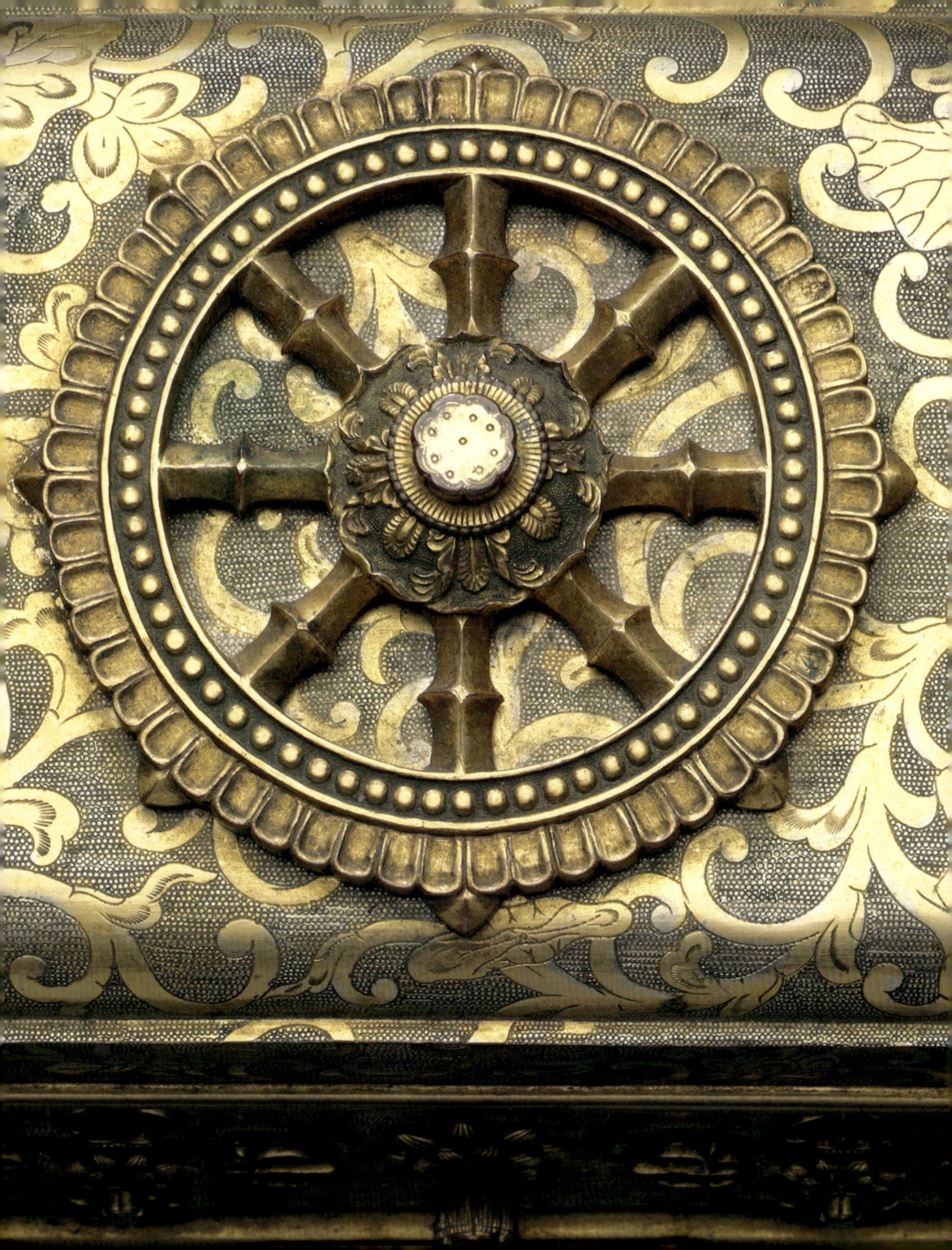

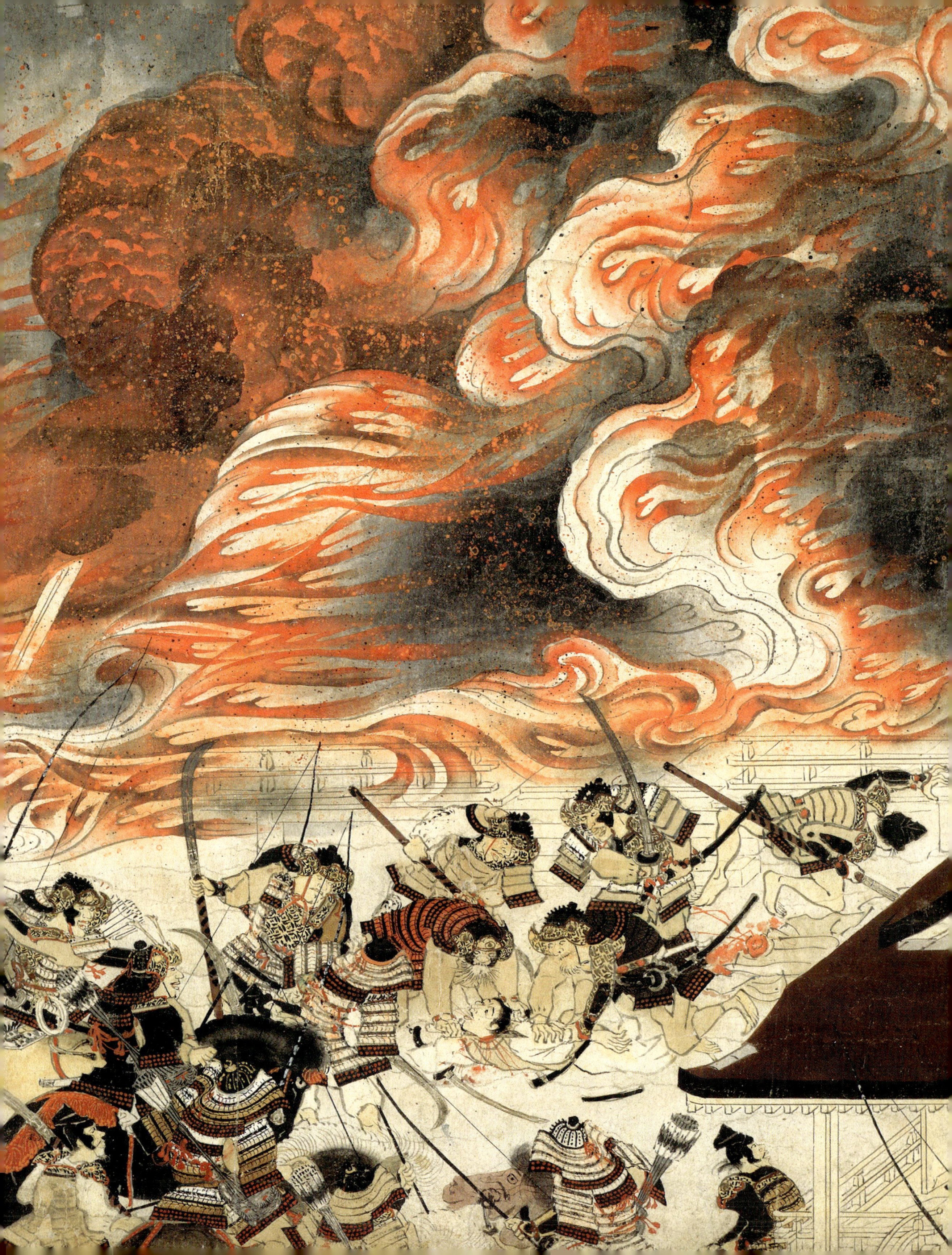

2 art of the RULING CLASSES

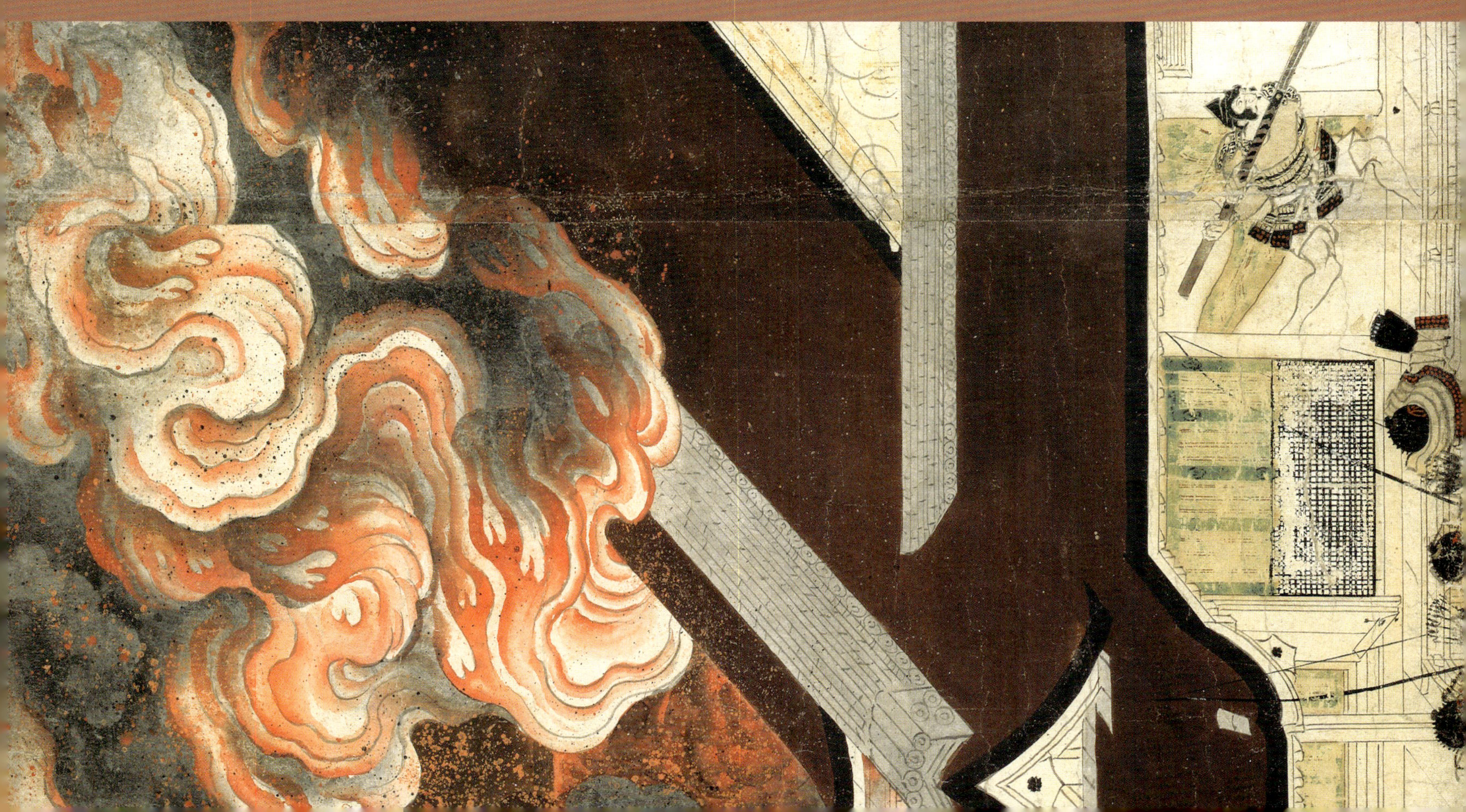

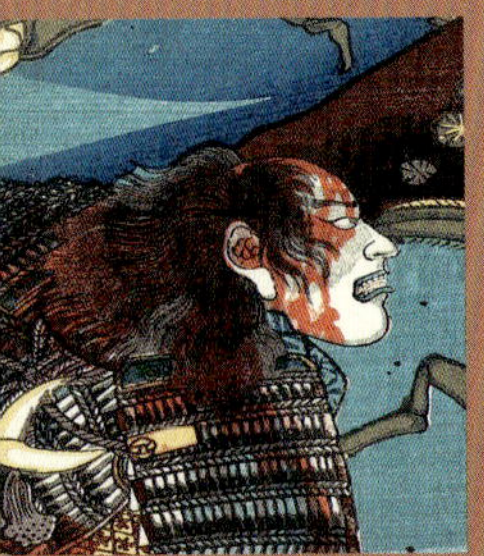
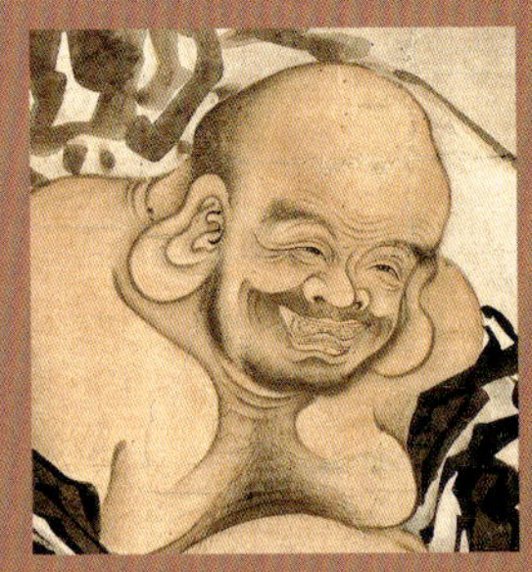
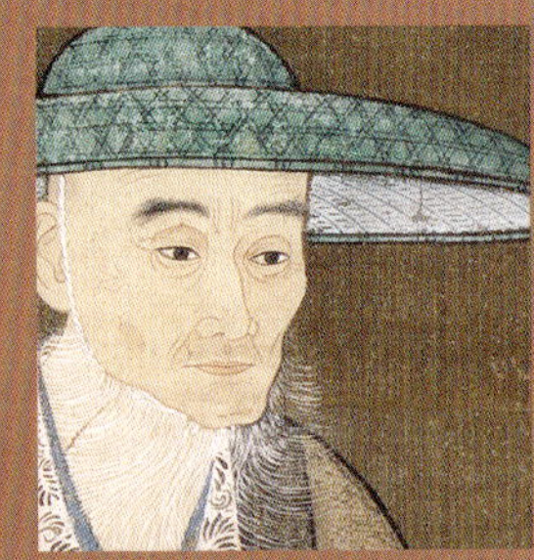
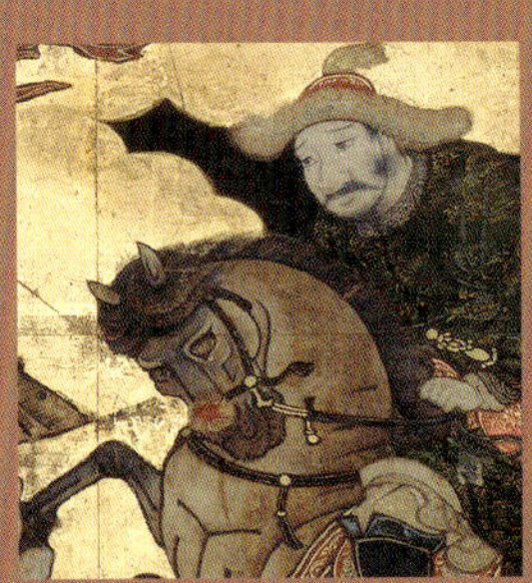
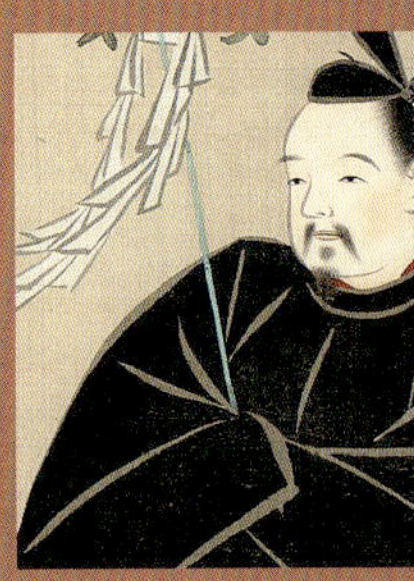

Art of the Ruling Classes

Rachel Saunders

> The sound of the Gion Shōja bells echoes the impermanence of all things; the color of the śāla flowers reveals the truth that the prosperous must decline. The proud do not endure, they are like a dream on a spring night; the mighty fall at last, they are as dust before the wind.
>
> –**The Tale of the Heike** (trans. Helen Craig McCullough)

These opening lines from the war epic *The Tale of the Heike* (*Heike monogatari*), written in the early thirteenth century, are strongly colored by the Buddhist sense of impermanence, reminding us that however concrete existence may appear to be, even the mightiest face death and the limitations of the body. Despite this awareness—or perhaps precisely because of it—the holders of power in Japan, like rulers in many other places, have used material art forms to symbolize their authority since the earliest times. Precious and unusual objects invested with an aura of beauty, value, or even spiritual power naturally distinguish their owners, signifying the wealth or influence necessary to obtain them. Possession of such objects indicates the ability to go where most cannot—to overcome distance if an object is from a foreign land, or time if it is from the remote past, or even the bounds of this world if the object has spiritual significance. In the realm of architecture, Japanese rulers have at times commissioned whole new worlds ordered according to their wishes. In the other arts, by accumulating objects through gift exchange and interacting with them, whether through display and appreciation or through performance rituals (such as Nō theater and tea practice), they have used art objects to regulate the hierarchy of human relations.

Evidence for the existence of structured society in Japan goes back at least to the Kofun period (300–538). But to study the ruling classes' engagement with art within the bounds of the MFA's collection, we can turn to two groups that gradually cultivated political power: imperial or courtly rulers, and warrior or samurai rulers. Imperial rule based on Chinese models began to emerge in the sixth

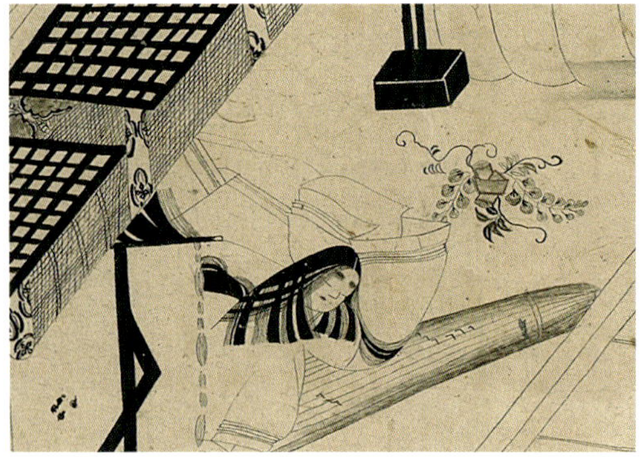

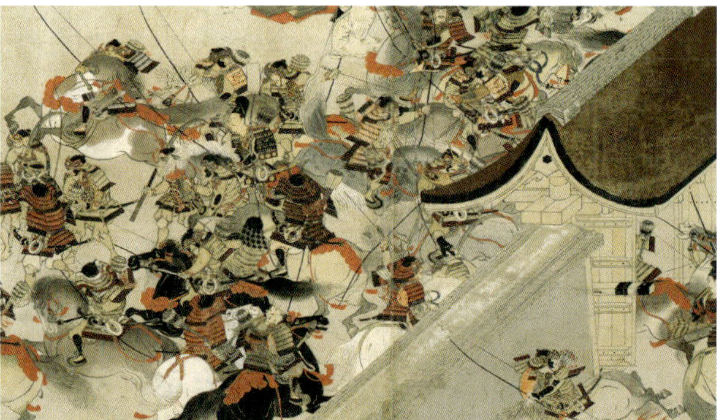

century, when power was channeled through—if not actually executed by—an emperor or empress. According to Japan's oldest historical records, imperial authority was mandated by the Sun Goddess, Amaterasu. The imperial line has theoretically remained unbroken to the present day, but the Heian period (794–1185) saw the zenith of elegant courtly rule. In the ninth and tenth centuries, the warrior class began to assert its presence through military campaigns, eventually resulting in the establishment of the position of shogun: de facto power passed to warrior rulers with the institution of the Kamakura military government (*bakufu*) in 1185. Warrior rule continued until the Meiji Restoration of 1868, when imperial government was restored with the emperor as figurehead to an oligarchy of powerful statesmen.

fig. 15 **The exquisitely refined lifestyle of imperial courtiers during the Heian period became the model of classical elegance, echoed in later works such as this painting by a sixteenth-century noblewoman.**

fig. 16 **After the rise to power of the warrior clans, painters catered to the taste of the new rulers by depicting complex battle scenes with careful attention to the details of armor and weapons.**

Because the distinction between courtly and warrior rule is a useful marker of change in Japanese history, it is easy to overstate the separation between the two groups and consider them binary opposites: effete courtiers versus brutal men of arms. Yet, especially in the earlier eras, their common goals in fact led to a degree of crossover and to the emergence of both warrior-courtiers and courtier-warriors. Furthermore, the shogun had to be officially appointed by the emperor and his actions sanctioned by the court. Power was thus delicately balanced between the two entities, and that balance shifted and changed over time. Nevertheless, however politically weak the imperial line became after hundreds of years of warrior rule by different houses, the emperor retained his divine status right up until the twentieth century.

From 710 to 794, the court resided in the city of Nara (then known as Heijō-kyō). As the court and emperor system were based on Chinese models, almost every aspect of courtly life was influenced by the continent, from the language used for official affairs to the adoption of Buddhism. Indeed, the growing power of the monks and temples of Nara is often cited as one of the prime reasons for the move of the capital city twenty miles north to Heian-kyō, or present-day Kyoto, in 794.[1] Heian-kyō remained the capital and seat of the court for more than a thousand years. At first the Heian period was characterized by continued borrowing from China, but in 894 contact with the continent was broken and a more inward-looking court, under peaceful domestic conditions, settled its attentions on the flowering of its own cultural practices.

At the beginning of the eleventh century, Lady Sei Shōnagon wrote in her *Pillow Book* (*Makura no sōshi*), one of the most important sources of information about the time, "Everyone should behave as elegantly as possible—women as well as men."[2] Her work reveals the depths of exquisite taste and cultivation, as well as the delicate political maneuvering, necessary to survive at the Heian court. Courtiers competed not with swords but more commonly with poetry, incense, or music. It was in this environment that Murasaki Shikibu wrote what has been called the world's first novel, *The Tale of Genji* (*Genji monogatari*), also in the early eleventh century. Genji's world, dubbed the "world of the shining prince" by the scholar Ivan Morris,[3] is filled with his elegant encounters with accomplished women. Yet it is also shot through with the Heian aesthetic of *mono no aware*, a sadness about the impermanence of things, influenced by the Buddhist idea that the world was about to enter a degenerate era in the late Heian period. Such an impression was no doubt encouraged by the growing disturbances that resulted from a steady shift of power from the imperial court to the provincial military clans.

fig. 17 **This illustration of a scene from *The Tale of Genji* shows the typical stylistic characteristics of *yamato-e* painting: bright colors, fine details, and flattened pictorial space.**

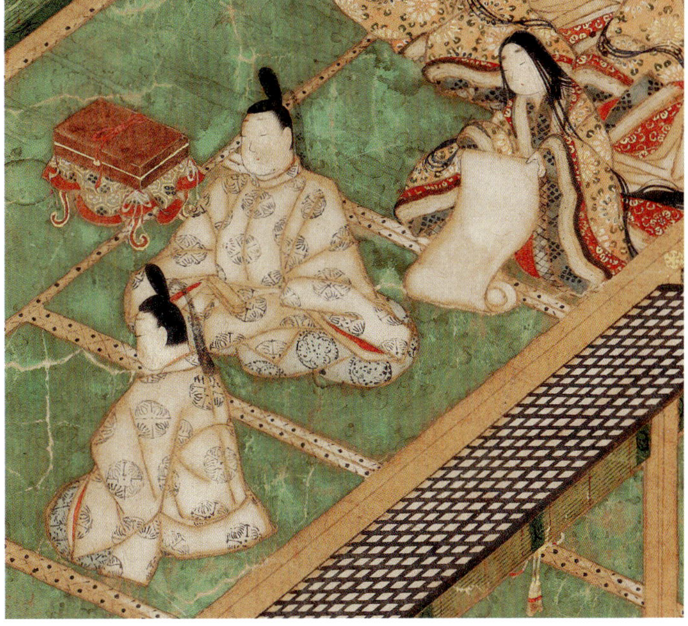

In the visual arts, the aesthetic expression of the Heian court has most often been linked to the development of *yamato-e* (Japanese painting), in opposition to imported *kara-e* (Chinese painting). *Yamato-e* is now associated stylistically with the luxuriant application of bright, flat planes of color, favored by the Heian court; but the term probably referred originally to subject matter, most likely recognizably Japanese (rather than Chinese) landscape and genre scenes painted on screens (although no large-scale Heian-period paintings survive to confirm this). In combination with the contemporaneous flowering of native poetry and literature, the twelfth century saw the development of the narrative handscroll, an intimate form of what we might now call an illustrated book. The link between image and text that was forged in the Heian period, when poems and tales were pictorialized, became a key marker of the classical courtly culture of this period.

Growing instability in the provinces outside the imperial capital eventually led to the outbreak of the Genpei War (1180–85) between the Minamoto and Taira warrior houses. The victorious Minamoto established a warrior government sanctioned by the imperial court, beginning the long political dominance of the warrior class. Because the seat of the *bakufu* was in Kamakura (in the east, about thirty miles from present-day Tokyo), the era of shogunal rule that lasted from 1185 to 1333 is known as the Kamakura period. Kyoto remained both the official and cultural capital, continuing to produce and renew the arts that had been lost to conflict and disorder.

If the Heian period was the world of the shining prince Genji, the Kamakura period was the golden age of the war tale, generating such major epics of warrior-courtier conflict as *The Events of the Heiji Era* (*Heiji monogatari*) and *The Tale of the Heike* (*Heike monogatari*). Probably written down in the early thirteenth century but set in the period just before the outbreak of the Genpei War, *The Tale of the Heike* in particular shows that as warriors surpassed the courtiers in power, they in turn were influenced by traditional courtly manners and aesthetics, which were signifiers of authority. Nevertheless, when contact was resumed with China, leading to the introduction of Zen Buddhism into Japan at the end of the twelfth century, the warrior elite were receptive both to the teachings of this sect and to the austere aesthetic of the monochrome ink paintings produced by Zen monks. Following the fall of the Kamakura *bakufu*, the Ashikaga warrior clan, who established a Kyoto-based shogunate that dominated the country from 1392 to 1568 (the Muromachi period), were the first to leave documents relating to their collection of Chinese ink paintings. These paintings, whose spare brushstrokes aimed to capture the spirit of the figure, landscape, bird, or plant depicted, rather than to leave a naturalistic representation, contrasted markedly with the colorful courtly aesthetic. Often appropriately understated and carrying the prestigious pedigree of China, they were first imported and then imitated and innovated by Japanese artists as a new aesthetic signifier for the ruling warrior class.

Monochrome ink paintings were not the only objects that traveling monks and traders brought back from China. The early Ashikaga shoguns, in particular, responding to the need to create an aura of cultural legitimization for their rule, surrounded themselves with symbols of high Chinese culture, including fine ceramics that they used in what is known popularly in the West as the "tea ceremony." The practice of drinking tea as an aid to meditation is thought to have arrived in Japan with Zen Buddhism. It developed into a ritual in which the appreciation of objects, carefully selected for their combined atmospheric effect, became key. The confined and highly controlled space of the tearoom, which brought competing warriors into close physical proximity as guest and host, has often been interpreted as a place of retreat from the world. But in late medieval Japan, it was also a space for codified competition, where the weapons were aesthetic objects. Simple implements became invested with the value of association with the dominant power holder, and the question of appropriate responses to them became deathly serious.

In the early days of the Ashikaga shogunate, the vessels used in tea ritual were showy: fine jade-green Chinese porcelains set on elaborate carved stands, for example. But the plain black wares used in Zen monasteries were also highly valued, and as time went on, the weathered aesthetic now known as *wabi*, which favored simple rusticity, came to be preferred over the perfection of high Chinese art. This aesthetic preference was fulfilled by the much rougher and famously "imperfect" wares produced in Korea and Southeast Asia, as well as domestically in Japan. It may well have been fueled by the almost complete destruction of Kyoto and collections of prestigious Chinese objects housed there during the Ōnin Wars of 1467–77, leaving a cultural vacuum that needed to be filled expeditiously.

The Ōnin civil wars unleashed forces that led to persistent conflict for roughly the next hundred years, out of which emerged the so-called three great unifiers of Japan: Oda Nobunaga, Toyotomi Hideyoshi, and Tokugawa Ieyasu. These men were powerful provincial warriors who sought control over the whole country. Nobunaga deposed the Ashikaga shogunate, ushering in the Momoyama period (1568–1615). His rule was followed first by that of Hideyoshi and then by Ieyasu, each of whom built on his predecessor's successes. The power of all three was based primarily in military strength, but patronage of the arts and the creation of their own visual programs formed an important part of the self-construction of these three men as rulers, particularly in the case of Ieyasu. These purposeful programs were spearheaded by the building of impressive castles and residences, which were decorated with suitably large-scale architectural screen paintings featuring fierce animals and enormous trees, often on gold backgrounds. The artists most strongly associated with these dynamic painting programs are the Kano school. Their hallmark was a monumental style that combined polychrome images of *yamato-e* subjects with Chinese ink-painting

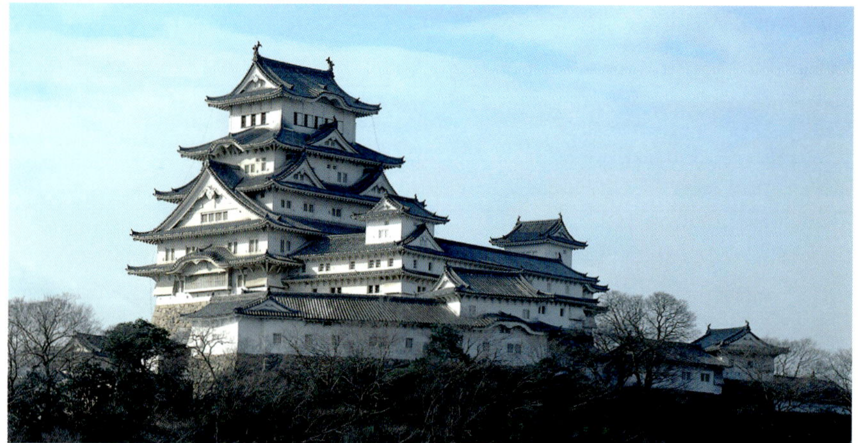

fig. 18 **Himeji Castle, built in 1601–18, is one of the finest surviving examples of an architectural form unique to Japan, inspired by the civil wars of the sixteenth century.**

techniques. In contrast, the Kyoto court, whose influence was further reduced by this next wave of warrior dominance, employed painters of the Tosa school. These artists produced highly detailed paintings in the *yamato-e* style depicting classical courtly and poetic subjects such as *The Tale of Genji*.

Ieyasu was the first in a new line of shoguns, the Tokugawa, who ruled from their new capital of Edo (present-day Tokyo) until the mid-nineteenth century. The early Tokugawa shoguns solidified their decisive military victories by creating a strong bureaucracy that allowed them to control land and potential rivals legally rather than simply by force. The Edo period (1615–1868) was remarkable for its lasting peace, after the centuries of combat that had preceded it. But this peace meant that the many samurai who had lived by the sword now had to adjust to lives as bureaucrats and politicians. Samurai remained at the top of the Neo-Confucian-inspired class system, but in fact it was the merchants, occupying the bottom rung of the social ladder, who truly prospered in the emerging urban economies of cities such as Edo and Osaka. As the Tokugawa pursued their grandiose architectural and collecting programs, samurai repackaged their hereditary arms and armor in gradually more arresting and less functional ways. Instead of essential weapons, these items became chilling markers of status to be worn on formal occasions, bridging the gap between past glories and present realities.

The Tokugawa established sufficient grasp on political power to place significant restrictions on the sovereignty of the emperor and the role of Kyoto's courtly aristocratic class, reducing them to figureheads, interfering in their traditional court duties, and greatly curtailing their freedom. In the early seventeenth century, a group of highly cultured Kyoto-based artists and wealthy townsmen, including Tawaraya Sōtatsu, Hon'ami Kōetsu, and the brothers Ogata Kōrin and Kenzan, began producing a range of sophisticated artworks now known under the rubric of the Rinpa school. They enlarged traditional *yamato-e* images and courtly poetics as symbolic motifs, investing them with a sense of loss and dislocation through the use of innovative materials and a penchant for silver, which—unlike gold—tarnishes dramatically over time. In a sense, Rinpa was an elegant form of protest art.

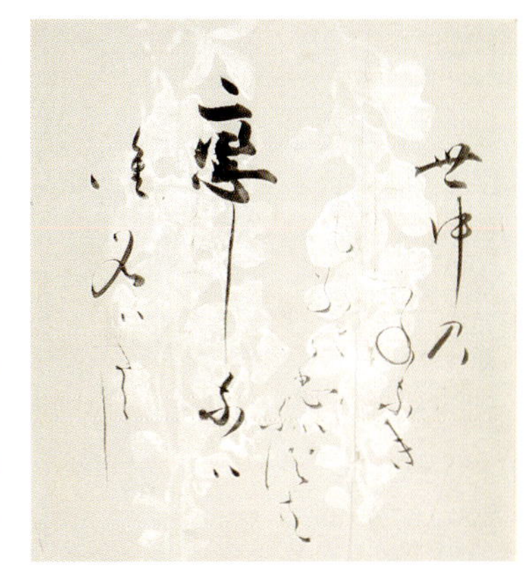

fig. 19 **Rinpa artworks, created in the face of increasingly intrusive warrior rule, are characterized by the use of gorgeous materials invested with a courtly nostalgia.**

The Tokugawa regime was eventually toppled in 1868 in a coup led by a group of samurai who wished to restore direct rule by the emperor, ushering in the Meiji era (1868–1912). While the premise for the overthrow may have been reversion to the ways of antiquity, the need to modernize in order to deal with foreign powers such as the United States and the nations of Europe on an equal footing was in fact a prime motivator. Modernization came to mean Westernization in many fields, and in the arts, Western techniques such as oil painting were pursued with an enthusiasm that was alarming to some. As Japan positioned itself on the international stage, a range of different types of artistic production were selected as symbolic of the country, rather than of a particular ruling class. Ultimately—and ironically—despite the long traditions and elegant complexities of the fine arts, it was "new" crafts such as metalwork that were perhaps the most successful representatives of Japanese art in the international arena. Under changing social and economic conditions, many venerable family collections migrated to museum collections, both domestic and international, in the early twentieth century. These institutions became the new repositories of the arts of Japan's historical ruling classes, housing the magnificent vestiges of people and times that have, as *The Tale of the Heike* predicted, disappeared like dust before the wind.

1 Although religious establishments such as temples and monasteries at times wielded great influence, they were never in a position of direct rule like the emperors and shoguns, but rather were corollaries to the political power held by those two groups.

2 Ivan Morris, trans. and ed., *The Pillow Book of Sei Shōnagon* (London, Melbourne, and Kuala Lumpur: Oxford University Press, 1967), 259.

3 Ivan Morris, *The World of the Shining Prince: Court Life in Ancient Japan* (New York: Knopf, 1964).

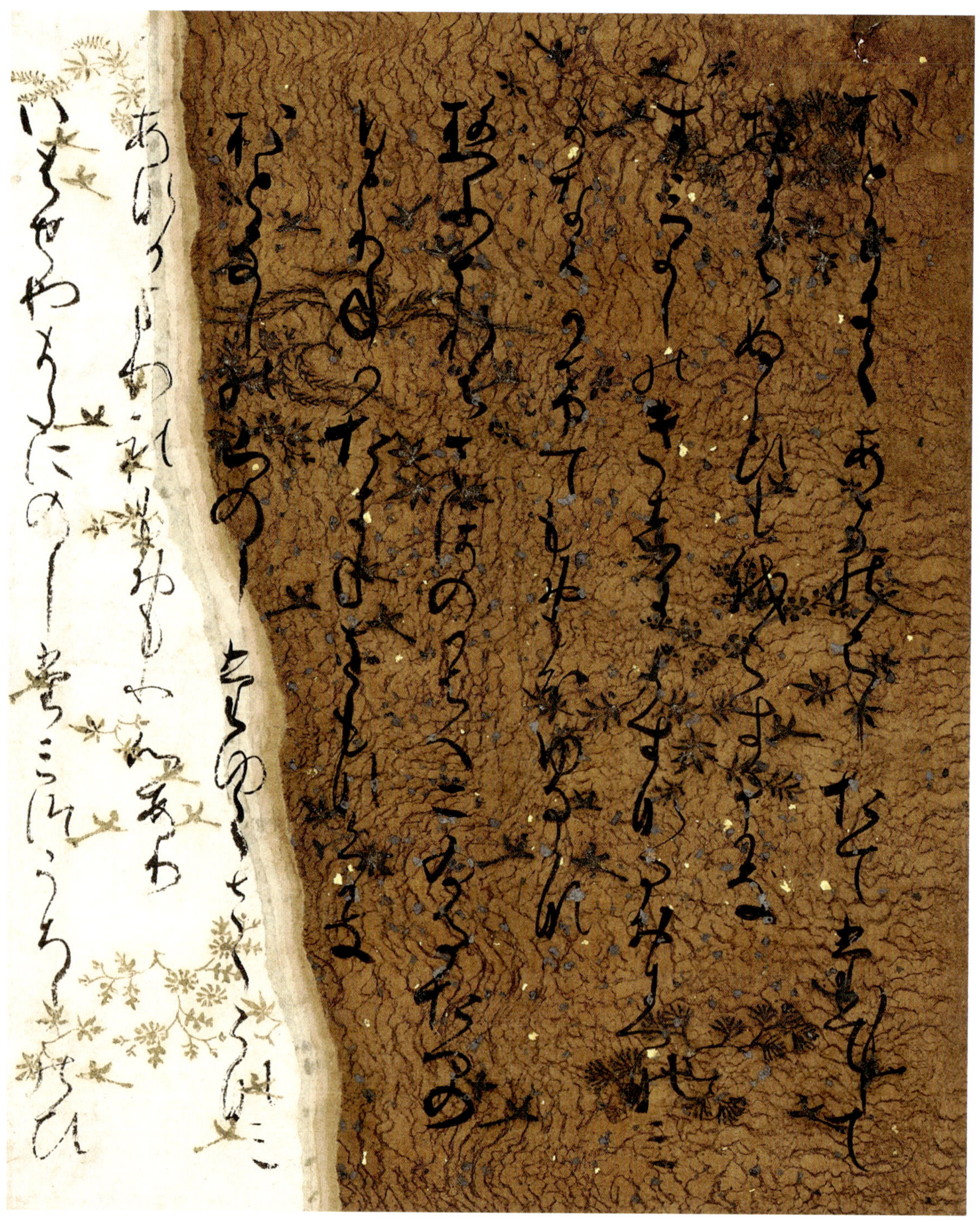

Five poems from the *Lady Ise Volume (Ise-shū)* of the *Anthology of Thirty-six Poets (Sanjū rokunin-shū)*, known as the *Ishiyama Fragments (Ishiyama-gire)*
Heian period, about 1112

Twelfth-century diaries record that to commemorate his sixtieth birthday, Retired Emperor Shirakawa (r. 1072–1086) presented his nine-year-old grandson Emperor Toba with a particularly lavish manuscript. Modern scholars believe that this gift was the *Anthology of Thirty-six Poets*, which was donated by the imperial household to the temple Hongan-ji at Ishiyama (the site of present-day Osaka Castle) in the mid-sixteenth century and subsequently transferred to Nishi Hongan-ji in Kyoto. Two of the thirty-nine volumes were dismantled and sold in 1929; the remaining volumes were designated as National Treasures.

Now mounted as a hanging scroll, this page bears fluid and elegant transcriptions of four verses by the tenth-century poetess Lady Ise. In each poem, a famous scenic spot serves as the point of departure for the poetess's melancholic musings on love:

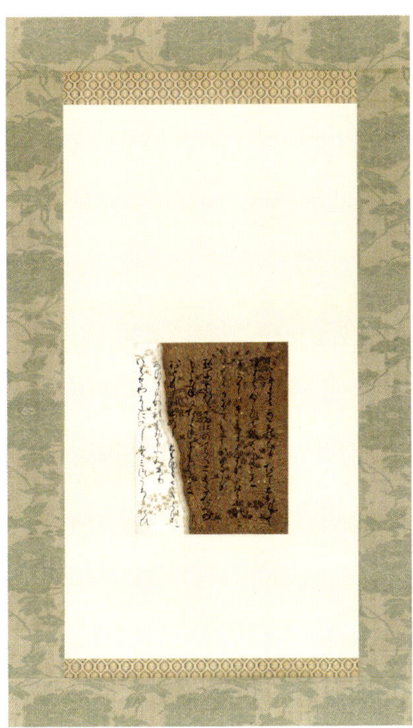

Famous far and wide
Ladderbridge Up to the Sky:
Though I climb and climb,
I can never climb to my love—
This ladder will not reach.

Sumiyoshi shore—
Rolling in come the breakers,
Waves from afar—
Over and over without pause
These thoughts of you sweep through me.

As evening descends
Along Saho riverbank
A lone crane standing . . .
Hard it is to sleep alone—
Just hear that desolate cry!

Down Soundless Mountain
Rush the little rippling waves:
Let them be still!
I too have such things on my heart
As could break the silence here.

(translated by Edwin A. Cranston)

A section of a fifth verse concludes the group. The poems are written on collaged paper embellished with mica and scattered, delicate silver patterns of birds and flowering branches. In its celebration of literary talents and its luxurious ornamentation, the *Anthology of Thirty-six Poets* represents the apogee of classical Heian-period taste.

Detached book page mounted as a hanging scroll; ink and gold and silver pigments on dyed, collaged paper
20.1 x 15.9 cm (7⅞ x 6¼ in.)
Promised gift of Sylvan Barnet and William Burto

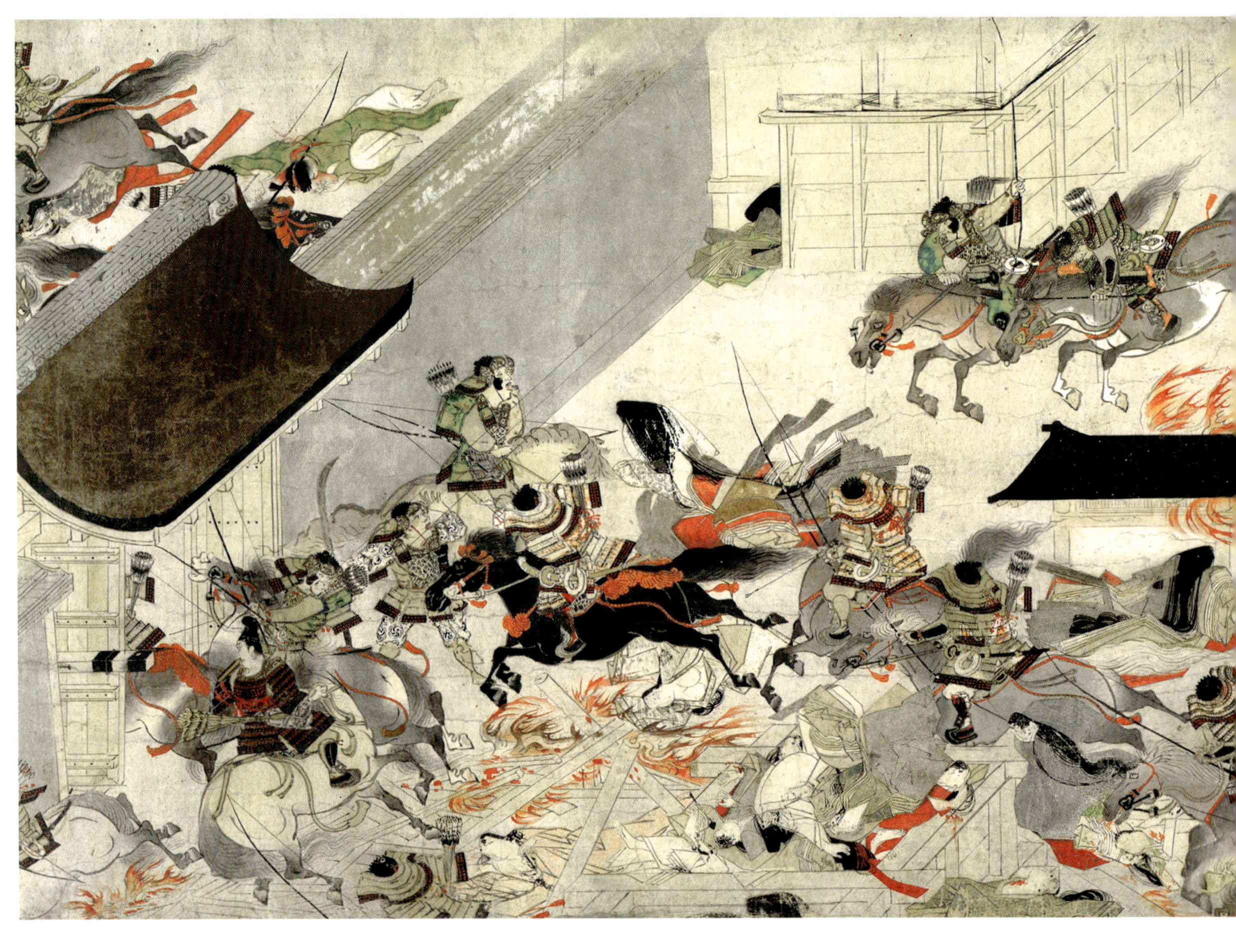

Night Attack on the Sanjō Palace, from the _Illustrated Scrolls of the Events of the Heiji Era_ (_Heiji monogatari emaki_)

Kamakura period, third quarter of the 13th century

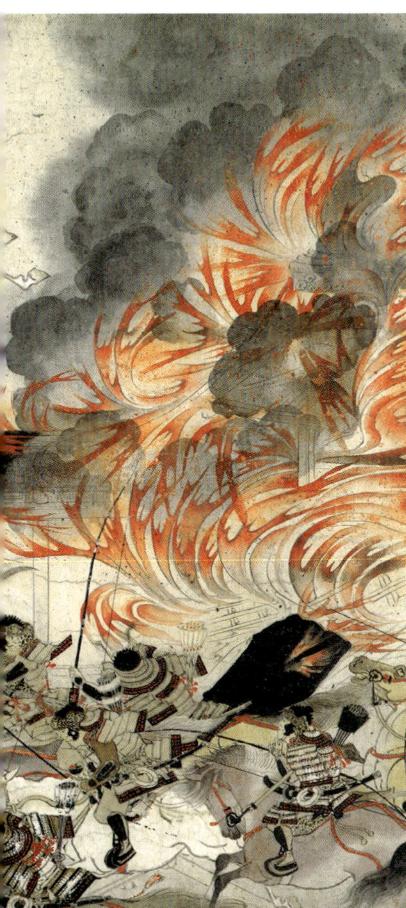

Universally considered the most powerful battle scene in all of Japanese art, *Night Attack on the Sanjō Palace* chronicles Retired Emperor Go-Shirakawa's violent abduction from his palace in 1159. This event took place during the Heiji Rebellion, one of a number of civil wars in the second half of the twelfth century that marked the end of aristocratic rule and the rise of governance by the military. The scroll begins at right with a text describing an early morning attack by several hundred warriors under the leadership of the upstart courtier Fujiwara no Nobuyori and his henchman Minamoto no Yoshitomo. The illustration that follows heightens the drama by setting forth the events in one continuous visual narrative.

In the first section, members of the court and other residents of the city rush toward the palace, desperate to learn the retired emperor's fate. On the far side of the wall that separates the palace from the street, warriors force Go-Shirakawa and his young sister into an ox-drawn carriage. In the next section, they surround and torch the palace, and all those who attempt to flee are "shot [with arrows] or hacked to death." Hoping to escape the flames, the court women jump into a well. The text relates that those at the bottom drowned, those in the middle suffocated, and those at the top burned to death. The animal-like faces of the lower-level warriors emphasize the brutality of their deeds.

This scroll, perhaps the most famous Japanese work of art outside Japan, is one of three remaining from what is believed to have been a set of fifteen scrolls describing the power struggle between the imperial family and competing warrior clans.

Handscroll; ink and color on paper
41.3 x 699.7 cm (16¼ x 275½ in.)
Fenollosa-Weld Collection 11.4000

Suit of armor in "great harness" (*ōyoroi*) style
The helmet bowl: Kamakura period, 14th century;
the other parts: Edo period, early–mid-19th century

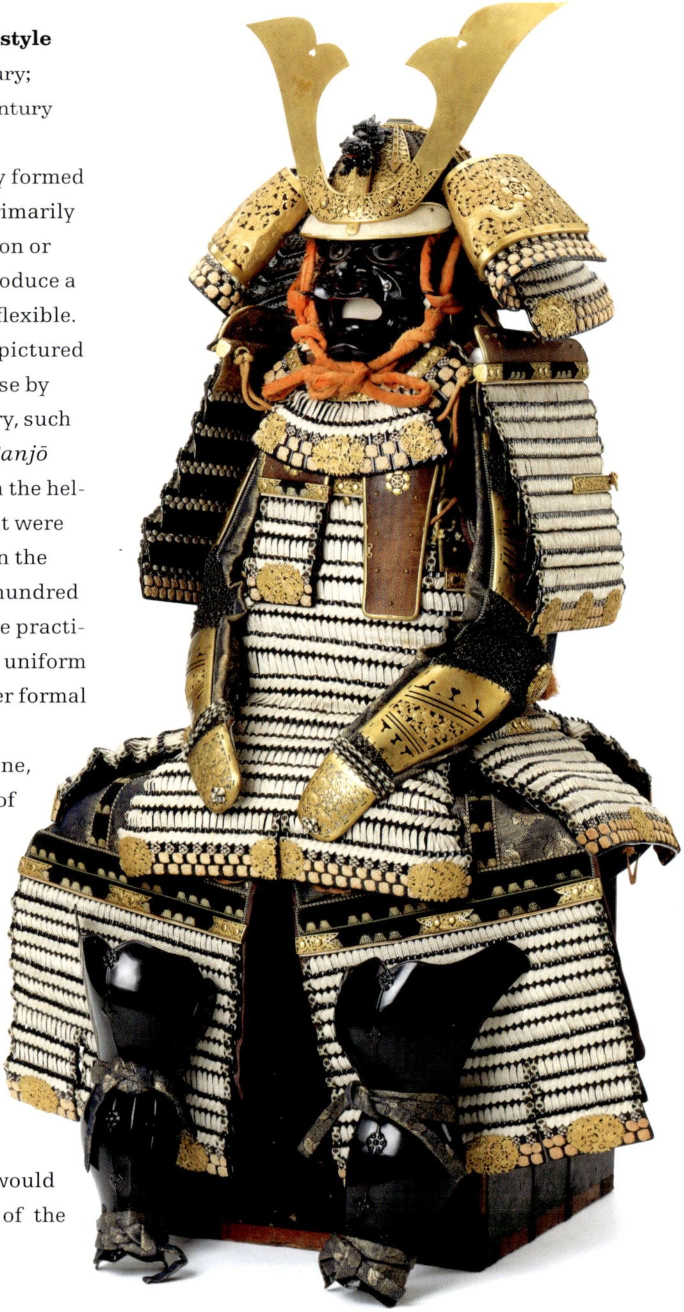

Unlike later European armor, which is usually formed from large metal plates, Japanese armor is primarily made up of many small pieces of lacquered iron or leather threaded together with silk cord to produce a scale-like texture that is both protective and flexible. The "great harness" (*ōyoroi*) style, as the type pictured here is known, was originally developed for use by eleventh- and twelfth-century samurai cavalry, such as those depicted in the *Night Attack on the Sanjō Palace* scroll (see detail, opposite). Apart from the helmet bowl, however, all components of this suit were actually made in the nineteenth century, when the country had already experienced nearly two hundred years of peace. Armor no longer had to provide practical protection but still played a vital role as a uniform to be worn in daimyo processions and on other formal occasions.

Since there was little real fighting to be done, the warrior class sought other methods of maintaining its status; codifying the "samurai way" (*bushidō*) and compiling books on the history of arms and armor were two such methods. A similar antiquarian spirit inspired the production of early-medieval-style armor such as this suit, with its highly decorated helmet turn-backs, chest ornaments, and arm plates. Armor became gradually more ostentatious and impractical, while maintaining the heart-stopping ferocity of its historic form. The wearer of this suit would truly have re-embodied the samurai spirit of the classic age of individual mounted combat.

Iron, lacquered iron, chain mail, gilded and silvered copper, silk cords, silk brocade, leather, stenciled leather, and ray skin
H. 152 cm (H. 59⅞ in.)
Charles Goddard Weld Bequest 11.12547

fig. 20 (right) **The medieval warriors depicted here depended upon their "great harness" style armor for protection.**

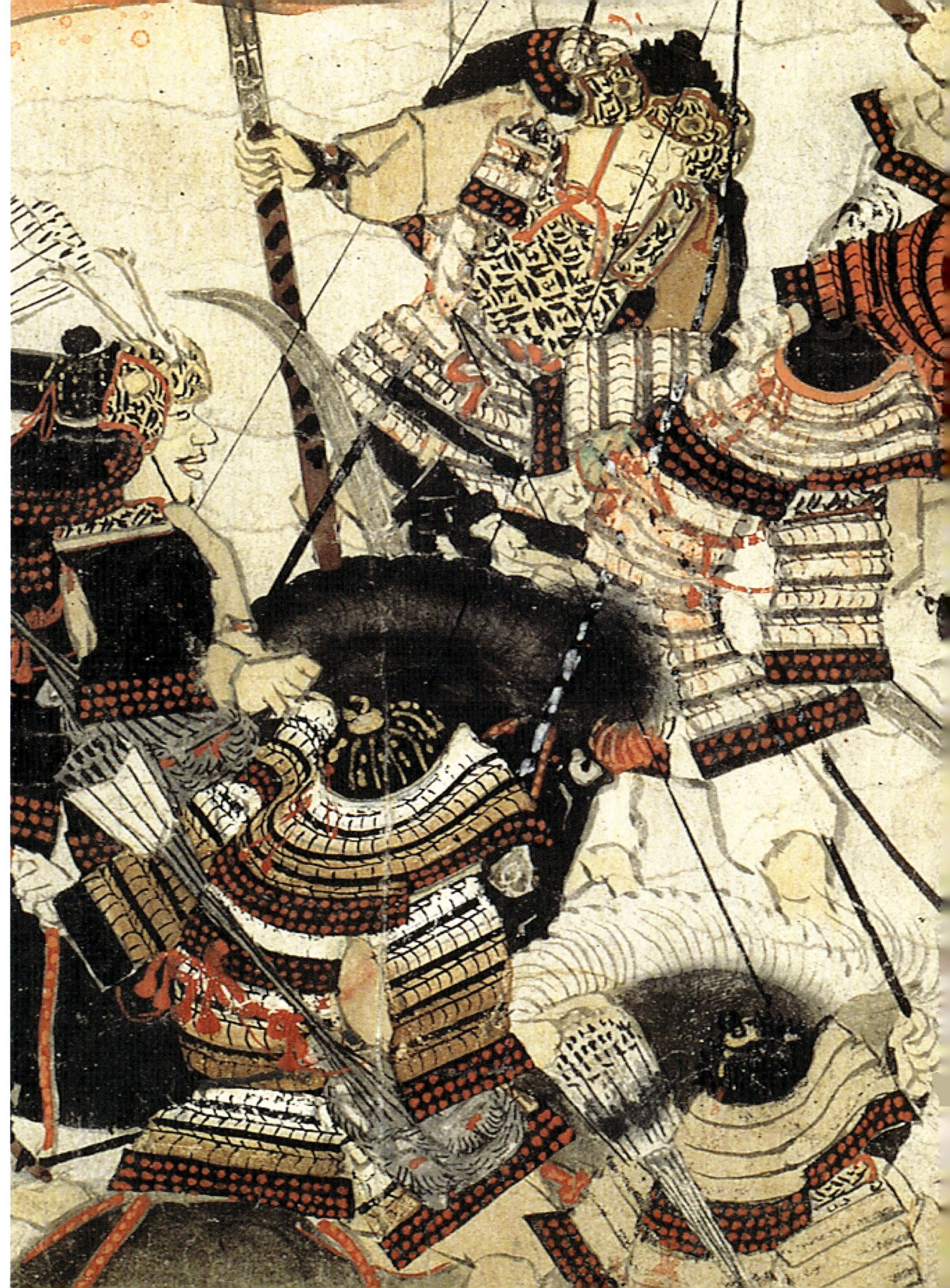

Blade for a dagger (*tantō*)

(*opposite page, left*)

Rai Kunitoshi (dates unknown)

Kamakura period, late 13th–early 14th century

Although it dates from a period when sword blades were beginning to be appreciated as much for their aesthetic as for their practical qualities, this dagger (*tantō*) was intended for actual warfare, as seen in this detail from *Night Attack on the Sanjō Palace*.

Like most Japanese blades, it is made of a soft iron core wrapped in a hard exterior layer forged from a block of steel that was repeatedly heated, hammered out, and folded. Once the dagger was roughly shaped, the smith covered it with a heat-resistant clay mixture that he partially scraped away, creating a distinctive border between the edge and the rest of the blade. He then reheated the dagger and plunged it into cold water. The surface grain seen here resulted from the forging process, while the secondary heating and quenching produced crystalline patterns along the border. These characteristics were subsequently brought out by filing, grinding, and polishing, and grooves were cut in both sides. Several times during the blade's long life, the entire surface was repolished to maintain its pristine beauty. The only section left unpolished was the tang, the part that fit inside the hilt when a blade was mounted, as in the example on the next page. The tang was once slightly shortened and an extra hole was drilled for the retaining peg, probably when the blade was given a new set of mounts.

Steel and iron

L. 36.8 cm (L. 14½ in.)

William Sturgis Bigelow Collection 11.11227

Blade for a sword of the *tachi* type

(*opposite page, center*)

Nagamitsu (dates unknown)

Kamakura period, late 13th–early 14th century

Because it has survived almost in its original form, unshortened and with only the addition of a second retaining-peg hole, this blade from the important swordsmithing center of Osafune in Bizen Province (present-day Okayama Prefecture) magnificently conveys the martial spirit of the late twelfth and thirteenth centuries. During this period, a military government was established in the then-remote eastern town of Kamakura, its power surpassing that of the court in Kyoto.

In addition to the features seen in the short dagger by Kunitoshi—a combination of harder steel and softer iron, and a razor-sharp edge—this classic blade has two more attributes, a central ridge and a backward curve, that characterize virtually all Japanese swords measuring more than sixteen inches in length made during the last millennium. The ridged cross-section insured the sword's unique combination of lightness and strength, with the thicker center of the blade compensating for the brittle, hardened edge. The curve not only contributed to the blade's elegance but also helped the samurai draw and strike in a single, unbroken movement: the shape forms a rough arc with its center at the user's shoulder and its radius, the length of his arm. The impressive size and pronounced curve are typical of *tachi*, swords that were generally worn slung from the waist by mounted warriors; later swords used by foot soldiers are somewhat shorter and have a gentler curve.

Steel and iron

L. 102.2 cm (L. 40¼ in.)

Gift of Mrs. Charles Goddard Weld 13.281

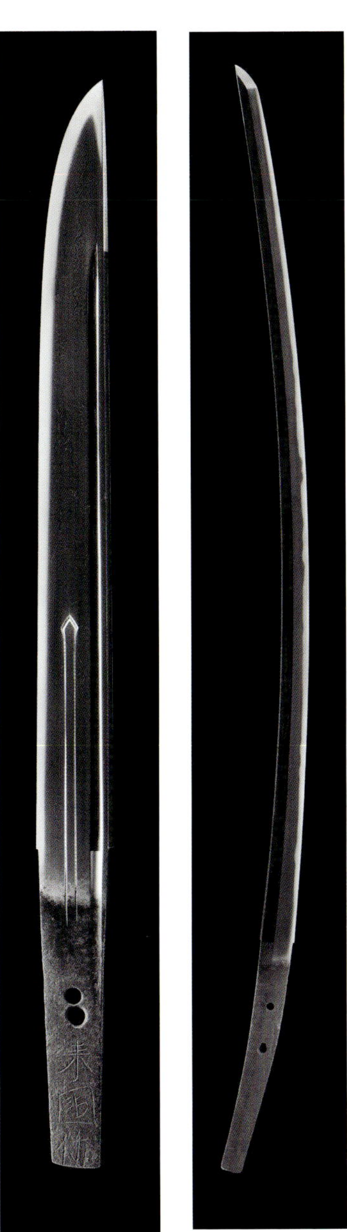

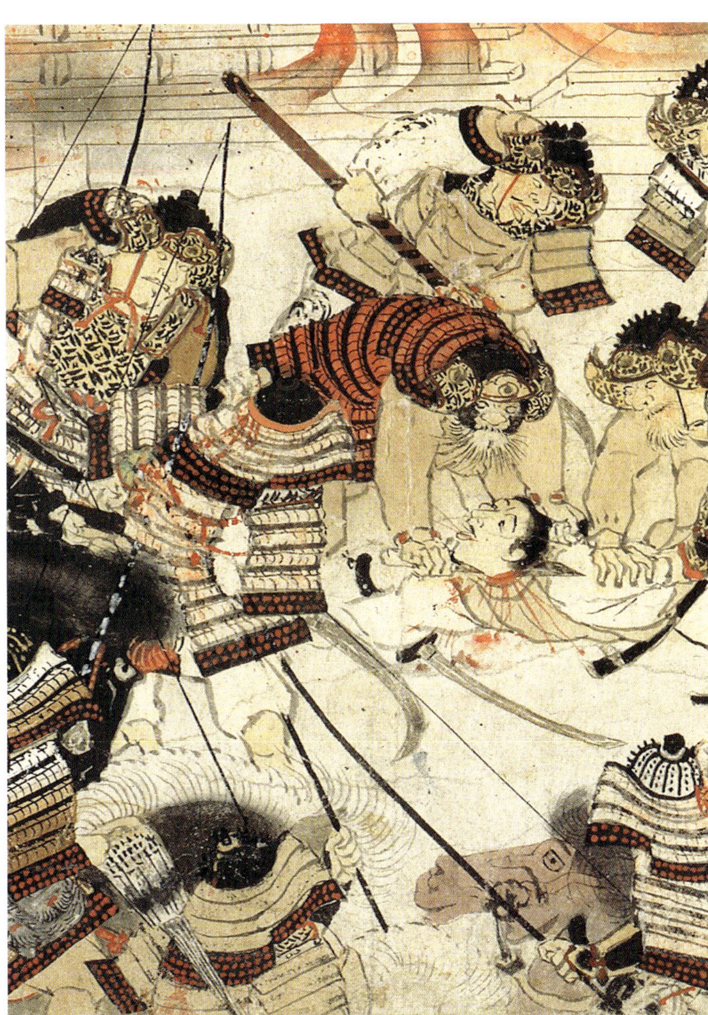

fig. 21 **This dramatic detail shows a *tantō* being used to decapitate a captive samurai.**

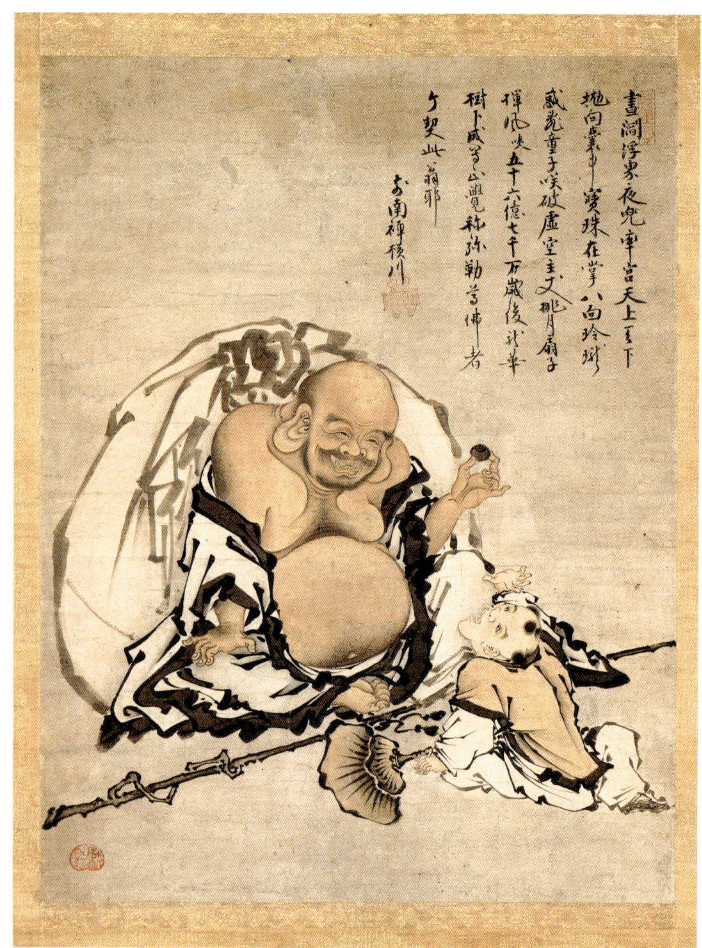

Hotei

Inscribed by Ōsen Keisan (1429–1493)

Muromachi period, 1479

The jovial Hotei (known in Chinese as Budai, literally "Cloth Bag") is characteristically depicted with a rotund belly, elongated ears, a voluminous sack, and a pilgrim's staff. Based upon a historical personage—the tenth-century Chinese itinerant monk Qici—he was revered as an incarnation of Maitreya (Japanese: Miroku), the Buddha of the Future. Later, Hotei also became known as one of the Seven Gods of Good Fortune, as well as a protector of children.

Although images of the eccentric deity were first displayed in Zen monasteries, by the fifteenth century they were attracting secular interest from members of the Ashikaga shogunate, who began to collect examples, first by leading Chinese masters of the Song (960–1279) and Yuan (1279–1368) dynasties, and then by Japanese artists. This painting, which shows Hotei playfully tempting a young Chinese boy with a wish-granting jewel, bears a commendatory inscription by the Zen prelate Ōsen Keisan in the upper-right corner. The identity of the artist remains unconfirmed, but the contrast between fine, detailed brushstrokes for the unkempt deity and dynamic, jagged lines for his robes and sack bears strong similarities to scrolls attributed to Kano Masanobu, founder of the Kano school, which would provide the official painters (*goyō eshi*) to the ruling military leaders for more than 350 years.

Hanging scroll; ink and color on paper
61.4 x 45.6 cm (24 3/16 x 17 15/16 in.)
Fenollosa-Weld Collection 11.4244

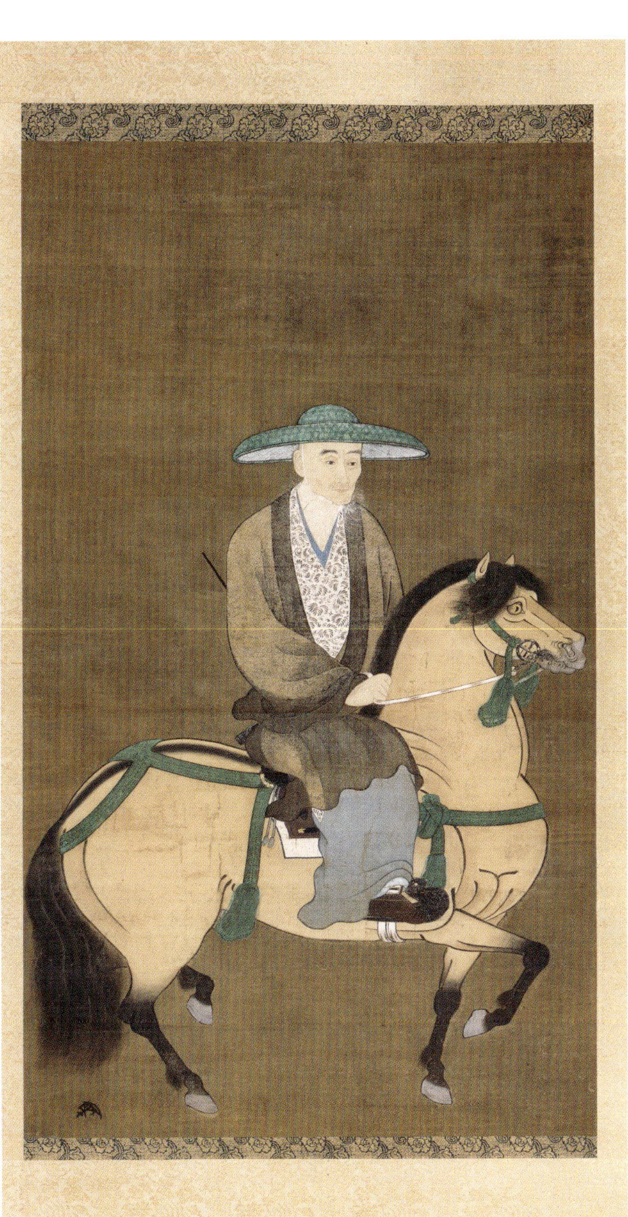

Portrait of Iio Sōgi

Attributed to Kano Motonobu (1476–1559)

Muromachi period, first half of the 16th century

Born into a humble provincial family, Iio Sōgi (1421–1501) grew up to become the preeminent poet of the late fifteenth century. Like many contemporary youths of limited means, he underwent Zen monastic training in Kyoto. Soon he proved himself more adept at literary than religious pursuits and gained the patronage of powerful members of the court. They encouraged Sōgi in his studies of classical Japanese literature, and he eventually became skilled at incorporating allusions to earlier poems in linked verse (*renga*), long poetic sequences that comprised one of the major literary genres of the late medieval period.

In this posthumous portrait, Sōgi is depicted astride a muscular, stylized steed—a reference to his tireless trips to eastern and northern Japan, where he was well received by local military leaders eager to elevate their cultural credentials. He wears the sedge hat typical of wandering poets, and wisps of straggly white beard bespeak his advanced age.

On the basis of the cipher in the lower-left corner, this sensitive depiction of the poet has traditionally been attributed to Kano Motonobu, who dominated painting production during the early sixteenth century as the second-generation head of the Kano school. Although recent scholarship has questioned the authenticity of the cipher itself, the painting continues to be celebrated as one of the masterworks of early Kano-school portraiture.

Hanging scroll; ink, color, and gold on silk
98 x 54.4 cm (38 9/16 x 21 7/16 in.)
Frederick L. Jack Fund 58.314

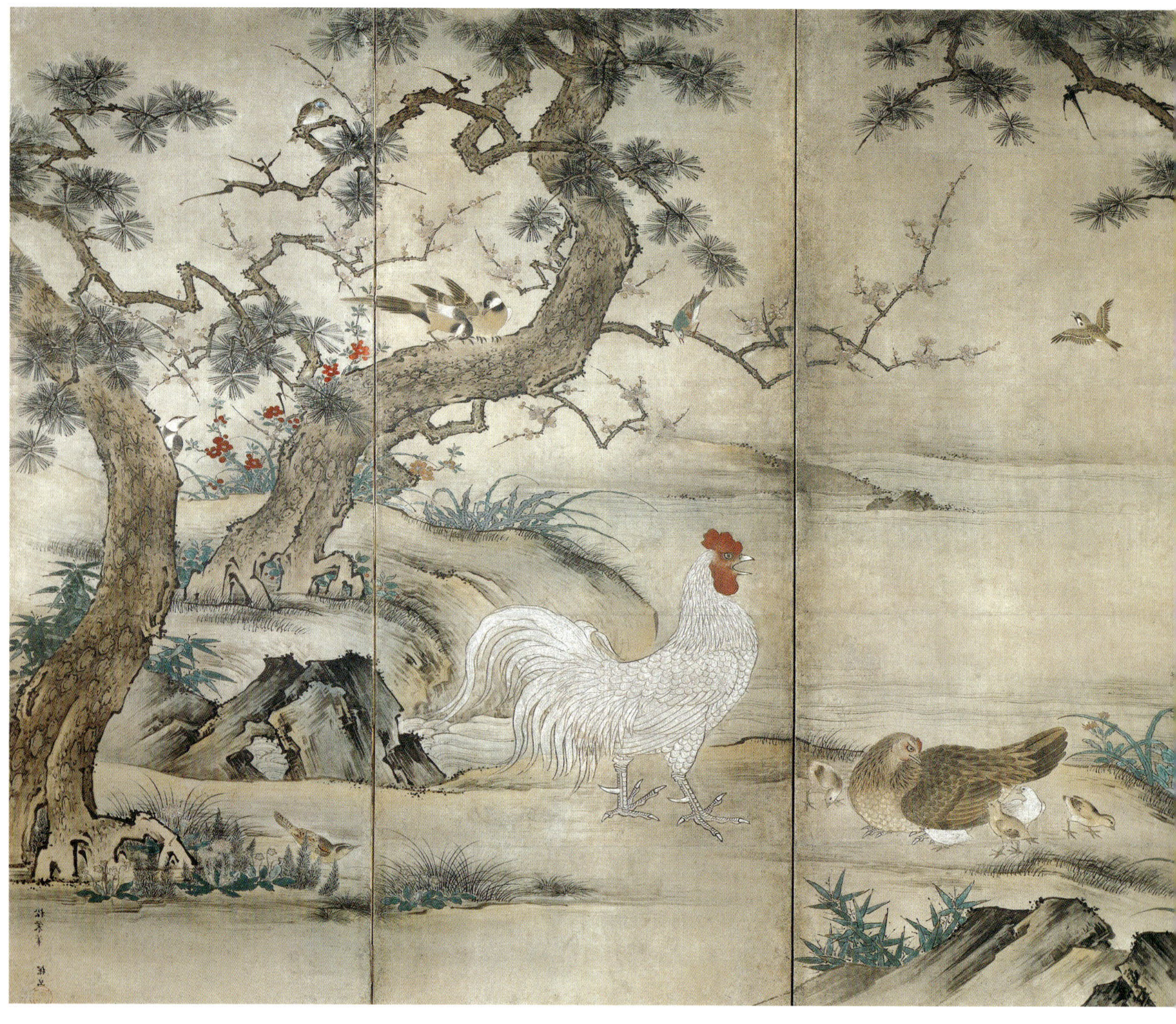

Fowl in Spring and Summer Landscape
Attributed to Kano Shōei (1519–1592)
Momoyama period, late 16th century

Blossoming plum branches and violets in the right foreground of this screen herald the arrival of spring, then give way to the peonies and water plantains of summer as the composition progresses from right to left through low-lying marshes. The remaining seasons would have been represented in a complementary screen, which has not survived. Monumental yet highly detailed paintings of flora and fauna of the four seasons were made popular during the early decades of the sixteenth century by Kano Motonobu, the second-generation head of the Kano school. His compositions ornamented the sliding doors (*fusuma*) of the subtemples of Kyoto's Zen monasteries, which often served as memorial chapels for powerful military families.

This screen does not bear an artist's signature or seal. In the lower-right corner, however, the Edo-period connoisseur and celebrated artist Kano Tan'yū

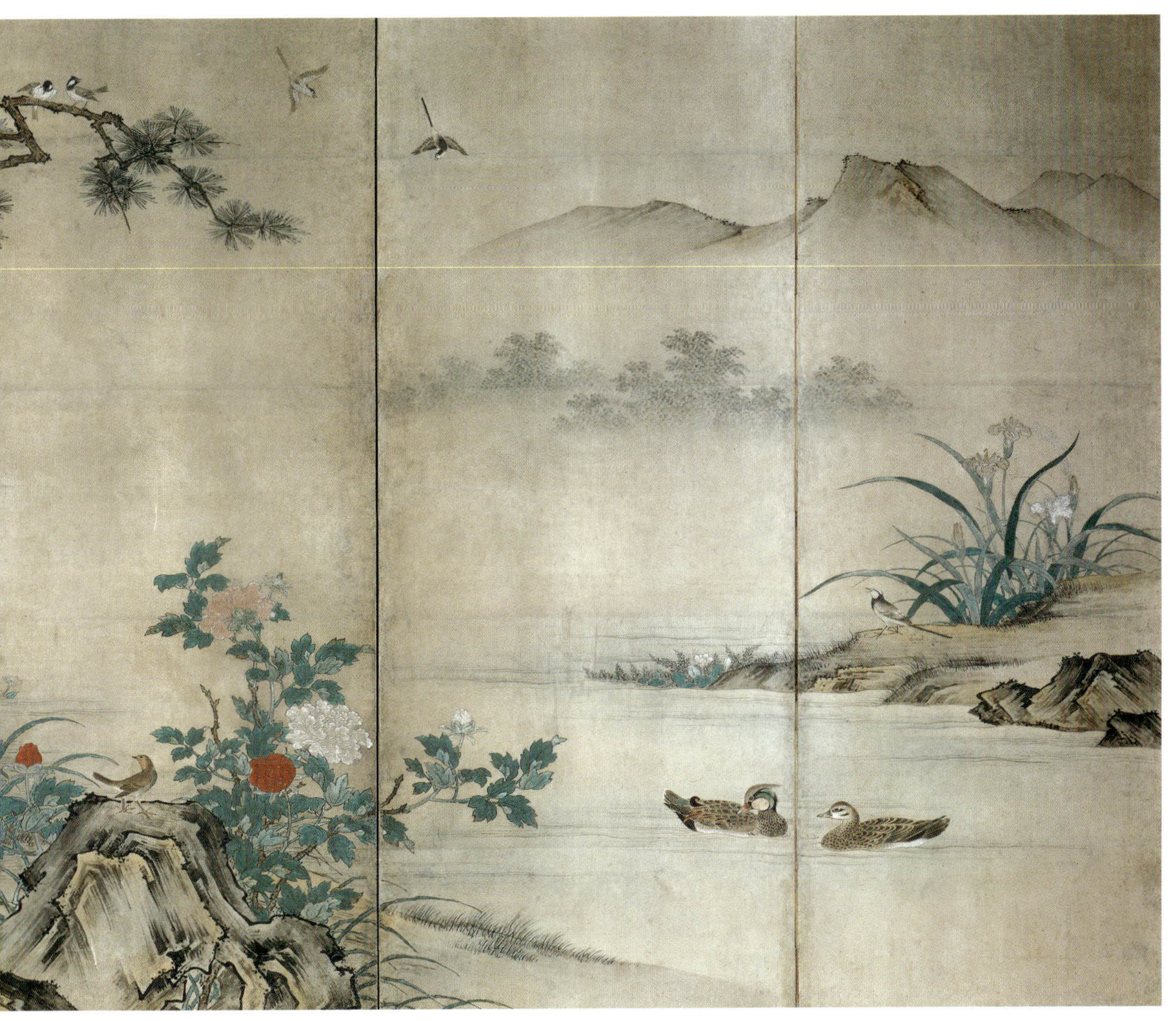

attributed the work to his great-grandfather, Kano Shōei, son of Kano Motonobu. Shōei is known for having distilled his father's style, which successfully synthesized Chinese-style ink painting (*kanga*) with Japanese polychrome painting (*yamato-e*).

Six-panel folding screen; ink and color on paper
151.5 x 372 cm (59⅝ x 146½ in.)
Fenollosa-Weld Collection 11.4347

Tartar Envoys Bringing Tribute

Attributed to Kano Eitoku (1543–1590)

Momoyama period, second half of the 16th century

Under the rule of the Ashikaga shoguns in the fourteenth and fifteenth centuries, official and commercial contact between Japan and China increased. Trade items included medicines and curiosities, as well as prestigious porcelains and ink paintings, which were particularly favored by the Japanese military elite. Fifteenth-century texts mention screens painted with Chinese boats, reflecting this new, more international outlook, but no examples of such early date are extant.

The exotic mounted figures in the foreground of this sixteenth-century screen are northern Chinese nomads, often called "Tartars," identifiable by their Central Asian features, fur-trimmed hats, and prominent weapons. The banners they carry suggest that the figure in the middle wearing a red-and-gold tunic is an envoy; standing behind him is an attendant carrying a gift of a tiger skin. Two ornate Chinese vessels at the top carry a variety of travelers, from scholars and officials to students and merchants. Several turn their faces eagerly toward the shore in anticipation of landing.

The spirited yet careful depiction of the facial features makes it likely that this screen was produced either by the renowned sixteenth-century official painter Kano Eitoku or under his supervision. The painting was originally attached to a *fusuma*, or sliding door. At some point in its history, it was cut down and remounted as this smaller screen. The scale and strength of the images suggest that it would originally have been part of a much larger ensemble in a grand architectural setting.

Two-panel folding screen; ink and color on gold-leafed paper
153.2 x 170.4 cm (60 5/16 x 67 1/16 in.)
Fenollosa-Weld Collection 11.4450

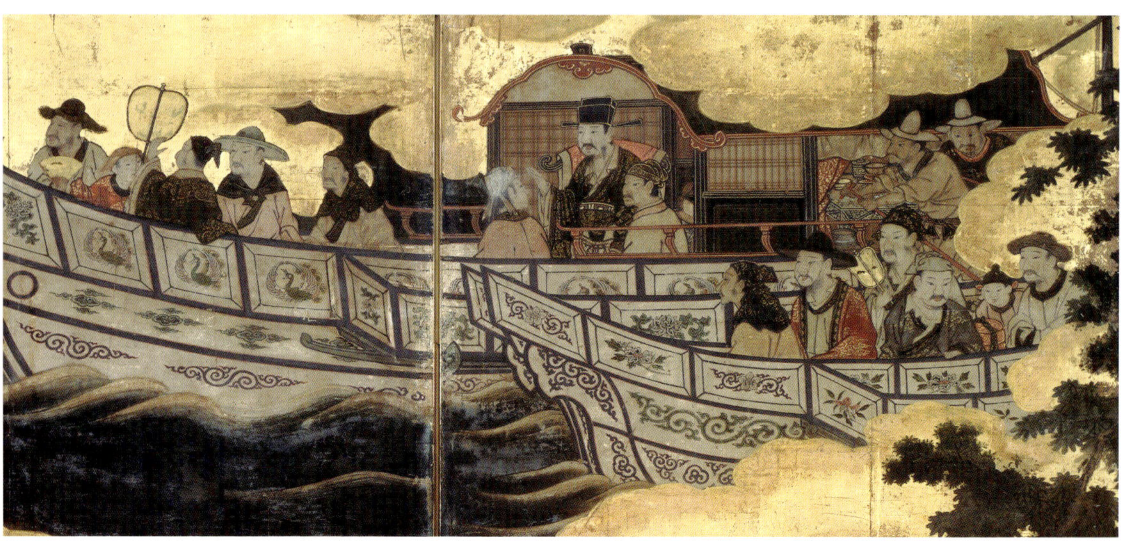

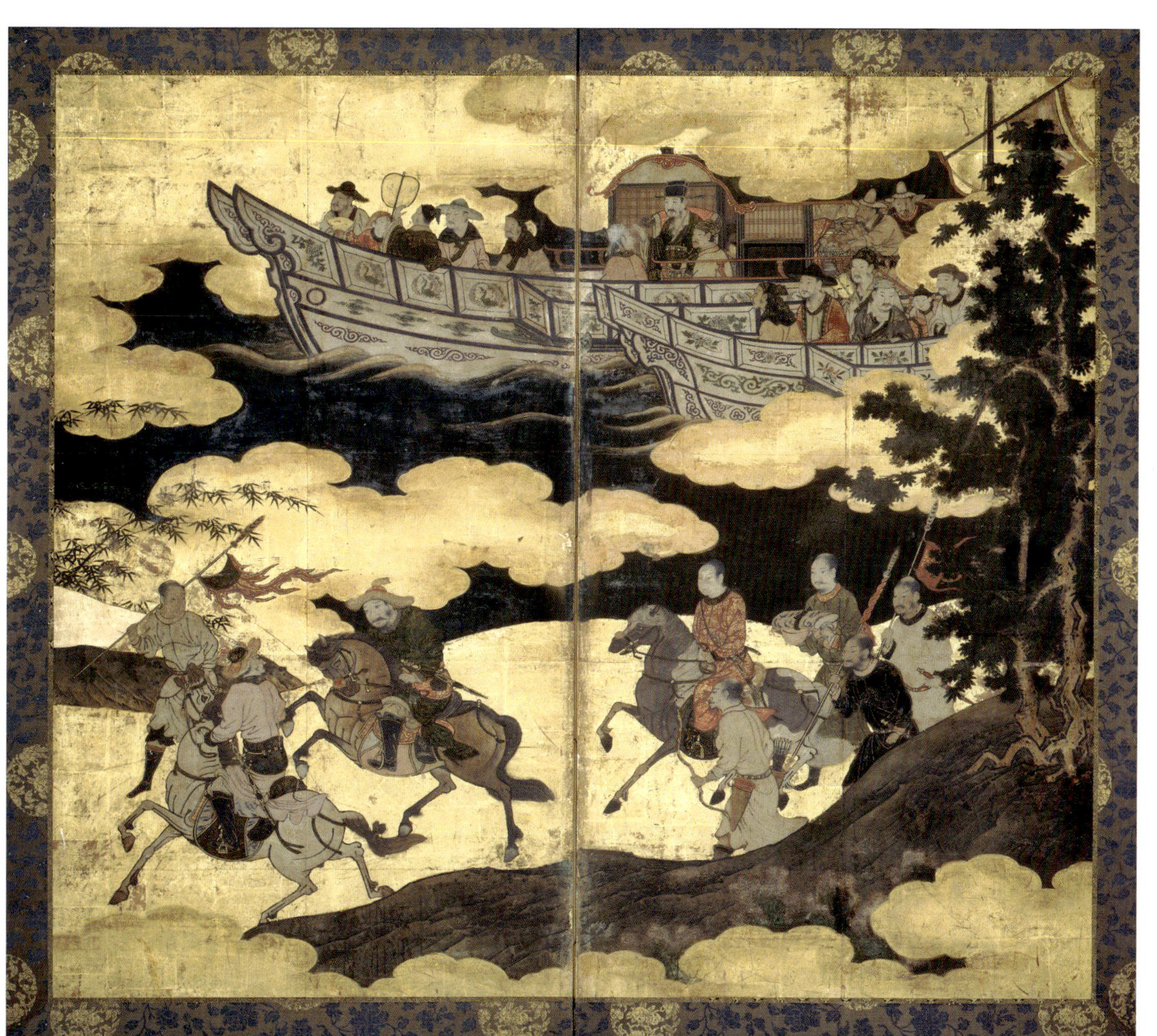

Nō mask of the *akobujō* type

Muromachi period, 15th–16th century

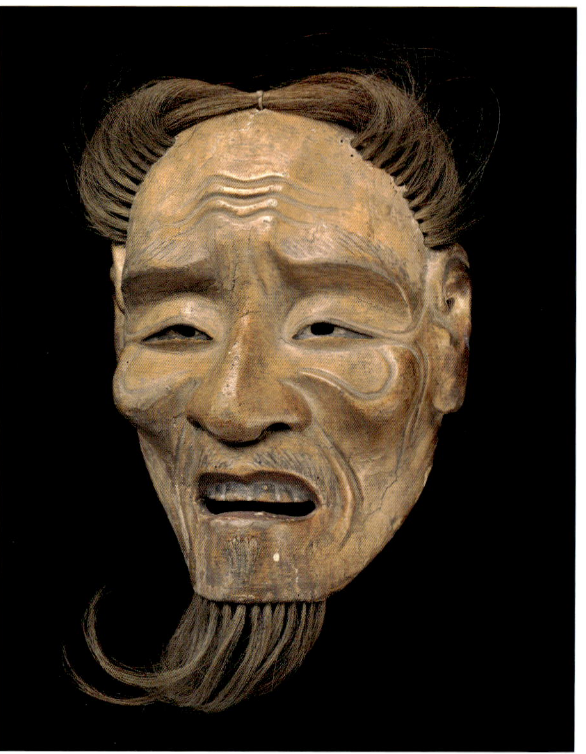

Nō drama developed out of folk performances into a highly stylized dramatic art that enjoyed great prestige among the upper classes. The plays, which are frequently based on episodes from the Japanese classics, deal with human emotions and encounters with spirits in an ethereal dream world where time can move in any direction. Performed by a small number of actors on a bare wooden stage with minimal props, Nō plays are accompanied by spare music and chanting. Every movement is carefully choreographed; the pace of action can be likened to a greatly enlarged still photograph depicting a human emotion, which is mysteriously animated in slow motion.

Otherworldly masks are key to the illusory world of Nō. This finely carved example, embellished with real hair, is craggy with the lines of age. Well worn, it appears to have been used often for its designated purpose of transforming an actor into an elderly man. During the Muromachi period, Nō was formalized into several distinct schools, with particular types of mask assigned to particular roles. This one would have been used by the main actor in the first part of a play. In Nō drama, elderly men are often revealed to be gods, and the importance of these roles meant that masks for them were created relatively early in the development of Nō.

Japanese cypress, with gesso, pigment, and hair
20.2 x 15.2 x 8.2 cm (7 15/16 x 6 x 3 1/4 in.)
Special Chinese and Japanese Fund 05.226

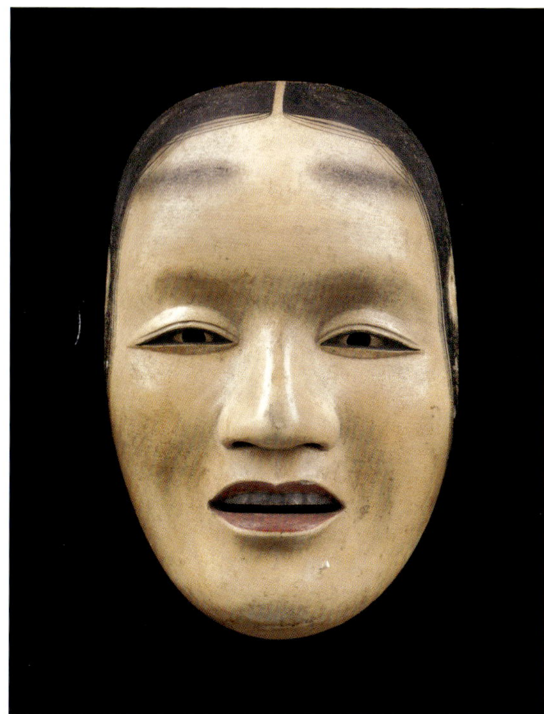

Nō mask of the *fukai* type

Deme Mitsushige (died in 1719)

Edo period, early 18th century

Nō is performed by an all-male cast, making the wide range of female masks particularly important. This mask, of a type known in Japanese as *fukai*, would have been used to portray a middle-aged woman. The slight disarrangement of the hair and the serious, melancholy mien distinguish the mask from those designed to portray the energy of a younger woman, which are painted without a single glossy black hair out of place.

Nō masks are painstakingly carved from wood and then painted with layers of pigment over a gesso base. Actors treat them with great reverence, preserving them and passing them down through generations within each school. A particularly fine mask, like a highly esteemed tea caddy for use in tea ritual, could become the model for subsequent commissions. The reverse of this mask bears an inscription in gold and silver by the actor Kanze Dayū, which reveals that the carver, Deme Mitsushige, was asked to copy a famous Kanze-school *fukai* mask in the year 1707.

Japanese cypress, with gesso and pigment
21 x 13.5 x 7.5 cm (8¼ x 5⁵⁄₁₆ x 2¹⁵⁄₁₆ in.)
William Sturgis Bigelow Collection 11.5952

Nō robe of the *atsuita* type

(*right, top*)

Edo period, late 17th–early 18th century

Nō robes are among the finest and most luxurious textiles ever produced in Japan. Each robe is a unique garment, woven with techniques that seem almost impossibly complex. This robe is an *atsuita*, the basic garment for male roles, often worn underneath an outer jacket. The strong colors, bold peony design, and undulating lines of this very fine example would have been suitable for the role of a younger man. The patterning on the robe was achieved through the use of supplementary weft threads of silk and gold- and silver-leaf paper strips that were bound into the structure of the fabric, rather than embroidered. The word *atsuita* is thought to have originally referred to heavy, weft-patterned fabric imported from China that was wrapped around thick boards (*atsuita*); the term likely evolved to mean the garments made from such fabric, finally identifying this type of Nō robe.

The Nō stage itself is a very simple environment. The actor chooses his robe with great care, since it is one of the principal devices by which he evokes the mood and emotional intensity of his performance as he moves to the chanting of the chorus and the accompanying music. The flattened, bold designs of many Nō robes would combine with the masks worn by the actors to transport the audience to an otherworldly plane of mysterious refinement known in Japanese as *yūgen*.

Silk twill with supplementary silk and gilt-paper patterning wefts
143.5 x 139.7 cm (56½ x 55 in.)
William Sturgis Bigelow Collection and James Fund
15.1155

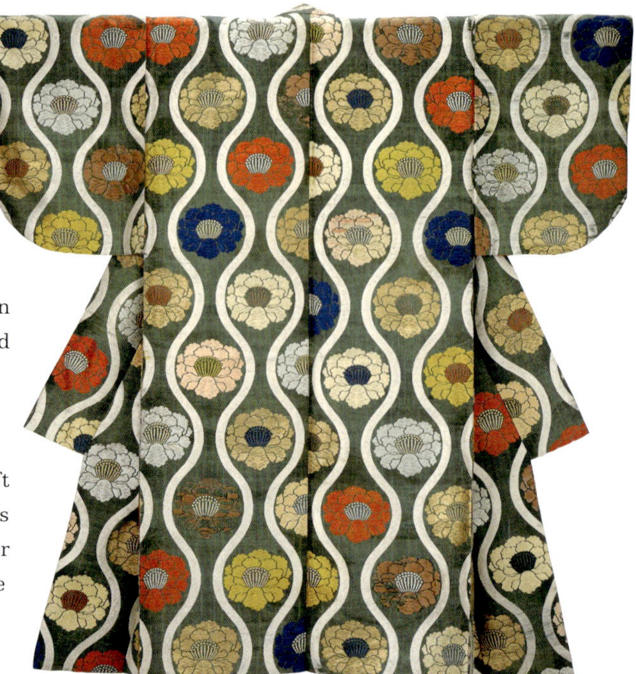

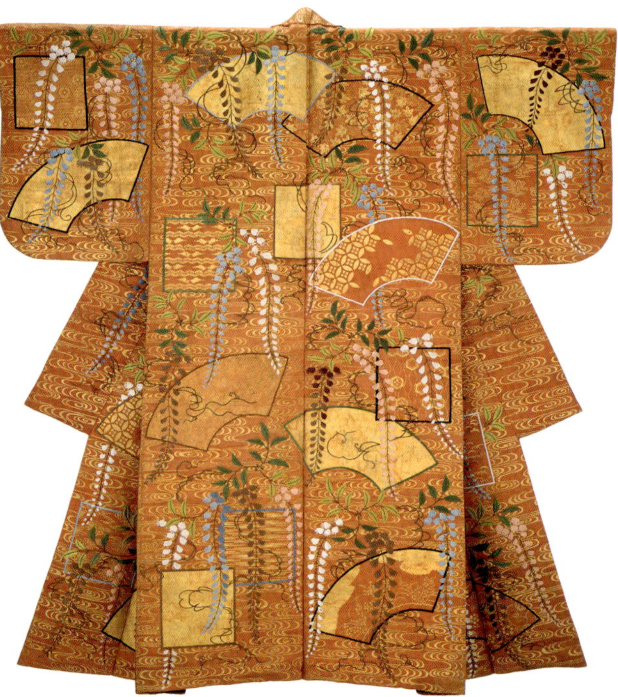

Nō robe of the *nuihaku* type

(opposite page, bottom)

Edo period, 18th–19th century

Nuihaku refers both to a type of Nō robe and to the techniques used to embellish it: embroidery (*nui*) and gold- and silver-leaf stenciling (*haku*). *Nuihaku* are worn for female roles, and the motifs are more delicate than those used for male garments. This pliant robe is decorated with a design of poem cards, fans, and elegantly trailing wisteria on a background of stylized water rendered in gold.

Early in the formalization of Nō, the dramatic genius Zeami Motokiyo emphasized that actors' garments should closely resemble those worn in real life. Nō robes continued to follow street fashion until the late sixteenth century, when they began to become conventionalized stage costumes. Patrons of Nō and guests of honor at performances traditionally made gifts of robes to actors, and this patronage, largely by powerful warriors who also performed Nō themselves, enabled the textile industry to produce these superb examples of artistry and craftsmanship.

Silk twill embroidered with silk and stenciled with gold leaf
151.8 x 141 cm (59¾ x 55½ in.)
William Sturgis Bigelow Collection 21.165

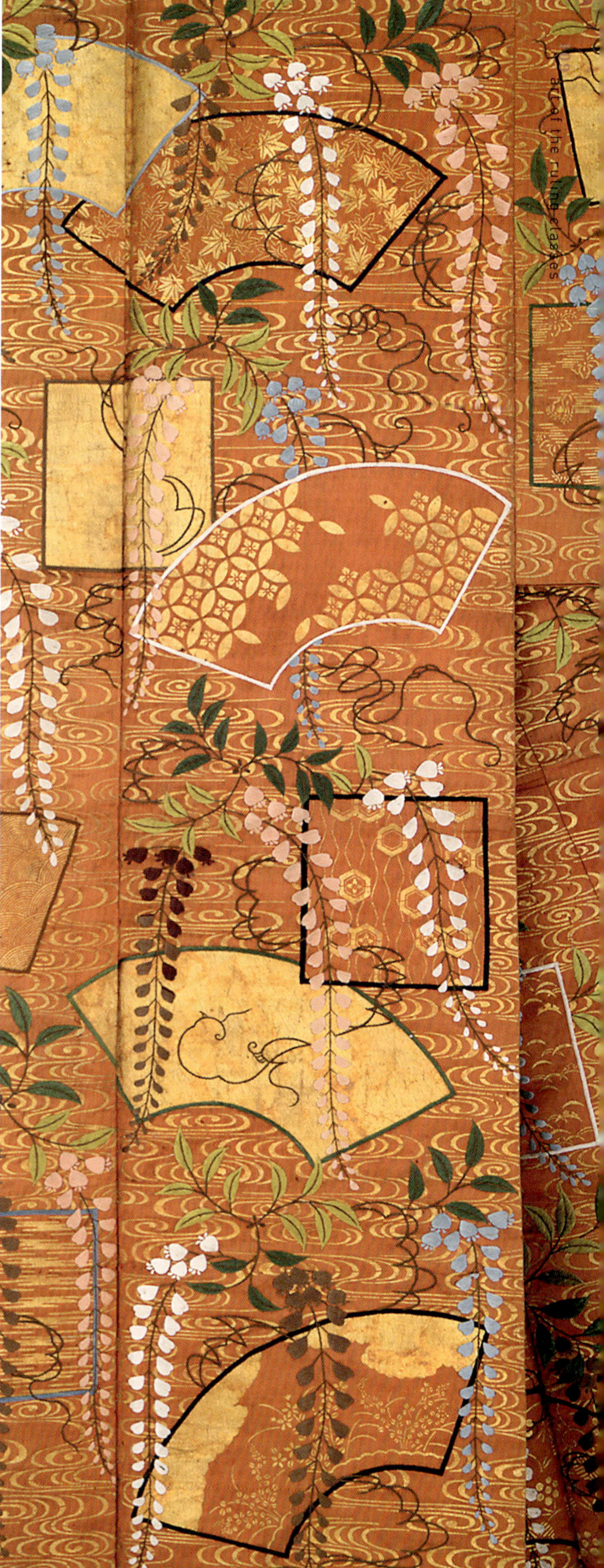

Dish with design of grasses

Momoyama–Edo periods, late 16th–early 17th century

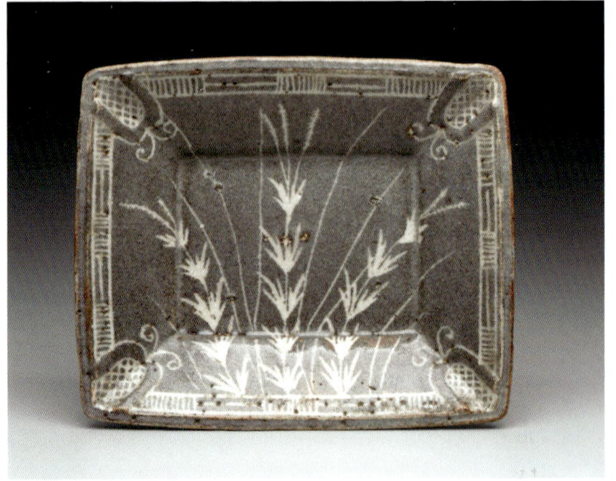

This small dish was likely used to serve food during the formal meal known as *kaiseki* that precedes tea ritual. It was first thrown on a potter's wheel and then reshaped into a rectangle with sloping sides. The white body was covered in a layer of darker, iron-rich clay that, once dry, was scratched away to form the design.

Although Japan boasts a pottery tradition dating back about twelve thousand years, the surface finish of most early ceramics relied on incidental glazing caused by flying wood ash in the kiln. It was not until the sixteenth century that improvements in kiln technology enabled potters to create a wide range of deliberately glazed vessels, which often were decorated with lively, sketchy motifs. Many of these new wares were made in the Mino region of central Honshu, an important power base for each of the three successive warlords (Oda Nobunaga, Toyotomi Hideyoshi, and Tokugawa Ieyasu) who brought Japan under unified control during the Momoyama period.

All three warlords were keen devotees of tea practice, and the first two, Nobunaga and Hideyoshi, engaged the services of Japan's most famous tea master, Sen no Rikyū, who committed suicide in 1591 on the latter's orders. Although the very idea of decorated ceramics was inspired by fashionable Chinese models, Rikyū's authority is evident here in the rustic simplicity of the design and the unusual form that was intended to emulate a wooden prototype.

Mino ware (Gray Shino type); stoneware
with iron slip and feldspathic glaze
4.3 x 22.9 x 19.7 cm (1¾ x 9 x 7¾ in.)
Morse Collection. Museum purchase with funds
donated by contribution 92.5399

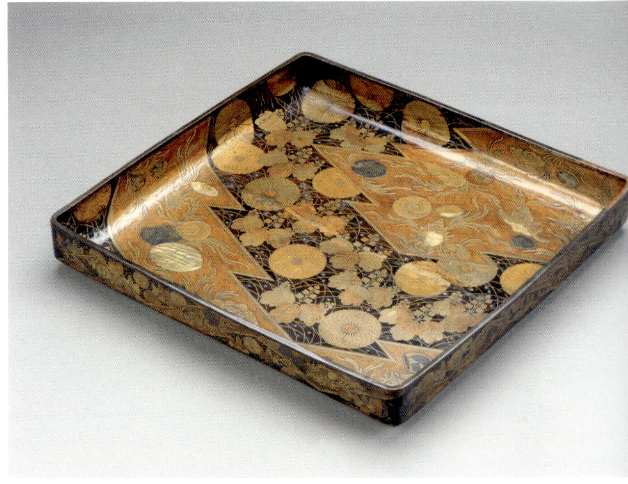

Tray (*midarebako*) with design of shells, weeds, grasses, and family crests

Momoyama period, late 16th–early 17th century

Traditional Japanese clothes are made up of narrow lengths of cloth with minimal tailoring, so that they are easy to fold into a small space. This shallow tray (*midarebako*), one of several new types of lacquer furniture that appeared in the late sixteenth century, would have been used to hold a court or samurai lady's formal garment.

The rich decoration is executed in a lacquering style known as Kōdai-ji *maki-e*, which is associated with the temple Kōdai-ji in Kyoto, founded in 1606 by the widow of warlord Toyotomi Hideyoshi. The Kōdai-ji style emerged in response to the extravagant tastes of Hideyoshi and his vassals, who demanded that large expanses of their castles and residences be flamboyantly—and rapidly—decorated. Instead of first being drawn on tracing paper in reverse and then applied to the black lacquer ground (as in earlier centuries), designs were painted directly onto the surface and then sprinkled with gold powder. Further details might be scratched into the gold-lacquer decoration while it was still wet, rather than being painstakingly reserved as nonpainted areas when the lacquer was first applied. Although this imposing tray is one of the more formally decorated examples of Kōdai-ji ware, parts of the decoration still have the immediate, painterly look that was made possible by these time-saving techniques.

Lacquered wood with gold and silver overlays
56.6 x 53.3 x 7.7 cm (22 5/16 x 21 x 3 1/16 in.)
Keith McLeod Fund 1998.58

Fragment from a *kosode*

Momoyama period, late 16th–early 17th century

This fragment is part of a kimono-like garment called a *kosode*. The motif of paulownia leaves in circles was produced by a sophisticated dying technique known as stitch-resist, in which areas to be dyed different colors are outlined with minute stitches. The stitches are then gathered together, and the area not to receive the dye is bound. Although paulownia leaves (seen also on the tray on the preceding page) were a symbol of the imperial family, they are used here simply as a decorative motif.

The term *tsujigahana*, literally "flowers at the crossroads," seems to have had different meanings at different times, and the low survival rate of early textiles has hampered efforts to determine exactly what it referred to when first used. Today it most often describes textiles such as this one decorated with a subtle blend of resist tie-dyeing and exquisitely fine shaded-ink painting, sometimes embellished with gold or silver leaf. Typical motifs include trees and flowers of the four seasons executed in ink, often with insect-eaten leaves or drops of dew nestled among petals. *Tsujigahana* is thought to have originated in the fifteenth century among the lower classes, but it was taken up and refined by the military elite during the turbulent and dynamic Momoyama period. Production declined in the subsequent Edo period, owing partly to the fashion for new kinds of figured Chinese-style silks, to which these painstaking techniques were not suited.

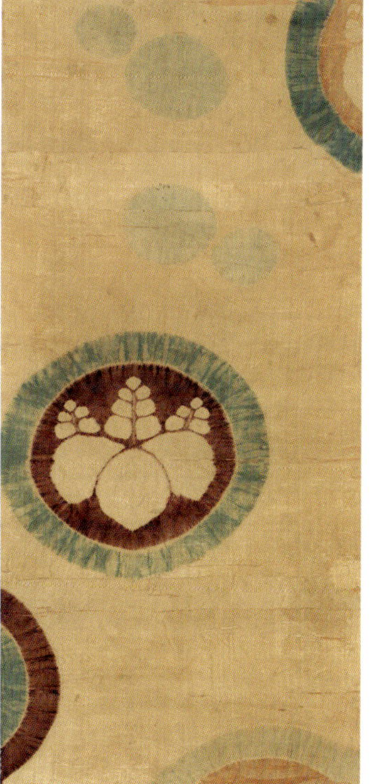

Plain-weave silk with stitch-resist tie-dye (*tsujigahana*)
82.6 x 39.7 x 1.9 cm
(32 1/2 x 15 5/8 x 3/4 in.)
Special Chinese and Japanese Fund
35.1939

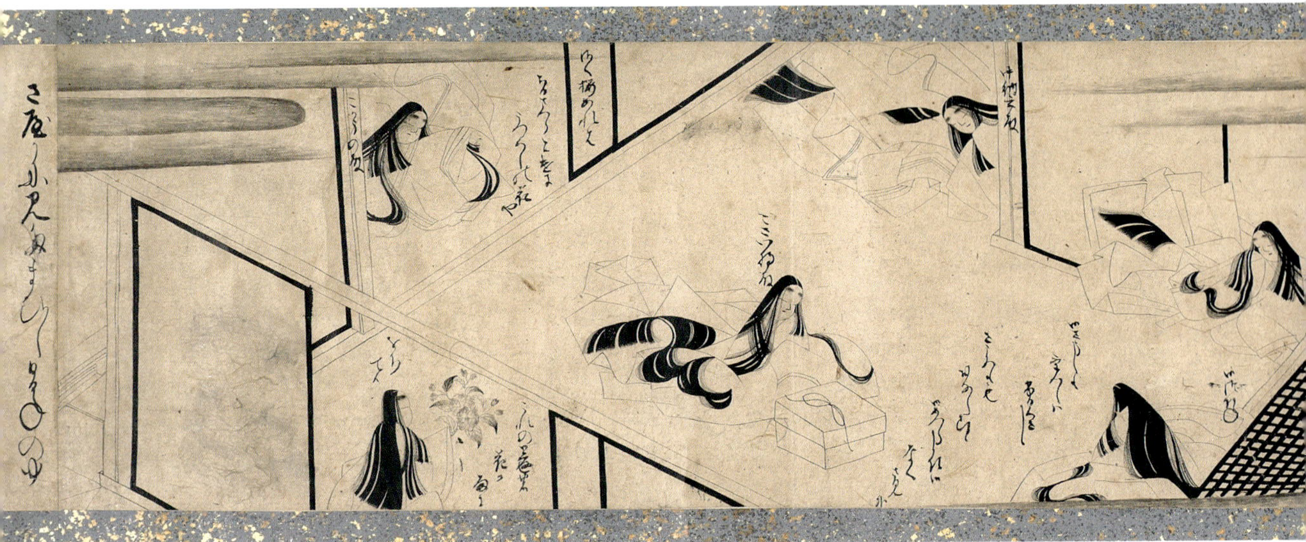

A Tale of Brief Slumbers (Utatane sōshi)
Muromachi period, 16th century

Written in imitation of the classic courtly romances of the Heian period, this late-medieval story tells of the love of a young noblewoman for a man she first encountered in a dream. The two scrolls were probably originally a single scroll, with alternating sections of text and pictures.

The special monochrome ink technique used for the illustrations is known as "white drawing" (*hakubyō*). Unlike Chinese-style ink painting, which exploits the calligraphic properties of a variegated line, this Japanese style uses fine lines of even thickness to outline the shapes, accented by areas of solid black representing architectural details, men's court hats, or ladies' floor-length hair. It is thought to have developed in the thirteenth century when underdrawings, originally intended to be colored over to create finished paintings, came to be appreciated as works of art in their own right. By the sixteenth century, this style of drawing had become strongly associated with amateur women painters, ladies of the Kyoto nobility who used it to illustrate classical Japanese poetry and fiction, often in small-scale works such as

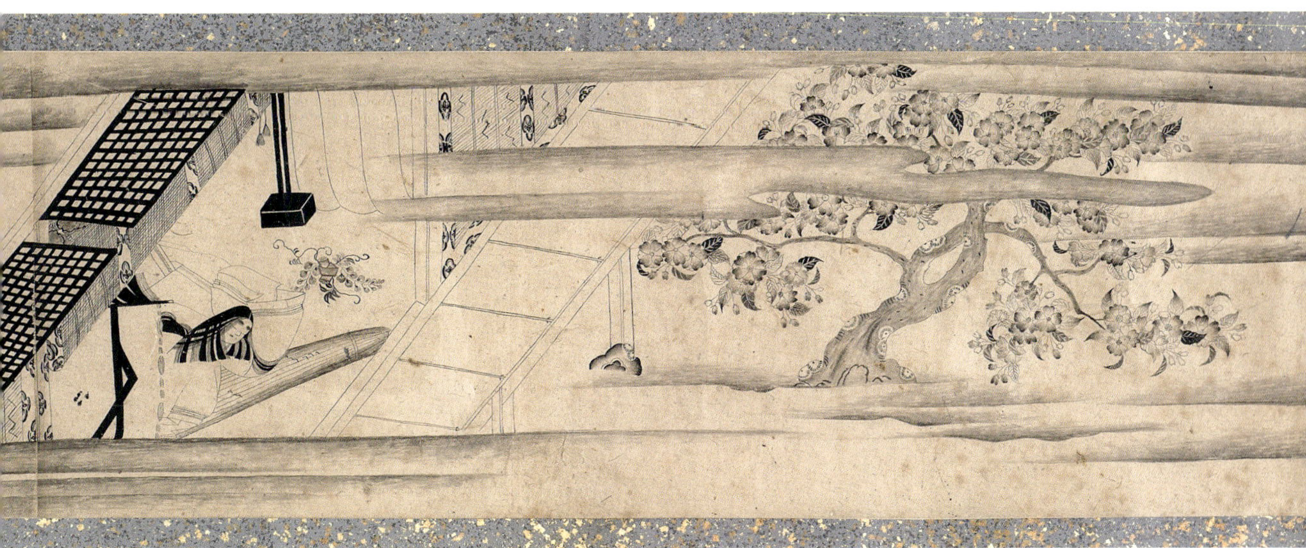

this one. Less than six inches in height, the tiny scroll was most likely a private treasure for the artist and her friends.

One of two handscrolls; ink on paper
13.5 x 521.5 cm (5 5/16 x 205 5/16 in.)
William Sturgis Bigelow Collection 11.9456

The Picture Contest, from *The Tale of Genji* (*Genji monogatari*)

Edo period, 17th century

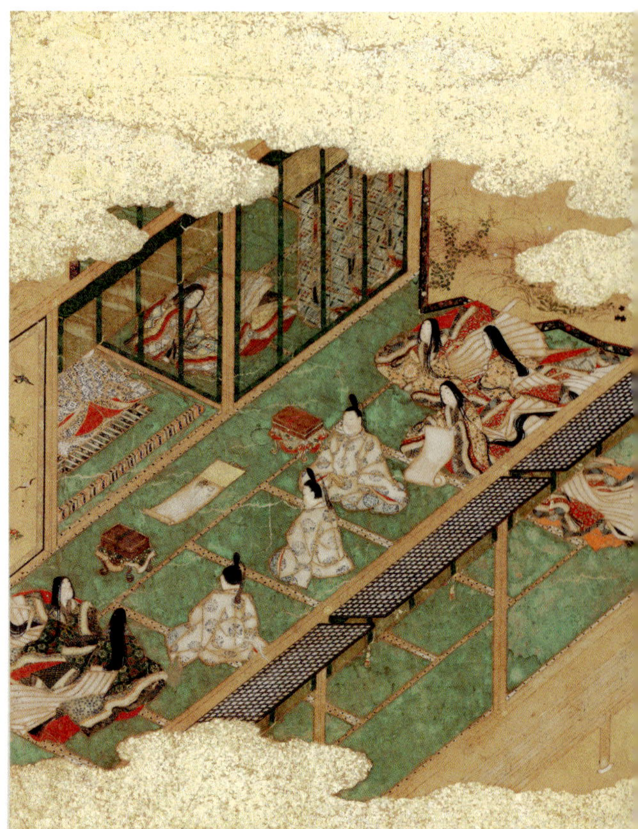

This exquisitely detailed miniature painting was once part of an album that probably included one illustration for each of the fifty-four chapters of *The Tale of Genji*, the greatest classic of Japanese literature. Written around the year 1000 by the court lady Murasaki Shikibu, the book describes the life and loves of Prince Genji and his descendants. In chapter 17, "The Picture Contest" (*E-awase*), two groups of courtiers compete in sponsoring the production of beautiful handscroll paintings to be judged by the emperor himself. The prize is of course awarded to Genji.

The painter of this miniature used a centuries-old compositional technique known as the "blown-off roof" (*fukinuki yatai*). The roof of the building is removed so that the viewer can look down into the room, observing in this case the emperor (his face hidden by a blind in deference to his high status), the court ladies and gentlemen, the paintings, and the elaborate boxes made to hold them. Gold clouds surrounding the scene create a dreamlike atmosphere of antique elegance.

Each painting in the original album would have been paired with a page of calligraphy that used a short quotation from the chapter to identify the scene. The patrons who commissioned the album—either courtiers or samurai who admired court culture—would most likely have requested the paintings from professional painters of the Tosa school, specialists in traditional courtly scenes,and would have brushed the calligraphy themselves.

Album leaf; ink, color, and gold on paper
24.6 x 18.5 cm (9 11/16 x 7 5/16 in.)
William Sturgis Bigelow Collection 11.7131

Poem from the *Anthology of Ancient and Modern Poems* (*Kokin-shū*) with design of wisteria
Calligraphy by Hon'ami Kōetsu (1558–1637)
Momoyama period, early 17th century

On a sumptuous yet understated album leaf, printed in mica with a design of wisteria, Hon'ami Kōetsu inscribed lines from a poem that had been included in the tenth-century imperial anthology, the *Kokin-shū*. The poignant verse, by the Heian-period courtier Kiyowara no Fukayabu, reads,

> I should die of love,
> It will not be another's name
> People will talk about—
> For all you say that life is short
> In a world where nothing stays.
>
> (translated by Edwin A. Cranston)

During the early seventeenth century, Kōetsu was instrumental in reviving classical Heian culture in Kyoto. Chafing under the imposition of Tokugawa military control over the imperial court, he and other wealthy townspeople expressed their support for the emperor by commissioning works of art that recalled Japan's aristocratic past. In this calligraphy, Kōetsu's selection of a verse from an imperial anthology expresses his personal bond with the past, and his choice of luxurious paper is reminiscent of twelfth-century works such as the *Anthology of Thirty-six Poets* (p. 93).

At some later date, connoisseurs had the leaf mounted as a hanging scroll so that it could ornament an alcove during a tea gathering. Particularly luxurious seventeenth-century textiles were used for the mounting, including some that had been tie-dyed and then hand-painted (*tsujigahana*) with motifs of long-tailed birds, and some embroidered with floral patterns.

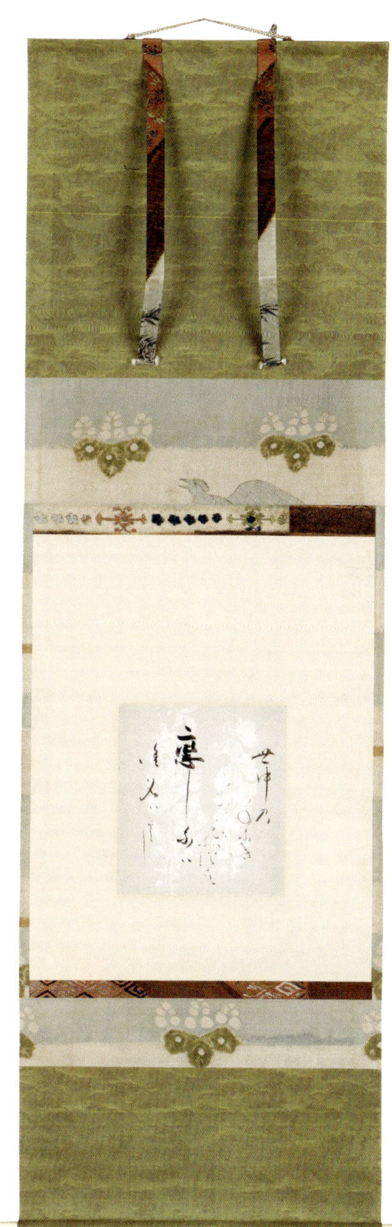

Album leaf mounted as a hanging scroll;
ink and mica on paper
Image: 19.9 x 17.2 cm (7¾ x 66¾ in.);
overall scroll: 128 x 41.2 cm (50½ x 16¼ in.)
Promised gift of Sylvan Barnet and William Burto

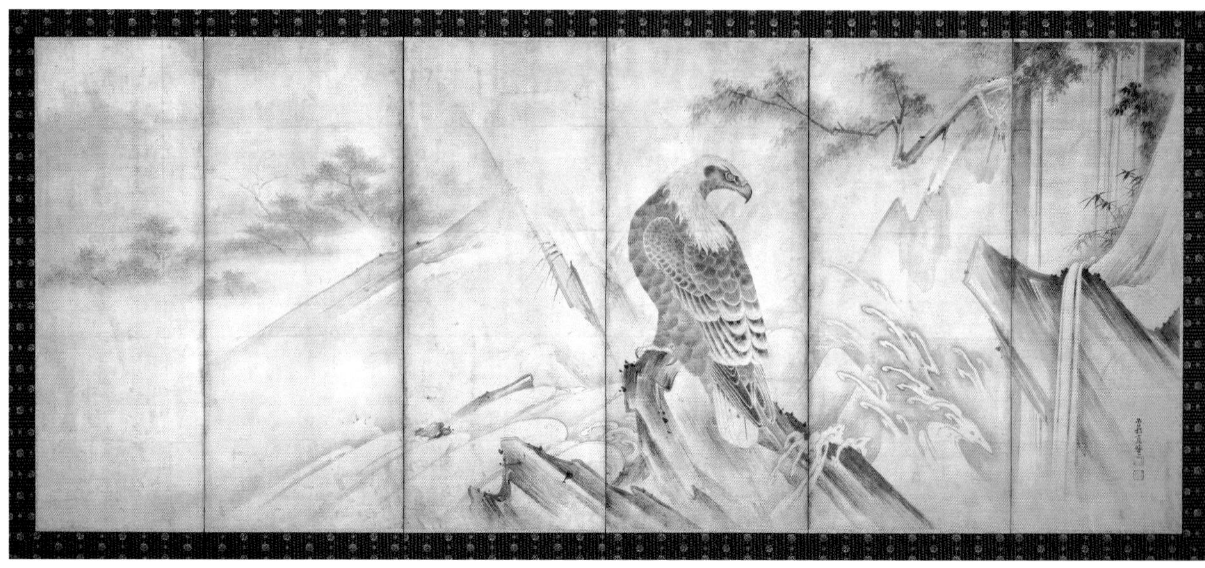

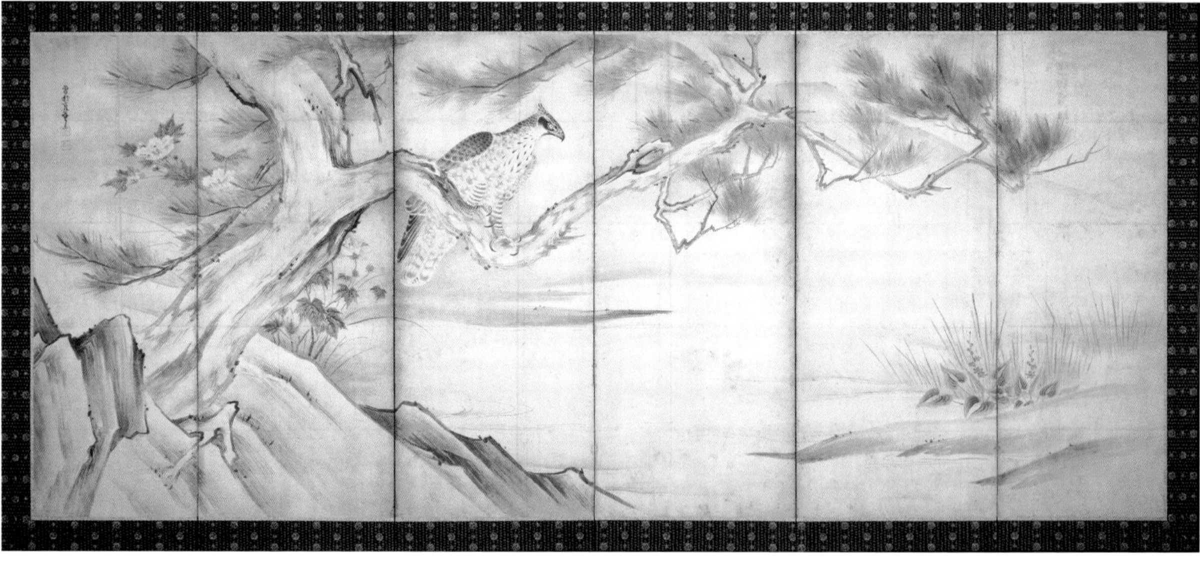

Eagle on a Rock **and** ***Hawk-Eagle in a Pine Tree***

Soga Nichokuan (active about 1625–1660)

Edo period, 17th century

In the course of the seventeenth century, the warrior class had to adapt to ruling through bureaucratic means rather than by brute force, and powerful samurai collected art to add legitimacy to their theoretical position at the top of the social order. Birds of prey were considered suitable painting subjects, partly because of their innately fierce and predatory nature, and partly because the right to practice falconry was a status symbol granted only to the most senior samurai, the daimyo.

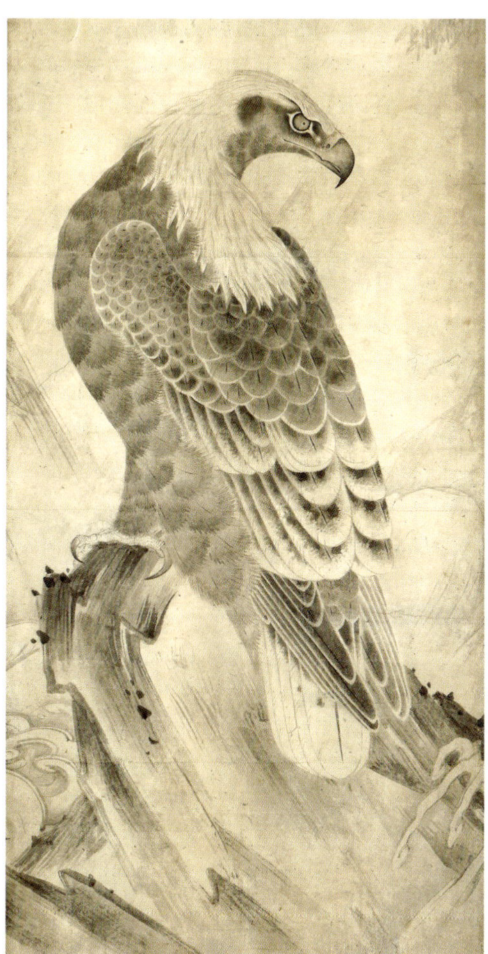

These two screens, depicting two of the largest birds of prey known in Japan, are painted purely in ink, a severe aesthetic that was favored by the military leaders of the Edo period. They would not necessarily have been displayed side by side but would have been positioned so as to define space at formal social gatherings where guests sat on the floor on mats. Sitting near either screen could put the viewer in the intimidating position of a sparrow or small rabbit just spotted by the imposing birds, with their hooked beaks and razor-sharp talons.

Details of the lives of the painter Soga Nichokuan and his father Soga Chokuan remain shadowy, but the fact that they are known to have specialized in paintings of birds of prey attests to the demand for this subject.

Pair of six-panel folding screens; ink on paper
151.9 x 348 cm (59 13/16 x 137 in.) and
151.7 x 348.6 cm (59 3/4 x 137 1/4 in.)
William Sturgis Bigelow Collection and Fenollosa-Weld Collection 11.6912, 11.4809

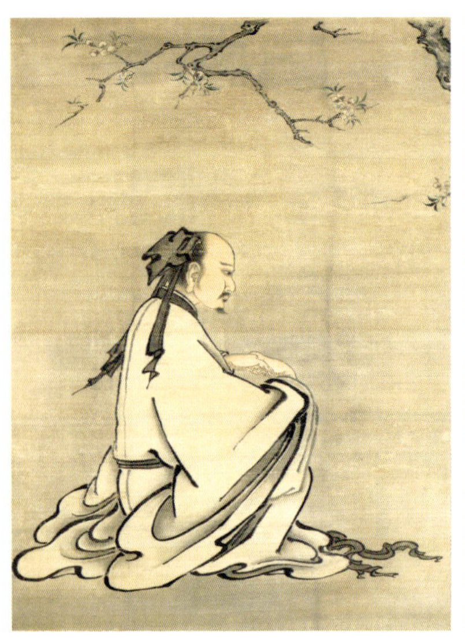
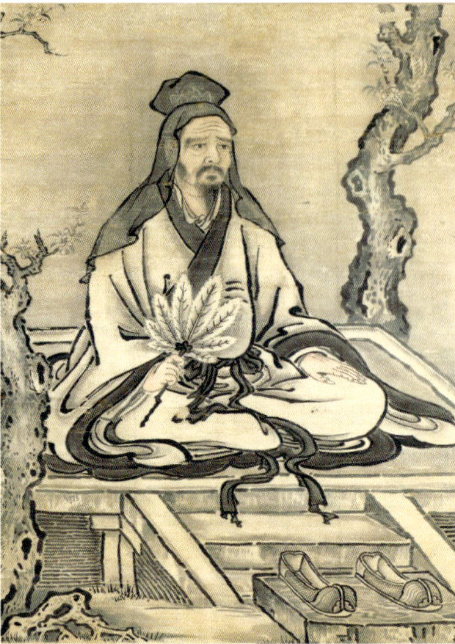
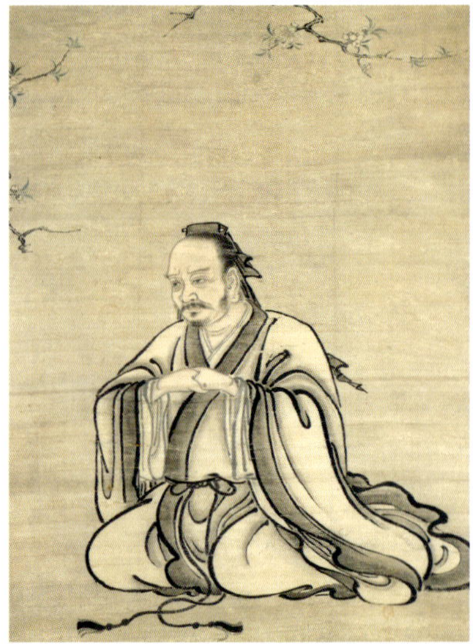

Confucius with His Disciples Yanzi and Huizi at the Apricot Altar
Kano Tan'yū (1602–1674)
Edo period, mid-17th century

The celebrated Chinese philosopher and educator Kong Qiu (551–479 B.C.E.), popularly known in the West as Confucius, is depicted with his two leading disciples in this rather austere set of portraits executed in ink with touches of light color. Branches of two gnarled flowering trees, which extend across the three paintings, suggest that the setting is the Apricot Altar, where Confucius is said to have delivered his lectures.

It is unclear when Confucian teachings were first introduced to Japan, but by the early seventeenth century the Tokugawa military leaders actively promoted Confucianism. Its emphasis on ethics and the maintenance of the proper relationship between the ruler and the ruled supported the highly regulated and hierarchical society that they had established.

Although these paintings are unsigned, they have been attributed to Kano Tan'yū, the official painter to the Tokugawa shogunate, who dominated artistic production during the early to mid-seventeenth century. Boston collector Ernest Fenollosa wrote that he acquired the set from the last direct descendant of Tan'yū in 1882. He also claimed that Tan'yū copied the works from an earlier set by the fifteenth-century Kano master Masanobu.

Set of three panels; ink and light color on silk
104.3 x 74.4 cm (41 1/16 x 29 5/16 in.) each
Fenollosa-Weld Collection 11.4399, 11.4400, 11.4401

Hand guard (*tsuba*) with design of paulownias, gourds, and snowflakes

Probably Momoyama period,
late 16th–early 17th century

This hand guard (*tsuba*), one of the largest in the MFA's collection, is made from a disk of iron pierced with four different motifs—two paulownia crests, two gourds, six circular dewdrops, and many stylized snowflakes. The three other piercings are functional: a large hole in the center through which the blade would pass, and a smaller pair to left and right that allows the handles of implements slotted into the scabbard (as in the mountings shown on p. 121) to protrude a short distance along the sides of the hilt. The pieces of copper at top and bottom of the central hole were added as a means of adjusting its size when the guard was fitted to a variety of different blades over time.

Although many plain early sword guards used in the civil wars of the fifteenth and sixteenth centuries were also made from iron, two features of this piece suggest that it was not intended for combat. Its size, about 50 percent larger than normal, suggests that it may once have been fitted to one of the extra-long, showy blades sported by the kind of fashionable young men depicted in the Museum's famous screen *Scenes from the Pleasure Quarters of Kyoto* (pp. 140–41). Furthermore, the guard's thinness and the removal of a large percentage of metal to create the design would have compromised its ability to protect its owner's hands in a swordfight.

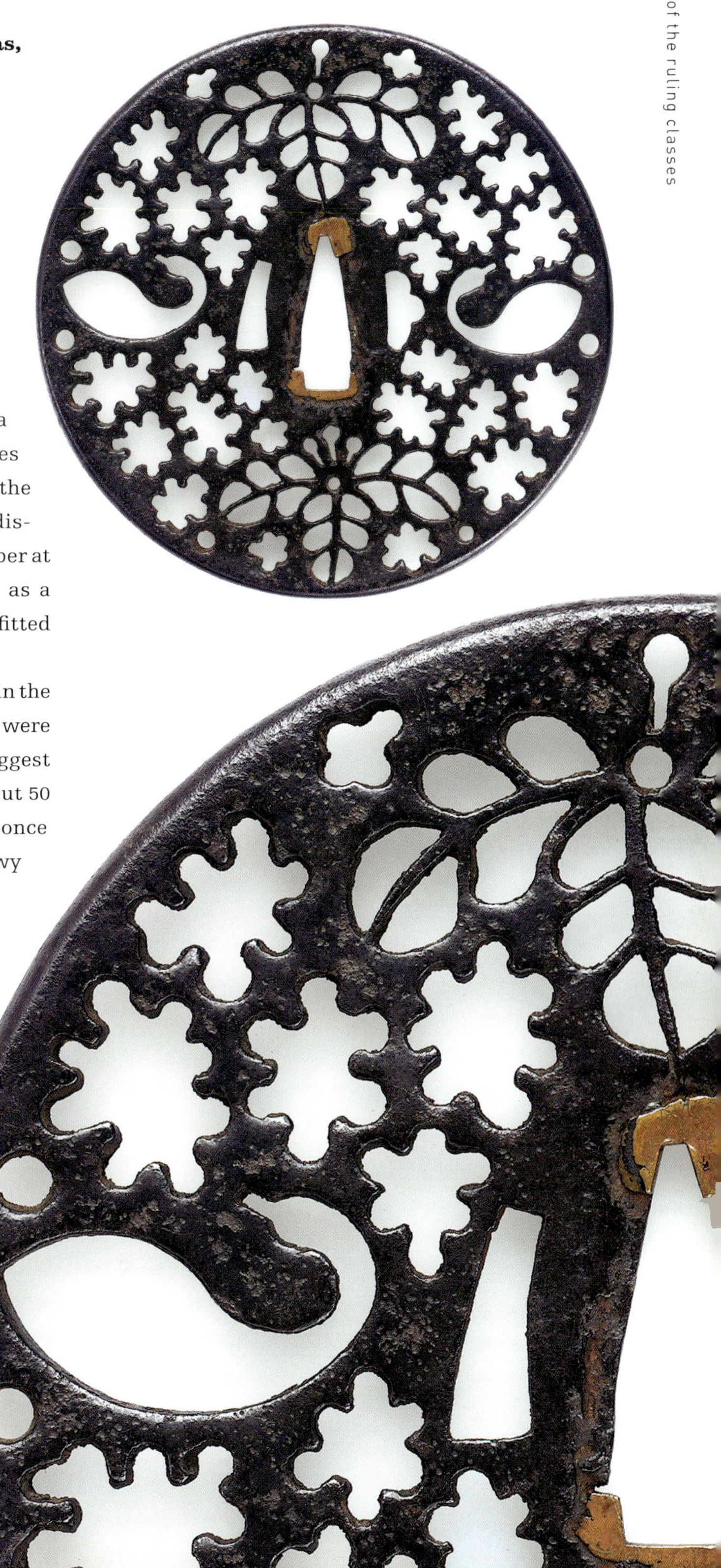

Iron, with punched surface and piercing
11.1 x 11.1 cm (4 3/8 x 4 3/8 in.)
Denman Waldo Ross Collection 06.233

Mounting for a sword of the *tachi* type with design of family crests

Edo period, 17th century

This mounting, the oldest in the MFA's collection, was made for a blade by Kanemitsu, a fourteenth-century successor of Nagamitsu (see p. 98). For most of its first three centuries, the Kanemitsu blade was likely carried in a durable lacquered-leather scabbard and hilt. Few of those plain early mountings have survived. Because of changes in warfare during the sixteenth century, *tachi* assumed a more ceremonial role and came to be mounted in the less practical, luxurious style seen here, known as "thread-wrapped" (*itomaki*).

The term *itomaki* refers to the fact that the silk bands not only cover the hilt but also extend to the first third of the scabbard, where they supposedly protected the lacquer surface from damage by contact with the wearer's armor. Despite this practical measure, in all other respects the decoration bears eloquent testimony to the *tachi*'s transition from feared cavalry weapon to formal symbol of senior samurai status. As with the *daishō* mounting on the following page, the lacquer, the gold and copper-alloy mounts, and the silk bands would all have been highly susceptible to damage in combat. Nearly all the metal fittings, however, are markedly different in shape from those used on *daishō*, and the elite character of the *tachi* is conveyed by the formal family crests that are the only decorative motif.

The scabbard: gold-lacquered wood partially wrapped with silk bands; the hilt: wood covered in ray skin wrapped with silk bands; the metal fittings: gold, silver, and copper alloys; the tying cords: leather and silk

L. 109.2 cm (L. 43 in.)

Charles Goddard Weld Collection 11.5097a–c

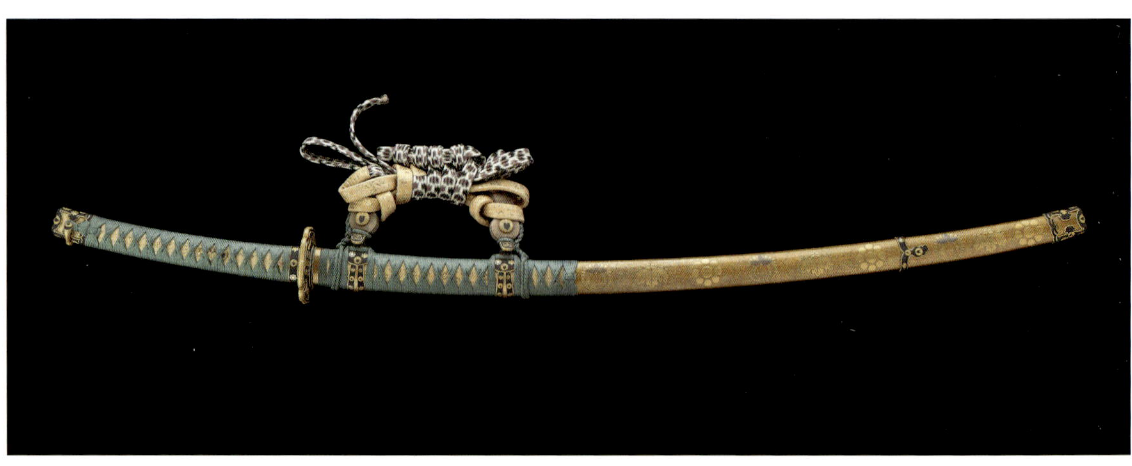

Set of matched mountings for a long and a short sword (*daishō*) with design of autumn plants and insects

Takeshiba Toshiteru (dates unknown) and others

Edo period, mid-19th century

The fifteenth and sixteenth centuries witnessed rapid economic growth, the dispersal of power to local warlords in various regions of the country, and almost incessant civil war. With increased resources at their disposal, daimyo could command the services of large armies of foot soldiers. Consequently, the curved cavalry sword (*tachi*) was replaced by the slightly shorter and straighter *katana*, worn on the wearer's left side in a scabbard that was thrust, edge upwards, between sash and waist. It soon became customary for middle-ranking and senior samurai to carry a second sword known as the *wakizashi*, about two-thirds the length of the katana, creating a combination known as "large and small" (*daishō*).

During the Edo period, the mountings for these *daishō* sets grew increasingly elaborate, employing fragile materials such as lacquer, silk, gold, and soft copper alloys. This example features a unified design of autumn grasses and insects, supposedly based on a painting by Kano Tan'yū. The metal fittings include the pommel (*kashira*) and collar (*fuchi*) covering each end of the hilt, which were made as a matching set; the *menuki*, a pair of fittings underneath the hilt's silk wrapping, intended to improve the grip; the hand guard (*tsuba*) at the beginning of the polished, sharp part of the blade; the handle of a small knife (*kozuka*) carried in the scabbard; and a skewer-like implement, the *kōgai* (not visible here), carried in the opposite side of the scabbard.

The scabbards: gold-lacquered wood; the hilt: wood covered in ray skin wrapped with silk bands; the metal fittings: gold, silver, and copper alloys; the tying cords: silk

L. 71.4 and 99.2 cm (L. 28⅛ and 39 in.)

William Sturgis Bigelow Collection 11.11291, 11.11292

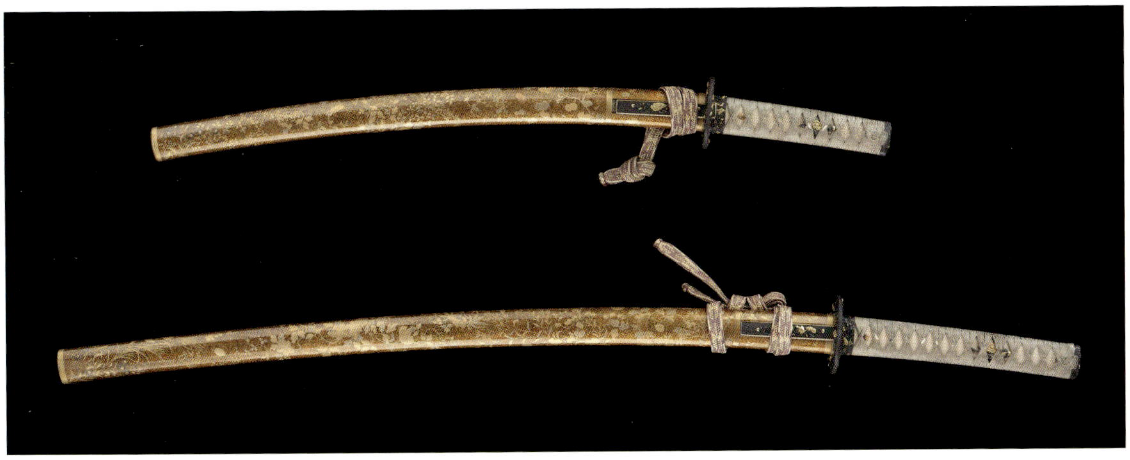

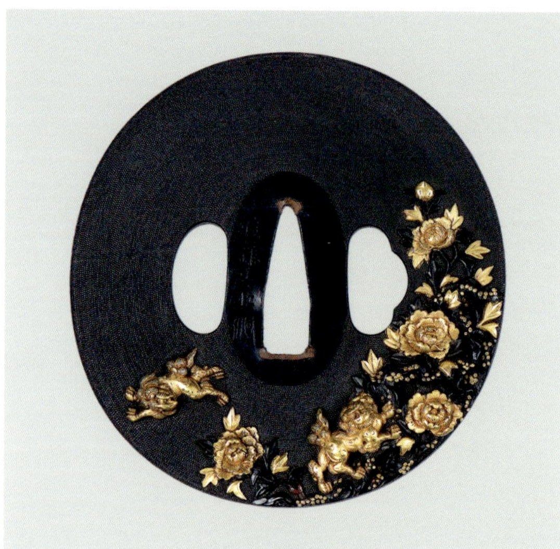

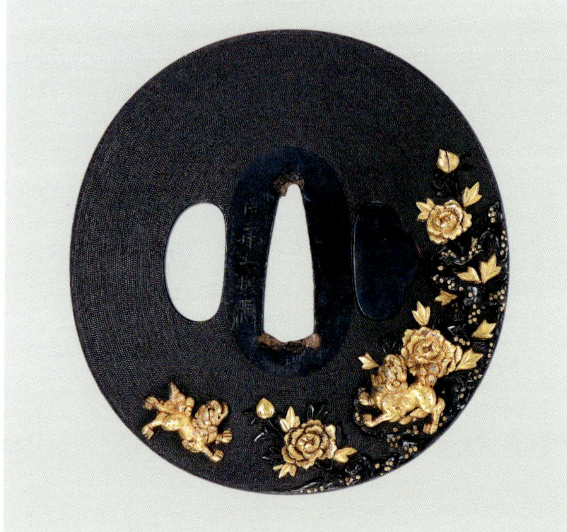

Set of two matched hand guards (*tsuba*) for a long and a short sword (*daishō*) with design of mythical lions (*shishi*) and peonies

Gotō Mitsuhiro (also called Mitsusato, 1797–1845)

Edo period, early–mid-19th century

After iron, the most common material for Japanese metal sword-fittings is an alloy of copper with a small percentage of gold (*shakudō*), textured with a tiny, precise pattern of circular granulations (*nanako*, literally "fish roe") and patinated to a blue-black hue. The so-called *shakudō nanako* came into its own toward the end of the fifteenth century, when its sober appearance appealed to the sometimes austere taste of shogun Ashikaga Yoshimasa. Originally pioneered by Yūjō, founder of the Gotō family of shogunal metalworkers and mintmasters, the combination of *shakudō nanako* with gold was adopted over the centuries by a host of other workshops.

These two hand guards, one very slightly larger than the other, were made for a matched set of a long and a short sword. The artist, a late artistic descendant of Yūjō, used mercury amalgamation to apply a thin sheet of gold to high-relief designs already worked in the *shakudō*, leaving some areas polished but ungilded to create an almost polychromatic effect. The motif of lions and peonies, a favorite in later Japanese art, refers to the Stone Bridge (*Shakkyō*) legend (discussed on p. 164).

Copper alloy with granulated surface and high-relief carving inlaid with gold
8.2 x 7.8 cm (3¼ x 3 1/16 in.) and
7.7 x 7.2 cm (3 x 2 13/16 in.)
Charles Goddard Weld Collection 11.5418, 11.5442

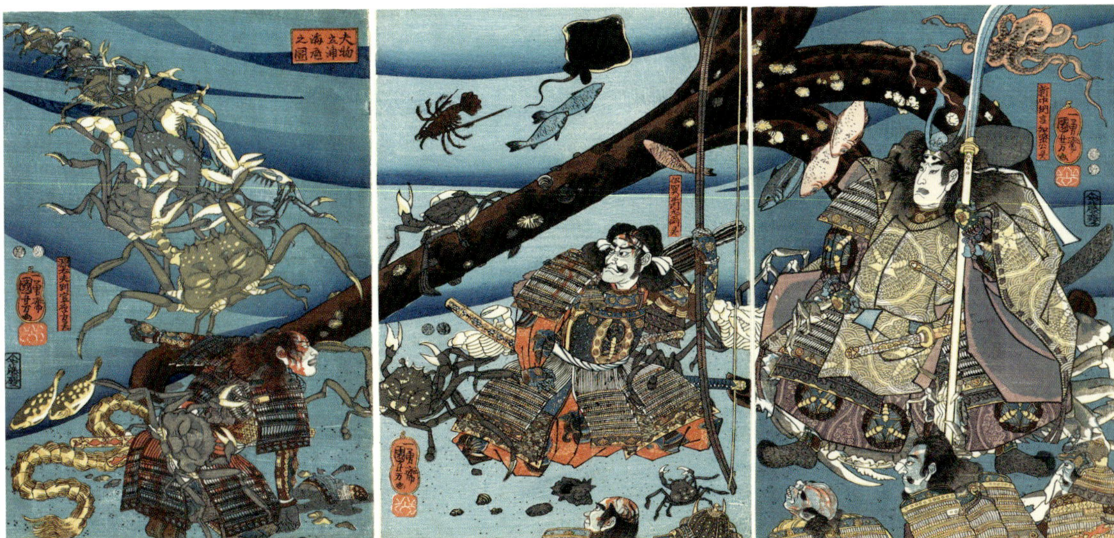

At the Bottom of the Sea in Daimotsu Bay

Utagawa Kuniyoshi (1797–1861)

Edo period, about 1851–52

During the nineteenth century, a romantic image of the great samurai warriors of past ages was popularized in color woodblock prints. The Taira warrior clan controlled Japan for almost thirty years before committing mass suicide by drowning after the rival Minamoto clan defeated them at the great naval battle of Dan-no-ura in 1185, thus concluding the Genpei War. The clan members' spirits are said to be reincarnated in the crabs of the bay, whose shells have markings that resemble a scowling human face. This triptych print by Utagawa Kuniyoshi shows the ghosts of the Taira—deep beneath the waves of the bay but still clad in splendid armor and brocade robes—gathering to plot supernatural revenge on the Minamoto.

Prints such as this were a commercial product intended primarily for urban commoners, who enjoyed visualizations of stories that they knew from books and Kabuki plays; however, such works also appealed to the samurai themselves, who were now government bureaucrats rather than actual warriors. In order to speed production and keep prices down, this large picture was made from three sheets of paper printed separately and then assembled. This accounts for the slight discrepancies in coloring among the three sheets.

Woodblock print (*nishiki-e*); ink and color on paper
36.3 x 74.3 cm (14 5/16 x 29 1/4 in.)
William Sturgis Bigelow Collection 11.30560, 11.30561, 11.30562

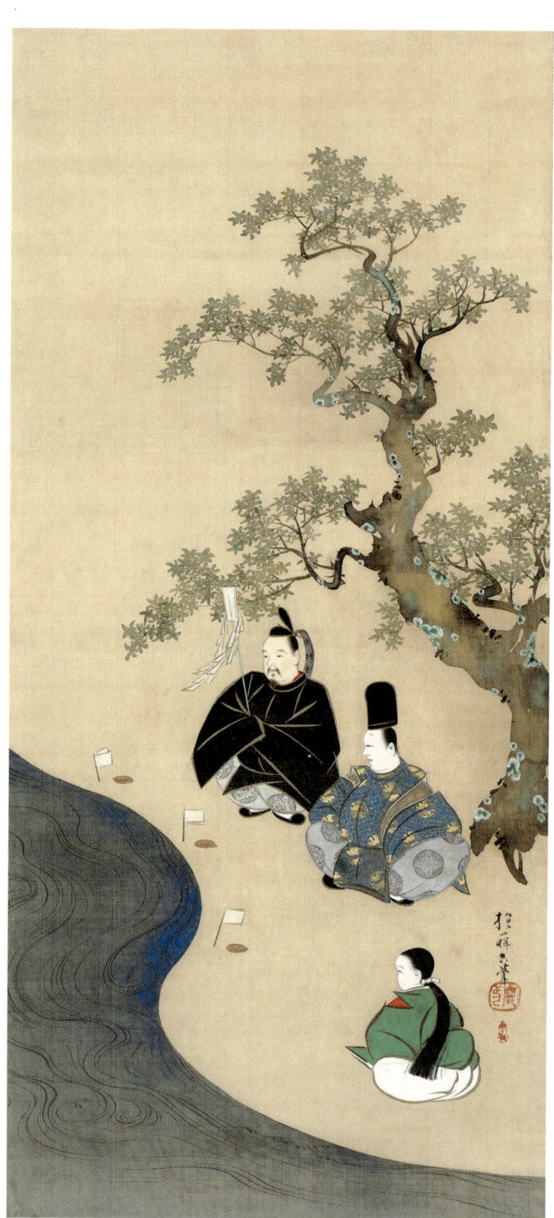

Purification Ritual (_Misogi_) from the _Tales of Ise_
Sakai Hōitsu (1761–1828)
Edo period, early 19th century

During the Edo period, members of the ruling military families and sophisticated aesthetes from the merchant class adopted literary themes from Japan's courtly past to legitimize their political and social authority.

The second son of a daimyo, Sakai Hōitsu became fascinated by the paintings of the eighteenth-century Rinpa master Ogata Kōrin, whose works were well represented in his family's collection. He expressed his admiration by copying several of Kōrin's well-known compositions, including his rendering of the *Misogi* scene from the tenth-century *Tales of Ise*, now in the collection of the Hatakeyama Memorial Museum of Art, Tokyo.

In both Kōrin's and Hōitsu's versions of the *Misogi* scene, the renowned ninth-century poet Ariwara no Narihira, seeking relief from an obsessive love affair, undergoes a Shinto purification ritual along a riverbank. Seated under a maple tree, he is accompanied by a diviner and a priestess. Whereas Kōrin's scroll is characterized by the boldness of its form, Hōitsu's copy delights in the exquisite details of the brocaded robes and the pooling of color that suggests the abstracted trunk of the tree.

Hanging scroll; ink, color, and gold on silk
111.5 x 50.4 cm (43 7/8 x 19 13/16 in.)
Museum purchase with funds by exchange from the William Sturgis Bigelow Collection 2005.622

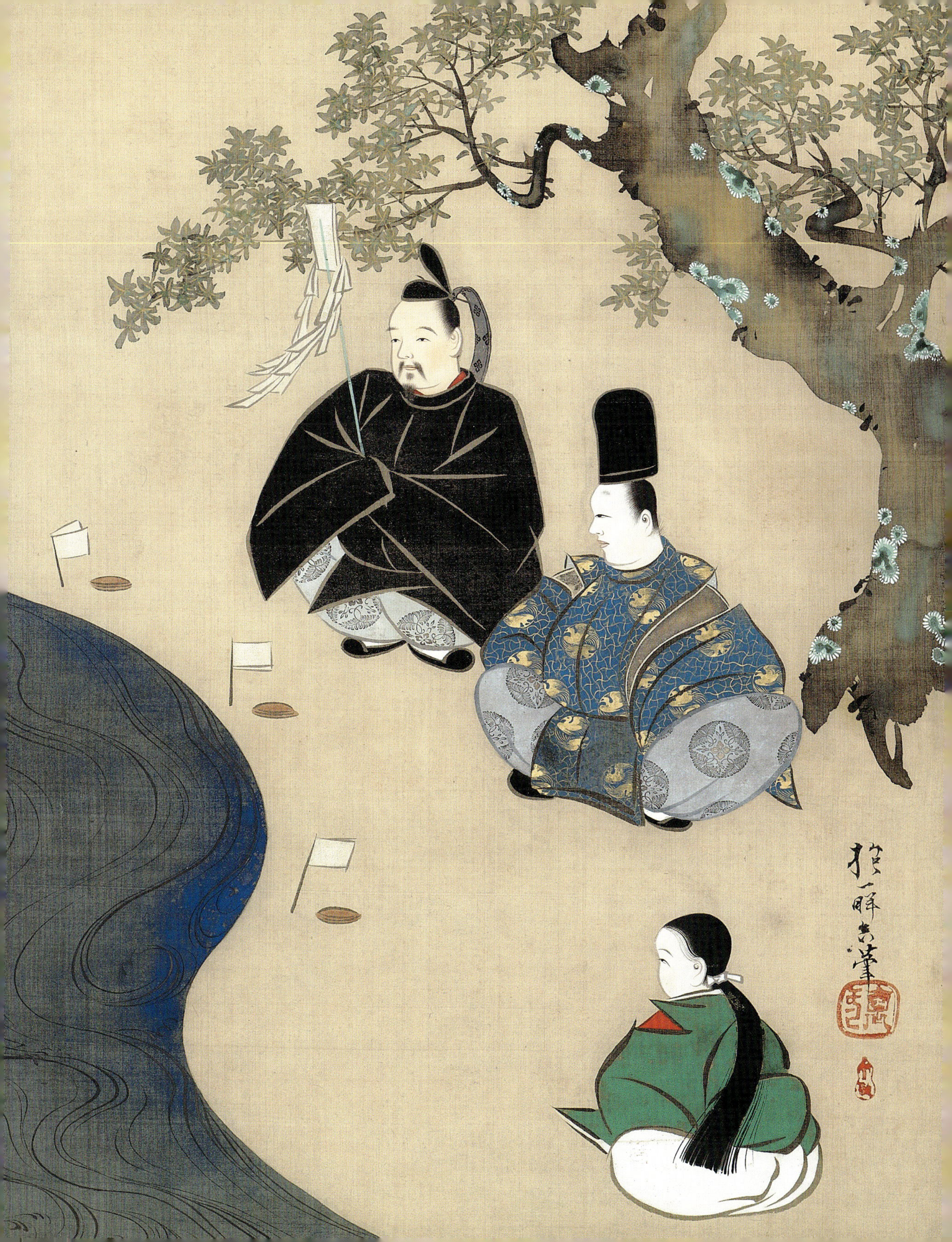

Drum, drum box, and wrapper with design of Mount Utsu
Designed by Kamisaka Sekka (1866–1942); lacquered by Kamisaka Yūkichi (1886–1938)
Taishō era, about 1925

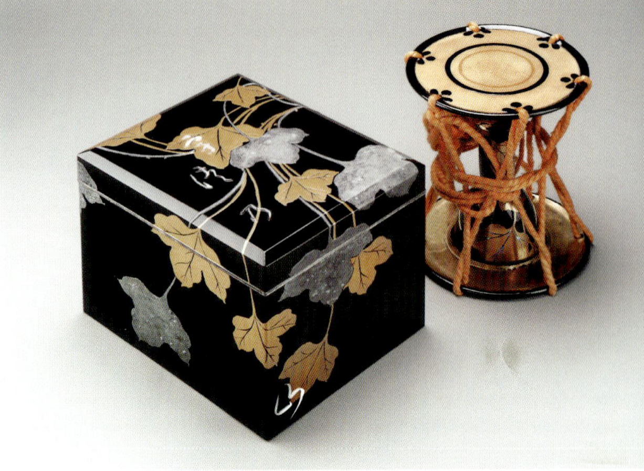

All three components of this set are decorated with motifs alluding to a scene from the tenth-century *Tales of Ise*, in which the poet Ariwara no Narihira comes to a gloomy, overgrown pass and meets an elderly priest he remembers from his former life in the capital. The poet asks the old man to remember him to a lady he loved during his time at court, and recites a verse:

> In far Suruga
> By Mount Utsu's gloomy slopes
> We can never meet—
> Neither in reality
> No, nor even in my dreams.
>
> (translated by Joe Earle)

The first few syllables of the poem are inlaid on the box's lid and side.

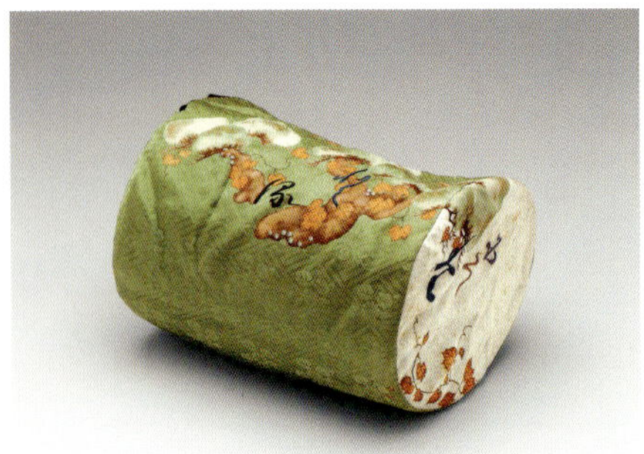

Kamisaka Sekka revived the seventeenth-century Rinpa style in the changed circumstances of the early twentieth century, an achievement that made him in effect the father of modern design in Japan. He worked frequently with artists in other media, especially textiles and lacquer; here, he designed a set that was executed by his brother. Rinpa lacquers had developed three centuries earlier under the direction of Hon'ami Kōetsu, who is credited with introducing the dramatic use of large sheets of lead and bold shell inlay, as well as encouraging the incorporation of themes from courtly literature. The Rinpa lacquer style was revived three times: first by Ogata Kōrin and artists such as Tsuchida Sōetsu in the early eighteenth century; then a century after Kōrin's death by Hara Yōyūsai; and finally, another century later, by Sekka himself.

The drum and box: lacquered wood, with shell and lead, silk cords, and leather skins; the wrapper: silk brocade
L. of drum: 26.5 cm (10¾ in.);
box: 28.2 x 23.2 x 22.9 cm (11⅛ x 9⅛ x 9 in.)
Keith McLeod Fund 2005.194.1–3

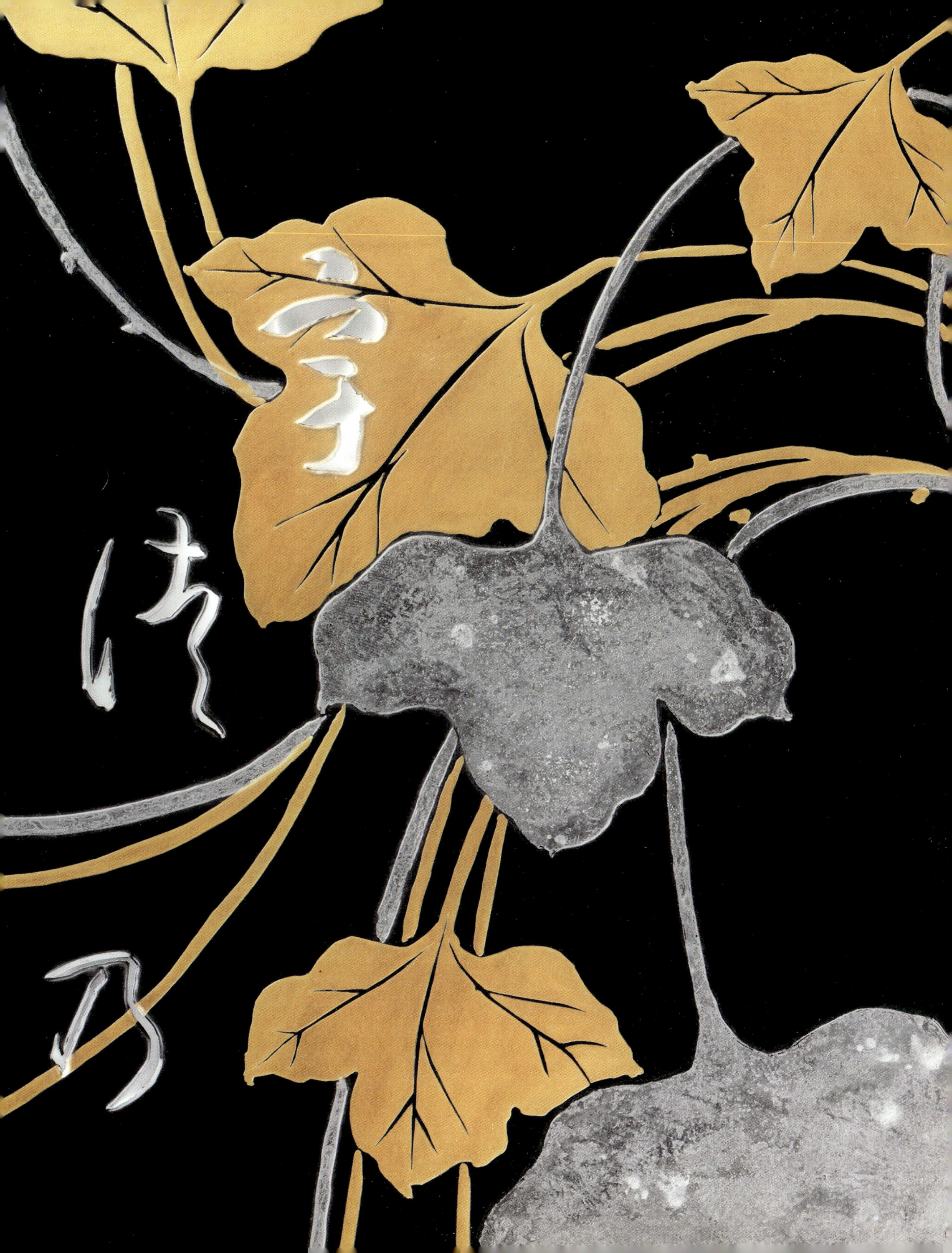

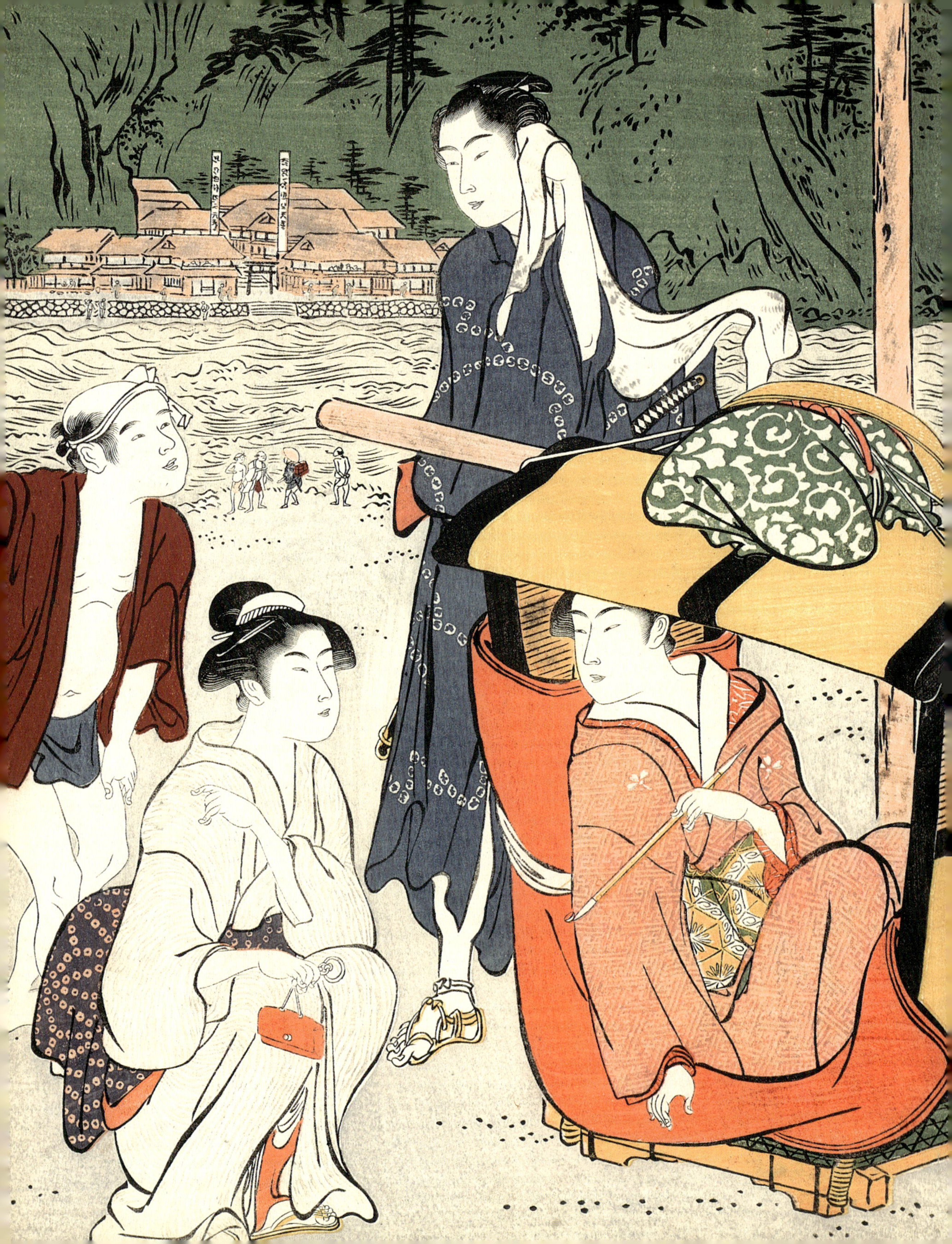

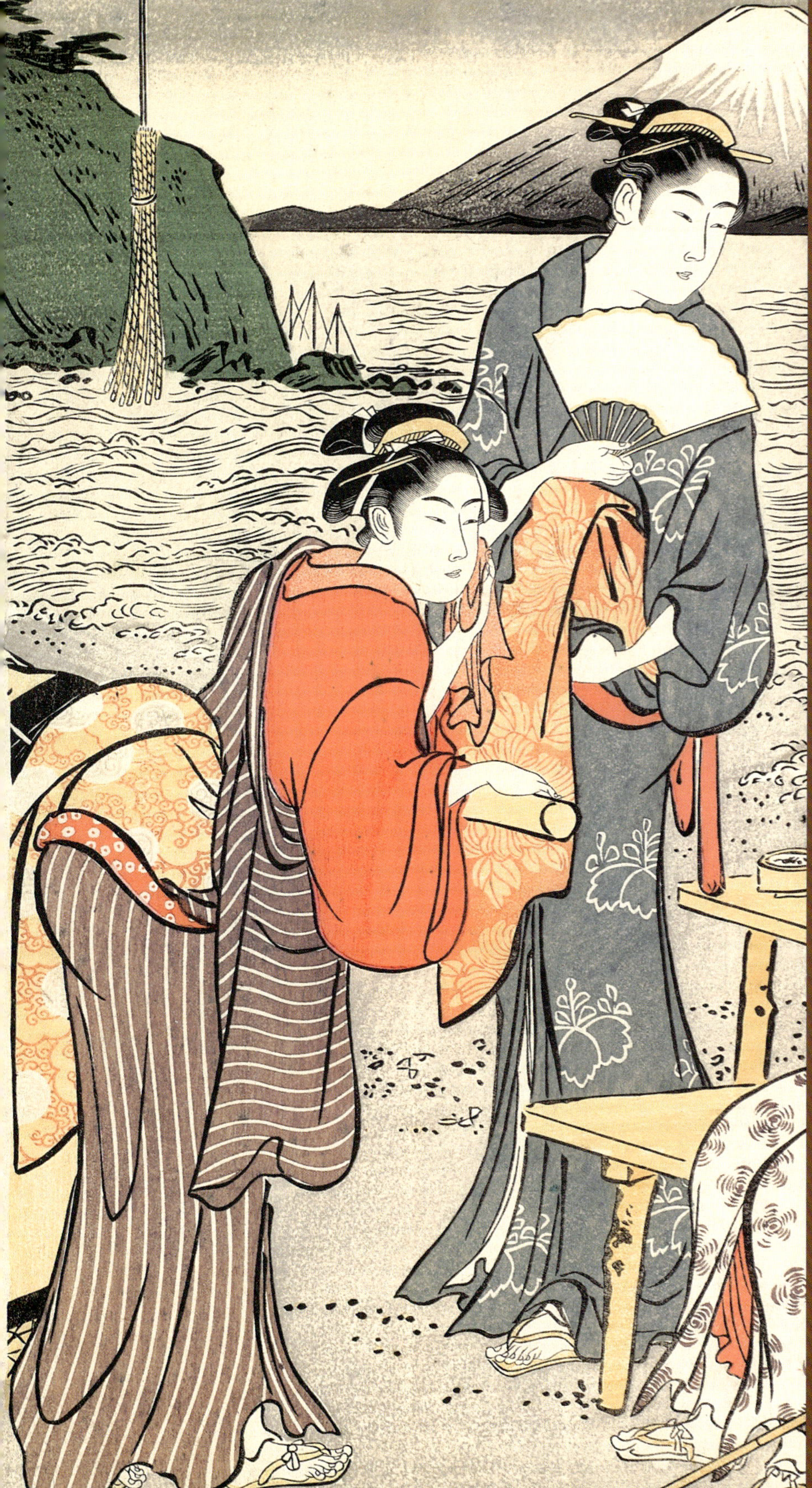

3 art of the TOWN

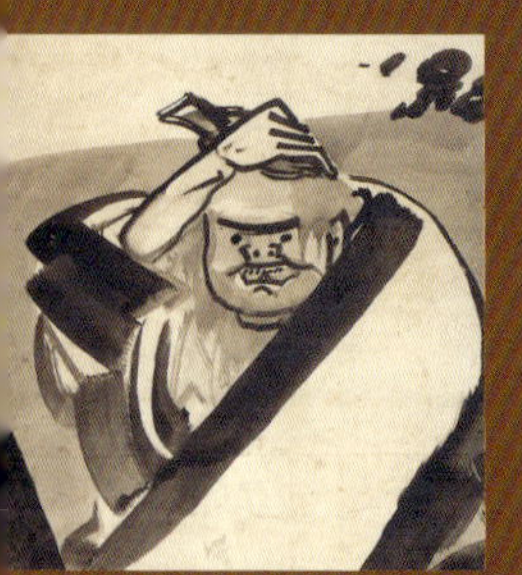

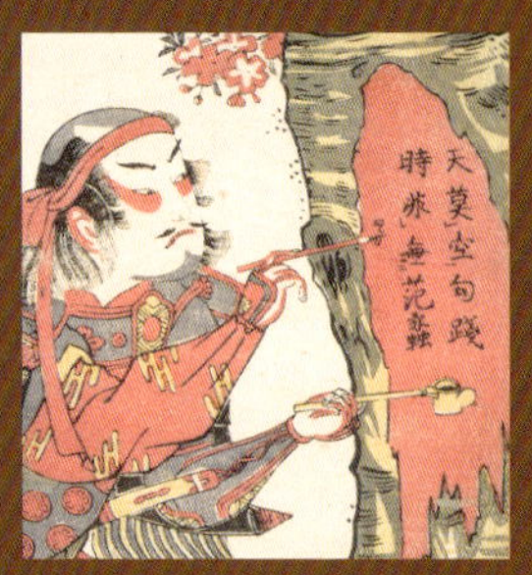

天莫空句踐
時非無范蠡

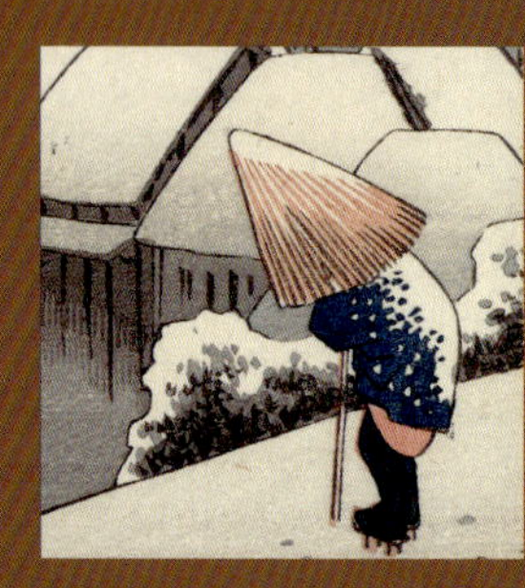

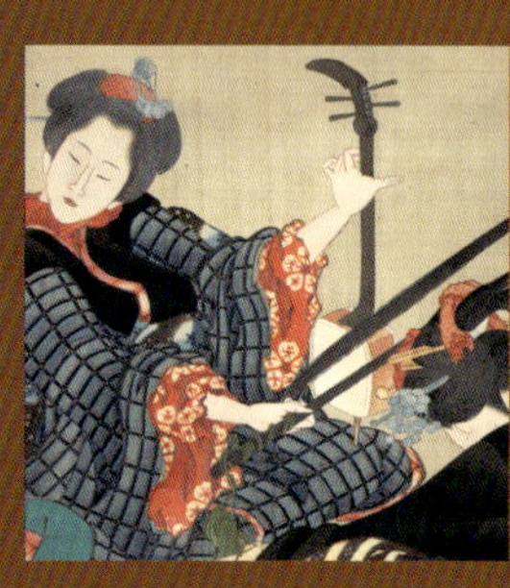

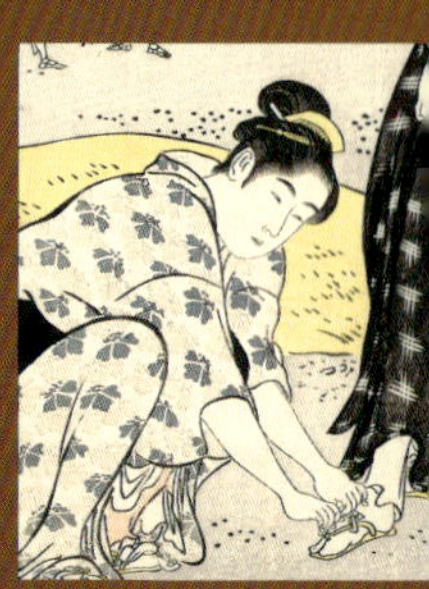

Art of the Town

Sarah E. Thompson

> Living only for the moment, turning our full attention to the pleasures of the moon, the snow, the cherry blossoms and the maple leaves; singing songs, drinking wine, diverting ourselves in just floating, floating; caring not a whit for the pauperism staring us in the face, refusing to be disheartened, like a gourd floating along with the river current; this is what we call the *floating world.*
>
> –Asai Ryōi, **Tales of the Floating World** (trans. Richard Lane)

The century of civil wars that had divided Japan into competing factions ended in 1568 when the warlord Oda Nobunaga occupied the city of Kyoto, the imperial capital since 794. Lavish rebuilding of the almost-destroyed city began under Nobunaga and continued under his successor Toyotomi Hideyoshi, who ruled from a spectacular castle in nearby Osaka. A lasting military dynasty was achieved by the third of the great warlords, Tokugawa Ieyasu, who wrested power from Hideyoshi's heirs and moved his own administrative center from western to eastern Japan, establishing the city of Edo (present-day Tokyo) in 1603. The formation of modern Japanese culture took place in these three cities, accompanied by a remarkable flowering of the visual, literary, and performing arts.

During the Edo period (1615–1868), the eastern part of Japan, centered on the shogun's headquarters at Edo, and the western part of the country, centered on the imperial capital of Kyoto and the merchant city of Osaka, were connected by the famous Tōkaidō (literally "Eastern Sea Road"), part of a well-maintained network of roads that facilitated communication and commerce throughout Japan. One important reason for the existence of these roads was the Tokugawa policy known as alternate attendance (*sankin kōtai*), which required the daimyo, the feudal lords who governed the provinces on behalf of the shogun, to spend every other year personally attending the shogun at his court in Edo; their families remained in the city permanently as hostages. A compulsory annual journey with a large number of retainers, carried out in the lavish style befitting persons of high station, kept the daimyo busy and consumed financial resources that might otherwise have been used for plots against the shogun. The resulting unification of the country through the improvement of the transportation infrastructure was a side benefit. News and fashions from the cities spread rapidly throughout the country, and products from the various provinces poured into the cities.

The alternate-attendance policy also resulted in the presence in Edo of large numbers of young single men, samurai brought by their lords from the provinces for temporary duty on the annual visits. The resulting sexual imbalance in the city, with far more men than women, was a major factor in the rise of the Yoshiwara licensed brothel district, which became even larger and more spectacular than its counterparts in Kyoto and Osaka. Far more than just a place of sexual release, the Yoshiwara set the fashion trends followed by the entire city and was an inspiration to musicians, poets, novelists, dramatists, and painters. The standing of a man-about-town who could cut a dashing figure in the Yoshiwara (or Shimabara in Kyoto, or Shinmachi in Osaka) was determined by money and sophistication, not by his hereditary social position in the four-class system of samurai, peasants, artisans, and merchants that was theoretically in effect at the time (though becoming increasingly blurred).

Another policy that the Tokugawa shoguns instituted to tighten their control, which profoundly affected the society of the Edo period, was the semi-isolation of Japan from the outside world. In the 1630s, distrust of the activities of European missionaries in Japan—exacerbated by a peasant uprising led by a charismatic teenager who claimed to be the second coming of Christ—resulted in a harsh crackdown on Christianity and the expulsion of all Europeans except the Dutch. The only countries with which Japan maintained formal diplomatic relations were Korea and the Ryūkyū kingdom (now Japan's southernmost prefecture, Okinawa), but informal trade was permitted with the Netherlands and China. The foreigners were restricted to the port city of Nagasaki, and Japanese were not permitted to travel abroad at all. A few selected scholars were allowed to travel to Nagasaki to study foreign learning, but for most Japanese, knowledge of the outside world came from imported goods and books.

Strict though it was, the Tokugawa regime was a welcome relief after the decades of civil war that had caused so much suffering. For some 250 years the country was peaceful and for the most part prosperous, and these circumstances led to social developments similar to the changes happening in Europe around the same time: urbanization, the development of a money economy, and above all, the rise of a middle class. Japanese society, especially in the cities, began to take on features familiar to people of today; for this reason, the Edo period is often characterized by scholars of Japanese history as the Early Modern period. Political power was still limited to the hereditary samurai class, but in the absence of wars, the samurai were no longer warriors but government bureaucrats. Commercial development put de facto financial power increasingly in the hands of the supposedly lowly merchant class, the group who would become the primary patrons of the arts of the town.

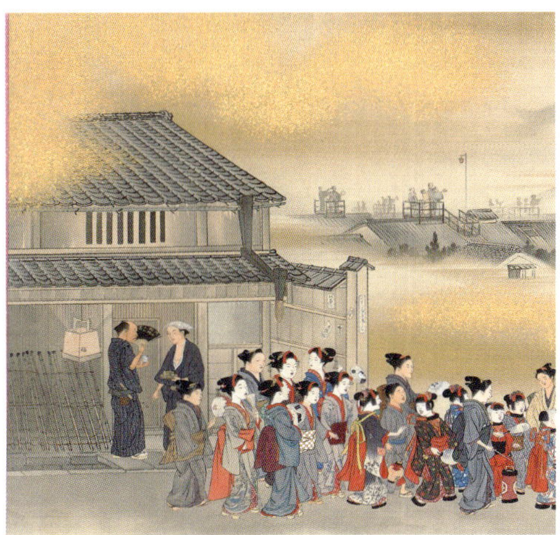

fig. 22 **The background of this painting of an evening festival shows two-story wooden townhouses typical of middle-class homes in nineteenth-century Kyoto.**

The rising economic power of the merchants, and the resulting impact on the visual arts, began in Kyoto. In the later part of the Muromachi period (1392–1568), the prominence of merchant-class rice brokers and money-lenders was accompanied by the appearance of commercial picture shops offering ready-made works by *machi eshi*, or "town painters," independent artists who were not necessarily affiliated with the great painting schools (such as the Kano and Tosa) that worked on commission for the aristocracy. By the seventeenth century, the artistic trend-setters of Kyoto were a class of wealthy merchants known as *machishū* (literally "town people"), many of whom were purveyors of luxury goods to the imperial court. The Rinpa school—named for its most famous member, Ogata Kōrin—grew out of the desire of these newly affluent consumers for art that reflected the heritage of the imperial court but reinterpreted the classical themes in a stylish, updated, eye-catching manner. Rinpa artists created not only paintings but calligraphy, lacquer designs, and ceramics; Kōrin's younger brother Kenzan was a leading potter. Like many Rinpa-school works, Kenzan's ceramics were intended for use at tea gatherings, a custom that had begun among the samurai but had now spread throughout society.

The elegance and luxury of the imperial court were emulated in the lower levels of Kyoto society as well. The glamorous demimonde that later came to be known as the "floating world" (*ukiyo*) originated in the Shimabara licensed brothel district and the Shijō riverbed theaters. Courtesans, like courtiers, were garbed in the finely dyed silk fabrics that were—and still are—one of the best-known traditional products of the city of Kyoto. The more expensive houses of pleasure were decorated to resemble palaces, and courtesans were trained in

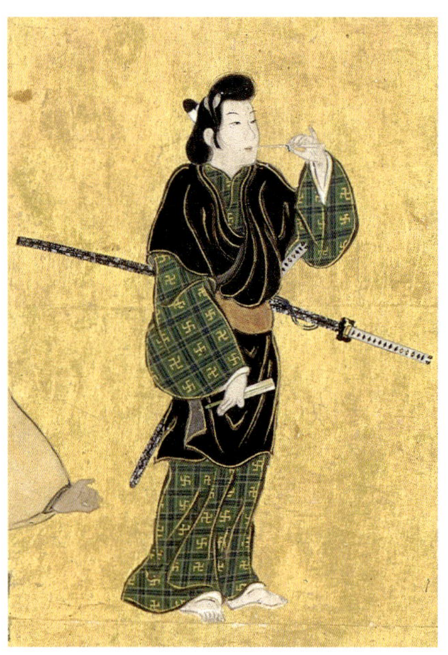

arts such as calligraphy, poetry, and painting, so that an affluent customer could fantasize that he himself was a prince surrounded by cultivated noblewomen, like the hero of an ancient courtly romance. Seventeenth-century genre paintings, the forerunners of the *ukiyo-e* school, depict this new urban subculture, in which privileges formerly limited to the aristocracy were made available to anyone who could pay for them.

fig. 23 **An elegantly dressed young man of the samurai class (indicated by his two swords) saunters through the pleasure quarters of Kyoto.**

The Kyoto painting world of the eighteenth century was remarkable for its great variety, incorporating many different schools and styles catering to the tastes of a wide range of patrons. In contrast to the Rinpa style, with its sources in traditional Japanese painting, the literati style (called *bunjinga* or *nanga* in Japanese) was based on Chinese concepts and models. Such models were not acquired in China itself, as Japanese were forbidden to go there, but through the medium of printed books imported through Nagasaki after the general ban on foreign books was lifted in 1722. While Rinpa painting typically emphasized bold colors and shapes, literati painting relied for its effects on the use of calligraphic brushstrokes and finely graded tonalities of ink. It appealed to intellectuals of assorted social backgrounds who shared a love of Chinese culture and a longing for the high-minded scholarly lifestyle idealized in Chinese painting and poetry. The literati style was practiced in various parts of Japan, but it is most strongly associated with the Kyoto painters Ike Taiga and Yosa Buson. Talented literati painters from other areas, such as Yamamoto Baiitsu of Nagoya, tended to move to Kyoto to enjoy the congeniality of literati circles there.

The influence of Western art appears in the work of Maruyama Ōkyo, who as a young man studied and copied Western-style pictures using vanishing-point perspective. He also drew studies of landscapes and living creatures from life, probably inspired by the meticulously detailed realism of Chinese professional paintings brought in through Nagasaki, and perhaps also by Western prints or book illustrations. In the second half of the eighteenth century, Ōkyo became Kyoto's leading painter thanks to the brilliant eclecticism of his mature style, using elegant brushstrokes to construct highly detailed images of traditional subjects set in realistically three-dimensional pictorial space.

Some of the finest painters of eighteenth-century Kyoto cannot be classified into any school, although they are sometimes grouped together as the so-called Eccentrics. Soga Shōhaku claimed artistic descent from a noted fifteenth-century school of Chinese-style ink painting, but his own exuberant use of ink went far beyond anything seen earlier. Itō Jakuchū, the heir to a prosperous grocery business, turned to Buddhism and painting, expressing his deep belief in the inherent Buddha nature of all living things through paintings of animals and birds that are highly detailed and at the same time extremely individualized.

The town of Edo was little more than a village surrounding a provincial castle when Tokugawa Ieyasu made it his headquarters in 1603, but by the end of the seventeenth century it had overtaken Kyoto as Japan's leading city. Edo in the eighteenth century is thought to have had a population of about one million and may well have been the largest city in the world at that time. Here, the new urban commoner culture of the floating world—*ukiyo*—reached its fullest development. Originally a Buddhist term denoting the sadness of impermanence, the word *ukiyo* came to be used first for the entertainment quarters on the outskirts of the major cities, and later for urban pleasures in general. In the late seventeenth century, this floating world became the theme of new kinds of literature and art that reached a wider audience than ever before, thanks to the development of the printing industry.

Woodblock printing had been employed in the context of Japanese Buddhism since at least the eighth century for replication of prayers, images, and scriptures, but the use of printing technology for secular, commercial book produc-

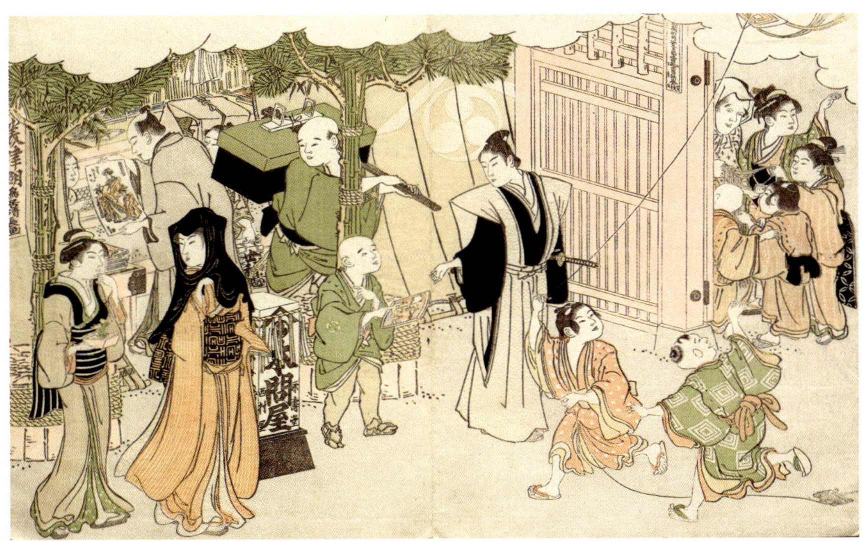

fig. 24 **At a bookstore decorated for the New Year holiday, customers select from the first prints and books of the year.**

tion dates from the seventeenth century. The rise of the merchant class led to an increase in the rate of literacy, further encouraged by the Tokugawa government's emphasis on education in keeping with its adoption of Confucianism as an official philosophy. Not only were more people than ever before able to read but there were now also substantial numbers of city dwellers with at least a little disposable income, enough to purchase a book or at least to rent one from a lending library. Suddenly, recreational reading matter was a potentially profitable commodity.

The earliest secular printed books were generally printed versions of works already widely known in manuscript form (often illustrated), including courtly romances such as the *Tales of Ise*, war stories such as *The Tale of the Soga Brothers*, and Nō plays, among others. Some of these books experimented with movable type, a technology that originated in Korea and was brought to Japan (as was the knowledge of porcelain making) as the result of Hideyoshi's two unsuccessful invasions of Korea in the 1590s. Gradually, however, the use of movable type was abandoned, and books were printed from carved wooden blocks of entire pages, with texts and illustrations both reproduced in the same way. By the middle of the seventeenth century, stories were being written specifically for publication in printed form; these works are known as *kana-zōshi*, or "*kana* books," because they were written mainly in the phonetic, easy-to-read Japanese *kana* script, with limited use of the more difficult Chinese characters (*kanji*) used for serious, scholarly works. For the newly literate popular audience, Chinese characters often had to be glossed with phonetic readings in *kana*, and the complexity of this dual writing system, together with the desire for copious illustrations, were among the reasons why movable type fell into disfavor. Block printing also made it easier to produce reprint editions of books that sold well, without the need for resetting the type each time.

It was the *kana-zōshi* author Asai Ryōi—the first known professional writer in Japan—who popularized the term *ukiyo* in his *Tales of the Floating World* (*Ukiyo monogatari*), published in the early 1660s. His stories, however, were often heavily didactic and moralizing in tone (not surprising, given his samurai-class origins). Literature that truly reflected the frivolous nature of the floating world itself began in 1682, when the Osaka author Ihara Saikaku published his first novel, *The Life of an Amorous Man* (*Kōshoku ichidai otoko*). The works of Saikaku and similar authors came to be called *ukiyo-zōshi*, or "floating-world books." The beginning of the school of art known as *ukiyo-e*, or "pictures of the floating world," can be dated to 1684, when Saikaku's book was published in Edo in a new edition with illustrations by Hishikawa Moronobu, who is considered the first *ukiyo-e* artist. Moronobu blended the graceful elegance of earlier genre paintings with the strong ink lines of woodblock-printed book illustrations to create a chic new style ideally suited to the illustration of the new form of literature. In addition to his book illustrations, he created designs for single-sheet prints that were produced in the same way as the books and sold in the same bookstores.

Moronobu's paintings of the theaters and pleasure quarters of Edo are clearly derived from the earlier Kyoto tradition, and his new *ukiyo-e* style was practiced by some Kyoto artists such as Nishikawa Sukenobu. For the most part, however, *ukiyo-e* was strongly associated with the city of Edo, and with the commoners—known as *chōnin*—rather than with the samurai ruling class (although many samurai participated as customers and sometimes as artists). Like the earlier Kyoto term *machishū*, the word *chōnin* translates literally as "town people," but refers to a broader social group: not just the wealthiest and most prestigious of the merchants, like the purveyors to the imperial court in Kyoto, but the full range of artisan and merchant-class residents of Edo. The spread of printing made literature and art available to a wider segment of the population than ever before.

Ukiyo-e artists typically produced three kinds of pictures: print designs, book illustrations, and paintings. All three of the large cities—and several smaller cities as well—had book-publishing industries, and painters could of course work anywhere. The single-sheet woodblock print, however, was a specialty of the city of Edo. Many of the shops selling these prints were located on roads leading out of the city, for the convenience of travelers returning home and needing to buy souvenir gifts for family and friends in the provinces. The most common subject matter of the prints drew on the two great attractions of the floating world: the Yoshiwara pleasure district, and the Kabuki theater. Early prints included many explicit erotic scenes, but from the 1720s on these were technically illegal (although the law was never strictly enforced, and all of the major *ukiyo-e* artists produced erotic works that were sold on an under-the-counter basis). Legal prints focused on the glorious costumes of leading courtesans, the fashion trendsetters of the city.

The Kabuki theater had originated in Kyoto at the beginning of the seventeenth century, founded by a female dancer, Okuni. During the course of the century, Kabuki underwent many changes, with women banned from the stage in 1629 and their successors, adolescent boys, banned in 1652. In the latter half of the century, Kabuki took on its mature form, with sexy song-and-dance routines replaced by intricately plotted dramas of wrenching emotional conflicts. A more flamboyant, macho style of acting became popular in Edo in the 1690s and led

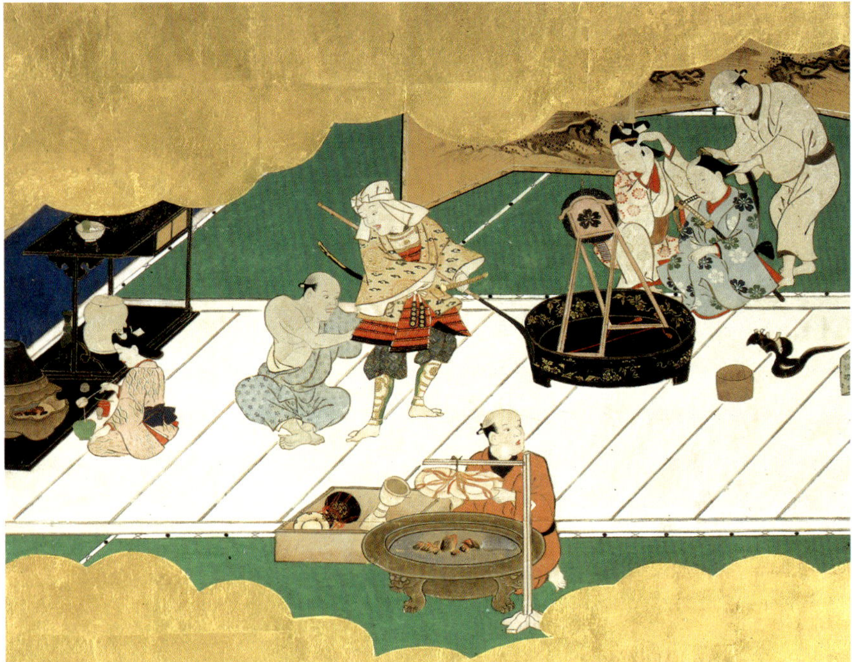

fig. 25 **Backstage at the Nakamura Theater in Edo, Kabuki actors dress for their parts while an assistant prepares tea.**

directly to a boom in the popularity of actor prints that showed the heroes of the stage—and the heroines, also played by male actors. Throughout the eighteenth century, the realistic portrayal of actors' faces and bodies steadily increased until, with the work of the mysterious Sharaku in the 1790s, depictions extended past literal realism into caricature, resulting in striking close-up portraits that are greatly admired even today.

Ukiyo-e prints were mass-produced commercial products; the artist was responsible only for drawing the design. Wooden blocks—one for each color, in the case of color prints—were carved by professional block cutters, and prints were made from the blocks by professional printers. The entire process was controlled by the publisher, who sold the finished works in his bookshop along with printed books. The technology of woodblock printing developed steadily throughout the first part of the eighteenth century. The earliest single-sheet prints designed by Moronobu in the 1680s had been monochrome ink woodcuts, but because prints were commercial products sold to the public on a competitive basis, publishers were constantly on the lookout for ways to make their own products more attractive. Appealing colors were an especially good way to attract the eyes of potential customers, and so the colors that had been added by hand to early book illustrations began to be used for prints as well, featuring at first an orange-colored, lead-based pigment (called *tan*). Around 1718 the large prints colored in the orange tones were replaced by smaller prints hand-colored with a palette based on a bright rose-pink (*beni)*, sometimes with special features such as metallic flakes. In the 1740s, simple color prints made with two or three color blocks in addition to the black outline block began to appear; and in 1765 the process of full-color printing, with five or more color blocks, came into commercial use. This process was so satisfactory that it continued to be used until the beginning of the twentieth century for commercial pictures (and was still used even beyond that as a fine art form). Full-color prints were known as *Azuma nishiki-e*, or "brocade pictures of the East," a joking reference to the famous brocades of Kyoto, implying that this rival Edo product was equally fine.

In the nineteenth century, the repertoire of subject matter depicted in *ukiyo-e* prints expanded greatly. In addition to beautiful women and popular Kabuki actors, landscapes and historical prints, especially scenes of legendary warriors, became major subgenres. Landscape series such as *Thirty-six Views of Mount Fuji* by Katsushika Hokusai and *Fifty-three Stations of the Tōkaidō* by Utagawa Hiroshige utilized a version of Western perspective, just as the Kyoto painter Maruyama Ōkyo had done in the previous century. By the 1830s, this way of seeing the world was familiar enough to the Japanese to make the landscape series bestsellers at home—and popular collectors' items abroad a few decades later, when Japan once again opened up to foreign trade in the 1860s. Another newly popular subject was historical adventure stories, often with a fantasy twist, as in the works of Utagawa Kuniyoshi. The world of the *ukiyo-e* print expanded not only thematically but geographically, and in the nineteenth century actor prints began to be made in Osaka as well as in Edo.

The colorful world depicted in *ukiyo-e* prints and paintings also found expression in three-dimensional form in the costumes and personal accessories treasured by well-dressed city dwellers. Though simple in basic construction, kimono during the Edo period were highly elaborate in decoration. Dyeing and embroidery were often combined to create lavish effects in costumes for both men and women, though fashions for commoners were sometimes restricted by sumptuary laws. For men, much attention was paid to elegant small accessories such as tobacco pouches, layered medicine boxes (*inrō*), and the toggles that held these items in place at one's belt (*netsuke*). The *netsuke* in particular are exquisitely carved miniature sculptures, another example of the availability of art to ordinary citizens that was one of the remarkable features of life in Edo-period Japan.

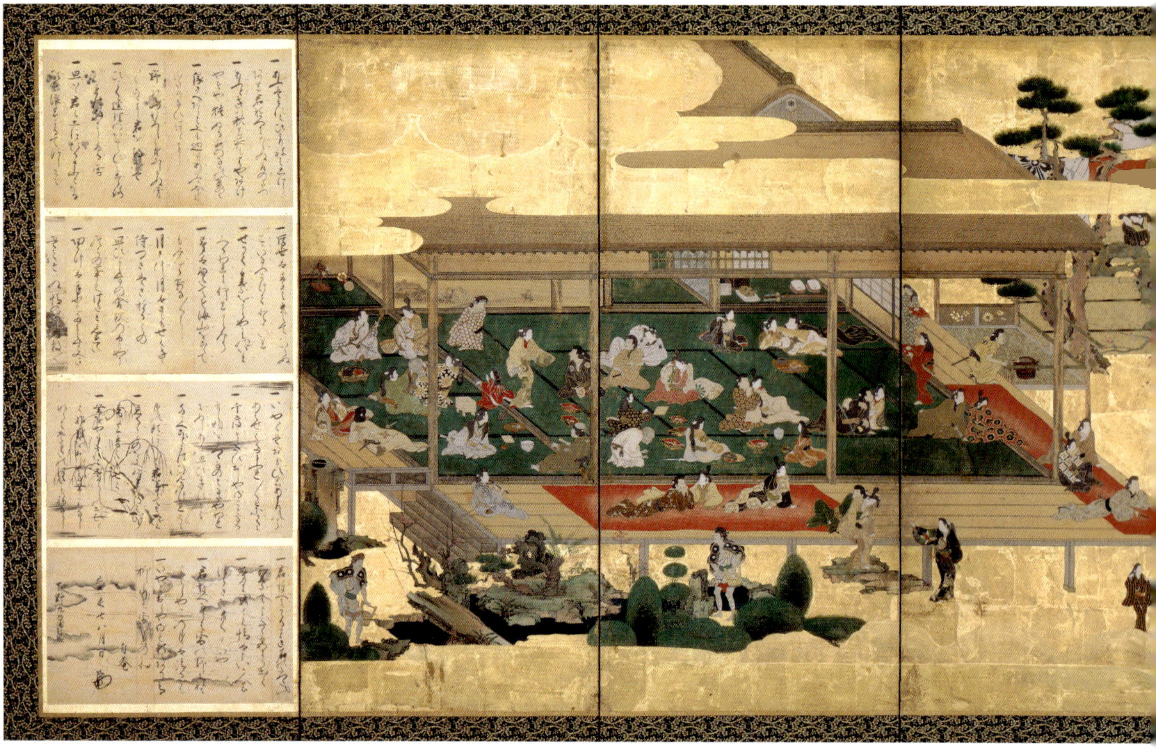

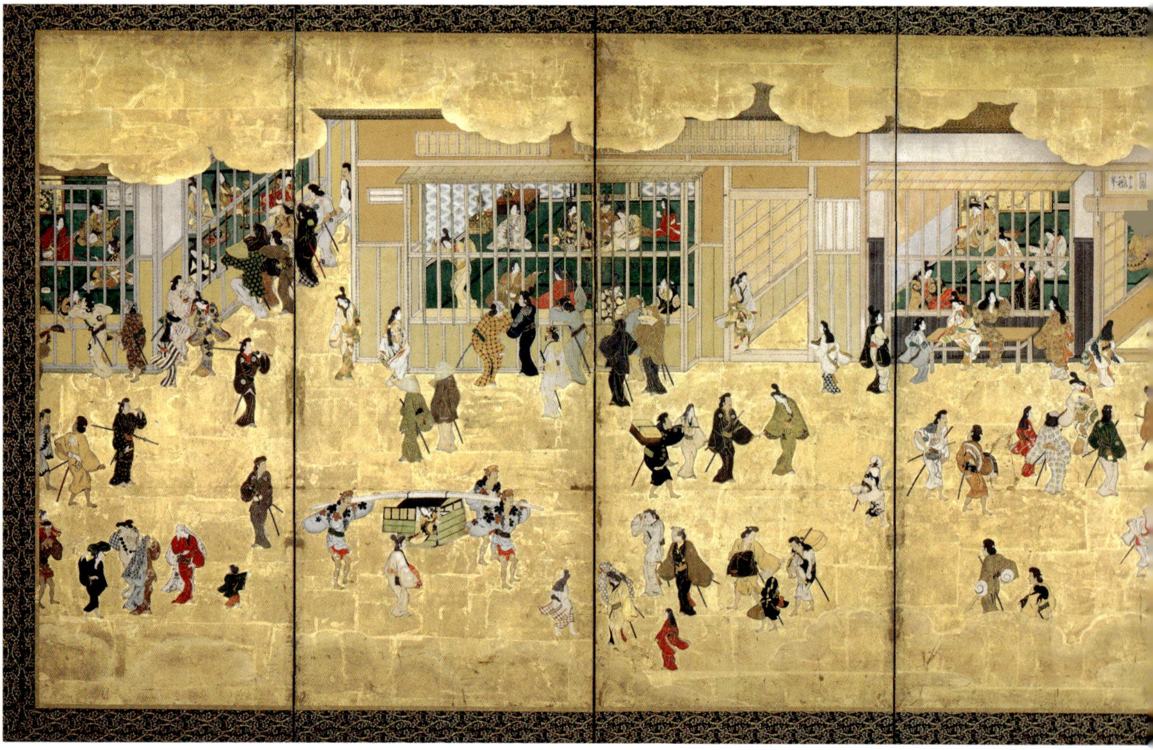

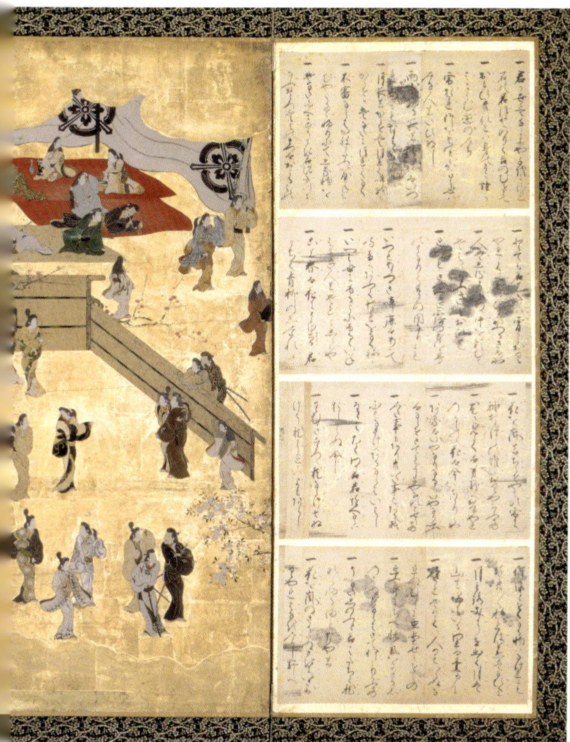

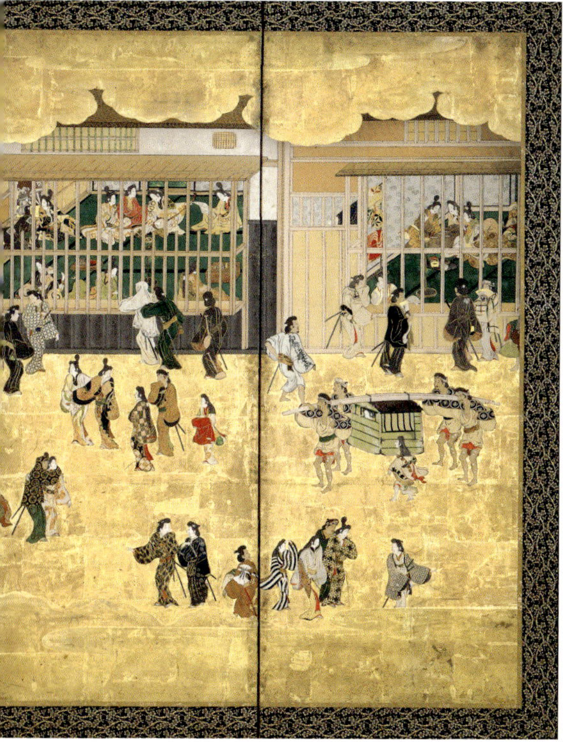

Scenes from the Pleasure Quarters of Kyoto

Edo period, 1630s–early 1640s

In the first years of the seventeenth century, following their consolidation of military and civil authority, the Tokugawa shoguns established their presence in Kyoto, Japan's ancient capital, by constructing an ostentatious palace complex at Nijō. As part of a plan to institute clearer social distinctions between ruler and ruled, they removed the brothels from that area, first to a location a few miles to the south and then, in 1640, to a tightly regulated compound known as Shimabara, on the western outskirts of the city.

The exact location of the brothels depicted in these vibrant screens cannot be identified, since the works are not precisely dated, but talismans from Kyoto's Gion Shrine depicted above the lintel of one of the buildings in the left screen make it clear that the setting is one of the two pleasure districts mentioned above. The left screen provides a panoramic view of a bustling avenue lined with latticed establishments, where stylish prostitutes pass the time strumming samisens or playing board games while they are ogled by prospective clients. The complementary screen presents a house of assignation, a grand building with luxuriously appointed rooms and gardens where the highest-ranking courtesans entertained their guests.

In order to enhance the screens' decorative effect, a previous owner replaced the first and last panels on the right screen with sections from an early-seventeenth-century calligraphic handscroll. The text includes lines from the tenth-century *Kokin-shū* imperial poetry anthology that now appear in Japan's national anthem, *Kimigayo*.

Pair of six-panel folding screens; ink and color on gold-leafed paper
104.4 x 260.8 cm (41 1/8 x 102 11/16 in.) each
Denman Waldo Ross Collection 06.286, 06.287

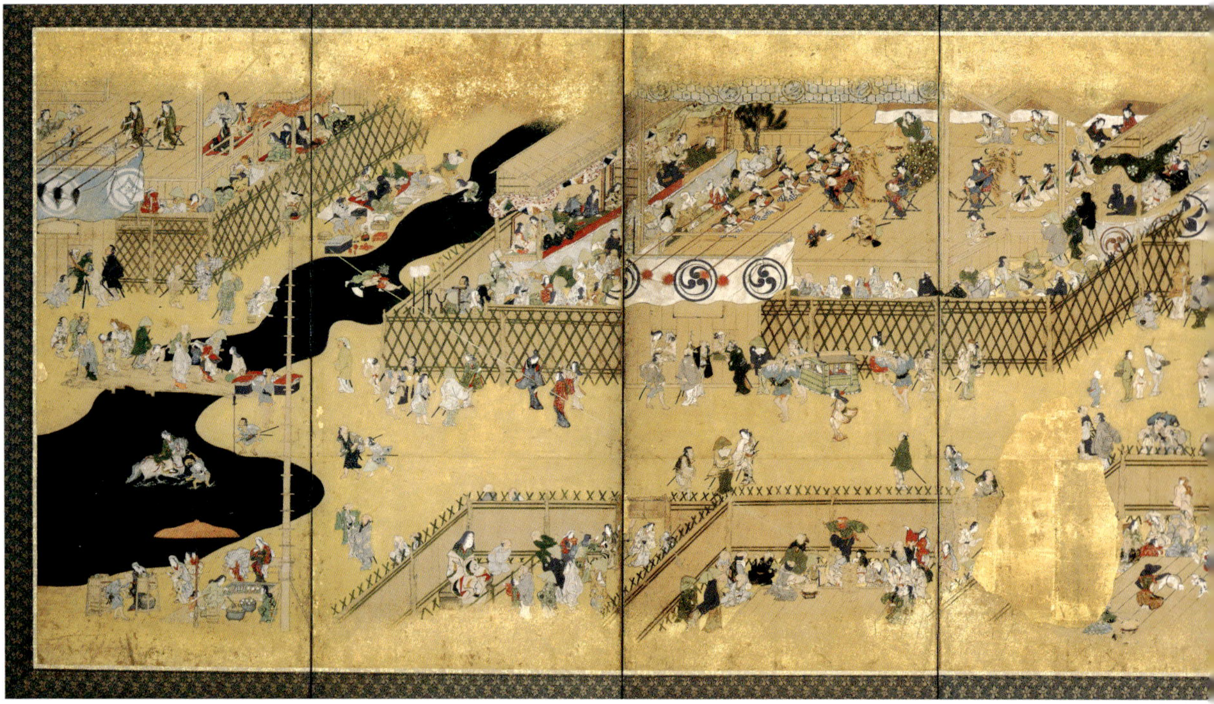

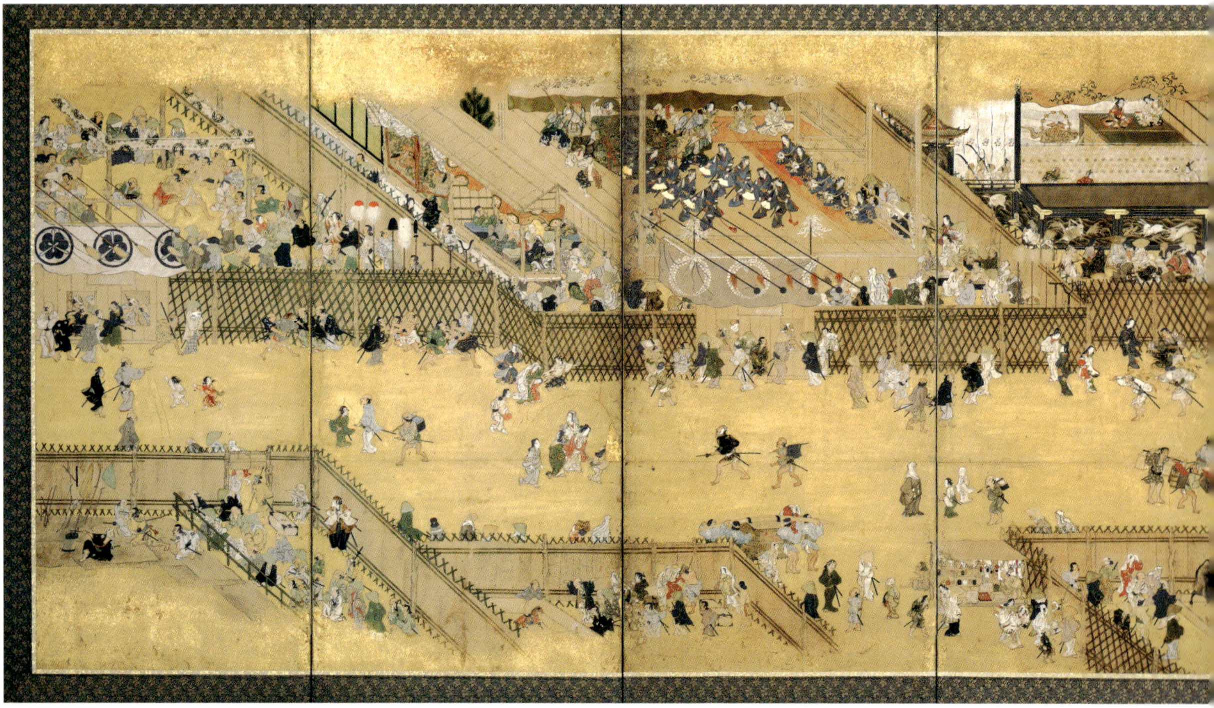

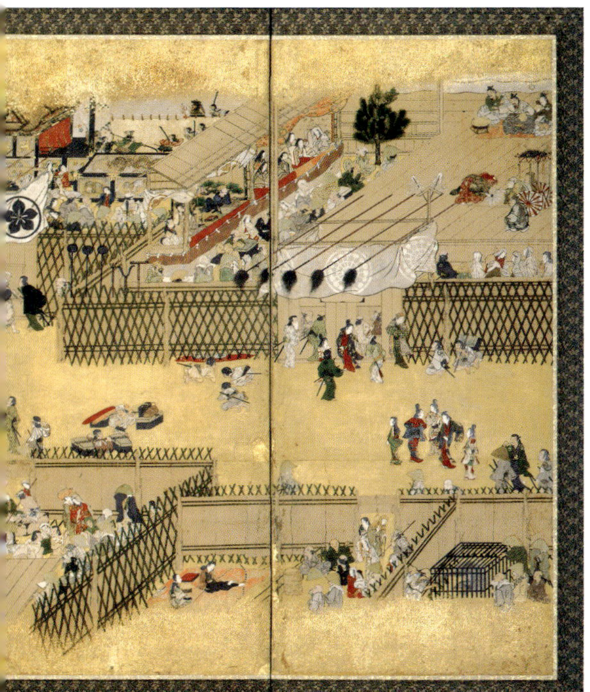

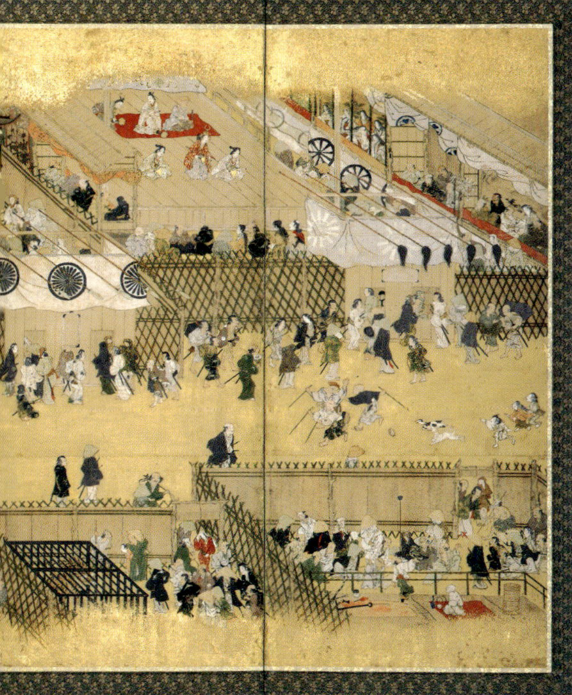

Amusements at the Dry Riverbed, Shijō

Edo period, 1660s–early 1670s

Many aspects of the urban popular culture of early modern Japan originated in seventeenth-century Kyoto, in the dry bed of the Kamo River where it crosses the street named Shijō (or Fourth Avenue), then and now the city's major shopping district. Since the riverbed was sometimes flooded, it was unsuitable for permanent buildings, and so it became a fairground filled with temporary structures housing a wide variety of entertainments and attractions. The Kabuki theater began here about 1603, when the shrine dancer Okuni of Izumo and her troupe performed alluring song-and-dance routines interspersed with comic skits.

Among the handful of surviving screens showing activities in the Shijō riverbed, the MFA examples are especially rich in variety and detail. The theatrical performances depicted along the upper register of this pair of screens include Kabuki shows both by women (banned from the stage in 1629, ostensibly on moral grounds) and young men (banned in 1652 for similar reasons); two puppet theaters; a performance of Nō, the masked theater usually associated with the military elite; and a sumo wrestling match. Across the street, along the lower register, are additional fenced enclosures where spectators view carnival-like attractions including wild animals such as a caged tiger and porcupine; an armless woman who shoots a bow with her feet; a trainer of performing dogs wearing an exotic foreign-style costume; a gigantic woman twice the size of a normal person; and a charming miniature horse. Lively depictions of many visitors of assorted ages, genders, and social classes emphasize the universal appeal of the famous entertainment district as it would have appeared several decades before this nostalgic work was painted.

Pair of six-panel folding screens; ink and color on gold-leafed paper
103.9 x 289.2 cm (40⅞ x 113⅞ in.) each
Fenollosa-Weld Collection 11.4591, 11.4592

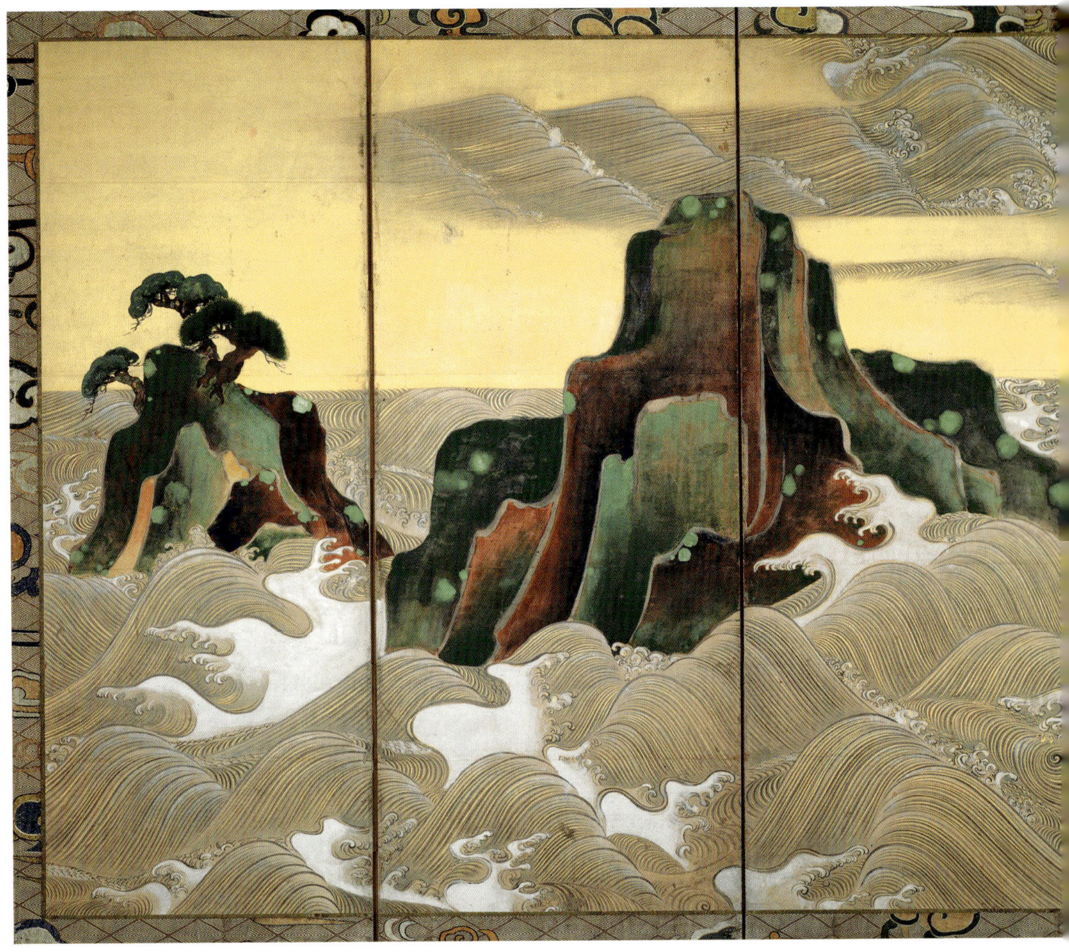

Waves at Matsushima
Ogata Kōrin (1658–1716)
Edo period, early 18th century

A cluster of small pine-clad islands off the northeastern coast of Japan, known as Matsushima, has been famed since the early seventeenth century as one of the country's three most scenic places. It became a favored subject of a group of painters loosely associated with Tawaraya Sōtatsu and later Ogata Kōrin. Taking the last syllable from Kōrin's name, this group, admired for its striking sense of design, has come to be called Rinpa (the "Rin school").

Kōrin and his brother Ogata Kenzan belonged to a prosperous dry-goods merchant household in Kyoto. Due to a lack of business acumen and an excessive fondness for wine and women, however, Kōrin was forced to seek a living as an artist. He first collaborated with Kenzan in the production of ceramics, but later turned to the execution of large-scale paintings. Partially in homage to Sōtatsu and partially as painting practice, Kōrin copied several of the earlier mas-

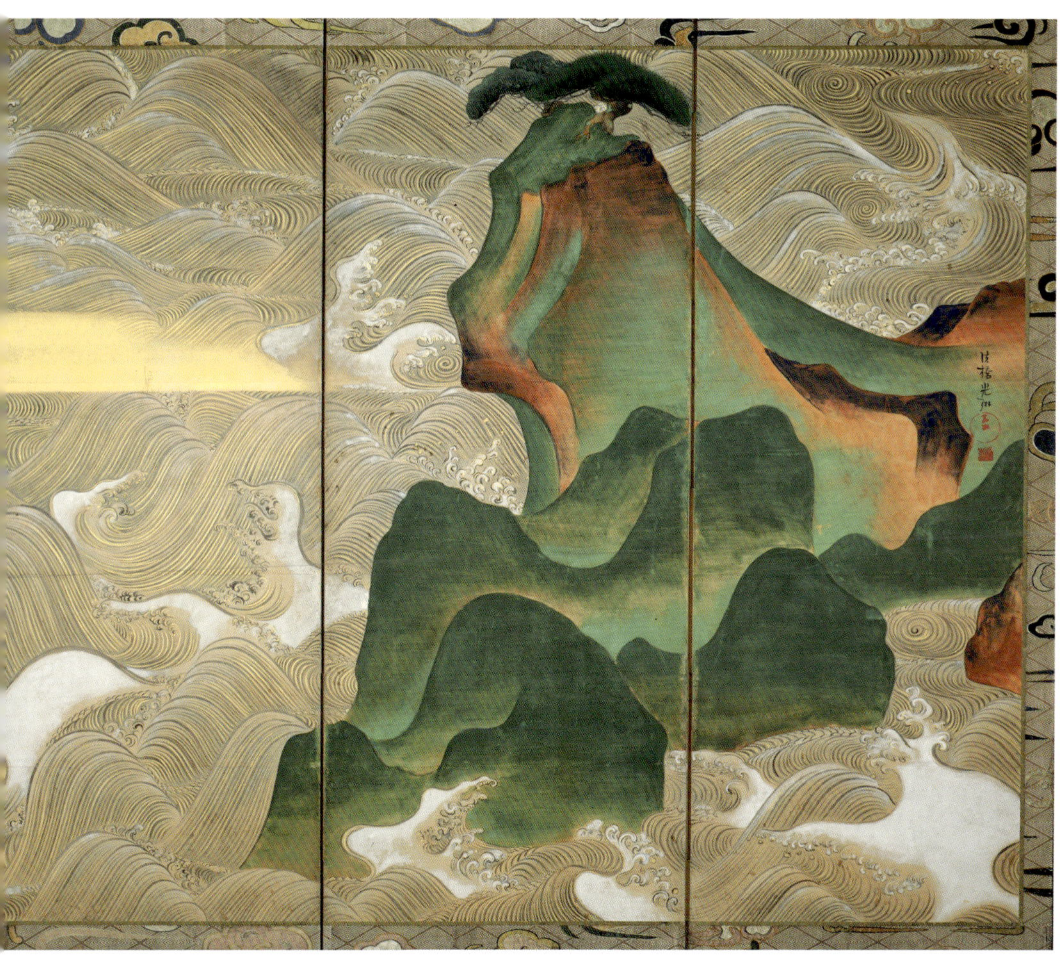

ter's works. This screen, which once would have been the right-hand side of a pair, is patterned on Sōtatsu's Matsushima screens, now in the Freer Gallery of Art in Washington, D.C., with their roiling waves and polychromed islands.

Although Sōtatsu had been patronized by Kyoto merchants who promoted a courtly aesthetic, by Kōrin's time large commissions were not forthcoming in western Japan. Therefore, the artist was compelled to relocate to Edo, where the military elite were eager to acquire his works. The exact provenance of this screen is not known, but the collector Ernest Fenollosa claimed that it had belonged to a prominent warlord family.

Six-panel folding screen; ink, color, and gold on paper
150.2 x 367.89 cm (59 1/8 x 144 13/16 in.)
Fenollosa-Weld Collection 11.4584

Ember pot with design of peonies and vines
Ogata Kenzan (1663–1743)
Edo period, early–mid-18th century

When in use, this container would have been filled with a thick layer of ash that supported a small pile of charcoal embers. Aromatic smoke, given off by a few slivers of rare, imported incense wood placed on the embers, would have perfumed a room used for an elegant pastime such as a tea gathering.

The base bears the signature of Japan's most celebrated ceramic artist, Ogata Kenzan. Born into a wealthy Kyoto merchant family, Kenzan spent his early adult years as a cultivated recluse engaged in calligraphy, music, literature, and tea practice, but in 1699 he established a sizeable ceramic production center northwest of the city. Unlike many other renowned Japanese potters, Kenzan is not thought to have been directly involved in working with clay. He assumed the role of craft and design entrepreneur, leaving the actual manufacture to his employees.

Many of his early productions are decorated with inscriptions (often executed by Kenzan himself) and designs (often by his brother Kōrin) that evoke Chinese and Japanese literary and painterly themes. The motifs on this piece, in contrast, were inspired by a regional Chinese ceramic ware known as *Cizhou*. Kenzan first took this ware as a model in 1706, probably because its relative looseness and freedom of execution were well suited to his skillful exploitation of a casual, unaffected look. Such a style earned him great commercial success and has inspired countless imitators, in both Japan and the West. Kenzan continued to produce wares with the same style of decoration after he moved his facility to downtown Kyoto in 1712.

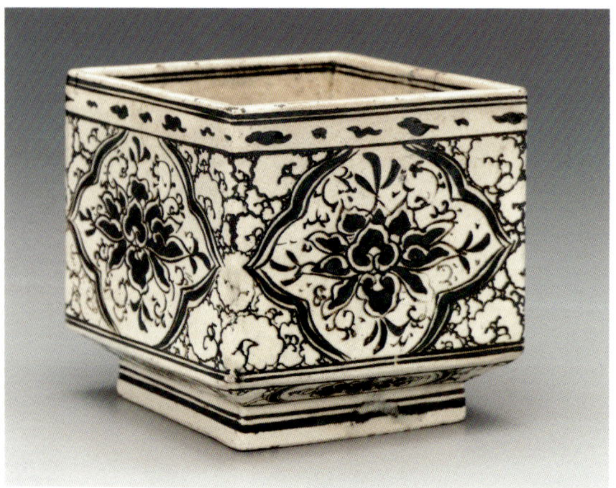

High-fired ceramic decorated in underglaze iron
11.7 x 11 x 11 cm (4⅝ x 4⅜ x 4⅜ in.)
Morse Collection. Museum purchase with funds donated by contribution 92.6498

The Four Sages of Mount Shang
Soga Shōhaku (1730–1781)
Edo period, about 1768

In the early seventeenth century, the Tokugawa shoguns transferred civil and military authority from Kyoto to their headquarters in Edo. Soon thereafter the four major lines of the Kano school of painters, which had historically been sponsored by members of the military elite, followed them to Edo, thus allowing eighteenth-century Kyoto artists to enjoy unprecedented creative freedom. Newly prosperous merchants provided patronage for works that often expressed disaffection with the political establishment, and artists were no longer compelled to follow the conventions of the traditional masters.

No artist embodied the zeitgeist of eighteenth-century Kyoto more than the eccentric Soga Shōhaku. Although he briefly received instruction from a minor Kano painter, Shōhaku is described as having adopted extremely untraditional techniques, such as painting with straw or rags. In an almost abstract play of dynamic, sweeping strokes of the brush, here he suggests the forms of three sages and their attendant under a monumental pine tree that extends across both screens; the form of the fourth sage riding a donkey can only be interpreted through simple lines and the dots for the beast's eyes and muzzle. Generally venerated as symbols of moral rectitude, the Four Sages are said to have retreated to Mount Shang during a period of political oppression in China at the end of the third century B.C.E. Shōhaku's representation, however, is exceedingly irreverent: the sages wear befuddled expressions and sit with sake cups in hand, clearly having indulged in drink.

Pair of six-panel folding screens; ink and gold on paper
154.7 x 361.2 cm ($60\frac{7}{8}$ x $142\frac{3}{16}$ in.) each
Fenollosa-Weld Collection 11.4513, 11.4514

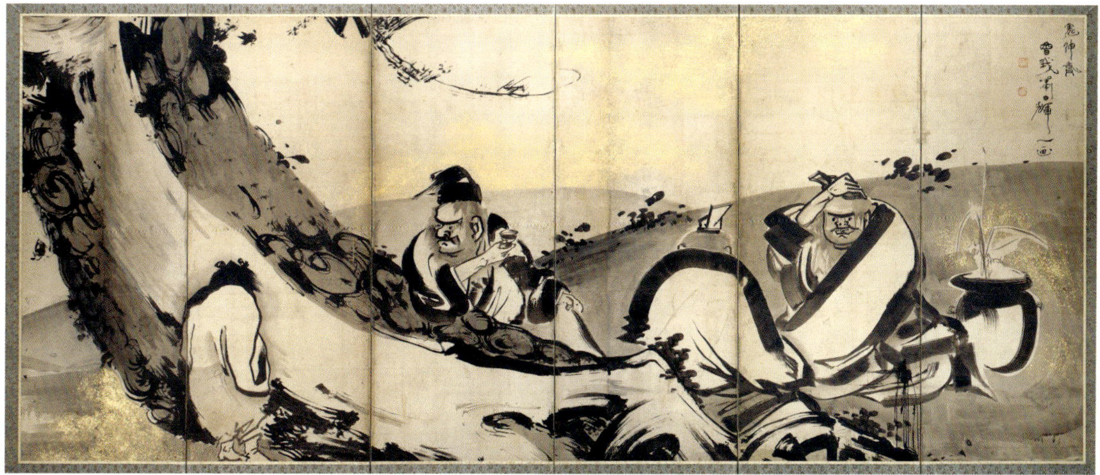

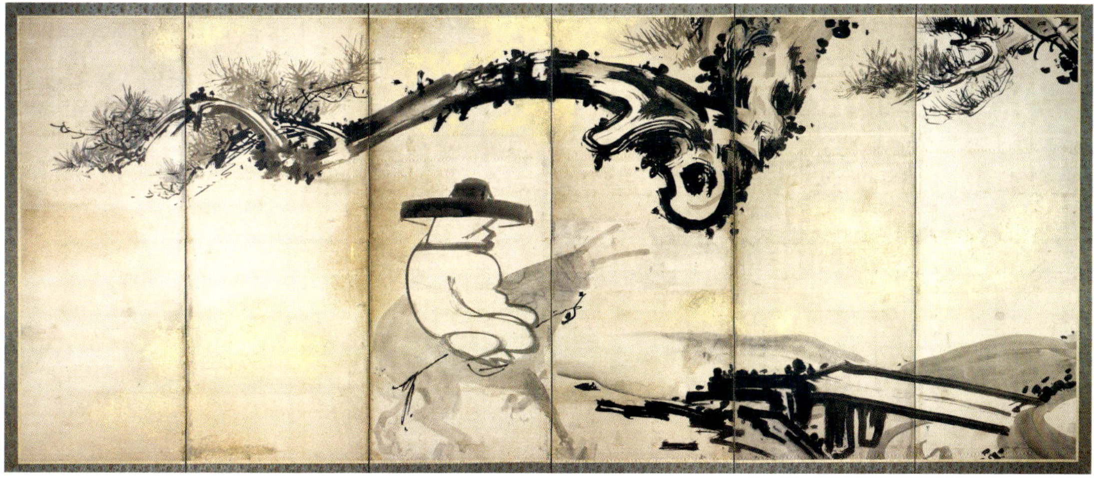

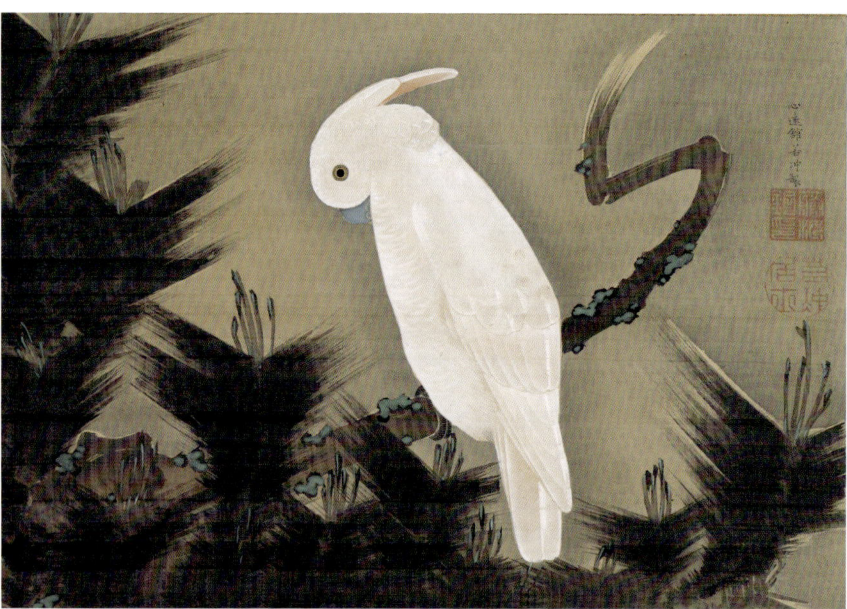

White Cockatoo on a Pine Branch

Itō Jakuchū (1716–1800)

Edo period, about 1755–57

Born into a line of Kyoto greengrocers, Itō Jakuchū was compelled to head the family business until his forties, when he became a lay Buddhist and dedicated himself to painting. Through his wholesale establishment, he made the acquaintance of a high-level monk who later became the chief abbot of Shōkoku-ji, one of the city's leading Zen temples. Soon thereafter, about 1757, the artist began creating a celebrated set of some thirty scrolls depicting creatures from the natural world, entitled *The Colorful Realm of Living Beings* (*Dōshoku sai-e*), as an act of devotion. This exquisite painting of a cockatoo perched on a lichen-covered branch amid pine needles was executed during the same period, when Jakuchū had begun to internalize the lessons of ancient as well as contemporary Chinese bird-and-flower paintings and to realize his own highly individual style.

The naturalism of the cockatoo recalls the avian forms in colorful Chinese scrolls of the Qing dynasty (1644–1911) that entered Japan through Nagasaki at that time. But the meticulous handling of the exotic bird's individual feathers, delicately built up in layers of shell white, also demonstrates the artist's insistence on direct observation of his subject (in fact, colleagues related that he kept ornamental fowl for study). For the pines, in contrast, Jakuchū attacked the silk with broad strokes of ink that yield an abstracted yet energized setting for the refined bird.

Hanging scroll; ink, color, and gold on silk
40.1 x 55.6 cm (15 13/16 x 21 7/8 in.)
Bequest of Charles Bain Hoyt 50.1493

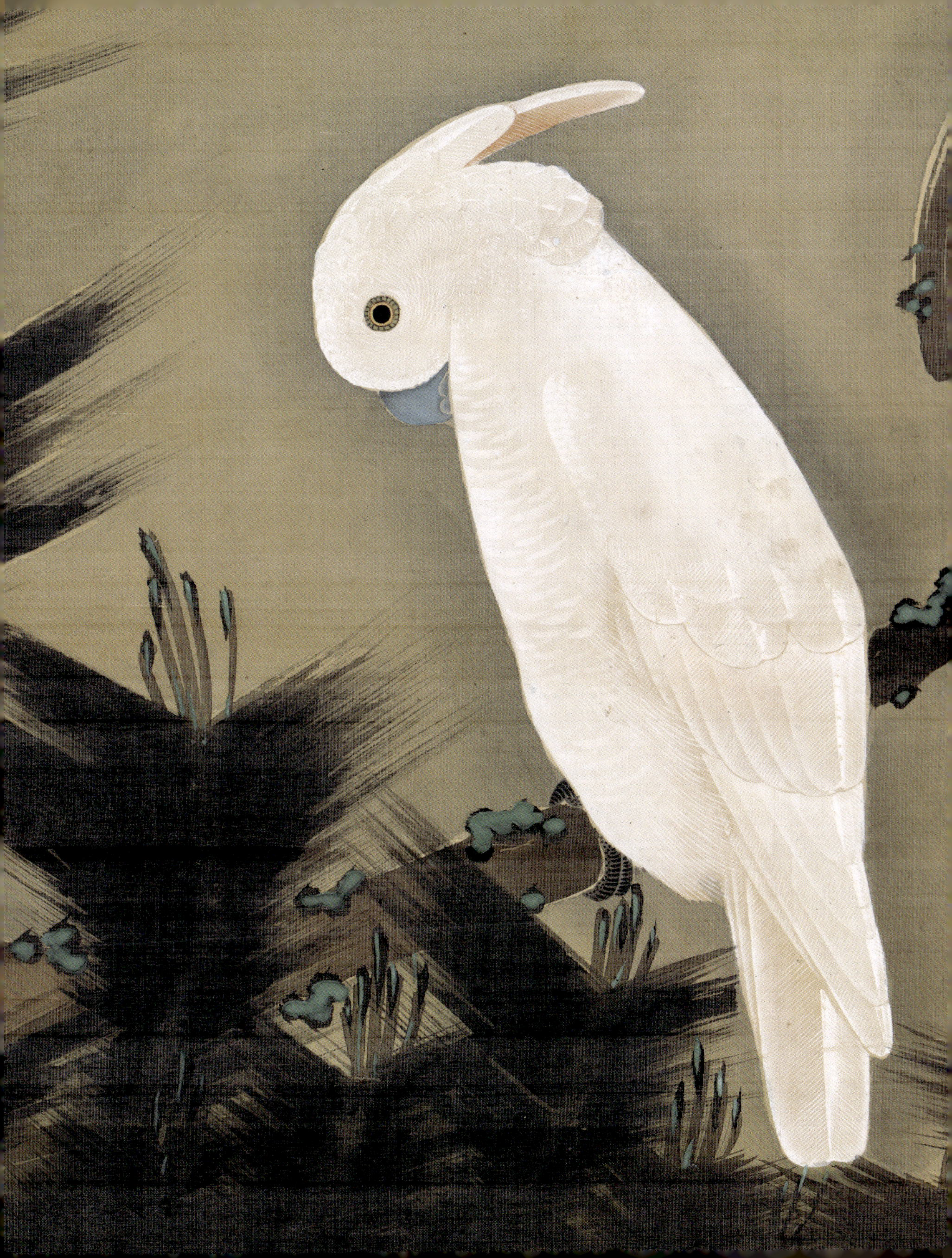

Boating Under the Willows* and *Outing by the Hills

Yosa Buson (1716–1783)

Edo period, late 1770s

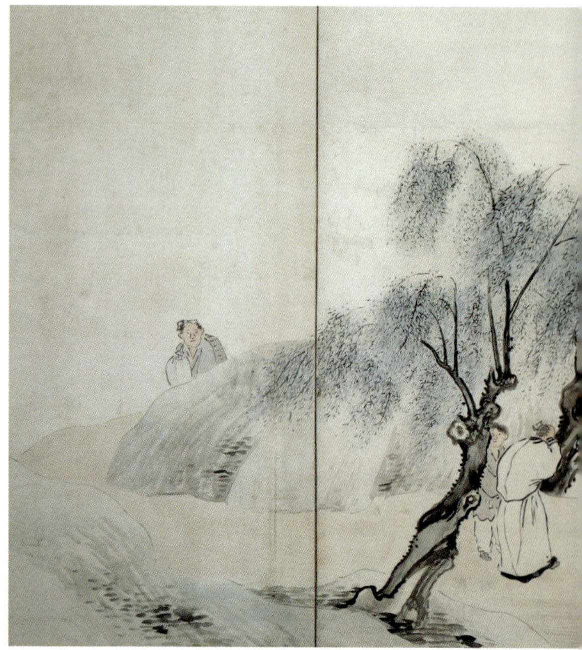

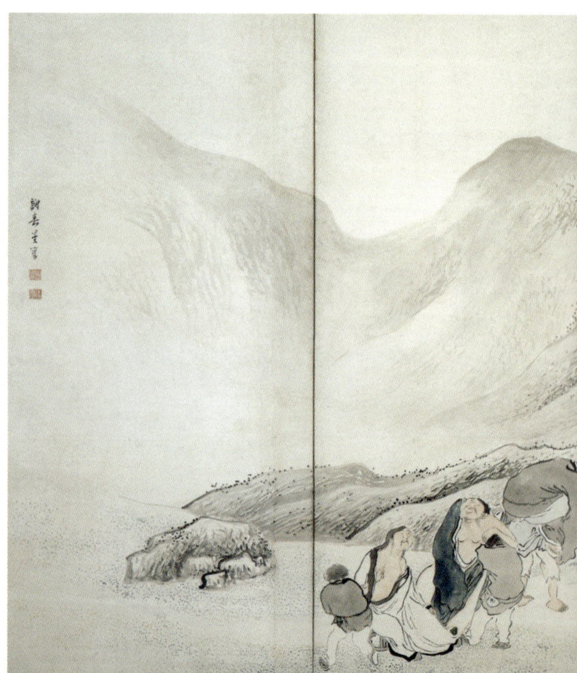

Yosa Buson is equally famous as a haiku poet and a literati painter—so accomplished in both fields that he ranks as one of the leading figures in each. Literati painting, called *bunjinga* in Japan, had been practiced in China from at least the fourteenth century but was little known in Japan until the eighteenth century. (It was also sometimes called *nanga,* or "Southern painting," a term derived from Chinese art criticism that likened the skillful brushwork of this style to the "sudden enlightenment" form of Zen Buddhism practiced in southern China.) In theory, literati painting was supposed to be practiced not by professional painters but by gentleman amateurs who disdained superficial prettiness and created deliberately simple, naïve compositions of calligraphic brushwork in ink that expressed the lofty character of the painter.

Because Edo-period Japanese were forbidden to travel abroad, it was not possible for Japanese painters to study in China. Instead, they taught themselves literati painting techniques using imported Chinese printed books. By the late eighteenth century, second-generation literati painters such as Buson had mastered the new style and adapted it to Japanese taste, creating works that were notably warmer in feeling and more decorative in appearance than their relatively austere Chinese prototypes. This pair of screens depicts the carefree, convivial, nature-loving lifestyle regarded as ideal by Chinese scholars: setting out on a boat trip, perhaps to view a scenic spot, in the right screen; and staggering happily home, supported by servant boys, after enjoying wine and poetry amid mountain scenery on the left.

Buson's finest works were created in the last decade of his life, and it is thought that he painted these screens when he was around sixty.

Pair of six-panel folding screens; ink and color on paper
139 x 363 cm (54¾ x 142 15/16 in.) and
139.4 x 363.6 cm (54⅞ x 143⅛ in.)
Frederick L. Jack Fund 58.952, 58.953

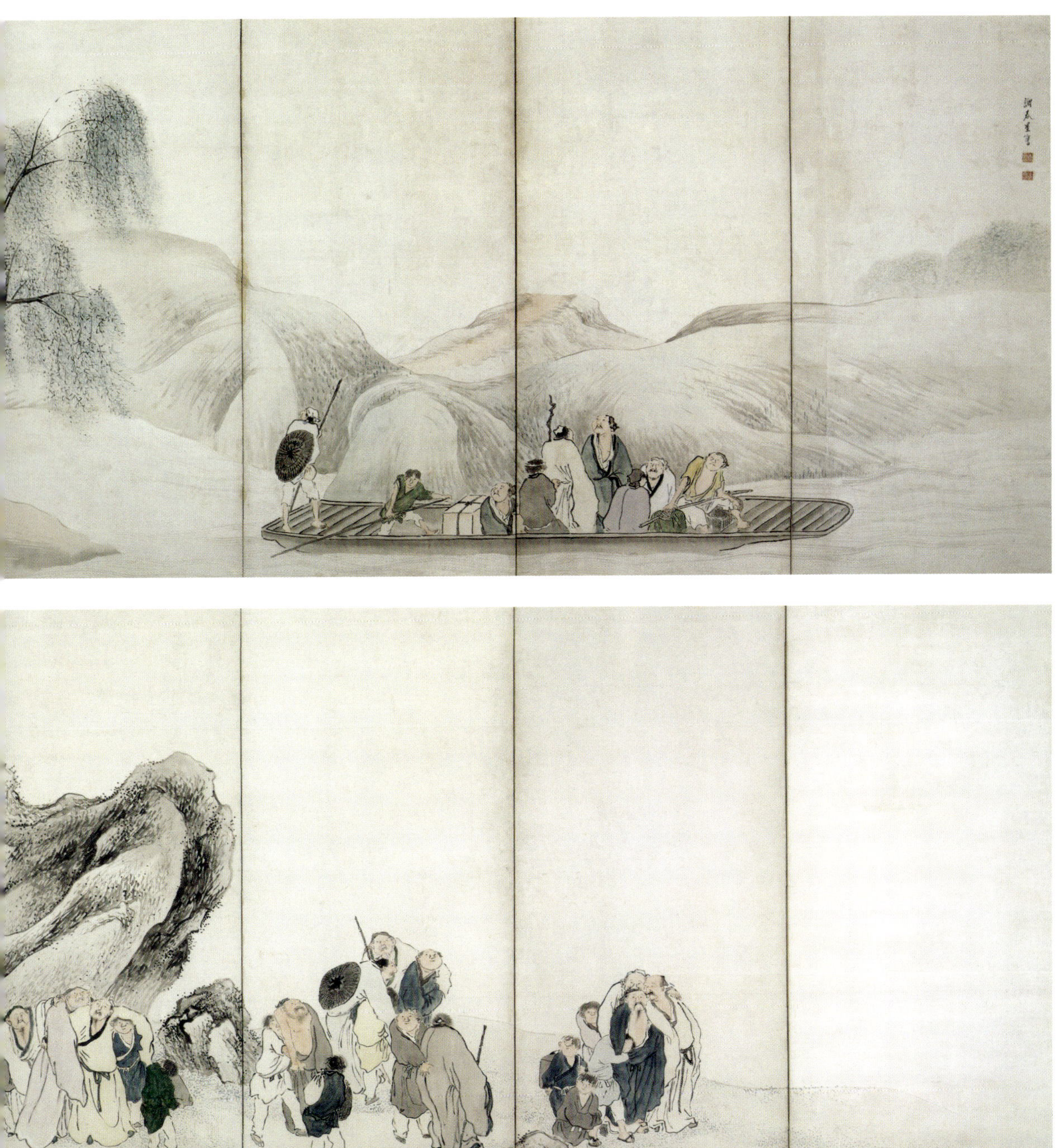

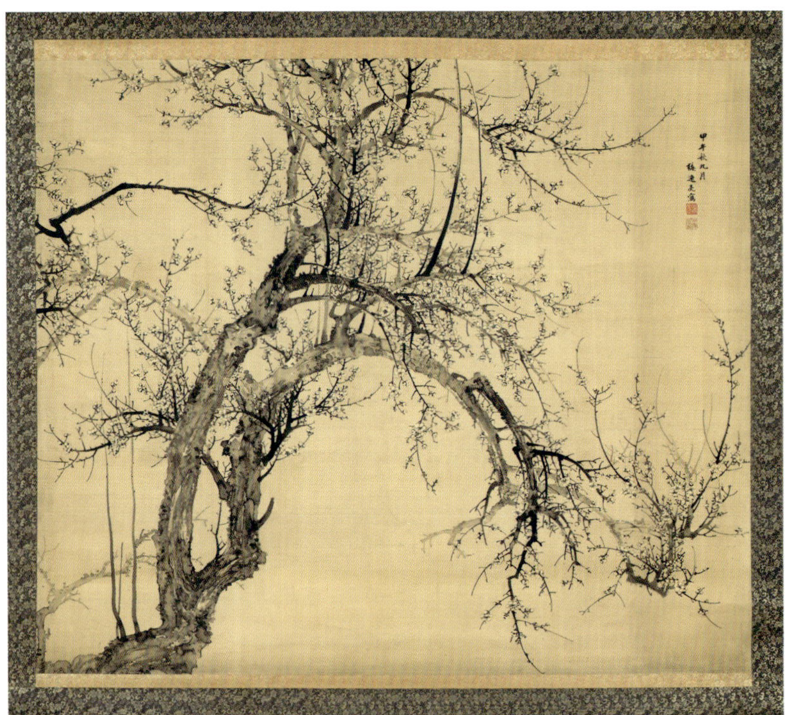

Flowering Plum Tree
Yamamoto Baiitsu (1783–1856)
Edo period, dated 1834

Yamamoto Baiitsu, an early-nineteenth-century literatus from Nagoya, has been acclaimed as one of the consummate painters of bird-and-flower compositions. Like most Japanese scholar-artists who wished to emulate their Chinese counterparts, he dedicated himself not only to the creation of works of art but also to music, poetry, and the connoisseurship of Chinese painting and calligraphy. Although Baiitsu and his colleagues held lofty ideals and sought to distance themselves from professional painting schools that were beholden to military and civil authorities, they did have to resort to selling works in order to secure their livelihoods.

Throughout his career, Baiitsu held particular admiration for scrolls of blossoming plum trees by the Chinese master Wang Mian of the Yuan dynasty (1279–1368); supposedly the artist name "Baiitsu," which literally means "plum leisure," was conferred on him after he viewed one of Wang's works in a Nagoya temple. In this monumental scroll, Baiitsu pays homage to the Chinese literati tradition in his adoption of the plum motif, a symbol of moral fortitude, and specifically to Wang Mian in his embrace of the Chinese artist's arrangement of the magnificent twisted branches. Baiitsu's lush use of ink, however, which pools in areas along the gnarled trunk and creates sensuous plays of dark and light in the luminous blossoms of early spring, is distinctively Japanese.

Baiitsu's signature dates the painting to 1834, two years after the artist moved from Nagoya to Kyoto, seeking company with a wider community of scholars. Although he occasionally returned to his hometown for exhibitions, the square relief seal naming the Gyokuzen studio indicates that this impressive scroll was executed in Kyoto.

Hanging scroll; ink on silk
147.3 x 167.6 cm (58 x 66 in.)
Museum purchase with funds by exchange from the William Sturgis Bigelow Collection and a Gift of Dr. Ernest G. Stillman 2007.105

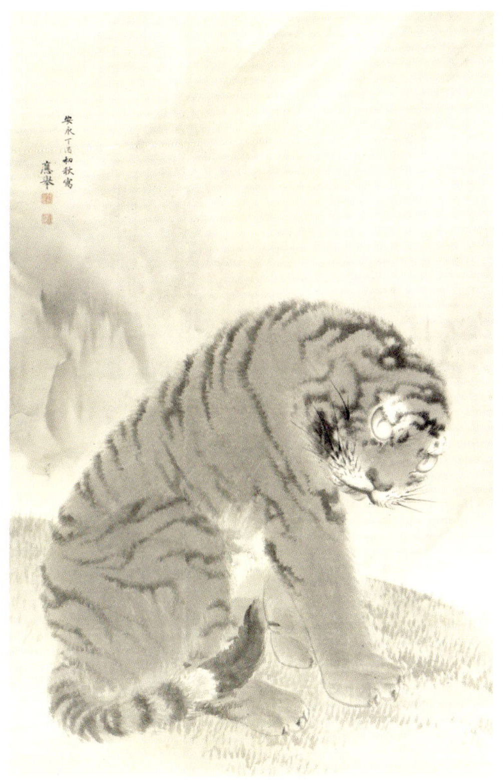

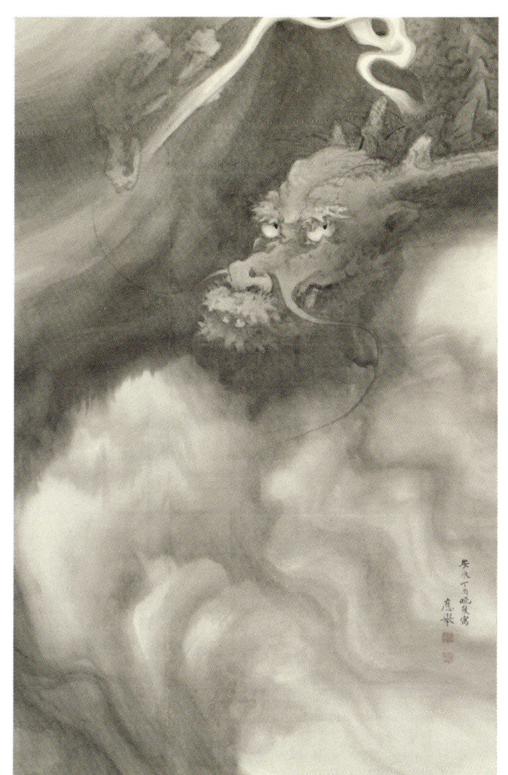

Dragon* and *Tiger
Maruyama Ōkyo (1733–1795)
Edo period, 1777

In ancient Chinese mythology, the dragon and tiger symbolized powerful natural forces: the dragon controlled water and rain, while the force of the tiger's roar generated the wind. The two animals also represented the directions east and west, respectively. The most powerful of mythical animals and the mightiest of living beasts were frequently depicted together in the arts of China, Korea, and Japan. In Japan, where there were no living tigers, both creatures were effectively mythical; Maruyama Ōkyo's realistic depiction of the tiger's fur was probably based on an imported skin.

The founder of the Maruyama-Shijō school of painting, Ōkyo rose to the top of the art world in eighteenth-century Japan by revitalizing traditional subjects with an exciting new style that incorporated Western techniques such as shading and linear perspective, which he had learned as a young man by studying imported pictures. His tiger and dragon have the appearance of solid forms in three-dimensional space while at the same time displaying the consummate mastery of ink brushwork that was traditionally the most important criterion of fine painting.

This pair of scrolls was created at the height of Ōkyo's career. A guide to notable persons in the city of Kyoto, published in 1775, listed him first among all of the city's painters—an especially impressive achievement considering that his competition included such brilliant artists as Yosa Buson, Itō Jakuchū, and Soga Shōhaku.

Pair of hanging scrolls; ink on paper
134.7 x 89.4 cm (53 1/16 x 35 3/16 in.) each
William Sturgis Bigelow Collection 11.8498, 11.8499

The Tale of the Soga Brothers
(Soga monogatari)
Edo period, 1627

This depiction of a wrestling match comes from an extremely rare printing of the classic early-medieval revenge epic *The Tale of the Soga Brothers*. The pictures were printed in the usual manner from a carved woodblock but were subsequently colored by hand using mineral pigments including red (*tan*) and green (*roku*). About 120 titles produced in this way are known today by the term *tanrokubon*, literally "red and green books." The earliest *tanrokubon*, like this example, were professionally colored using a larger and subtler range of pigments than is found in later editions. Another mark of this book's early date is the fact that the text was not printed from a single carved block but was instead set from wooden movable type, a technology used in early modern Japan for a brief period starting in the late sixteenth century, after metallic fonts were looted during two invasions of Korea.

About 1650, movable type was gradually abandoned in favor of a return to carving both texts and images from woodblocks. Possible explanations for this change include the enormous number of characters needed for written Japanese, the difficulty and expense of casting metallic type, the fragility of the wooden type alternative, the importance of the individual calligraphic hand in the presentation of a text, and the ease with which wooden blocks could be preserved, making it convenient to produce reprints at a later date. Although the period of movable type was short, its use by the shogun Tokugawa Ieyasu (1543–1616) to produce secular texts effectively ended the Buddhist temples' monopoly on printing and paved the way for an extraordinary explosion of publishing culture in Edo-period Japan.

Woodblock-printed illustrated book with movable-type text and hand-coloring
27.8 x 18.6 cm (10 15/16 x 7 5/16 in.)
Denman Waldo Ross Collection 2006.1538

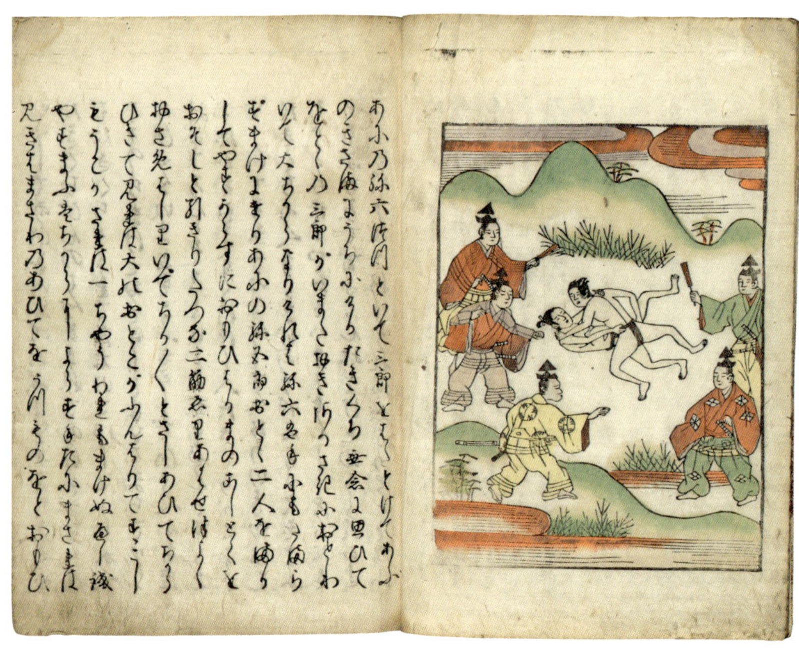

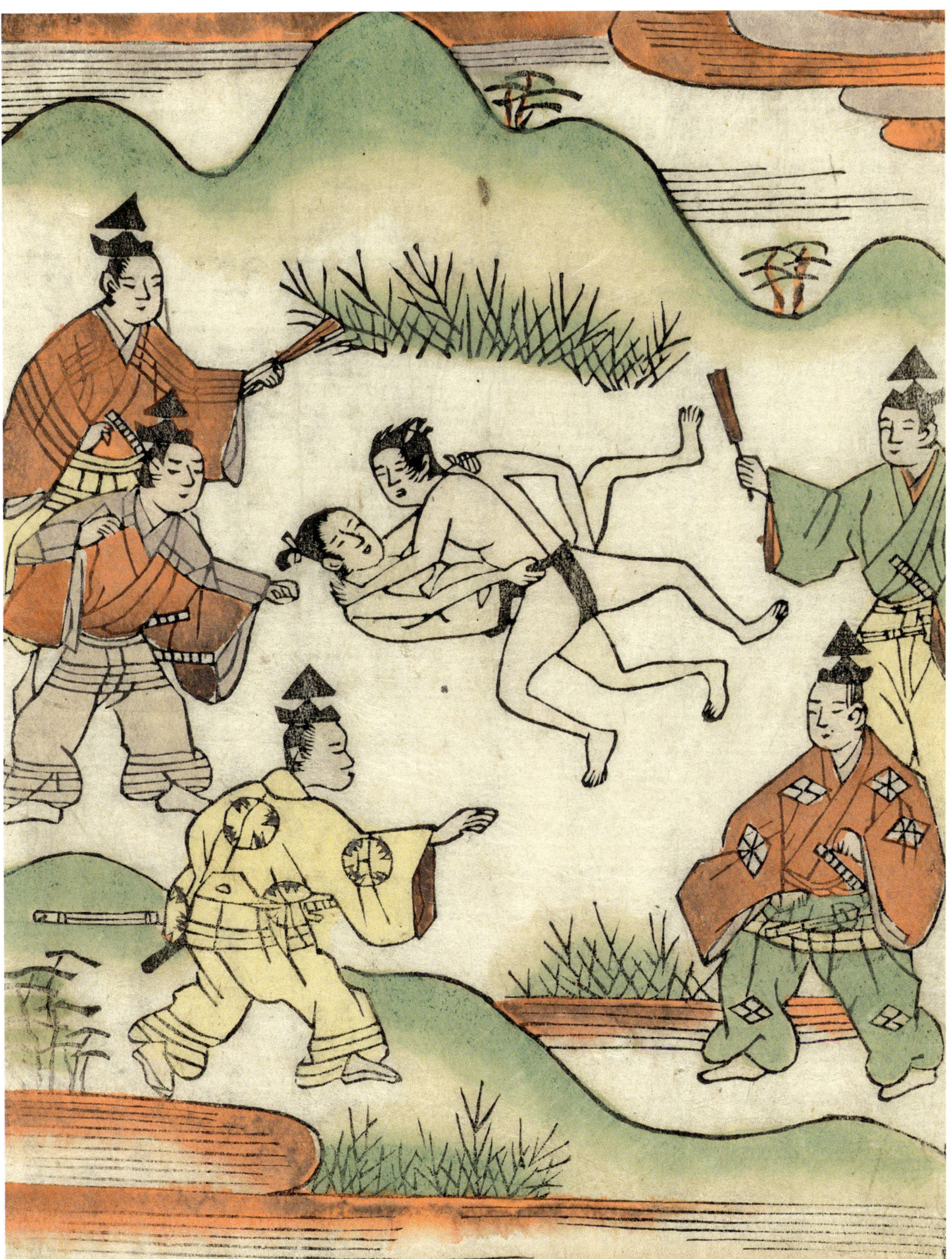

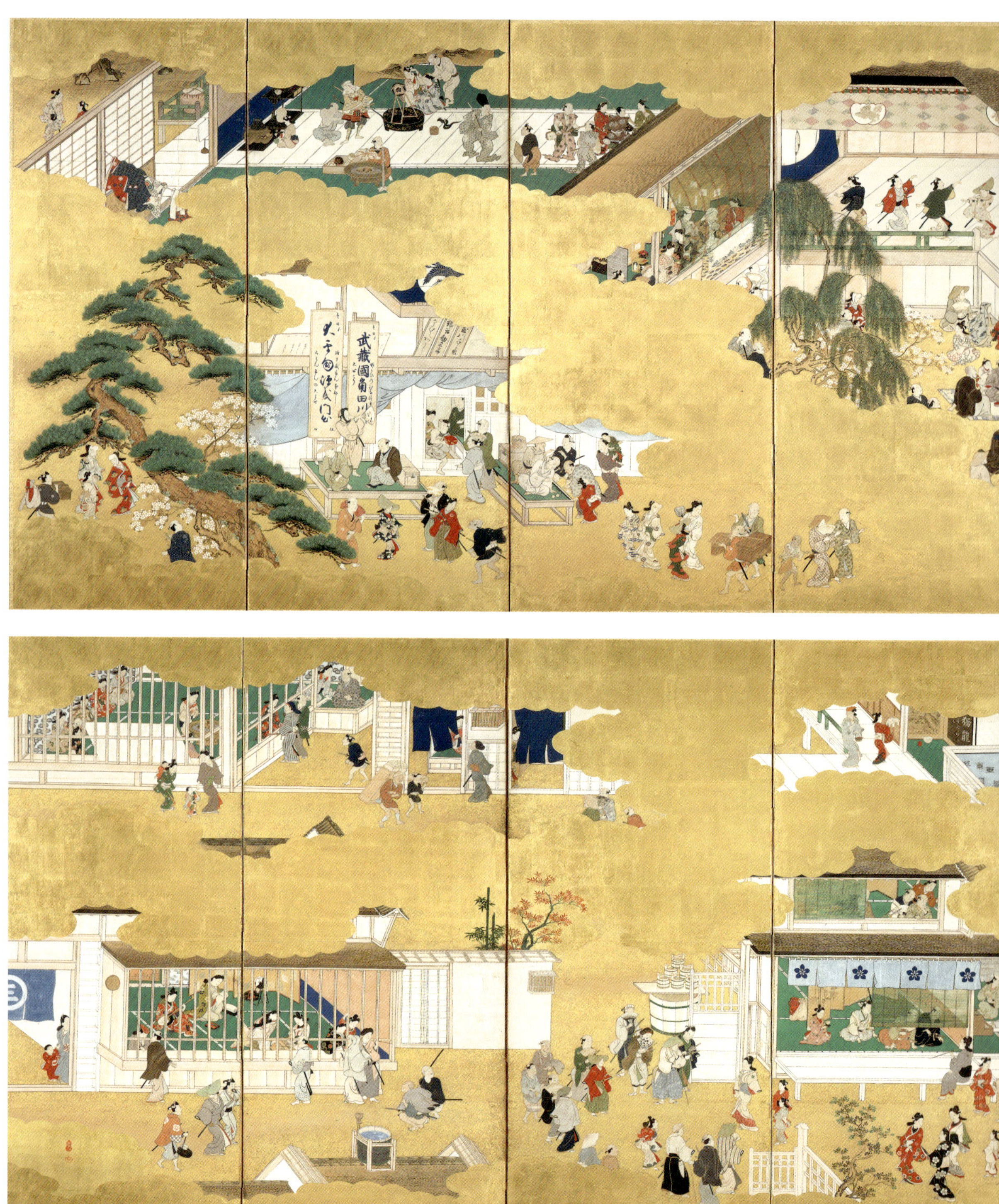
武蔵國角田川

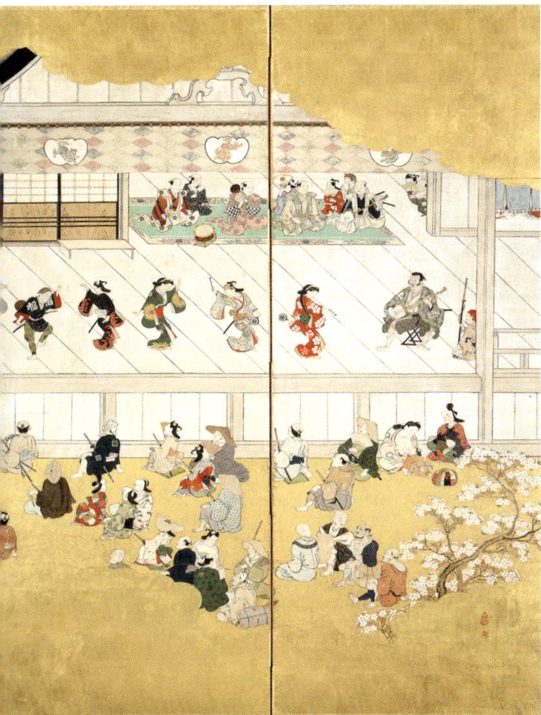

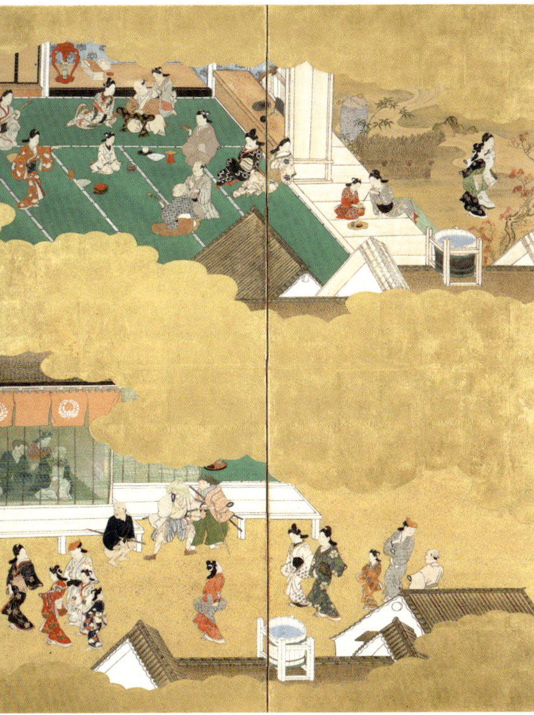

Scenes from the Nakamura Kabuki Theater and the Yoshiwara Pleasure Quarter
Hishikawa Moronobu (died 1694)
Edo period, about 1684–94

During the early seventeenth century, the Tokugawa shogunate established Edo (present-day Tokyo) as the seat of military and civil authority and decreed that warlords and their subordinates establish residences within the city. Attempting to exert control over the brothels that were emerging around this largely male-populated town, the government sanctioned the development of a pleasure district known as the Yoshiwara. An area was also designated for popular Kabuki theaters, where actors delivered stylized performances of high drama.

Hishikawa Moronobu was among the first artists to draw subject matter from this so-called *ukiyo* (floating world), creating paintings, book illustrations, and prints—known generically as *ukiyo-e* (pictures of the floating world)—that capture the fashionable preoccupations of urban trendsetters in the two *akusho* (bad places) of Edo. The right-hand screen of this pair is dominated by the Nakamura Theater, one of the four leading Kabuki stages in the city. In the lower left corner, Moronobu depicts the bustle of activity at the entrance, where a barker encourages passersby to attend the day's performances. At right is a wooden stage on which a procession of actors in male and female roles wends its way toward a samisen player.

The left screen is dominated by the main avenue of the Yoshiwara, where the highest-ranked courtesans promenade with their attendants on their way to houses of assignation in the early evening. Men gawk at these almost unattainable embodiments of feminine charm, while the inhabitants of lower-level brothels in the upper registers are displayed to those in search of sexual adventure.

Pair of six-panel folding screens; ink and color on gold-leafed paper
139.8 x 355.2 cm (55 1/16 x 139 13/16 in.) each
Gift of Oliver Peabody 79.468, 79.469

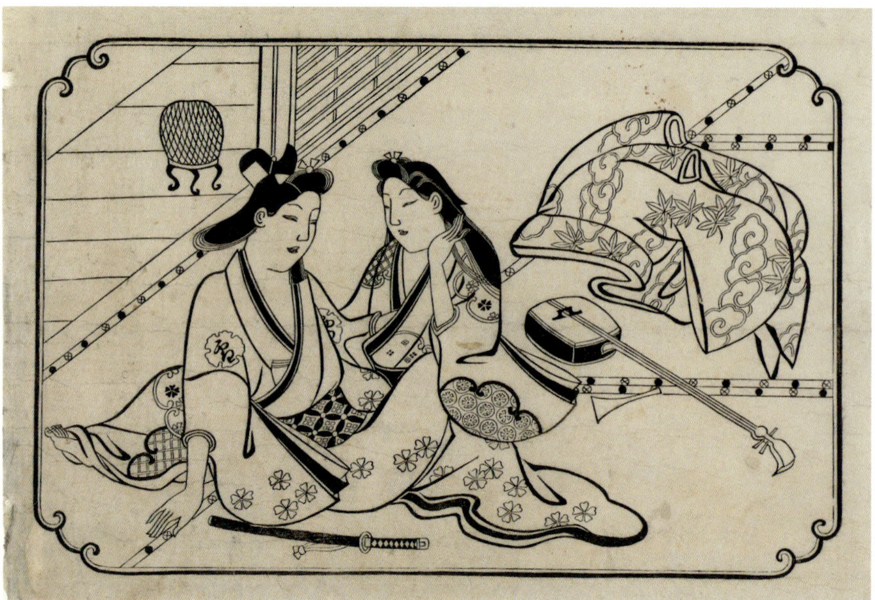

***A Young Man Dallying with a Courtesan*, from an untitled series of twelve erotic prints**
Attributed to Hishikawa Moronobu (died 1694)
Edo period, about 1680

About 1680, publishers of woodblock-printed illustrated books in the city of Edo began to produce single-sheet printed pictures as well. This new form of pictorial art became very popular with urban commoners as an affordable alternative to painting, launching a publishing boom that continued until the beginning of the twentieth century. Like paintings and book illustrations created by the same artists, early prints drew their subject matter primarily from the floating world of hedonistic big-city amusements such as the theater and the licensed brothels.

Moronobu's monochrome prints, celebrated for their "singing line," combine the techniques of woodblock illustration with the fashionable subject matter of genre painting, creating visual variety even without color by the deployment of skillfully modulated calligraphic lines. The brushstrokes of the preliminary drawings were translated into printed form through the skills of professional block cutters and printers, all under the supervision of the publisher.

Many early prints depicted amorous subject matter, as explicit erotica was not made illegal until the 1720s. Erotic prints were generally published in sets of twelve, with a unifying border design. It was customary for such a set to include several nonexplicit scenes such as this view of an elegantly dressed couple, probably a courtesan with the young son of a samurai or wealthy merchant family. Her samisen, his sword, and someone's outer robe have all been set aside as the lovers begin to concentrate their attention on each other.

Woodblock print (*sumizuri-e*); ink on paper
26 x 36.8 cm (10¼ x 14½ in.)
William S. and John T. Spaulding Collection 21.5813

Actor Tsutsui Kichijūrō in the Spear Dance

Attributed to Torii Kiyonobu I (1664–1729)

Edo period, 1704

The exuberant kinetic energy of the Kabuki theater during the Genroku era (1688–1704) was captured on paper by artists of the Torii school, who dominated the field of actor prints throughout the first half of the eighteenth century. This unsigned print is attributed to the founder of the school, Kiyonobu I, because it shows the powerful lines and dynamic composition typical of his work. The vertical format of hanging-scroll paintings has been adapted here to the print medium, creating a large-scale work that must have delighted theater fans.

The handsome young actor Tsutsui Kichijūrō came to Edo from Kyoto in 1704. At the Nakamura Theater's season-opening performance in the eleventh month of that year, he performed a dance with two spears to great acclaim. The spears depicted here are decorative, tipped with pompoms and ribbons rather than points, and the star wears a fashionable jacket with a pattern of cherry blossoms and horses in luxurious trappings. His personal crest is shown on the curtain overhead, and his name is written at far left. The inscription also notes that he has come from Kyoto, so the print probably represents his famous first performance after his arrival in Edo.

Many prints of this period were hand-colored with a palette featuring the bright orange pigment red lead (*tan*), and were therefore known as "red-lead pictures" (*tan-e*). This unusually elaborate example includes yellow and purple as well.

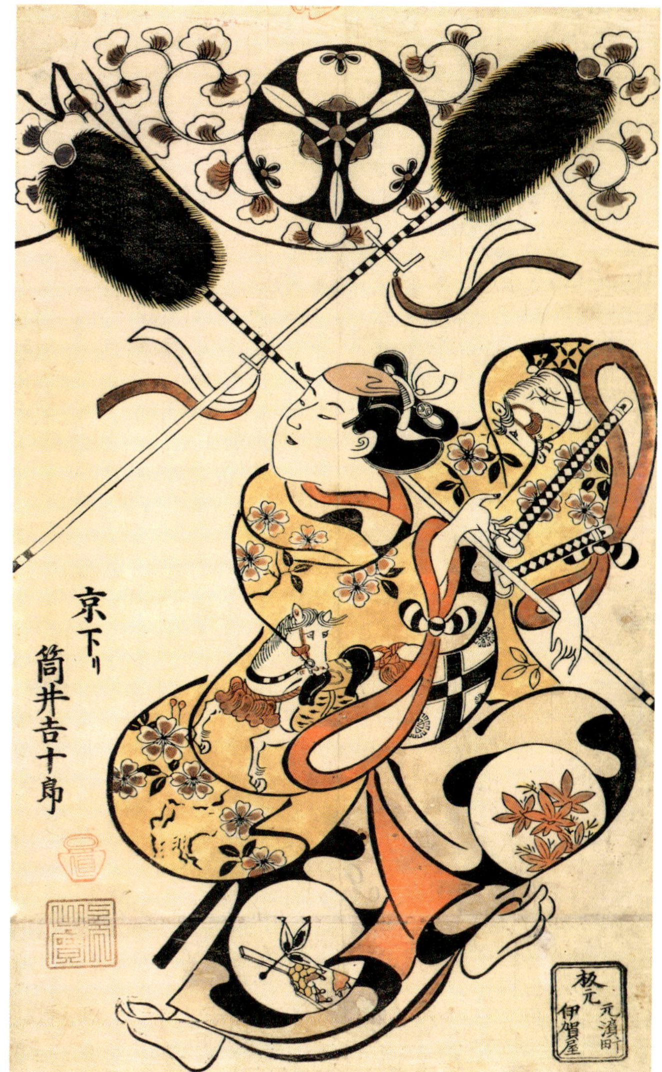

Woodblock print (*tan-e*); ink on paper, with hand-applied color

53.5 x 31.5 cm (21 1/16 x 12 3/8 in.)

William S. and John T. Spaulding Collection 21.5644

Actor Fujimura Handayū II as Ōiso no Tora

Torii Kiyomasu I (active about 1696–1716)

Edo period, 1715

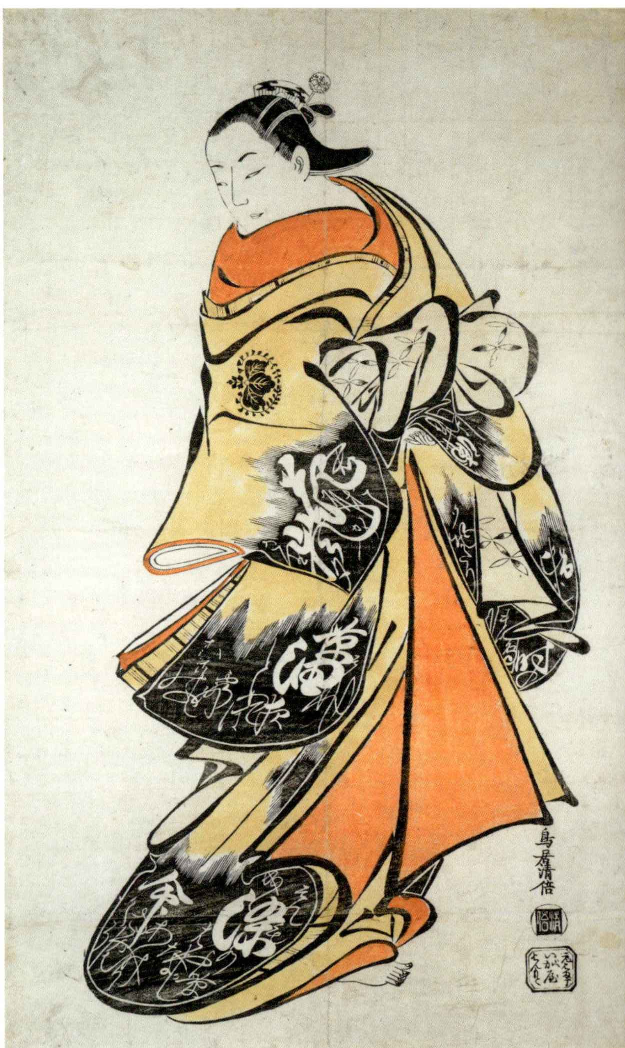

A beautiful courtesan casts a lingering glance over one shoulder, her hands coyly tucked inside her loosened robes. The lovely feminine figure is actually a male Kabuki actor, Fujimura Handayū II, who played women's roles on stage in accordance with laws dating from the early seventeenth century that banned women from acting in public. Handayū is identified by the personal crest that appears on the sleeve of his outer garment and his round hairpin. The role is most likely that of the courtesan Ōiso no Tora, the lover of legendary warrior Soga no Jūrō, which Handayū played on various occasions, including the New Year performance of 1715. With the cheerful anachronism typical of Kabuki, Handayū performs the twelfth-century courtesan as a modern beauty in a high-fashion costume: a kimono decorated with swirling calligraphic phrases from love letters in white against a black background, probably meant to represent resist-dyeing.

Large hand-colored prints of courtesans and Kabuki actors were popular during the first two decades of the eighteenth century. In this exceptionally well preserved example of the type known as "red-lead pictures" (*tan-e*), bright orange and yellow colors applied by hand contrast with the black-and-white patterns of the underlying woodblock print. The artist, Kiyomasu I, is thought to have been a son, younger brother, or pupil of Kiyonobu I, the founder of the Torii school. His style is similar to that of Kiyonobu but somewhat gentler in feeling, well suited to depictions of fashionable beauties.

Woodblock print (*tan-e*); ink on paper, with hand-applied color
52 x 31.7 cm (20½ x 12½ in.)
Special Fund 54.216

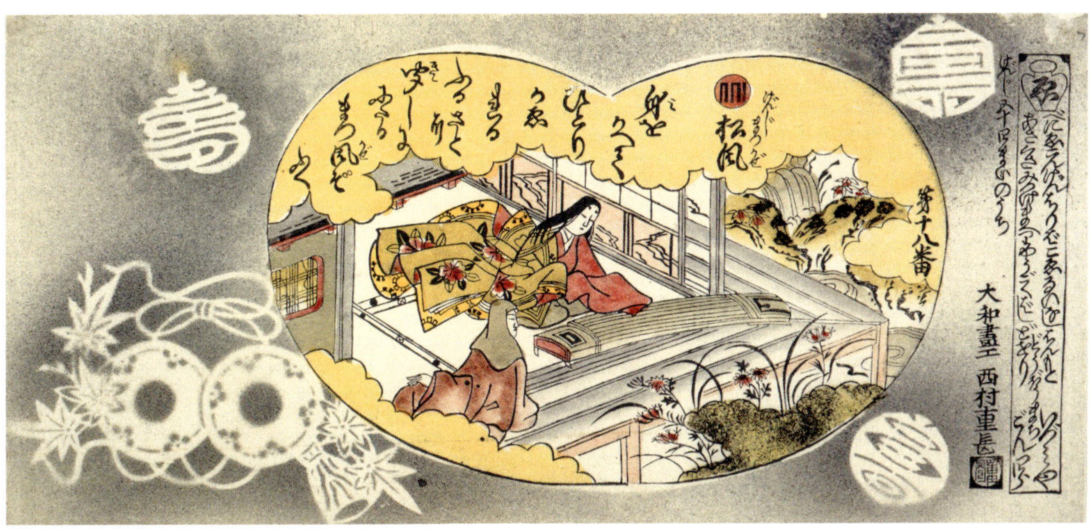

The Wind in the Pines, chapter 18 from the series _The Tale of Genji in Fifty-four Sheets_
Nishimura Shigenaga (about 1697–1756)
Edo period, about 1735

The thematic repertoire of *ukiyo-e* print artists included not only scenes of contemporary life but older pictorial traditions as well. This image comes from a lavishly hand-colored series of illustrations of the fifty-four chapters of *The Tale of Genji*, the eleventh-century novel of courtly life considered to be the greatest classic of Japanese literature. The series was codesigned by Nishimura Shigenaga, who executed the first half, and Torii Kiyonobu II, who completed the second. In chapter eighteen, one of Genji's consorts, a lady from the coastal area of Akashi, is staying with her mother at a villa on the outskirts of Kyoto. The two women exchange poems expressing nostalgia for the sound of the wind in the pines in their old home (hence the title of the chapter).

The finely detailed drawing style, scalloped clouds, and brilliant coloring all emulate painted Genji albums treasured by the upper classes. An inscription at the right explains that these prints may be used to decorate ladies' sewing boxes (inscriptions on other prints in the series suggest pasting them on screens and sliding-door panels as well), and claims that the publisher, Izumiya Gonshirō, is the originator of the hand-coloring method known as "red pictures" (*beni-e*). Used from the late 1710s to the mid-1740s, *beni-e* coloring employed a palette centering on safflower red (*beni*), often with special features such as the brass filings sprinkled here in imitation of the gold leaf that decorated paintings. This deluxe set, one of the finest known examples of *beni-e*, also includes color sprayed over stencil patterns to create an elegant background for each of the fan-shaped pictures.

Woodblock print (*beni-e*); ink on paper, with hand-applied and stenciled color and metallic filings
16.2 x 33.8 cm (6 3/8 x 13 5/16 in.)
William Sturgis Bigelow Collection 11.19132

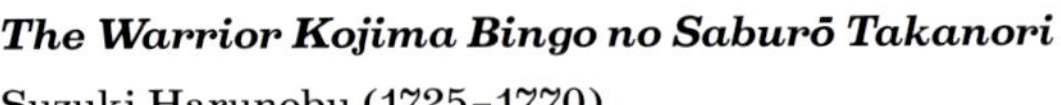

The Warrior Kojima Bingo no Saburō Takanori

Suzuki Harunobu (1725–1770)

Edo period, about 1762–64

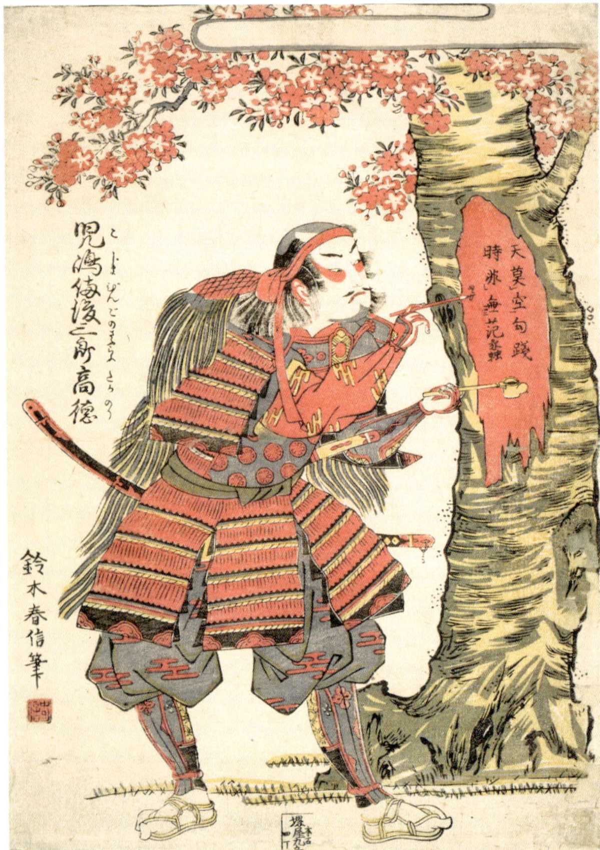

This print is one of the finest surviving examples of the early color printing process known as *benizuri-e* (literally "red-printed pictures"), which used two or three color blocks in addition to the black key block. Printers began using the technique for single-sheet commercial prints in the early 1740s, and by the end of that decade the process had almost completely supplanted earlier hand-coloring methods. It continued in use for some twenty years, until it was in turn superseded by full-color printing after 1765.

This fully developed example of *benizuri-e* uses three different colors—rose-red (*beni*), blue, and yellow—with blue and yellow overprinted to create a green tone in areas such as the tree trunk and the warrior's sash and straw raincoat. Harunobu's skillful deployment of this restricted color scheme to create a gorgeous effect suggests why he was the artist chosen, just a few years later, to design the first full-color prints.

Harunobu specialized in appealing scenes of contemporary life, but he was equally competent in the depiction of historical subjects such as this well-known episode from the civil wars of the fourteenth century, when Emperor Go-Daigo rebelled unsuccessfully against the military dictatorship of the shoguns. Takanori, a warrior loyal to Go-Daigo, secretly followed as the captured emperor was taken into exile. On a tree that he knew Go-Daigo and his jailers would pass, he wrote an encouraging poem in classical Chinese with historical allusions that only the emperor would understand.

Woodblock print (*benizuri-e*); ink and limited color on paper
39.3 x 27.6 cm (15½ x 10⅞ in.)
William Sturgis Bigelow Collection 11.19633

The Koto Player

Suzuki Harunobu (1725–1770)

Edo period, about 1767–68

Suzuki Harunobu was the first artist to design single-sheet prints in full color, using five or more color blocks in addition to the basic black outline block. The technology of polychrome printing had originated in China and was used on a limited scale in both China and Japan for deluxe art books, but it was not applied to large-scale production until 1765, when pictorial calendars designed by Harunobu were printed in color. They were an immediate success, and full-color woodblock printing continued to be used for commercial picture-making until the beginning of the twentieth century. Full-color prints became known as "brocade pictures of the East" (*Azuma nishiki-e*), in joking suggestion that these colorful products of the eastern city of Edo rivaled the renowned textiles of the western city of Kyoto.

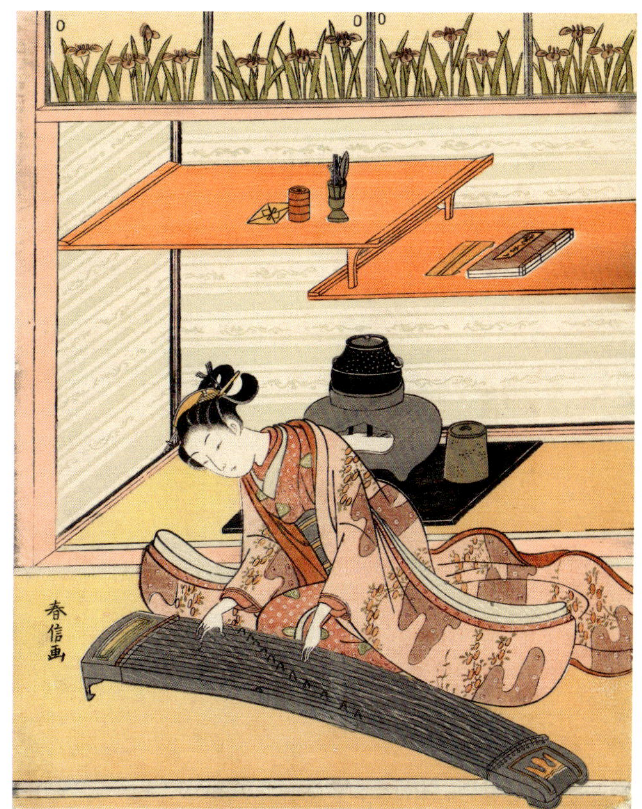

Harunobu is best known for his charming designs of delicate, childlike figures in elegant settings. Here, a young lady in a long-sleeved pink kimono plays the *koto* (zither) in a lavishly decorated room, where painted irises decorate the doors of overhead cabinets above a wallpapered alcove. The tea kettle heating on a brazier suggests that tea practice may be another of her accomplishments, while the books and equipment for an incense game displayed on the open shelves complete the picture of refined pastimes. Like most of Harunobu's full-color prints, this example is in a relatively small format, about the size of a modern sheet of letter paper. The modest size encourages a feeling of intimate connection with the subject, as if the viewer were in the same room as the *koto* player.

Woodblock print (*nishiki-e*); ink and color on paper
28.3 x 21 cm (11 1/8 x 8 1/4 in.)
William S. and John T. Spaulding Collection 21.4439

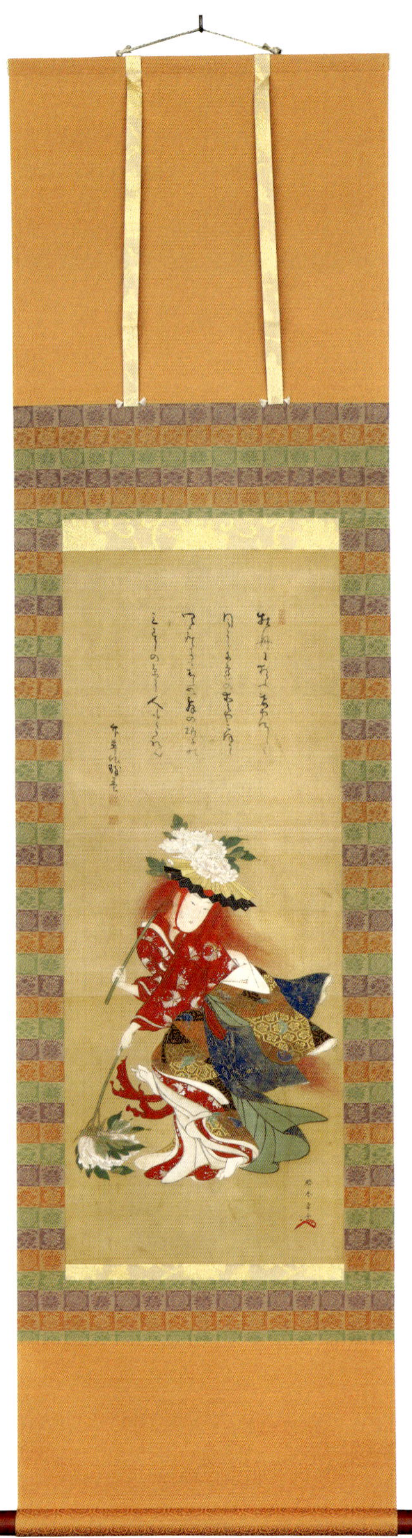

Shakkyō, the Lion Dance

Katsukawa Shunshō (1726–1792)

Edo period, about 1787–88

By 1780, when Katsukawa Shunshō had firmly established his reputation through his highly individualized woodblock portraits of Kabuki actors, the artist felt that he could now devote himself almost exclusively to paintings of beautiful women. Yet in this hanging scroll Shunshō returns to a theatrical theme. A feminine figure with delicate features wears a distinctive, unruly red wig and a peony-adorned headdress made of two layered folding fans. The large stems of peony blossoms held in the figure's hands sway to the movements of the lively dance. Intricate patterns of wheeling cranes and flitting butterflies on the layered robes further contribute to the sense of motion.

The headdress and floral props indicate that the dance is related to the Stone Bridge (*Shakkyō*) legend, in which the eleventh-century Japanese monk Jakushō made a pilgrimage to Mount Tiantai in southeastern China. There, at a celebrated narrow stone bridge, he had a vision of a lion (the mount of Monju, Bodhisattva of Wisdom) frolicking with a peony. This miraculous tale became the subject of a chant for the Nō theater and then of an agitated Kabuki dance, in which a princess is transformed by the spirit of the lion.

In 1787, about the time that Shunshō executed this scroll, the actor Iwai Hanshirō IV performed the Shakkyō dance. Whether the figure here is a depiction of Hanshirō, who was a celebrated *onnagata* (a male actor specializing in female roles), or a female entertainer performing the popular dance cannot be determined, but Shunshō has created an animated image of feminine allure.

Hanging scroll; ink, color, and gold on silk
82.5 x 32.5 cm (32½ x 12 13/16 in.)
William Sturgis Bigelow Collection 11.7762

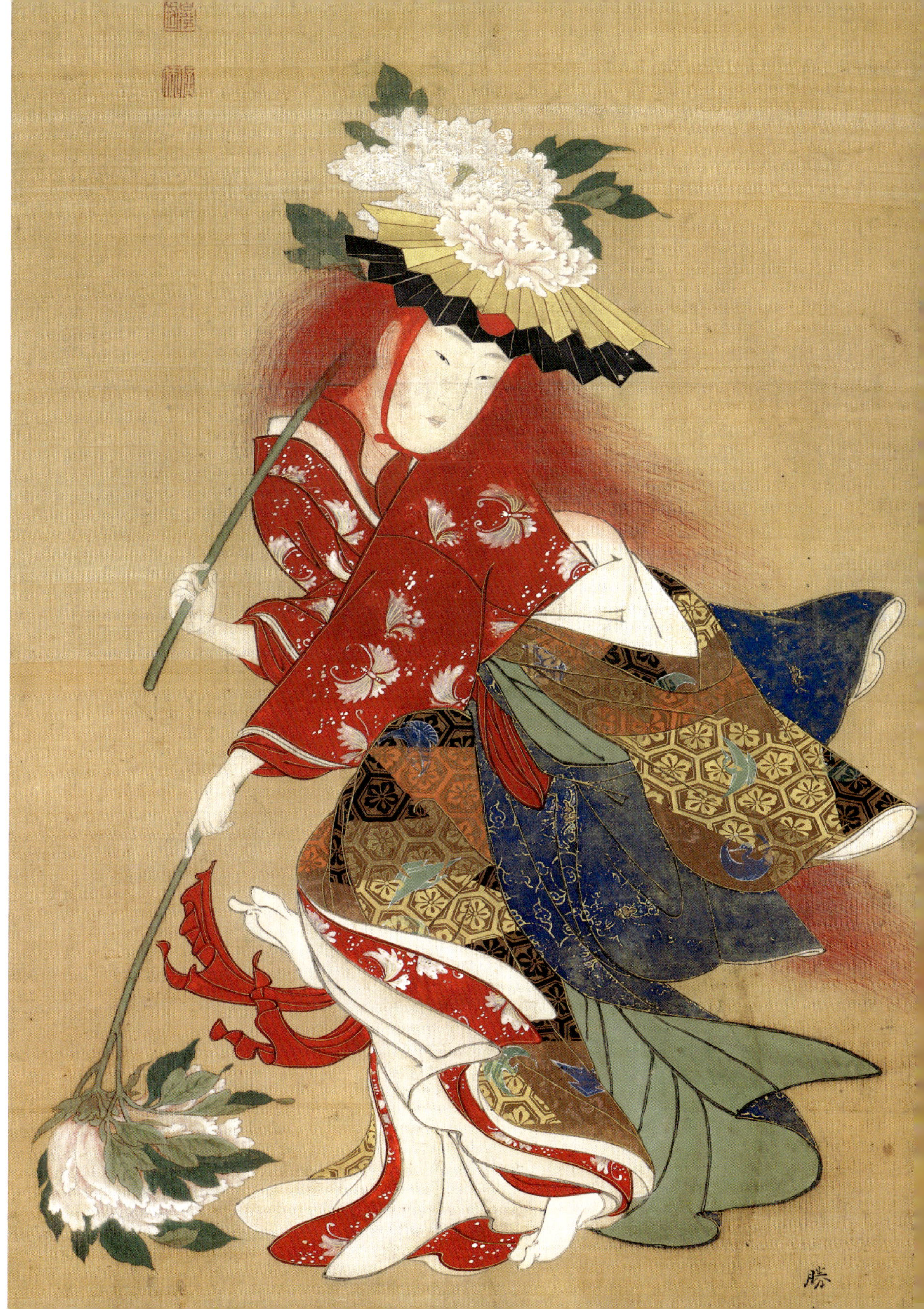
勝

A Pilgrimage to Enoshima

Torii Kiyonaga (1752–1815)

Edo period, about 1789

During the 1780s, Torii Kiyonaga was the leading designer of prints of beautiful women; he is still admired today for his superb draftsmanship and skillfully balanced compositions. He introduced a new, elongated type of figure (in contrast to the shorter women seen in the work of earlier artists), and to portray them, he used a larger sheet of paper, twice the size of the sheets most often used by his predecessor Harunobu. Kiyonaga often combined two or three separately printed sheets of paper to create even larger designs, such as this spectacular composition showing travelers on the seashore at Enoshima, a short journey from Edo.

The large island in the background was the location of an important shrine dedicated to the goddess Benzaiten, the ostensible reason for visiting the area. Pilgrims to the shrine could also enjoy the features that make Enoshima a popular summer resort even today: beautiful scenery, with a distant view of Mount Fuji, and an extensive white sand beach. Here, a high-ranking samurai lady who has arrived by palanquin, accompanied by several ladies-in-waiting and a handsome young man, pauses for a smoking break at an open-air teahouse on the beach. Her attendants adjust their traveling hats and sandals. The local boy standing next to the palanquin and gesturing toward the island is probably soliciting business for the porters seen beyond him in the distance; for a suitable fee, they would carry visitors on their shoulders through the shallow waves to the sacred island. Small children play in the surf at far left.

Woodblock print (*nishiki-e*); ink and color on paper
39.1 x 78.2 cm (15 3/8 x 30 13/16 in.)
William S. and John T. Spaulding Collection 21.7344–6

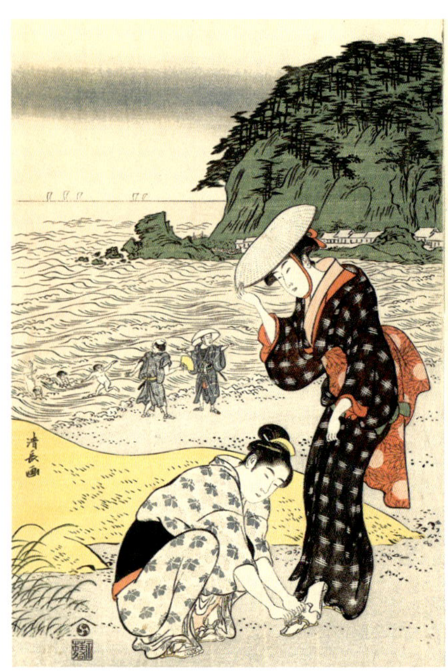

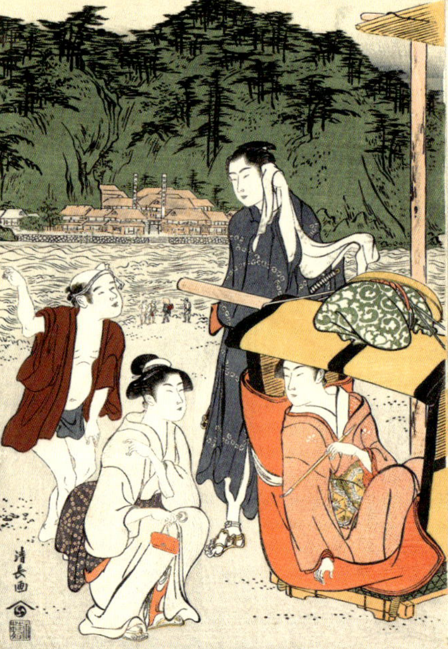

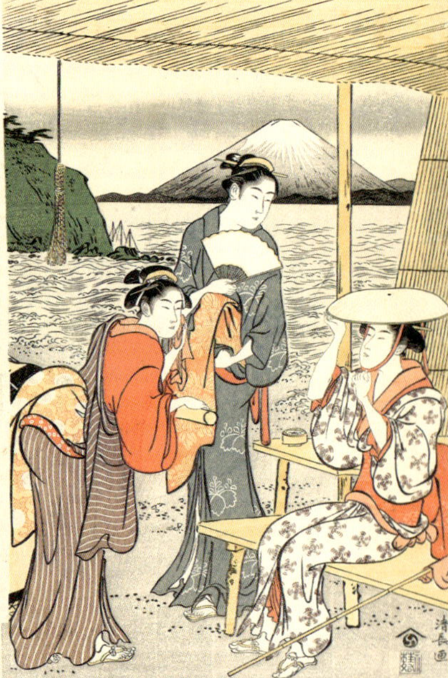

Gifts of the Ebb Tide (_Shiohi no tsuto_)

Kitagawa Utamaro (died 1806)

Edo period, 1789

A modestly sized volume of just ten pages encased by quietly dignified indigo covers, *Gifts of the Ebb Tide* is an utterly deceptive package overflowing with wit and delicate beauty. Opening the book, readers are presented with a cheerful scene of well-dressed people combing a beach for shells. On the next page, suddenly the distance between readers and beach has telescoped: the shells, superbly rendered on a sandy-textured background, are so close that we become beachcombers ourselves.

Six shells are illustrated in exquisite detail on each of six spreads, and above them are written six "mad verse" or comic poems (*kyōka*), one for each shell. These verses were composed by a poetry group, and the book is presented as being the private record of a beach outing. Luxury techniques—including blind printing (embossing) on fine-quality paper, and the application of mica to the shells to give them an authentic sheen—are used lavishly. Thanks to its charm and craftsmanship, the book was printed three times; this example is from the second printing.

Utamaro's accurate depictions make it possible to identify (from right to left) the plover shell, the board-roof shell, the abalone or ear shell, the reflection shell, the short-necked clam, and the washing shell. Each shell's name is given in the poem above, encouraging the reader to interact with both word and image. The last illustration shows a shell-matching game, and the book as whole can be viewed as a game-within-a-game in which readers participate as they read, rather than simply observing the visual forms. *Gifts of the Ebb Tide* reinvents the traditional fusion of poetry, painting, and calligraphy in a sophisticated articulation of the sparkling spirit of a new age.

Woodblock-printed illustrated book;
ink, color, and metallic pigments on paper
27.2 x 38.7 cm (10¾ x 15¼ in.)
Source unidentified 1997.953

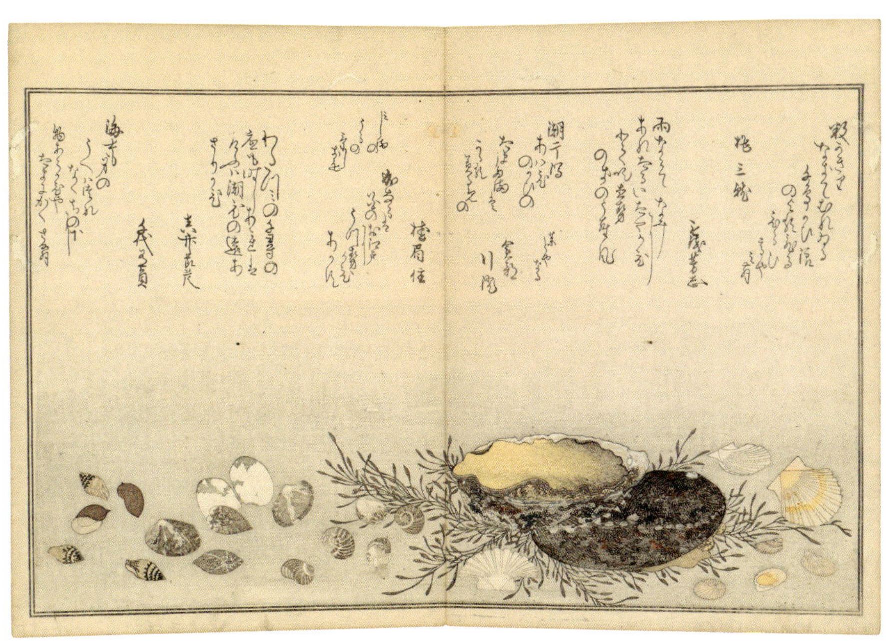

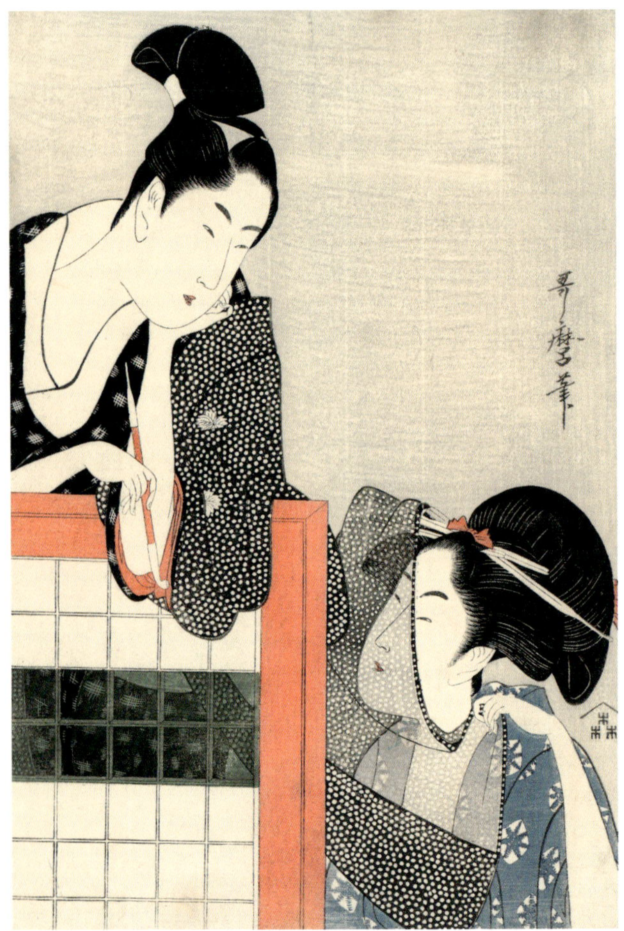

Couple with a Standing Screen

Kitagawa Utamaro (died 1806)

Edo period, about 1797

Kitagawa Utamaro's unique combination of elegance and sensuality made him the leading *ukiyo-e* artist of the 1790s, traditionally regarded by Western connoisseurs as the golden age of printmaking. In addition to fashionably elongated full-length figures, he designed many close-up bust portraits of beautiful women, as well as half-length compositions such as the charming young couple shown here.

Utamaro was fascinated by optical phenomena including reflection and translucency, and the extraordinary skill of the block cutters and printers who translated his designs into print form made it possible to convey these visual effects with uncanny clarity. In this remarkably well-preserved example, a young man in his late teens (his hairstyle indicating that he is not yet officially an adult) lounges against the wooden frame of a standing screen, resting his chin on his left hand and dangling a pipe in his right. A young woman, presumably his sweetheart, playfully peeps through the trailing edge of his black gauze summer jacket as it drapes over her hairpins. The motif of enticing glimpses seen through semitransparent materials is echoed by a green mesh panel set into the white paper surface of the screen, through which the young man's black garments are dimly visible.

When the brothers William and John Spaulding donated their world-renowned collection of Japanese prints to the Museum in 1921, they specified that the prints must never be displayed in the galleries, because their fragile colors fade rapidly when exposed to light. The visual impact of this unfaded print shows clearly why they made such an unusual requirement, and why the Museum agreed. The entire Spaulding collection is now accessible in digital form on the MFA's Web site, www.mfa.org.

Woodblock print (*nishiki-e*); ink and color on paper

38 x 25.1 cm (14 15/16 x 9 7/8 in.)

William S. and John T. Spaulding Collection 21.6610

Sunrise on New Year's Morning

Eishōsai Chōki (active about 1780–1810)

Edo period, late 1790s

Standing in a garden and looking out over the sea, a slender young woman watches the sun rise on the first morning of the year, pulling her loose clothing more tightly around her to ward off the morning chill. The potted adonis plant resting on the stone basin is a New Year decoration symbolizing long life and good fortune. The sky above has been printed with silver-colored mica (now partly worn away); a graded wash of dark blue printed over the mica suggests the dark sky of early morning, just beginning to lighten as the sun rises. The water, also shaded, echoes the dark-to-light coloring of the sky.

Eishōsai Chōki was a contemporary of Utamaro and may have studied under the same teacher. He produced a relatively small number of works, but among them are some of the most striking designs in all of *ukiyo-e*. His figures share the elongated proportions favored by other artists of the period but have an ethereal beauty all their own. This print is one of four remarkable designs showing half-length figures of women against mica backgrounds that may have been intended as a set representing the four seasons. In the lunar calendar used in premodern Japan, the year began slightly later than in the modern solar calendar, and so the New Year was considered to mark the beginning of spring.

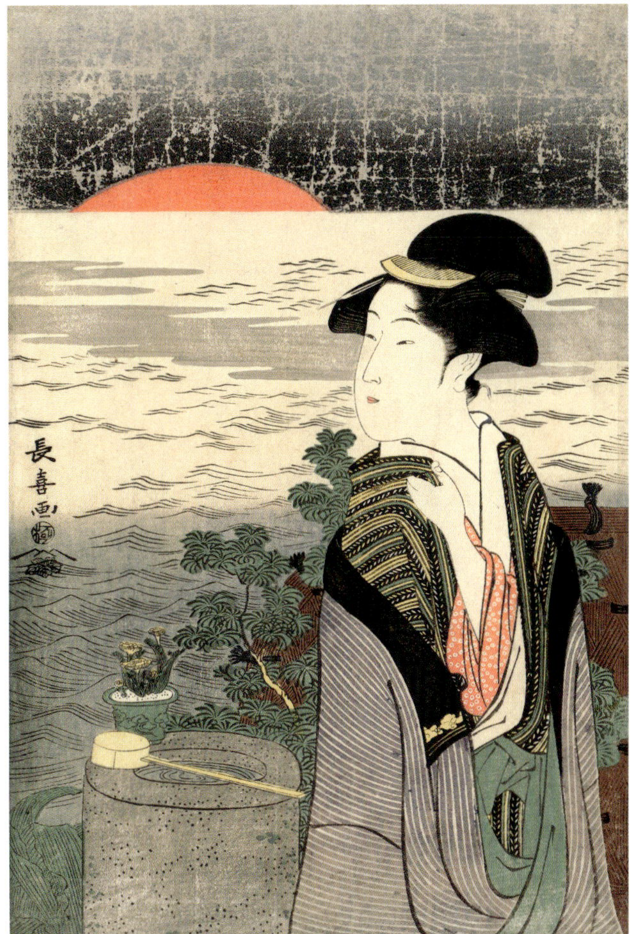

Woodblock print (*nishiki-e*); ink and color on paper
38.6 x 25.5 cm (15 3/16 x 10 1/16 in.)
William S. and John T. Spaulding Collection 21.4780

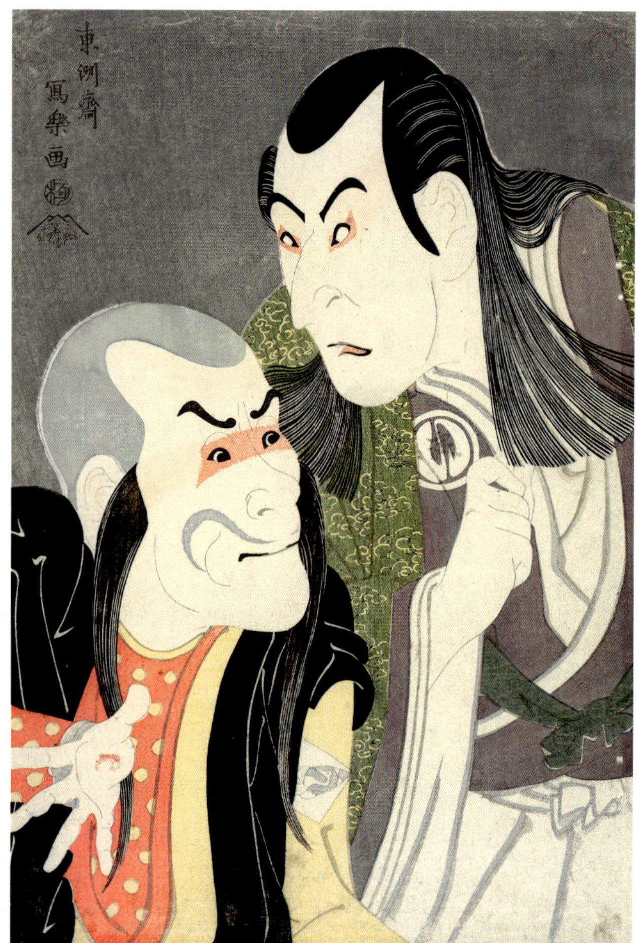

Actors Sawamura Yodogorō II as Kawatsura Hōgen and Bandō Zenji as Oni no Sadobō

Tōshūsai Sharaku (active 1794–1795)

Edo period, 1794

The enigmatic Tōshūsai Sharaku, known only by his pen name (meaning "Pleasure in Drawing"), is today the most highly admired of all Japanese print artists. Active for less than a year, from 1794 to the beginning of 1795, he designed about 150 known prints, almost all depicting Kabuki actors. The extreme, deliberately exaggerated, caricature-like style of his actor portraits generates an emotional intensity that still resonates with viewers more than two centuries later.

Most striking of all are his "big-head pictures" (*ōkubi-e*), close-up portraits often enhanced by glittering mica backgrounds. This double portrait juxtaposes good and evil characters from the same play, a technique used in several of Sharaku's prints. *The Thousand Cherry Trees of Yoshitsune*, one of the most popular plays in the Kabuki repertoire, is a highly fictionalized version of the life of the famous twelfth-century general Minamoto no Yoshitsune. In the scene depicted here, Yoshitsune and his followers have fled to the mountains of Yoshino (an area known for its scenic cherry trees), where they are sheltered from their enemies by Kawatsura Hōgen (shown at right). The scheming priest Sadobō (at left), whose long, catfish-style side-whiskers mark him as a disreputable character, plans to betray Yoshitsune in the hope of a reward. Kawatsura reacts with shock and disgust at such treachery. (Yoshitsune eventually escapes with the help of a magical fox.)

The actors are identifiable both by their faces and by the personal crests visible on their costumes, making it possible to pinpoint this production as that staged at the Kawarazaki Theater in the summer of 1794.

Woodblock print (*nishiki-e*); ink, color, and mica on paper
38.3 x 25.2 cm (15 1/16 x 9 15/16 in.)
William Sturgis Bigelow Collection 11.14676

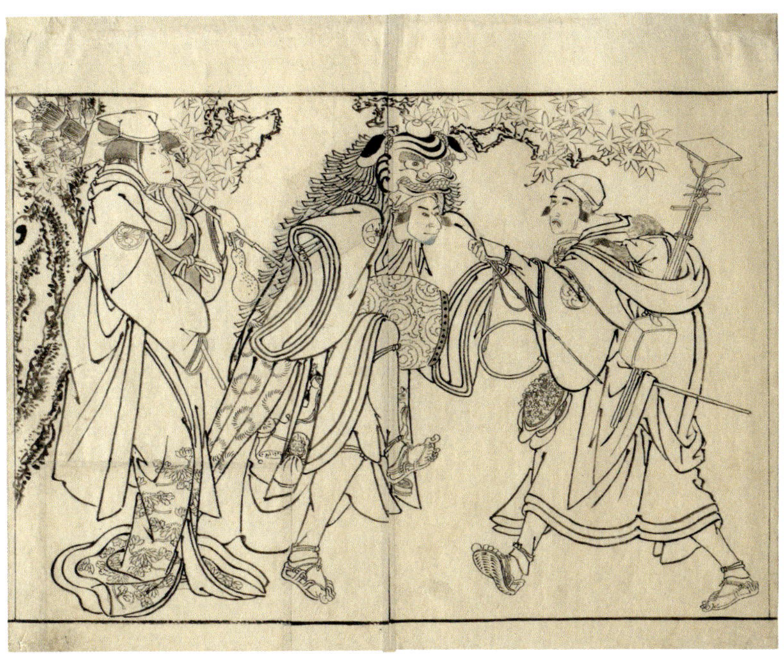

Actors Bandō Mitsugorō II, Ōtani Oniji III, and Segawa Kikunojō III

Tōshūsai Sharaku (active 1794–1795)

Edo period, about 1794–95

This unsigned drawing is one of a group of nine scattered in collections throughout the world; two are in the MFA, two in the Musée Guimet, one at the Art Institute of Chicago, and the rest in private hands. The Guimet drawings bear the signature of Sharaku, and the entire group shows his distinctive, exaggerated style. They were apparently intended as preliminary drawings for the illustrations of a printed picture book of actors that was never published.

This drawing for a two-page spread consists of two separate sheets of paper glued together. Outlines define the borders of the pages, including the central area (now trimmed and glued) where the pages would have been bound together in an actual book. The actors also appear in Sharaku's finished prints, but while the prints show scenes from specific plays, the drawings instead combine actors and roles freely to create a theatrical fantasia that would have appealed to sophisticated Kabuki fans.

Although Sharaku's true identity remains uncertain, there is some documentary evidence suggesting that he may have been an actor in the Nō theater, the formal masked drama of the samurai elite. The drawings illustrated here are from the last months of the artist's production, probably dating to the fall of 1794. It is tempting to speculate that he may have given up his career in *ukiyo-e* after less than a year—leaving projects such as this unfinished—because he was reprimanded by superiors who disapproved of his unseemly fondness for the boisterous Kabuki theater of the commoners.

Drawing for an unpublished book; ink on paper
26.2 x 31.4 cm (10 5/16 x 12 3/8 in.)
William S. and John T. Spaulding Collection 21.7256

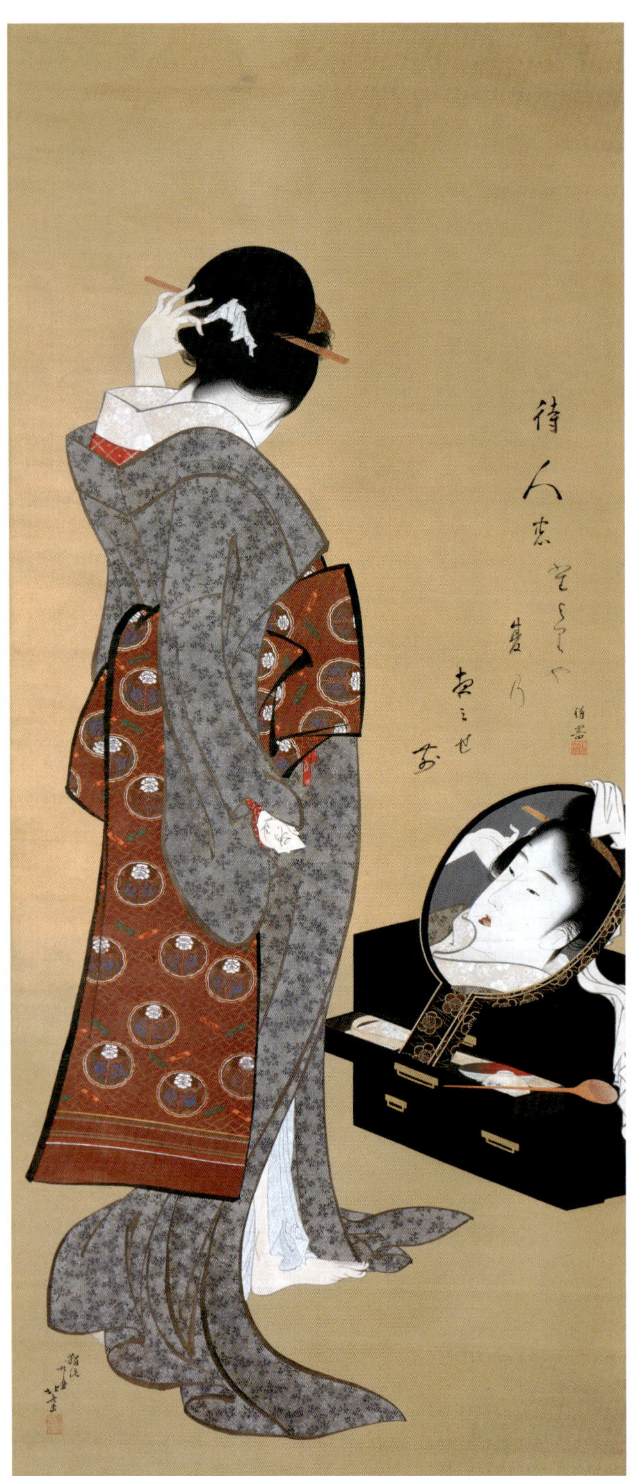

Woman Looking at Herself in a Mirror
Katsushika Hokusai (1760–1849)
Edo period, about 1805

Primarily known in the West for his series of landscape prints *Thirty-six Views of Mount Fuji,* Katsushika Hokusai was never content to create images of any one type. Throughout his career of more than seventy years, he explored extremely diverse styles and subject matter—from beautiful women to ghosts, from classical Chinese and Japanese poets to contemporary townspeople—in his paintings, prints, utilitarian objects, and illustrated books.

Frequently, Hokusai signaled his adoption of a new style by changing his artistic name or modifying his signature. The name Hokusai, by which he is commonly known today, was that of his studio (the "North Star Studio"). This exquisite hanging scroll includes a signature, "Painted by Kukushin Hokusai of the Independent Lineage," that the artist used for only a brief period about 1805 to declare his autonomy from his former teacher, Katsukawa Shunshō, and the Katsukawa school.

The seductive pose of a woman seen from the back as she adjusts her coiffure and gazes into a mirror had already been made popular by Shunshō and other late-eighteenth-century artists. Hokusai, however, imbues the figure with a new monumentality, emphasized by the S-curve of the robes, the calligraphic lines of the heavy, figured twill sash, and the gradations of gray that add volume to the folds. In contrast, subtle details such as the plum-blossom pattern in mica on the collar and the landscape in blue on the overturned bowl in the lacquer chest lend the image a pervasive sense of intimacy.

Hanging scroll; ink, color, gold, and mica on silk
138.7 x 57.5 cm (54 5/8 x 22 5/8 in.)
William Sturgis Bigelow Collection 11.7424

Fine Wind, Clear Weather, also known as "Red Fuji," from the series _Thirty-six Views of Mount Fuji_

Katsushika Hokusai (1760–1849)

Edo period, about 1830–31

Hokusai was about seventy years old and had already enjoyed a highly successful career when he created his most famous work, the series of landscape prints entitled *Thirty-six Views of Mount Fuji* (which actually includes ten extra designs, for a total of forty-six). The extraordinary success of the series made landscape one of the major themes of print designers, and for the next two decades Hokusai and the younger artist Utagawa Hiroshige vied with each other in designing views of spectacular scenic spots throughout Japan.

Thirty-six Views of Mount Fuji presents the mountain from many different angles and distances, at various seasons and times of day. The print nicknamed "Red Fuji," one of the most stunning designs in the series, shows the great mountain on a clear morning in summer or early fall, when the slope is colored red by the light of the rising sun. In the earliest impressions of the series (including this example), the outlines of the forms are printed not in the usual black but in the same deep blue used in a shaded wash (*bokashi*) to print the sky. This pigment, known as "Prussian blue" in Europe and "Berlin blue" in Japan, was a synthetic color imported from Europe that was first used in prints about 1828. The availability of this beautiful color, which was not only suitable for depicting water and sky but also did not fade as quickly as earlier vegetable-based blue dyes, may have helped inspire Hokusai to create this landmark series.

Woodblock print (*nishiki-e*); ink and color on paper
24.4 x 38.1 cm (9⅝ x 15 in.)
William S. and John T. Spaulding Collection 21.6756

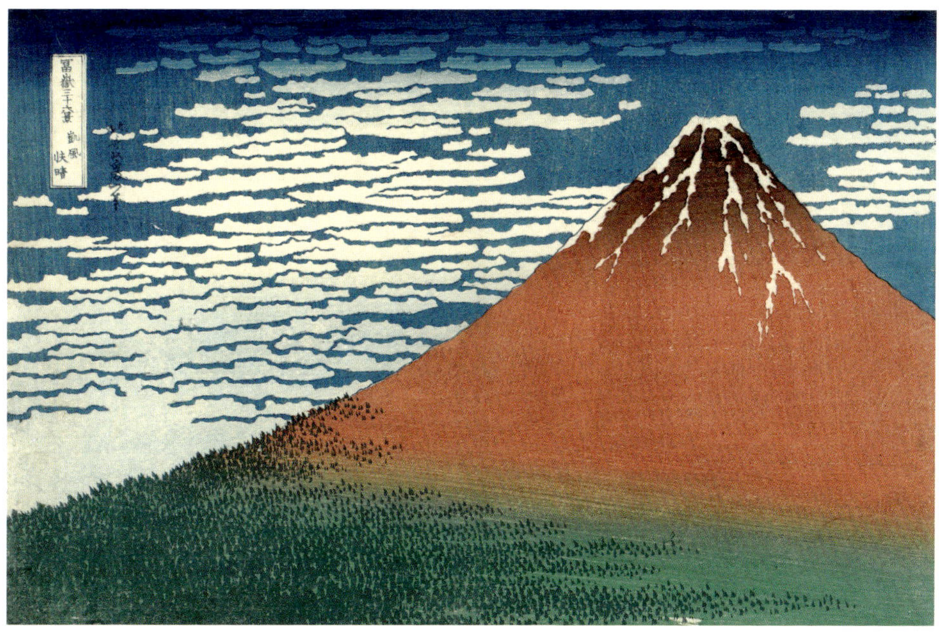

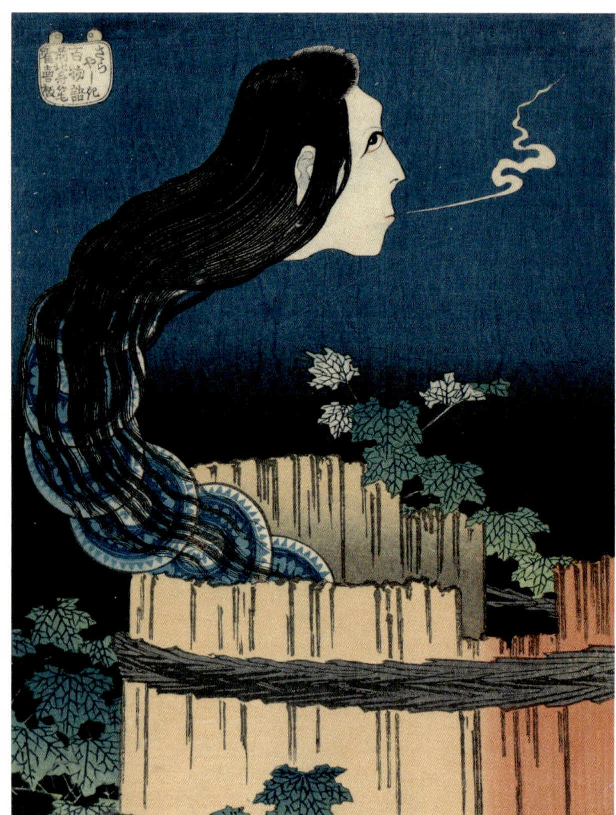

The Mansion of the Plates, from the series _One Hundred Ghost Stories_
Katsushika Hokusai (1760–1849)
Edo period, about 1831–32

The versatile Hokusai excelled not only at landscapes and figures but also at vividly imagined scenes of the fantastic, as in this series of five prints illustrating well-known ghost stories. The Mansion of the Plates was said to be haunted by the ghost of the unfortunate maidservant Okiku, who broke one of ten precious blue-and-white porcelain plates that were a family heirloom. She was murdered by the enraged master of the house, and her body was thrown into the well. In some theatrical versions of the story, the wicked master breaks or steals the plate himself and falsely accuses the innocent young woman in order to blackmail her into becoming his mistress, finally killing her when she refuses.

Night after night, the ghost rises from the well and counts the plates, wailing over the missing one that had caused her untimely death. Hokusai envisioned the dead woman not as a conventional ghost but as a spirit made up of the plates themselves, with ectoplasmic breath emerging from her lips as she begins her eerie count. He used the imported synthetic pigment Prussian blue in the decoration of the plates, the ghost's pallid complexion, and the eerie night sky in the garden.

Woodblock print (*nishiki-e*); ink and color on paper
23.7 x 17.6 cm (9 5/16 x 6 15/16 in.)
William S. and John T. Spaulding Collection 21.10236

Three Women Playing Musical Instruments

Katsushika Ōi (active about 1818–after 1854)

Edo period, about 1818–44

Gathered in a tight circle, three women perform in a traditional musical trio known as *sankyoku*. Although their individual identities are not made explicit, their positions in Edo society are clearly indicated by their robes and coiffures. Dressed in plaid layered over tie-dyed underrobes, a townswoman draws a bow across a *kokyū*, a folk instrument that became popular in Edo during the mid-eighteenth century. To the right, a geisha, wearing a somber plum-gray robe figured with plum blossoms, strums a three-stringed samisen with an ivory plectrum. In the center, with her back to the viewer, a young courtesan with elaborate dangling hairpins and a shorn neck artfully plucks at the zitherlike *koto*. Perhaps in a subtle commentary on the short-lived future of this young woman, her black long-sleeved robe is ornamented with butterflies flitting across dew-covered grasses, while her red underrobe is decorated with butterflies drawn to spider webs.

Always at her father Hokusai's beck and call, Katsushika Ōi took the name by which we know her today from the somewhat vulgar expression "come here" (*ōi*). Hokusai, however, greatly admired her talents and declared that when it came to paintings of beauties, he could not compare with her. As seen in the women's voluminous robes in this scroll, Ōi was particularly gifted at suggesting the illusion of depth by combining layers of thick mineral colors with thinner, almost translucent applications of vegetable pigments.

Hanging scroll; ink and color on silk
46.7 x 67.4 cm (18 5/16 x 26 9/16 in.)
William Sturgis Bigelow Collection 11.7689

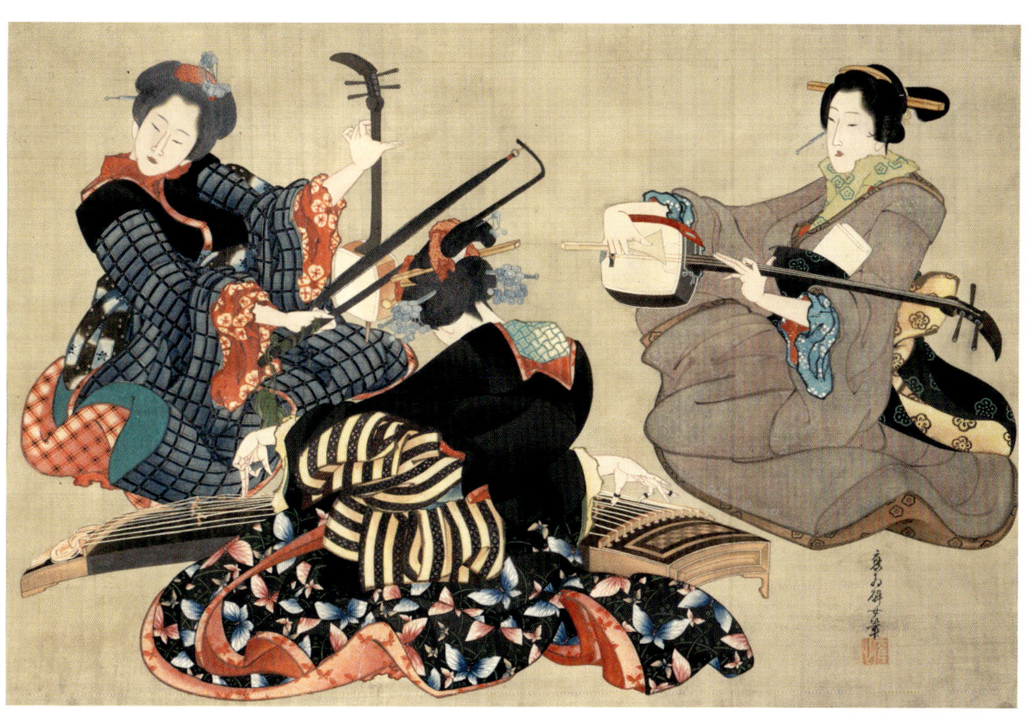

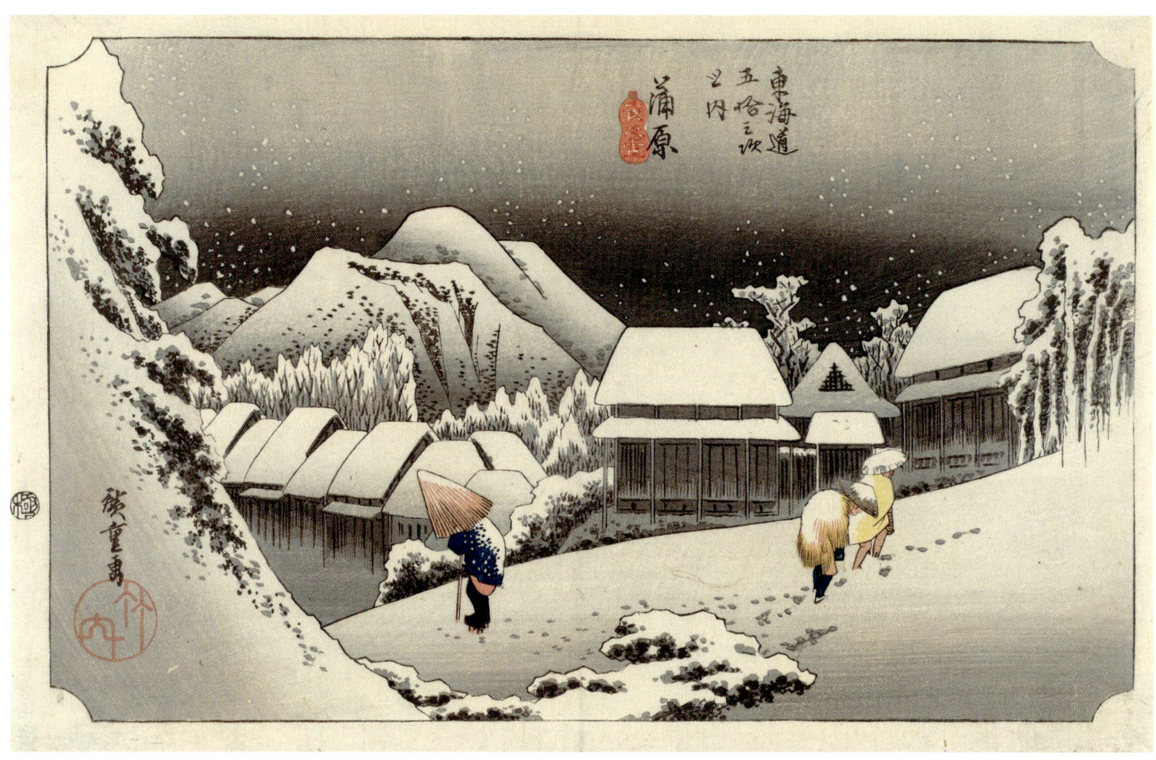

Night Snow at Kanbara, second state, from the series _Fifty-three Stations of the Tōkaidō_
Utagawa Hiroshige I (1797–1858)
Edo period, about 1833–34

The Tōkaidō, or Eastern Sea Road, ran between Japan's two main urban areas: Edo (present-day Tokyo), the administrative capital of the shogunate; and Kyoto, the ancient capital of the figurehead emperor (with nearby Osaka rivaling Edo as a commercial center). Today, high-speed trains make the trip in less than three hours, but during the Edo period, travelers walked the road for ten days to a month. Along the way, fifty-three towns were designated by the government as official rest stops, and were required to provide inns and other services. The artist Hiroshige made the trip himself in 1832, and over the next two years published his most famous set of prints, the *Fifty-three Stations of the Tōkaidō*. The series was an enormous success, selling thousands of each design, and established Hiroshige as the equal of Hokusai in the field of landscape prints.

Hiroshige traveled in the summer, but he used his imagination to show the post towns at all seasons of the year, including winter. In the very earliest impressions of this renowned snow scene, the dark shading of the sky is at the top; but someone—either the printer, the publisher, or Hiroshige himself—decided that shifting the dark area to the bottom of the sky would more effectively convey the chill of a winter evening. In addition, small lines were removed from the knee of the figure at far right. This print is one of the rare cases in which connoisseurs generally prefer the slightly later version to the original one.

Woodblock print (*nishiki-e*); ink and color on paper
24.6 x 37.5 cm (9 11/16 x 14 3/4 in.)
William S. and John T. Spaulding Collection 21.5032

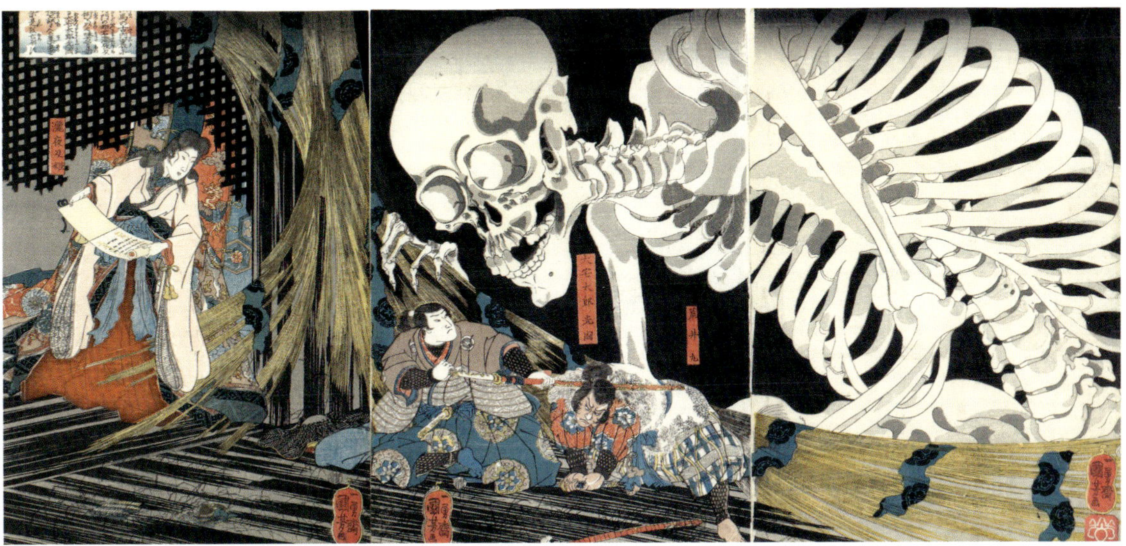

Masakado's Daughter Takiyasha Using Sorcery in the Ruined Palace at Sōma
Utagawa Kuniyoshi (1797–1861)
Edo period, 1843–47

The seductive sorceress Takiyasha (at left) reads spells from a magic scroll, summoning a monster in the form of a gigantic skeleton to attack the brave young samurai Mitsukuni (center). The fictional daughter of the historical tenth-century rebel Taira no Masakado, Takiyasha was the anti-heroine of a fantasy novel first published in 1806. In the novel, she and her brother study sorcery in order to avenge their father and carry on his rebellion. The headquarters of their supernatural conspiracy is the haunted ruin of the old palace at Sōma, with its broken lattices and bedraggled bamboo blinds.

Lengthy illustrated tales of fantastic adventures became extremely popular in nineteenth-century Japan. Successful books were dramatized as Kabuki plays and depicted in full-color woodblock prints. Utagawa Kuniyoshi, who had established warrior prints as a genre in the late 1820s, was the top artist in the field, and this print is considered one of his masterpieces. The precise, detailed drawing of the skeleton, and the use of chiaroscuro to give it three-dimensional form, suggest that Kuniyoshi was inspired by a European prototype. Although Japan was still largely closed to the outside world at this time, it was possible to obtain imported Western prints and illustrated books, and Kuniyoshi is known to have made a personal collection of these exotic images.

The text at the upper left states that this image is based on the novel, but in fact it was probably intended to suggest a recent stage production. As a result of reform edicts enacted in 1842, prints of Kabuki actors temporarily became illegal. Artists continued to depict scenes from plays, but pretended that they were illustrating history or fiction rather than drama.

Woodblock print (*nishiki-e*); ink and color on paper
36.2 x 74.1 cm (14 1/4 x 29 3/16 in.)
William Sturgis Bigelow Collection 11.30468–70

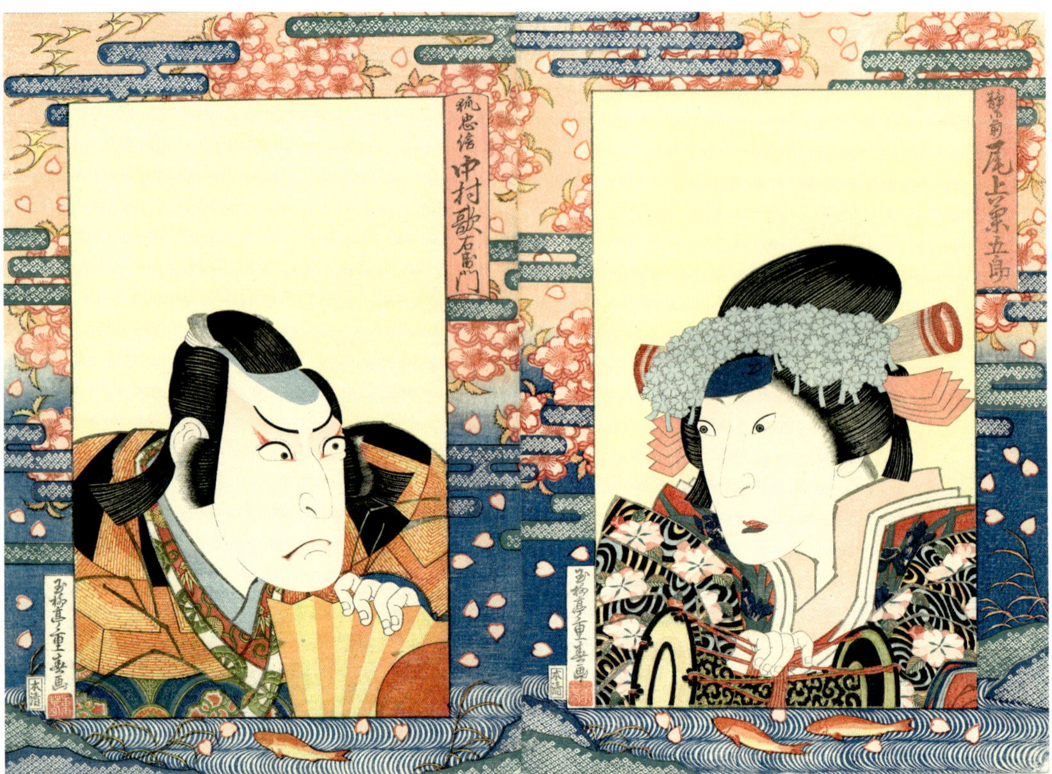

***Actors Onoe Kikugorō III as Shizuka Gozen* (right) *and Nakamura Utaemon III as the Fox Tadanobu* (left)**

Ryūsai Shigeharu (1803–1853)

Edo period, 1830

When color woodblock prints were first produced, they were considered a local specialty of the city of Edo; but from the 1790s on, a print-publishing industry developed in Osaka as well. Most Osaka prints depicted theatrical subjects. They were distinguished by the extremely high technical quality of the printing, which featured a wide range of brilliant colors as well as special features such as metallic pigments, and by an exaggerated drawing style—reminiscent of the work of Tōshūsai Sharaku—that captured the emotional intensity of theatrical performance.

An important subplot of the hit play *The Thousand Cherry Trees of Yoshitsune* features the beautiful dancer Shizuka, the lover of the general Minamoto no Yoshitsune. Shizuka (at right) holds a hand drum that she plays as she dances. A magical fox has taken the form of Yoshitsune's retainer Tadanobu (at left) in order to recover the drum, because it was made from the skins of the fox's parents. When kind-hearted Shizuka hears the story, she gives the drum to the fox, and he dances for joy. Later he uses his magic to help Shizuka and Yoshitsune escape from their enemies.

This close-up double portrait of two top actors is further enhanced by a trompe l'oeil border that mimics the dyed-textile mountings traditionally used to "frame" hanging-scroll paintings.

Woodblock print (*nishiki-e*); ink and color on paper
37.4 x 25.4 cm (14¾ x 10 in.) each
William Sturgis Bigelow Collection 11.36220a–b

Kosode

Edo period, first half of the 18th century

The term *kosode* literally means "small sleeves" and generally refers to garments with narrow sleeve openings. Like the T-shirt in the West, the *kosode* began life as an undergarment and was worn as a plain inner layer by Heian-period aristocrats. By the Muromachi period it had evolved into an outer garment for all classes, and during the seventeenth century it became a focus for the lively, exuberant taste of the merchant population in big cities like Kyoto, Osaka, and Edo. The showy, avant-garde fashions that resulted from this popular demand reached their peak during the Kanbun era (1661–1673), but the shogunal government regularly cracked down on such extravagance by issuing edicts specifying what fabrics, colors, and decorative techniques the townsmen could wear. Although these regulations were regularly flouted, *kosode* never again reached quite the same flamboyant heights after the banning of some particularly ostentatious and expensive techniques in 1683.

A number of Kanbun-era *kosode* have survived, and we also know from fashion books and paintings that they were characterized by large patterns that began at the back of one shoulder and swept in a dynamic arc to the opposite hem, using the entire garment as a canvas. Typical designs include traditional bird-and-flower motifs, objects from daily life, and even visual puns and puzzles. This *kosode* postdates the dazzling Kanbun era, but we can still see the arc-shaped sweep of the large-scale design, from the flower basket on top of the bamboo fence at upper right through the cascades of peonies to the lower left. The peonies have been stencil-dyed in blue and brown in imitation of the extremely labor-intensive (and therefore costly) minuscule tie-dyeing technique known as *kanoko shibori* (literally "fawn-spot dyeing"), one of the victims of the 1683 edict.

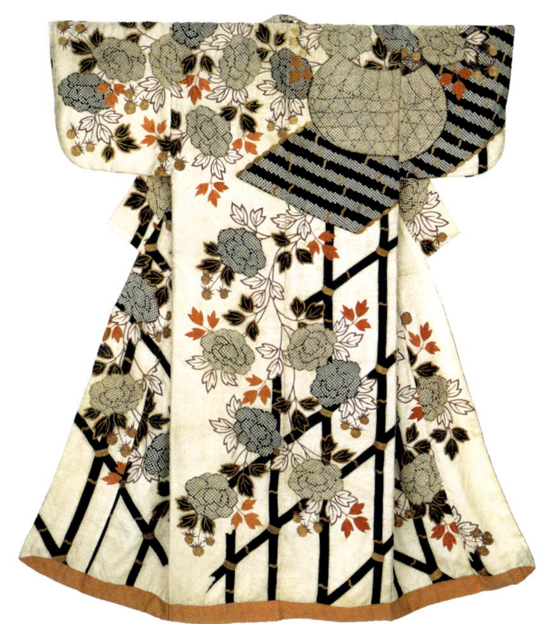

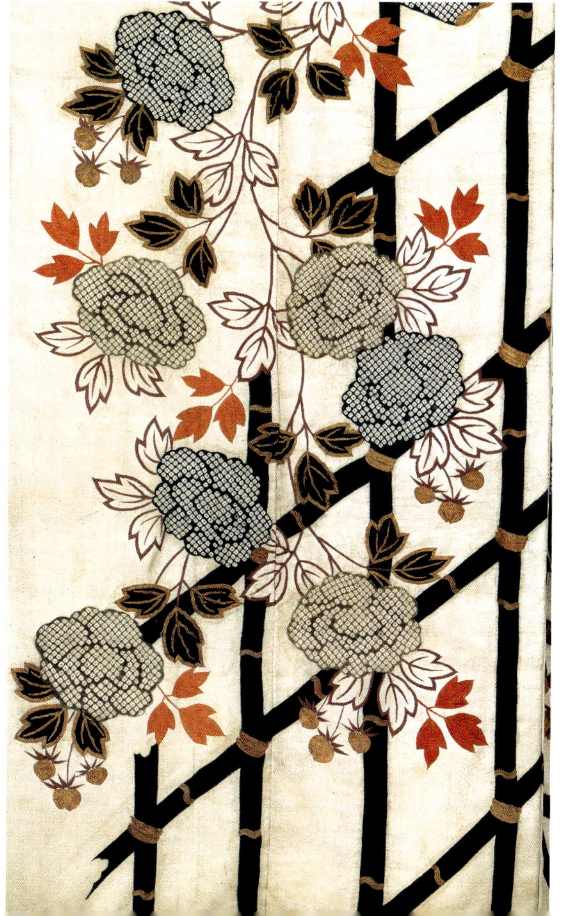

Self-patterned silk satin with resist- and stencil-dyeing, painting, and embroidery
162.6 x 124.5 cm (64 x 49 in.)
William Sturgis Bigelow Collection 11.3848

Medicine case (*inrō*) with design of pines, masts, and plovers, shown with bead (*ojime*) and toggle (*netsuke*)

Tsuchida Sōetsu (1660–1745)

Edo period, late 17th–early 18th century

Lacquered wood or paper with applied gold, lead, and shell; the bead (*ojime*): lacquered wood; the toggle (*netsuke*): carved and stained boxwood

9.5 x 4.7 x 3 cm (3¾ x 1⅞ x 1 3/16 in.)

William Sturgis Bigelow Collection 27.75a–c

Medicine case (*inrō*) with wave and rock design

Gotō Denjō (died 1712) and Masanori (dates unknown)

Edo period, late 17th–early 18th century

Lacquered wood or paper with applied silver, gold, and shell; silk cord

6.4 x 5.3 x 2.6 cm (2½ x 2 1/16 x 1 in.)

William Sturgis Bigelow Collection 11.9898

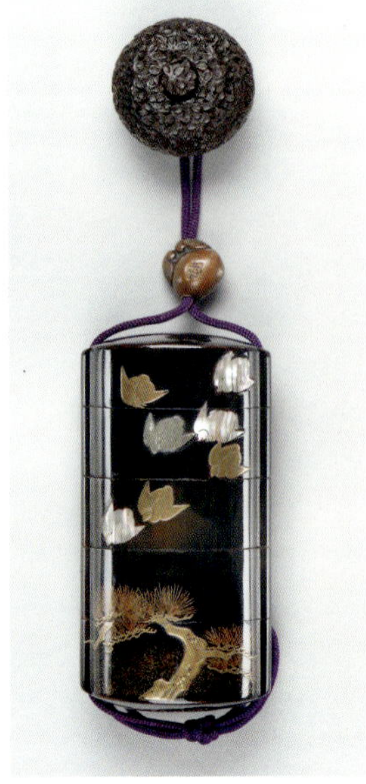

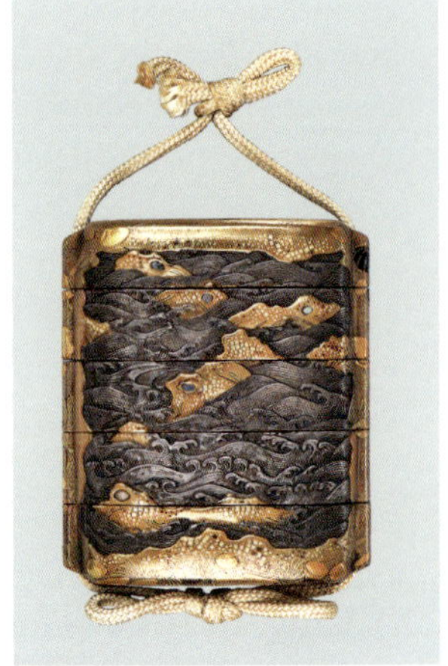

The miniature containers illustrated on these two pages are made up of interlocking lacquered compartments that were used to hold a selection of patent preparations with fancy names, such as Life-Prolonging Medicine (*Enreitan*) and Restorative Aromatic Compound (*Sogōkō*). In these photographs, the *inrō* are shown closed, but the horizontal lines visible on their sides are in fact divisions between the various sections. When these were pulled apart for use, the silk hanging cord kept them from getting lost or being put back in the wrong order. *Inrō* were generally worn only by men, suspended from the sash (*obi*) worn around the waist on a cord tightened with a bead (*ojime*); a toggle (*netsuke*) protruded above the sash and kept the whole assemblage from falling through. Together with their associated *netsuke*, *inrō* are an expression of the Japanese passion for fashionable accessorization that is still evident on any Tokyo subway train today.

Patent medicines grew popular during the early Edo period, and *inrō* are known to have been in use by 1636; in 1686 they were listed in a regional gazetteer as one of the craft products of Kyoto, where both examples on this page were likely manufactured. The larger *inrō*, complete with *ojime* and *netsuke*, was made by an artistic descendant of Hon'ami Kōetsu, and its design includes stylized plovers, or "wave birds," a classic courtly motif with roots in Heian-period literature. The smaller *inrō* is an unusual collaboration between a lacquerer and a member of the Gotō family of metalworkers, who contributed the silver waves.

Medicine case (*inrō*) with design of sea life
Koma Kansai II (1767–1835) and Shibayama Sōichi (dates unknown)
Edo period, early 19th century
Lacquered wood or paper with applied gold, silver, copper alloy, shell, crystal, horn, and stone; silk cord
9.7 x 5.1 x 2.9 cm (3 13/16 x 2 x 1 1/8 in.)
William Sturgis Bigelow Collection 11.9980

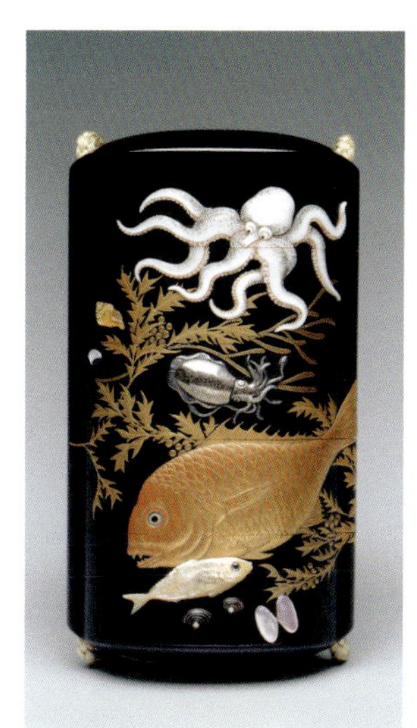

Medicine case (*inrō*) and box-shaped toggle (*netsuke*) with design of carriage wheels and waves
Nakayama Komin (1808–1870)
Edo period, mid-19th century
Lacquered wood or paper with shell; silk cord
8.8 x 6.3 x 2 cm (3 7/16 x 2 1/2 x 13/16 in.)
William Sturgis Bigelow Collection 11.9989a–b

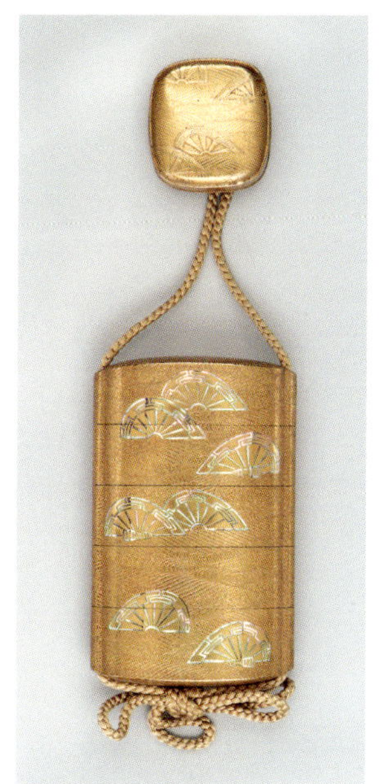

These two *inrō*, later than the examples opposite, were both made in Edo. The second Koma Kansai, who led one of Edo's most prolific lacquering ateliers, created a design that celebrated Japan's edible marine life including, on the side shown, an abalone, a left-eyed flounder with gold lacquer spots, a raised-lacquer blowfish (*fugu*), and a rockfish. The inlaid materials were applied by another artist, Shibayama Sōichi.

In contrast to the realism of the Kansai *inrō*, the decoration of the other *inrō* is rooted in ancient courtly customs and beliefs. The design, taken from a famous twelfth-century lacquer box, is conventionally said to owe its origins to the practice of soaking the wheels of courtly ox-drawn carriages in Kyoto's Kamo River to prevent them from drying out and warping. Another theory holds that the wheels are derived from a passage in a Buddhist sutra describing the glories of the Buddha Amida and his Pure Land, where lotuses with flowerlike carriage wheels are said to grow.

Toggle (*netsuke*) in the form of a hare scratching its chin with its right hind leg
Attributed to Garaku Risuke (dates unknown)
Edo period, early–mid-18th century
Carved and stained ivory with eyes inlaid in dark horn
2.7 x 4.8 x 2.5 cm (1 1/16 x 1 7/8 x 1 in.)
Gift of Major Henry Lee Higginson 18.221b

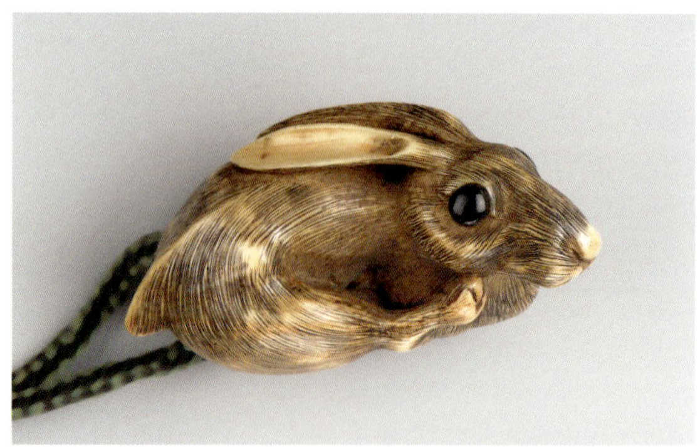

Toggle (*netsuke*) in the form of a *kirin*
Takaoka Ikkan (1817–1893)
Edo period, mid-19th century
Stained cherry wood and horn
3.2 x 3.6 x 2.7 cm (1 1/4 x 1 7/16 x 1 1/16 in.)
William Sturgis Bigelow Collection 11.23252

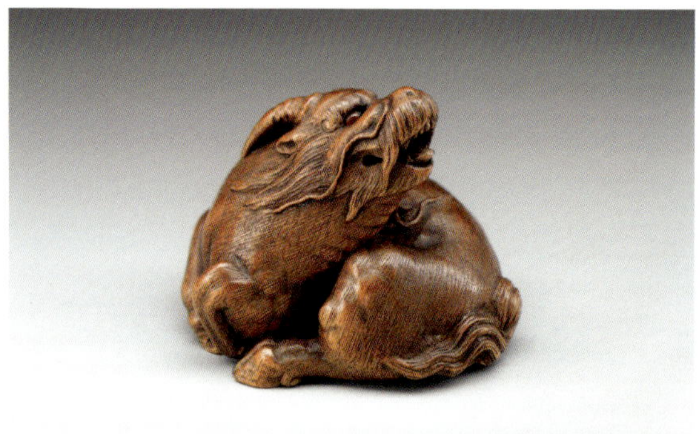

Toggle (*netsuke*) in the form of a boar sleeping on autumn plants
Kaigyokusai Masatsugu (1813–1892)
Meiji era, after 1863
Stained ivory, horn, and silver
2.5 x 4.2 x 3 cm (1 x 1 5/8 x 1 3/16 in.)
William Sturgis Bigelow Collection 11.23373

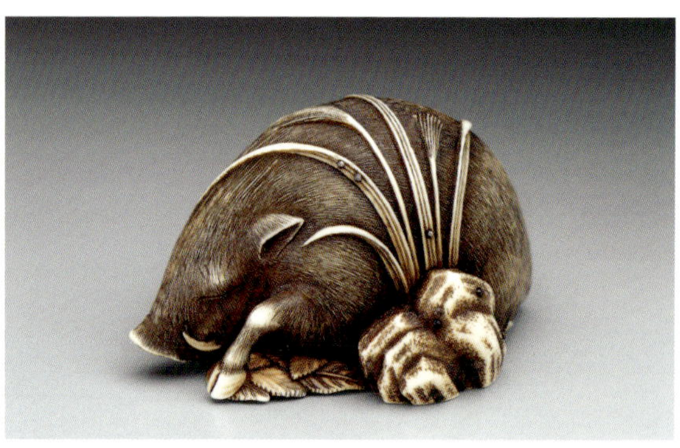

Netsuke are toggles used to secure items such as *inrō* suspended on cords from the wearer's sash. The earliest examples were probably simple ivory rings, but at some point in the seventeenth century, these were replaced first by imported Chinese carvings and then by figurative pieces produced in workshops in Kyoto and Osaka. Although the ivory hare illustrated here is unsigned, its powerfully carved, deeply stained fur, large inlaid horn eyes, and compact form all suggest the work of Garaku Risuke, who worked in Osaka.

In the later eighteenth century, *netsuke* production spread to other urban centers, including both Edo and Nagoya, and wood became increasingly popular as a less expensive alternative to ivory. Takaoka Ikkan worked in Nagoya during the nineteenth century, carving both Buddhist images and *netsuke* of popular subjects such as the *kirin*, a mythical beast of Chinese origin that appears on earth only during the rule of a virtuous monarch. Despite the imaginary nature of the *kirin*, Ikkan's naturalistic carving of its fur suggests the growing influence of the Maruyama-Shijō painting style.

During the Meiji era, Kaigyokusai Masatsugu earned a reputation among both Japanese and foreign buyers for his meticulous animal carvings. Like many popular *netsuke* subjects, his sleeping-boar *netsuke* is based on an illustration in an earlier woodblock-printed book.

Toggle (*netsuke*) in the form of two Guardian Kings (Niō) arm wrestling
Higo no Daijō (dates unknown)
Edo period, mid-18th century
Stained boxwood
3.5 x 8 x 3.9 cm (1⅜ x 3⅛ x 1⅛ in.)
Gift of Dr. Ernest G. Stillman 47.716

Toggle (*netsuke*) in the form of an *ashinaga* hugging a tree trunk
Edo period, mid-19th century
Fossilized sea pine, coral, and stag horn
19.6 x 2.5 x 4 cm (7 11/16 x 1 x 1 9/16 in.)
Gift of Dr. Ernest G. Stillman 47.705

Niō (Guardian Kings) often stand watch outside Buddhist temples, their muscular bodies making them ideal material for caricature in miniature—emphasized in this case by the irreverent positioning of a cord hole (not visible in this photograph) that is drilled between the buttocks of one of the kings. This humorous approach to tradition, a leitmotif of much later Edo-period art for urban clients, is one of the most endearing aspects of the world of *netsuke*.

Ashinaga ("long legs") and *tenaga* ("long arms") were perennial favorites with *netsuke* carvers. Although they do not seem to appear in Japanese art before the Edo period, they owe their origin to a written account of strange races in a Chinese text, the *Shanhaijing* (*Book of Mountains and Lakes*), that was compiled no later than the first century C.E. Both *ashinaga* and *tenaga* feature in sixteenth-century Chinese book illustrations, which quickly made their way to Japan. There they were seized upon by *netsuke* carvers eager to capitalize on a taste for the exotic that developed during the early decades of Japan's relative isolation from the outside world. This nineteenth-century depiction adopts the hairstyle and other features associated with earlier carvings of non-Japanese beings but replaces their caricatured expressions with a look of real terror. The use of sea pine, a type of coral, underlines the remote nature of the subject matter.

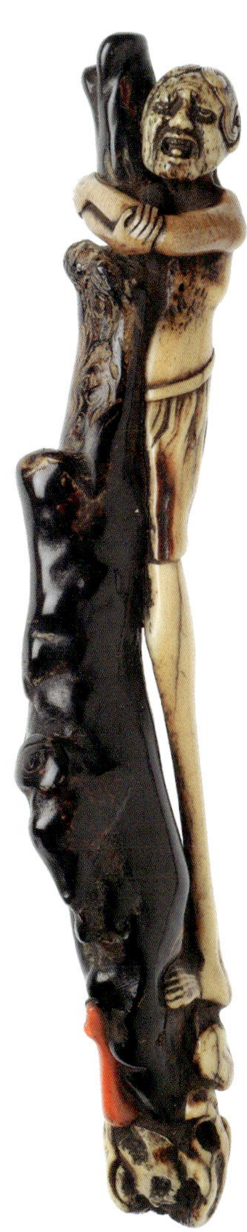

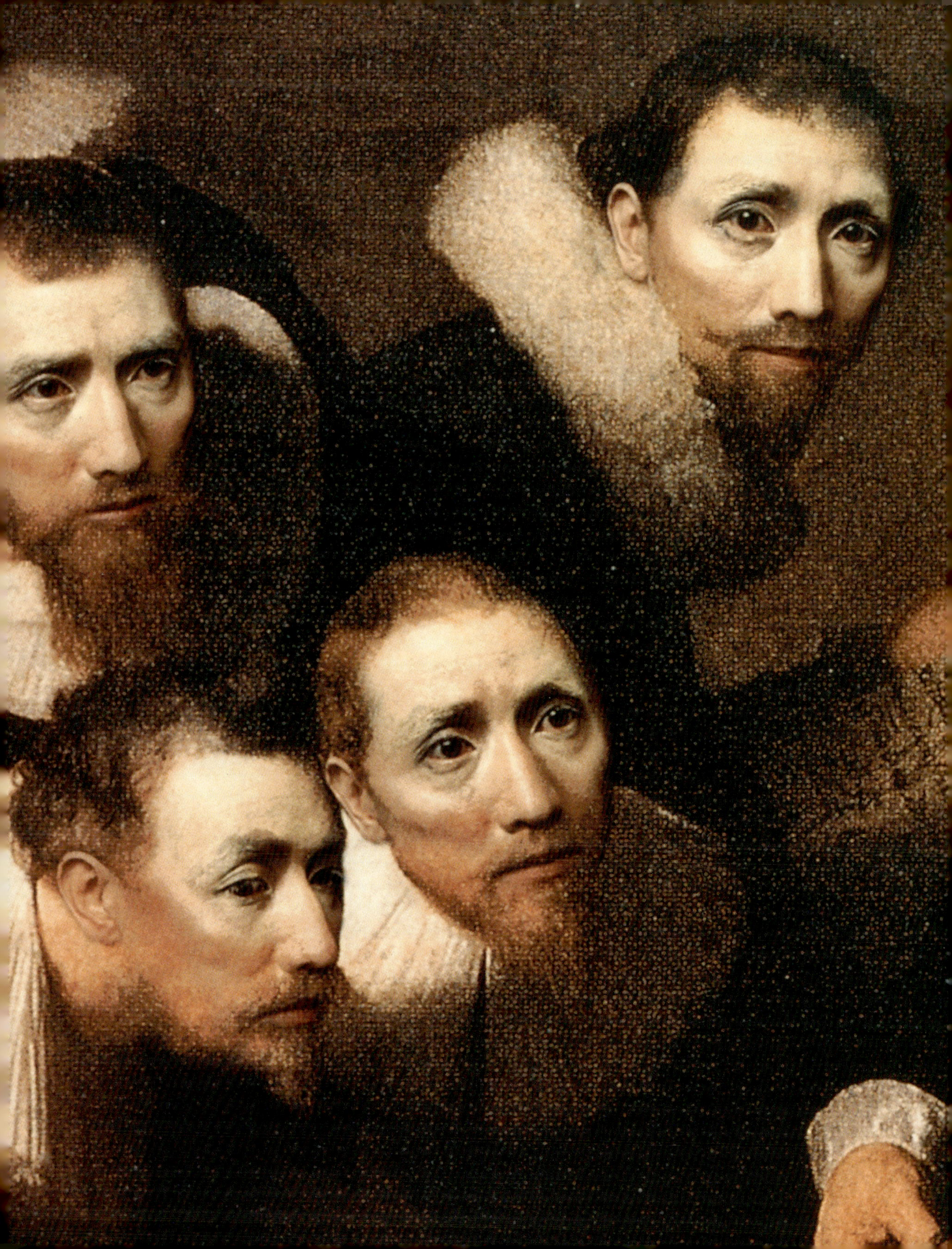

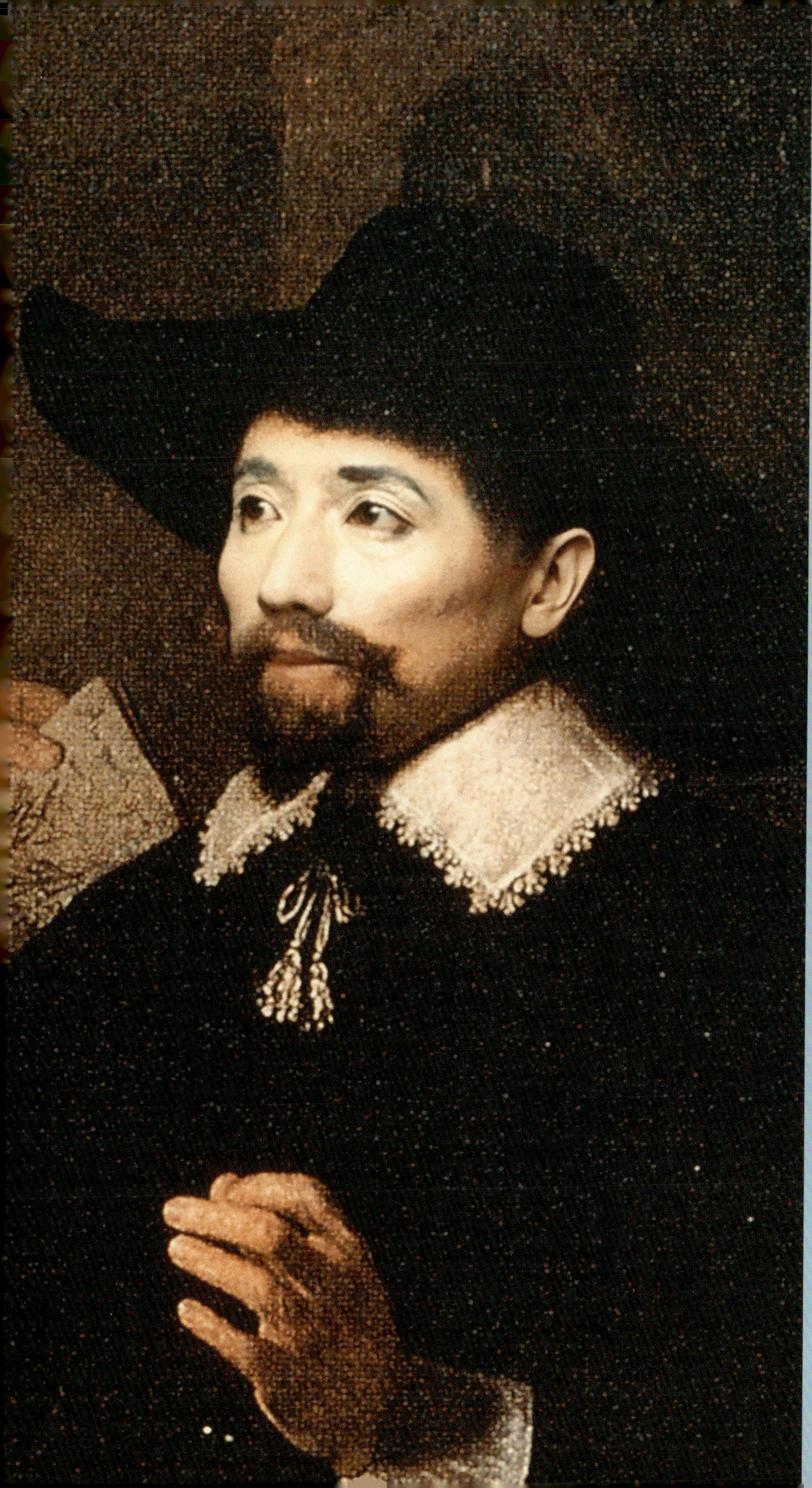

4 JAPAN and the outside world

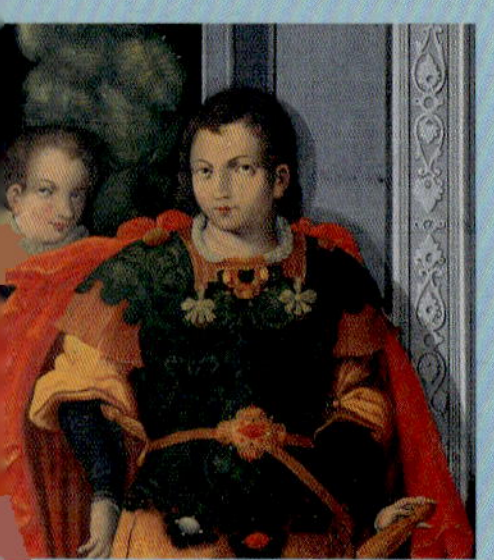
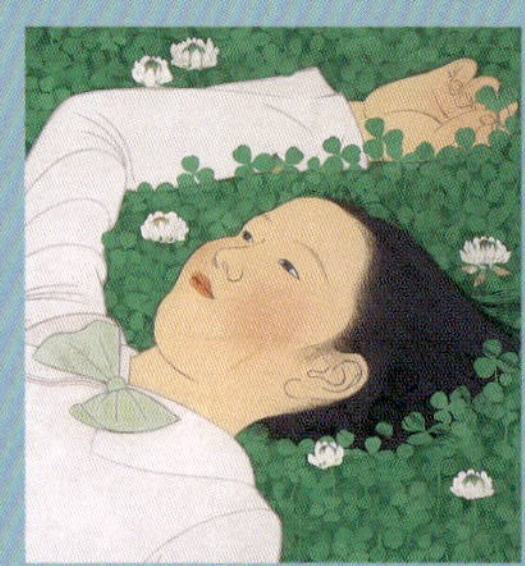
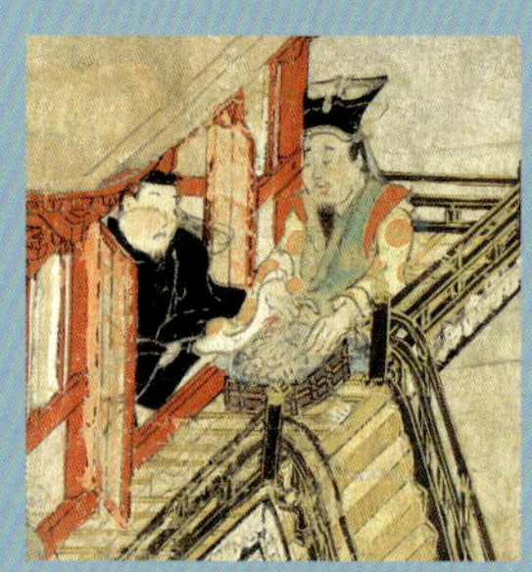
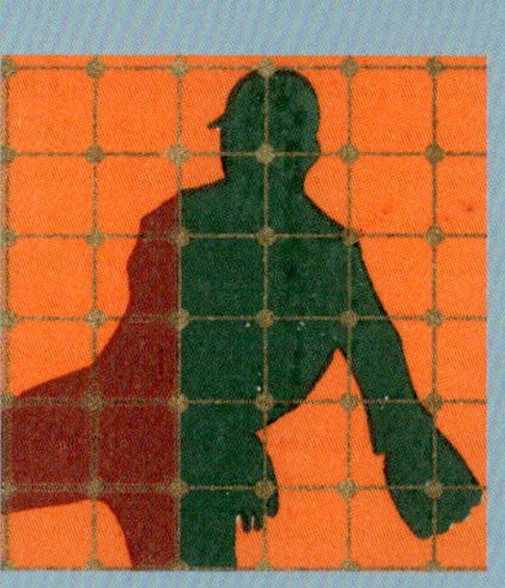
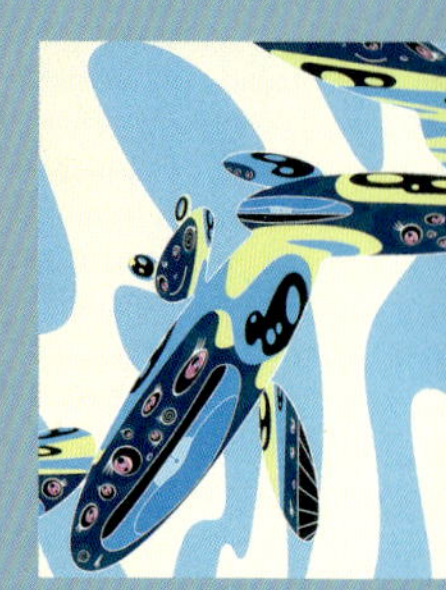

Japan and the Outside World

Joe Earle

> It would pay us . . . to establish an international suzerainty over Japan; to take away any fear of invasion or annexation, and pay the country as much as ever it chose, on condition that it simply sat still and went on making beautiful things while our men learned. It would pay us to put the whole Empire in a glass case and mark it, "*Hors Concours*," Exhibit A. –Rudyard Kipling, **From Sea to Sea**

British author Rudyard Kipling's 1889 vision of Japan—as a country that had developed an exquisite aesthetic sensibility thanks to lack of engagement with the outside world—was shared by many of his Western contemporaries. Japan had indeed been in a state of semi-seclusion for a little more than two hundred years when the American commodore Matthew Calbraith Perry's two visits to the country in 1853 and 1854 reopened it to more extensive foreign influence. Under a system perfected by the Tokugawa shoguns during the 1630s and early 1640s, Japanese were forbidden to travel abroad, while merchants from Korea, the Ryūkyū Islands (present-day Okinawa), the Netherlands, and China were allowed only limited, tightly controlled access to Japanese markets and people. But before the Edo period (1615–1868), Japan had enjoyed several long periods of interchange both with the Korean peninsula and with China. Even during the seventeenth to nineteenth centuries there existed a high degree of awareness of world events, Western technology, and Western objects, at least on the part of the ruling elite and a handful of educated individuals—particularly those who had learned to read Dutch books. All the same, the assumptions that bolstered Kipling's observations have continued to color our image of Japan in the pre-modern age.

We may attempt to correct that image by drawing together here a variety of objects, dating from the twelfth to the twenty-first century (and including several from those supposedly "closed" years of the Edo period), that bear witness to Japan's artistic and intellectual contact with the outside world—first with its

Asian neighbors (particularly China), and then, beginning in the sixteenth century, with distant Europe and America. It must be stressed, though, that many other works presented in this book also illuminate Japan's ongoing external interactions over the past fourteen centuries. The painted and carved icons in the "Art of the Temple" chapter, for instance, not only chronicle the enthusiastic adoption of Buddhism, which originated in India about a thousand years before it reached Japan in the sixth century, but also demonstrate how changing foreign patterns of belief, organization, and ritual could affect the evolution of Japanese religious art. Similarly, ink painting in Japan, shown in the "Temple" and "Art of the Ruling Classes" chapters, owes its origins to an influx of Chinese culture, when late-twelfth-century Japanese priests traveled to the Asian mainland in search of fresh religious inspiration and returned to found new monasteries.

Long before that, from about 50,000 to 10,000 B.C.E., parts of Japan were first settled by hunter-gatherers with a mostly nomadic lifestyle. Around 300 B.C.E., fresh waves of immigrants from southern China entered Japan by way of Korea and introduced rice cultivation. A fully agricultural society evolved from this time to 300 C.E. (some six centuries known as the Yayoi period), when bronze and iron were introduced by a new influx of settlers from the Korean peninsula. Later immigrants contributed to the formation of the unified political entity that would eventually become the Yamato state. At first a theocracy—with emperors who functioned both as heads of state and as high priests responsible for securing the goodwill of the Sun Goddess, Amaterasu, and other Shinto deities—Yamato began to become receptive to Buddhism toward the end of the sixth century, after visiting Korean delegates had introduced the religion. During the next two hundred years, the imported religion played an increasingly central role in national life, by the eighth century becoming virtually a state cult centered on the vast Tōdai-ji, or Great Eastern Temple, located in Nara, the capital at the time. Although Buddhism is of South Asian origin, the Buddhist texts that were brought to Japan were virtually all written in Chinese, a fact that contributed to the rapid adoption and adaptation of the Chinese script with its several thousand ideograms.

Japan's first era of intense cultural assimilation, then, took place from the sixth to eighth centuries and involved a great influx of Chinese culture. During that period, many Japanese scholars and diplomats traveled to the mainland to study the culture of the Tang dynasty (618–907), which they admired and considered more advanced than their own. The historical figure Kibi no Makibi, who made such a journey in the eighth century, can be seen as a symbol of this

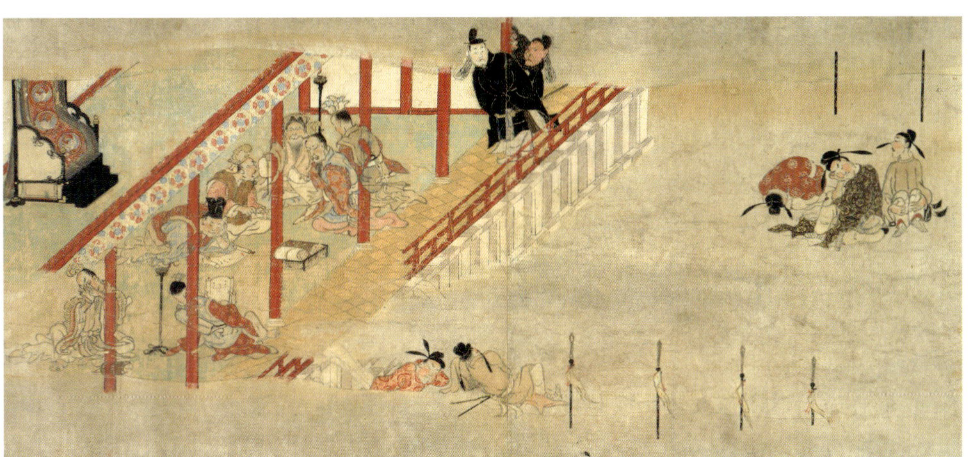

fig. 26 **Through the magical help of a friendly demon, the Japanese envoy Kibi is able to eavesdrop on the Chinese scholars who will test his knowledge the next day.**

phenomenon. But the biographic scroll (p. 194) that opens this chapter, painted about four centuries after Kibi's death, attests to the different attitude toward China that developed during the late twelfth century, a second period of engagement with Japan's great continental neighbor. Although inspired by factional politics between rival schools of divination, the Kibi scroll is also an eloquent expression of cultural self-confidence: instead of traveling to the mainland in a humble search for wisdom, Kibi aims to best his Chinese counterparts through superior intelligence, cunning, and skill. The narrative scroll (*emaki*), a uniquely Japanese form of visual expression that reached an early peak in the twelfth century, when the Kibi scroll was created, was also used to depict the events of Japan's most celebrated work of prose literature, the eleventh-century *Tale of Genji*, no more than a century after the *Tale* was completed. Other prose works had been pictured still earlier, although their illustrated versions are no longer extant. Narrative scroll painting was thus the ideal medium for a work that sought to assert Japan's cultural superiority over China.

Until the sixteenth century, Japan's exposure to the rest of the world was limited to Asia and was often facilitated by travel to the mainland on the part of monks, officials, scholars, and merchants. The earliest Japanese experience of European culture, in contrast, was almost wholly mediated by travelers to Japan, the only significant exception before the eighteenth century being a delegation that visited Portugal, Spain, and Italy in the 1580s. The first Europeans to reach Japan were three Portuguese sailors who were shipwrecked on the remote southern island of Tanegashima in the early 1540s, an initial contact that soon developed—thanks to the power and reach of the Iberian sea-borne empires—into a substantial presence, especially of Portuguese traders and

Roman Catholic missionaries. The pair of paintings (p. 196) depicting a Chinese port and "southern barbarians" at a Japanese port shows how this exotic new subject matter was seized upon by artists who were already developing bold new pictorial styles, especially in the folding-screen format, in response to changing tastes and the aspirations of a growing merchant class. The screen of a European king and members of his court (p. 195) is among the very earliest extant Japanese attempts at painting in a Western style, using a combination of native and European pigments and binders. Like the much later shop interior by Okumura Masanobu (p. 198), it demonstrates not only an enduring fascination with Western perspective but also the critical role played by prints, rather than paintings, in developing Japanese awareness of European pictorial conventions.

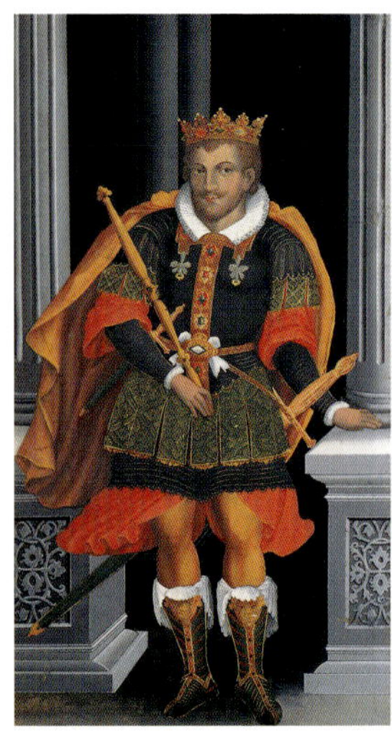

fig. 27 **The arrival of the Portuguese in Japan in the late sixteenth century sparked an interest in European subject matter and painting conventions.**

After the relaxation, early in the eighteenth century, of controls on the import of printed materials (provided they were not overtly religious), Japanese artists' perceptions of Western picture making were apparently based in large part on landscape and townscape etchings imported by the Dutch through the southern port of Nagasaki. The extreme linear recession of these popular views profoundly influenced not only Masanobu but also Maruyama Ōkyo, whose early peep-show scenes suggest an understanding of vanishing-point perspective not as a revelatory discovery but more as an ingenious, diverting invention. Far from displacing traditional methods of pictorial organization, in Ōkyo's case vanishing-point perspective was merely the starting point for a wider-reaching, highly sophisticated, and vastly influential project to combine different elements of Western naturalism with traditional East Asian brushwork. Shiba Kōkan, who emulated Western oil painting in his works, actually had direct contact with the Dutch at Nagasaki, in addition to making a close study of Western optical gadgets and producing several copperplate prints. The self-styled "Sō Shiseki" assumed a pseudo-Chinese name and sought out alternatives to conventional painting from Nagasaki's other foreign community, the Chinese, one of the few nationalities permitted to trade with Japan between the 1640s and 1850s. The experimental, playful, and open-minded spirit of Ōkyo, Kōkan, Shiseki, and their contemporaries did much to reinvigorate Japanese painting in the later eighteenth century, and contributed to the development not only of the artists in this chapter but also of the print designers Hokusai and Hiroshige. Even the familiar horizontal format of these print artists' early series depicting Mount Fuji and the Tōkaidō, so different from most earlier East Asian landscapes, reflects their awareness of European printed landscape formats.

Not only in the world of art but also in Japanese society at large, the years from the 1780s to 1860s were fraught with a mass of overlapping conflicts and contradictions, among them acceptance versus rejection of external influences; merchant versus samurai; rule by the shogun versus rule by the emperor; Chinese versus purely Japanese; economic freedom versus tight financial controls; and the native Shinto religion versus the imported but all-pervasive Buddhist faith. Even as Hiroshige published his later landscape prints, the arrival of Perry's naval squadron in Tokyo Bay began to bring these contradictions to a head. The Western powers soon forced Japan to sign a series of commercial agreements and to allow their merchants to reside in several cities, and the 1860s saw ever-increasing tensions between traditionalists who favored an unrealistic exclusionist policy and modernizers who understood the need to respond positively to foreign military and economic pressures. In 1867–68, the government of the shoguns was swept away by a coalition of reformist samurai, and the teenage emperor was installed as head of the new order. His era, named Meiji or "Enlightened Government" (1868–1912), is celebrated in a print (p. 205) by Toyohara Chikanobu, published in 1887 around the peak of the early Meiji enthusiasm for all things Western: at an imperial birthday ball held two years earlier, all but two of the Japanese ladies wore Western dress; and two years later, in 1889 (the date of Rudyard Kipling's observation), Western-style formal dress was required for those attending the promulgation of the new constitution. Yet Chikanobu, although making neat use of a recent triumph of advanced engineering, the iron- and brick-built Azuma Bridge, as a device for drawing the viewer's gaze deep into the composition, also places more time-honored motifs—temple pagodas and Mount Fuji—as reassuring focal points in the background.

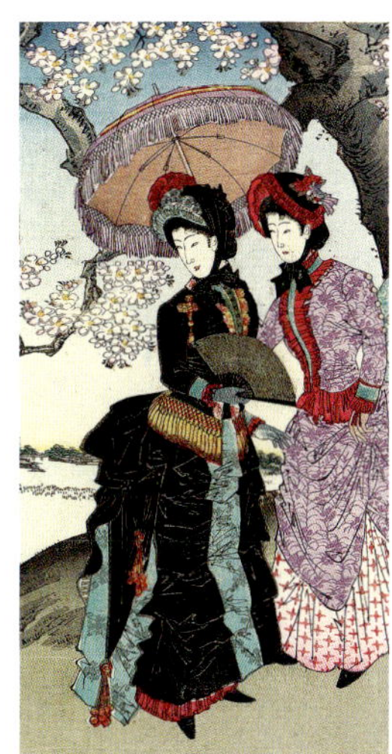

fig. 28 **In the nineteenth century, Japan not only embarked on a campaign of modernization but also embraced Western customs, manners, and dress.**

Chikanobu's eclectic choice of motifs (highlighted by lavish use of imported chemical pigments) reflects, at the level of popular art, some of the issues being addressed around the same time by a range of creative individuals, including poets, novelists, architects, craftspeople, and painters. Given the extraordinarily rich heritage of Japanese culture and the fractured nature of late-Edo society, the problem confronted by such artists was not one simply of Japanese versus Western. Before they could find an accommodation between native and non-native forms of expression, they had to establish just what parts of the Japanese tradition could be adapted to contemporary needs. In the case of painting, the American Ernest Francisco Fenollosa, a professor at Tokyo Imperial University, and his disciple Okakura Kakuzō played an important role in establishing a canon. Although recent critical writing has begun to question the significance of their interventions in Japanese art history, there is no doubt that their championing of the venerable Kano painting academy, founded in the fifteenth century, had a profound and lasting effect on both Japanese and non-

Japanese views of Japanese art throughout the twentieth century. Reaching four centuries into the past, Fenollosa paradoxically found what he considered most normative in Japanese pictorial art in a school whose origins were firmly based in the Chinese-style ink-painting tradition. With advice from Fenollosa and Okakura, two relatively obscure members of the Kano academy, first Kano Hōgai and then Hashimoto Gahō, combined their inherited brush manner with Western techniques (such as chiaroscuro) and a more subtle handling of perspective than had been seen in earlier prints, with results that were identifiably Japanese (even if Chinese in origin) but also unmistakably new—a process that was taken a stage further, at Okakura's prompting, by Yokoyama Taikan.

These American-inspired experiments in painting took place in the 1880s and 1890s, but ever since the 1860s the Japanese government had encouraged artists in other media—including ceramics, lacquer, metalwork, and the newly developed craft of enameling—to adapt their wares to foreign tastes and to exhibit them at great expositions, both nationally and internationally. Japanese applied arts at all levels of the market both attracted extravagant praise and earned significant foreign exchange at a time when the country was not yet ready to compete in the global market for machine-made goods. While the two examples included here (pp. 208–9) reflect the very highest quality that could be achieved—as well as the close linkage between developments in painting and in the crafts—they can only hint at the vast range and volume of goods that found their way onto world markets and earned Japan a reputation for manufacturing excellence that has lasted to the present. Before we assume that work of this kind was intended solely for foreign use, we should remember that many of the same specialist craftsmen were commissioned to work on both public and private buildings in Japan, and that photographs of the period often show interiors filled with a kind of Victorian clutter that is at odds with our preconceptions of traditional Japanese good taste.

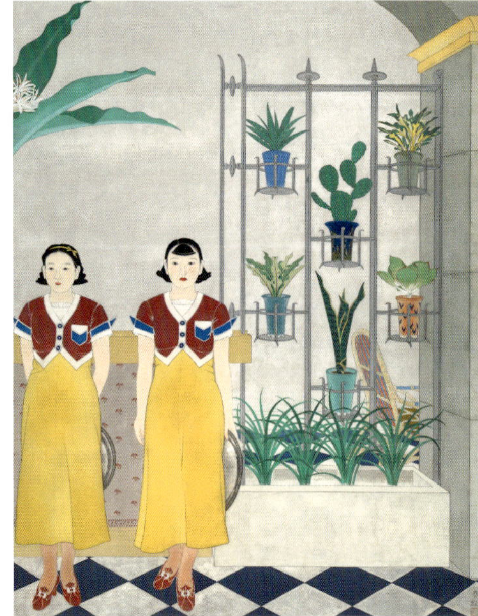

fig. 29 **During the 1920s and 1930s, Western-style tearooms and nightclubs with their "modern girls" and "modern boys" became popular painting subjects.**

During the early decades of the twentieth century, the further evolution of this complex process of reaction with tradition, adaptation of Western styles and techniques, and new subject matter reflecting a rapidly changing society is also seen in book design, postcards (a new art form in which Japan played a leading role), and academic drawing. While the history of Japanese painting during the modern age is still thinly represented in the MFA collections, the haunting and now celebrated *Clover* (p. 215) by Tateishi Harumi, the last work in this chapter that definitely predates World War II, gives a further hint of the rich possibilities that could be opened up by efforts to achieve a synthesis of Western and Japanese styles. Our selection of pieces representing the last six decades must, by its very nature, be seen as a work in progress, not only because this is an area that has received little curatorial attention until recently, but also because the sheer complexity of Japan's visual culture in a global age rules out any pretensions to the kind of magisterial overview of Japanese art history aimed at by Fenollosa and Okakura a hundred years ago. Our commentaries on these postwar works—baskets, fashions, furniture, photography, ceramics, prints, and paintings—often seek to identify a core of "Japaneseness." But even in the case of the two baskets (pp. 218–19, rooted in a seemingly ancient tradition that, in reality, dates back only to the Meiji era), we are constantly reminded that Japanese art has nearly always developed not in isolation, as Kipling hoped and thought, but in response—sometimes direct and immediate, sometimes less so—to outside stimuli. After two periods of intensive absorption of foreign culture, during the 1920s and again during the postwar American Occupation, a debate has developed over the last half century, just as it did during the 1880s, about the conflicting roles of modernization, Westernization, and (more recently) globalization in the evolution of Japanese culture and politics. This debate has been brought to worldwide attention by the fashionable artist, entrepreneur, and propagandist Murakami Takashi, but issues of national identity permeate the work of all of the artists featured in the closing pages of this chapter. We can only guess at the art of the future that will result from the further exploration of these issues.

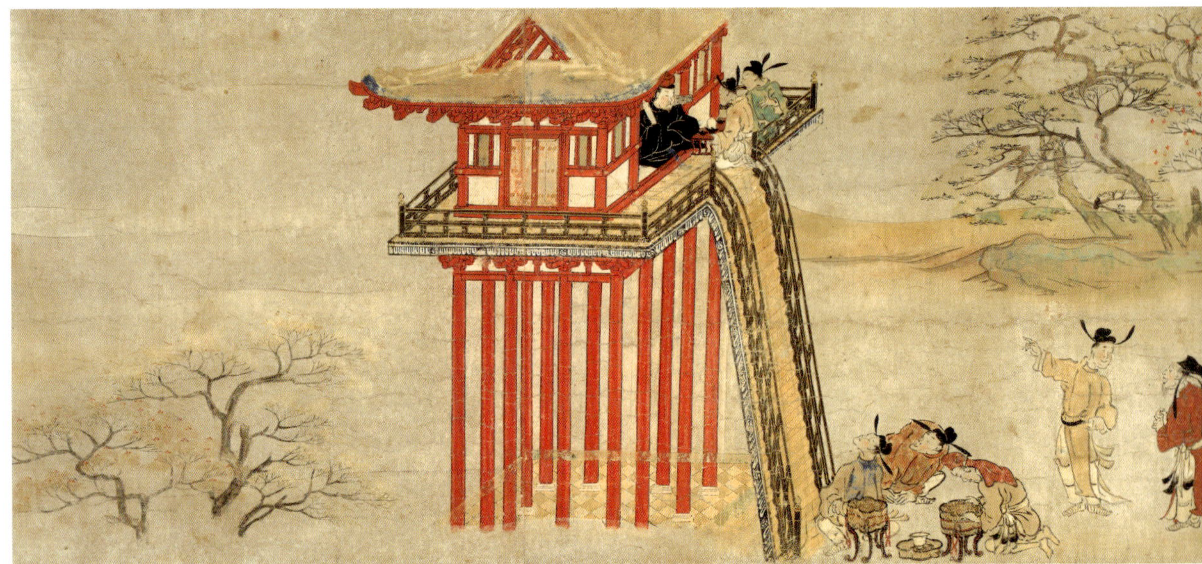

Minister Kibi's Trip to China
Heian period, late 12th century

The historical figure Kibi no Makibi visited China twice in the eighth century, first for nearly twenty years as a student and later, from 752 to 753, as an ambassador. He was one of numerous scholars and diplomats who made the arduous journey in order to study the advanced culture of the Tang dynasty (618–907), but four centuries later, when this scroll was painted, the Japanese were less awed by things Chinese and more concerned with internal rivalries. It is thought that the scroll was commissioned to uphold the prestige of a school of divination that claimed descent from Kibi.

In this celebrated pictorial biography, the same figures are depicted repeatedly at different moments in time, so that Minister Kibi, a demon, and various Chinese officials move through the landscape as the scroll is rolled from right to left. The lively, cartoon-like paintings show Kibi using magic tricks to outwit the Chinese in contests of intellectual skill, such as a game of Go, aided by a friendly demon who is the ghost of a previous Japanese ambassador. A concluding section, no longer extant, would likely have shown Kibi's final victories and triumphant return to Japan.

The Kibi scroll is one of the earliest surviving Japanese narrative picture scrolls and the only one of comparable date outside Japan. Its purchase by the MFA in 1932 resulted in the strengthening of Japanese laws regarding the export of cultural properties.

Set of four handscrolls (originally mounted as one scroll); ink, color, and gold on paper
32 x 2442 cm (12⅝ x 961 in.) total length
William Sturgis Bigelow Collection, by exchange 32.131

European King and Members of His Court

Momoyama period, 1601–14

In 1549, Portuguese missionaries traveled to Japan, bringing with them small oil paintings representing the Virgin Mary, the infant Jesus, and Christian saints. Toward the end of the sixteenth century, the Jesuits established a painting school, teaching Japanese artists to produce religious and secular images until the mission was shut down by the shogun Tokugawa Ieyasu in 1614. Although a Japanese delegation traveled to Portugal, Spain, and Italy from 1582 to 1590, for the most part knowledge of the European continent was acquired through printed books.

To create this very unusual six-panel screen, a Jesuit-trained Japanese artist transferred images of the Spanish king and members of his court from a group of European prints onto larger sheets of paper, using a grid of vertical lines that are now visible only under infrared light. Inconsistencies in the use of Western-style perspective indicate that the architectural elements must have been taken from other sources.

Recent analyses have shown that this screen was produced using mostly traditional Japanese colorants, with the addition of European copper resinate for the green of the armor worn by the figure in the fifth panel from the right. Many of the Japanese pigments were mixed with a Western-style oil binder, enhancing the sense of modeling and three-dimensionality of the figures.

Six-panel folding screen; ink, color, and gold on paper
127 x 333.6 cm (50 x 131 5/16 in.)
Fenollosa-Weld Collection 11.4312

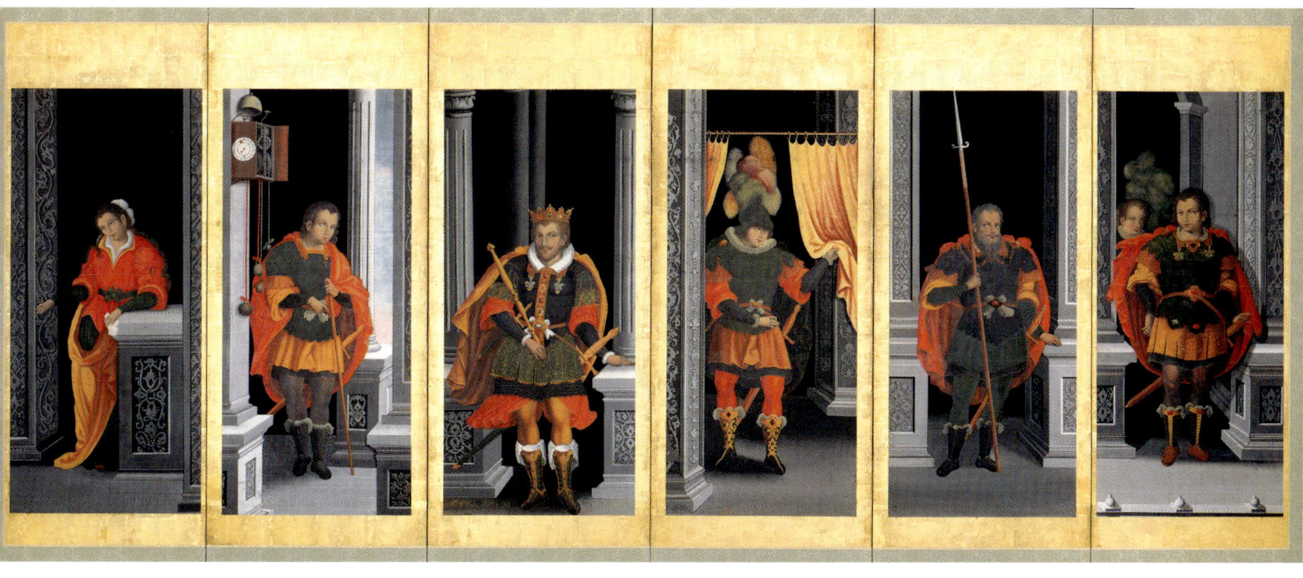

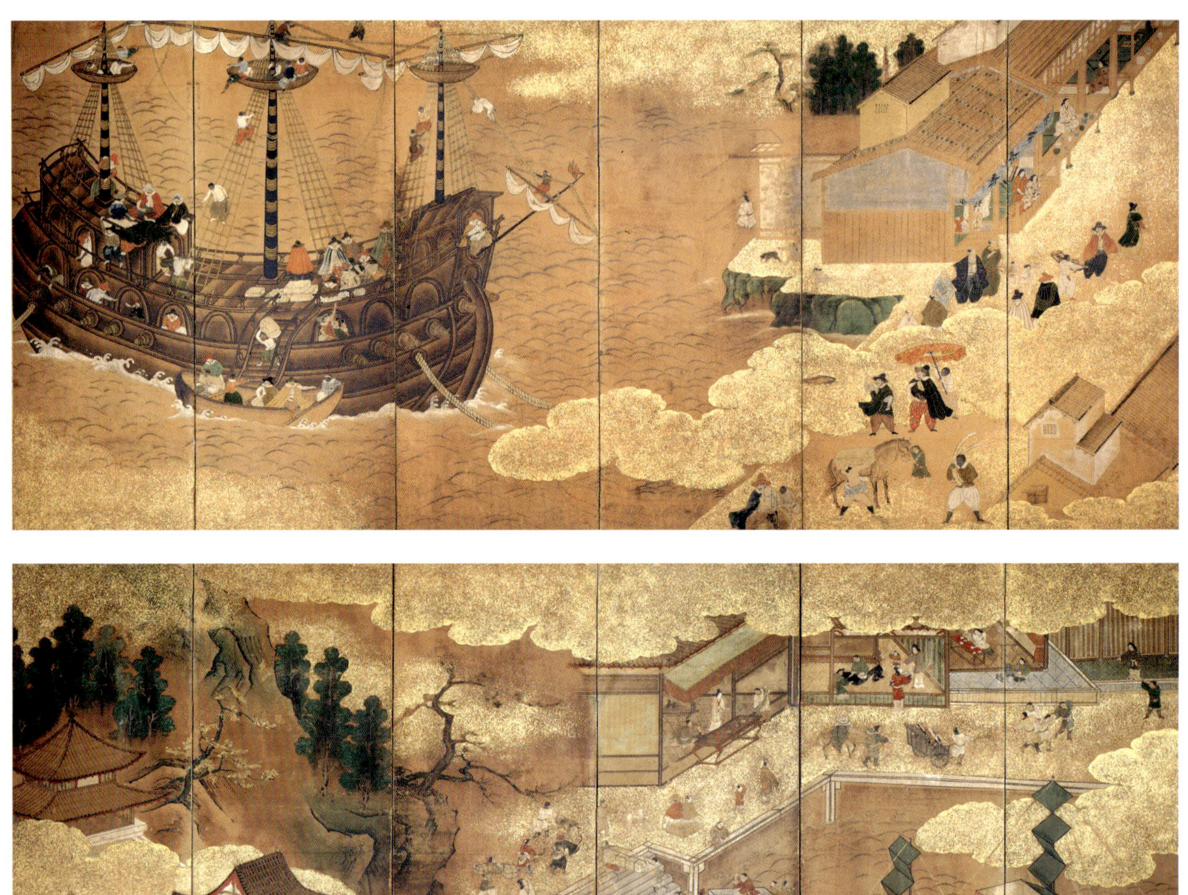

A Chinese Port and _Southern Barbarians at a Japanese Port_

Edo period, about 1624–35

The first Europeans to arrive in Japan, in the 1540s, were Portuguese sailors, soon followed by traders and Jesuit missionaries. The Japanese were fascinated by these strange new "southern barbarians" (*nanban*, so called because they arrived from the south), and about sixty pairs of screens depicting them survive today.

Most of the southern barbarian screens depict the arrival of a ship at a Japanese port in the left screen and the disembarkation of the foreigners in the right, but the MFA pair is unusual in that the left screen shows a Chinese port and the right, a Japanese one. The exotic atmosphere of the left screen is amplified by delicately rendered Chinese ladies at lower left and two Tartars, accompanied by a large civet and a white hunting dog, in the center. The right screen shows a Portuguese carrack about to dock, the traders aboard playing cards and a board game while above them darker-skinned sailors, probably Indians, scramble about in the rigging. On shore, a Portuguese dignitary looks on from under a ceremonial umbrella, while Japanese shopkeepers and children watch a procession of foreigners.

Recent scholarship has uncovered a pair of screens in Japan of similar composition to these, making it possible both to establish the approximate date of the MFA pair and to attribute them to a workshop influenced by the Kano-school painter Takanobu (1571–1618).

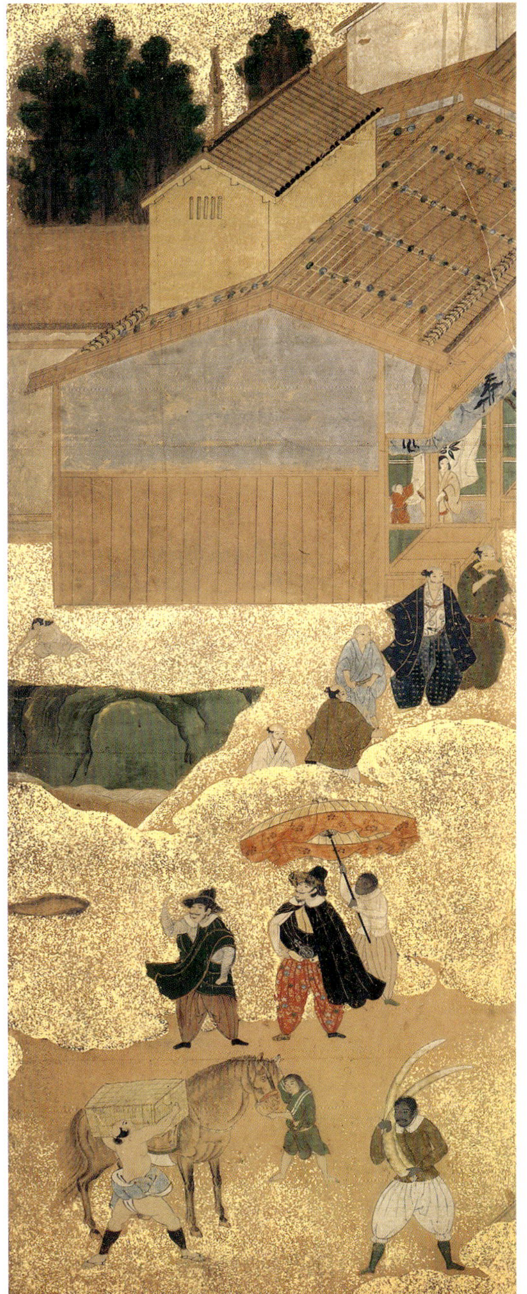

Pair of six-panel folding screens;
ink, color, and gold on paper
154.5 x 346 cm (60¾ x 136 in.) each
Fenollosa-Weld Collection 11.4168–9

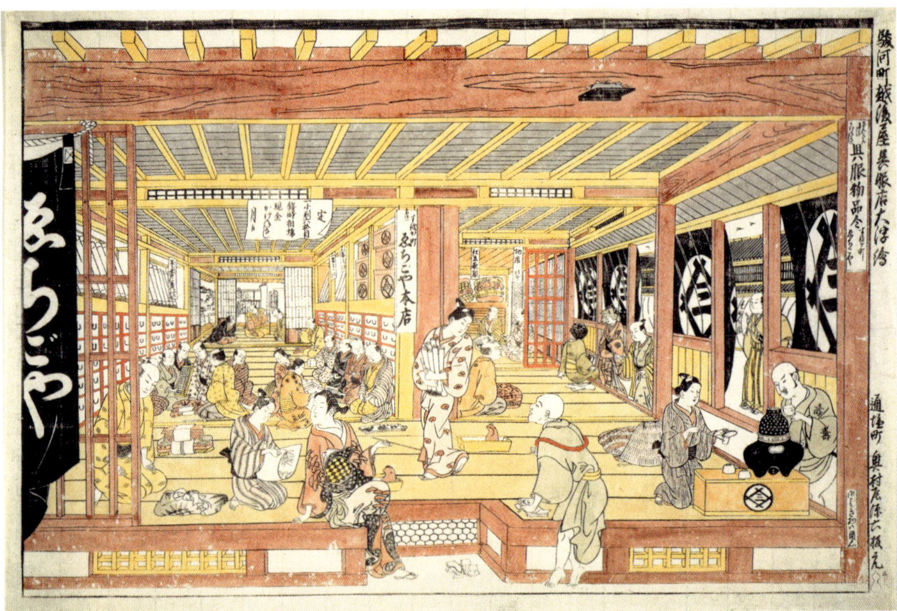

Large Perspective View of the Interior of the Echigo-ya in Suruga-chō

Okumura Masanobu (1686–1764)

Edo period, about 1745

This "floating picture" (*uki-e*) by Okumura Masanobu shows the great dry-goods store Echigo-ya, the direct ancestor of the famous Mitsukoshi department-store chain. The Echigo-ya sold fashionable kimono fabrics and accessories to customers like the elegant courtesan seen here in the left foreground, discussing patterns with a young clerk at the front of the store. Signs displayed throughout the large building present the store's name and logo, advertise its products, and explain its policies.

Masanobu's career spanned the entire first half of the eighteenth century, a time of exciting developments in printmaking, many of them pioneered by Masanobu himself. His flair for the commercial aspects of the print business made him especially quick to notice and exploit eye-catching trends such as Western-style vanishing-point perspective, reintroduced to Japan in the eighteenth century by means of imported European and Chinese prints and illustrated books. About 1745 Masanobu published a series of some half-dozen extra-large perspective prints that were among the earliest Japanese woodblock prints to employ the exotic technique. Their startling realism and novelty made them popular with the print-buying public, even though the rules of Western-style perspective were not yet fully understood or applied with complete consistency.

Woodblock print (*urushi-e*); ink on paper, with hand-applied color and glue (*nikawa*)
47.9 x 66.8 cm (18 7/8 x 26 5/16 in.)
William Sturgis Bigelow Collection 11.13343

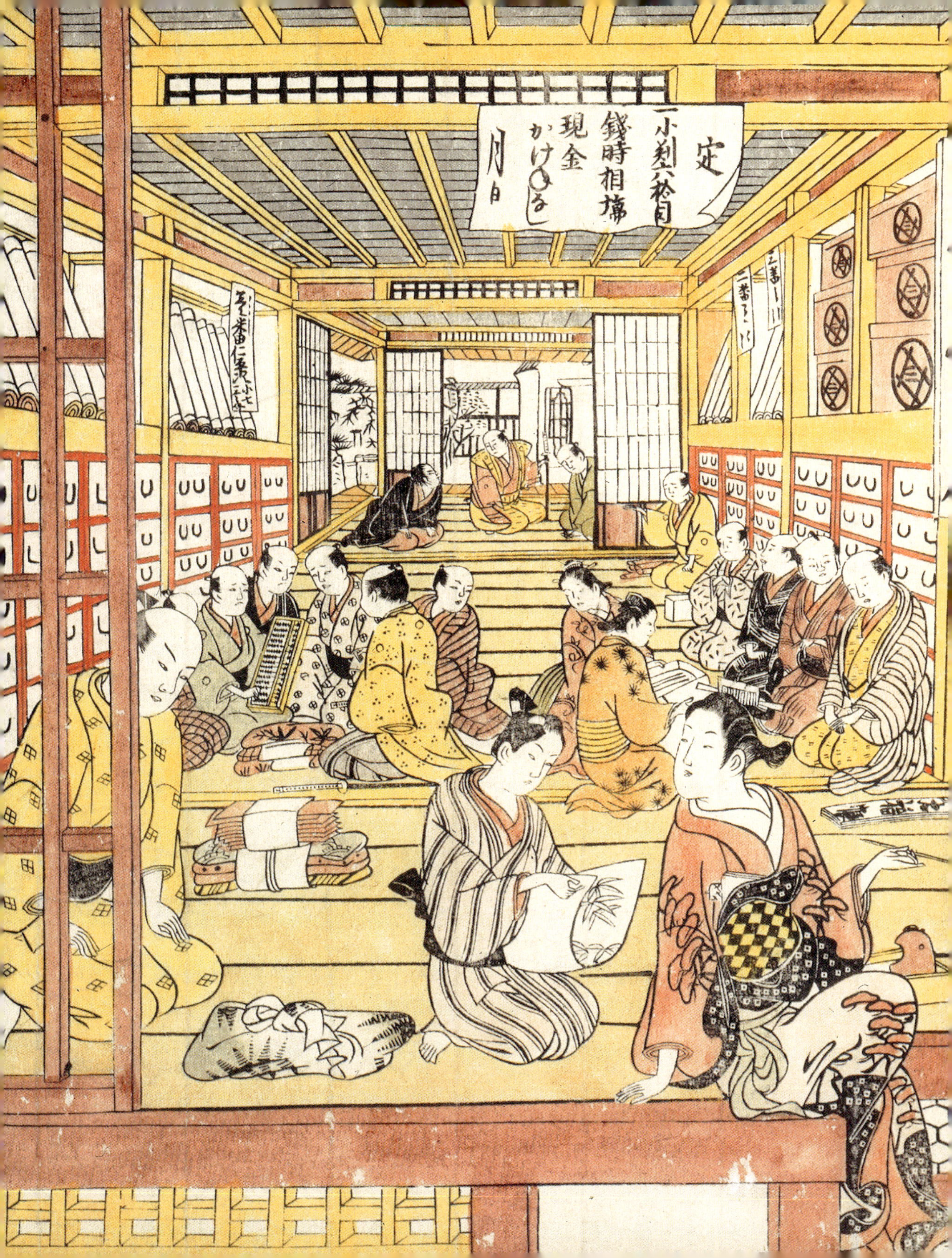
定
一小判六拾目
銭時相場
現金
かけねなし
月 日

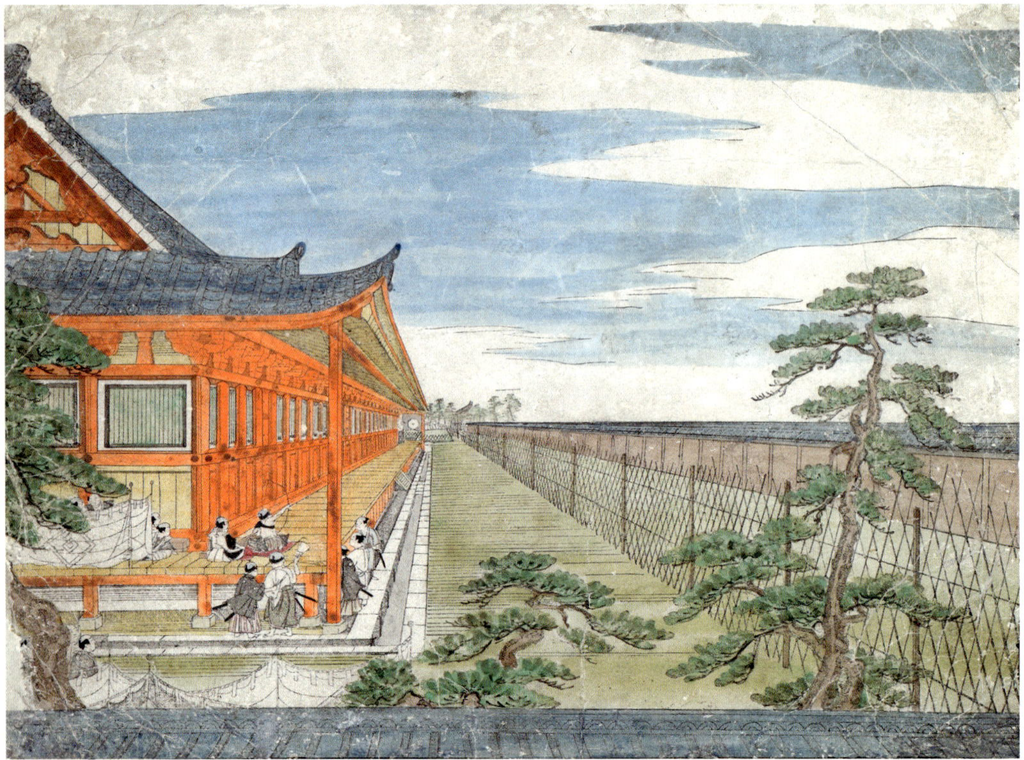

Archery Contest at the Sanjūsangendō
Maruyama Ōkyo (1733–1795)
Edo period, 1750s

The Sanjūsangendō, or Hall of Thirty-three Bays, is a thirteenth-century building in Ōkyo's hometown of Kyoto that is famous for its unusual length. This made it the ideal site for an annual archery competition in which contestants were required to shoot an arrow accurately along the veranda of the building. It is also well suited to perspective images such as this example, which Ōkyo is thought to have designed when he worked in a toy store as a young man. Since his employer hoped to sell as many copies as possible, the work is actually a woodblock print, with hand-coloring applied so thickly that it appears to be a painting.

About 1750 an optical contrivance for enjoying prints became wildly popular in Europe and was soon introduced by the Dutch to Japan. Ranging in size from small handheld versions to large ones used in carnivals, these devices were fitted with a picture—preferably an image like this print, with its exaggerated vanishing-point perspective—that was reflected in a mirror and then viewed through a lens, giving the effect of an actual vista seen through a tiny window.

Ōkyo's early experience in applying Western techniques to the depiction of Japanese subjects served him well in later life, when he achieved enormous success by combining the novelty of Western realism with the exquisite ink brushwork that was the traditional criterion of fine painting.

Woodblock print; ink on paper, with hand-applied color
20.9 x 27.2 cm (8¼ x 10 11/16 in.)
Denman Waldo Ross Collection 11.1868

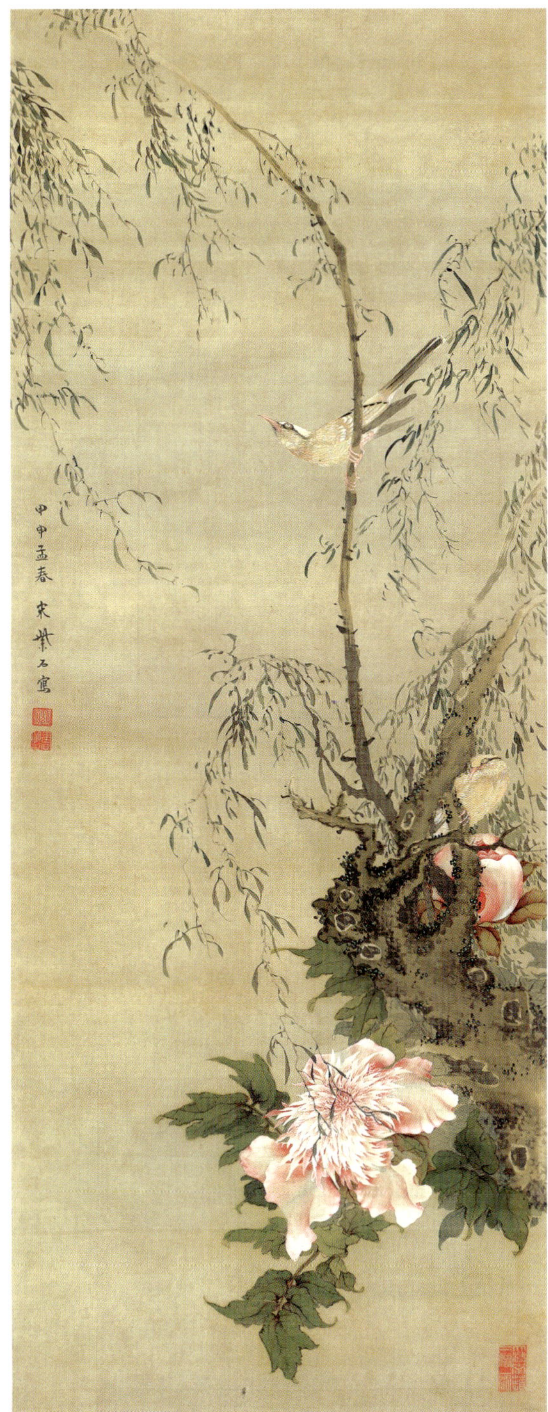

Willow, Flower, and Bird

Sō Shiseki (1712–1786)

Edo period, 1764

Following the souring of Japan's relations with Spain and Portugal in the early seventeenth century, the Tokugawa shoguns pursued a policy of national isolation. From 1639 to 1854, Japanese were strictly forbidden to travel abroad, and foreigners were allowed very limited access to Japan. Only merchants from China, Korea, the Ryūkyū Islands (which later became Japan's Okinawa Prefecture), and the Netherlands were permitted to trade at the port of Nagasaki. As it was no longer possible for Japanese painters interested in Chinese painting styles to travel to the continent, as they had done in previous centuries, the next best option was to visit Nagasaki in the hope of finding a resident Chinese artist willing to instruct Japanese pupils.

Sō Shiseki, originally from Edo, studied in Nagasaki under the Chinese painter Song Ziyan (Japanese: Sō Shigan) and changed his name to resemble that of his teacher. The style of painting that he learned from Song featured subjects from nature portrayed in lifelike detail, with fine brushstrokes for the feathers of the birds and volumetric, modulated color washes for flower petals and leaves, often combined with broader calligraphic ink brushstrokes representing branches or rocks. Shiseki returned to Edo and became the city's leading proponent of the Nagasaki style, teaching other artists (such as Shiba Kōkan) and publishing woodblock-printed books based on his paintings.

Hanging scroll; ink and color on silk
114 x 42.5 cm (44 7/8 x 16 3/4 in.)
Fenollosa-Weld Collection 11.4820

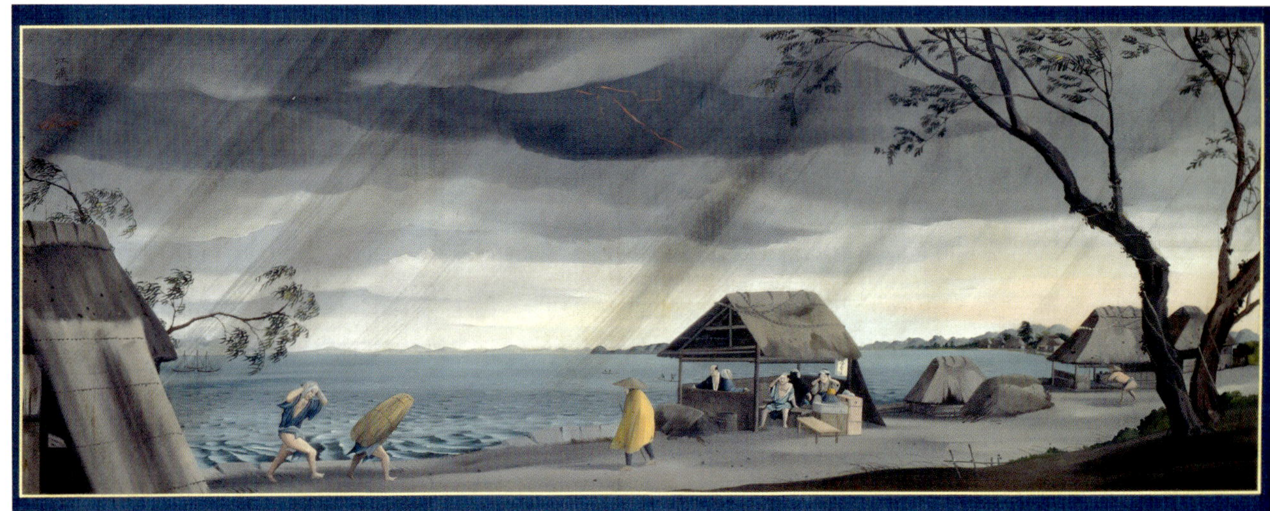

Sudden Shower off Shinagawa

Shiba Kōkan (1747–1818)

Edo period, late 18th–early 19th century

Shiba Kōkan, the creator of this intriguing image, was one of eighteenth-century Japan's most celebrated proponents of Dutch learning (*rangaku*) and Western art. From 1788 to 1789, he traveled to Nagasaki to learn Western painting directly from the small Dutch community that was allowed to live on the island of Deshima in Nagasaki harbor. Kōkan had already tried to master European methods of foreshortening and perspective by copying engravings from imported books, then available in Japan thanks to the reversal (in 1720) of an earlier ban on foreign printed materials. He was so determined to improve his skills that he made the 600-mile journey from Edo to Nagasaki on foot.

After his arduous trip, Kōkan produced a small group of scenes of famous places in Japan. Shinagawa, depicted in this painting, lay just to the south of Edo and was celebrated for its views of the bay. Here Kōkan juxtaposes the thatched buildings in the foreground with a low shoreline, a perspectival device that he adopted from European works. Infrared analysis has revealed that the artist made repeated attempts to place the pillars of the central structure in order to suggest its recession in space.

Panel; ink and color on silk
59 x 155.1 cm (23 1/4 x 61 1/16 in.)
Fenollosa-Weld Collection 11.4686

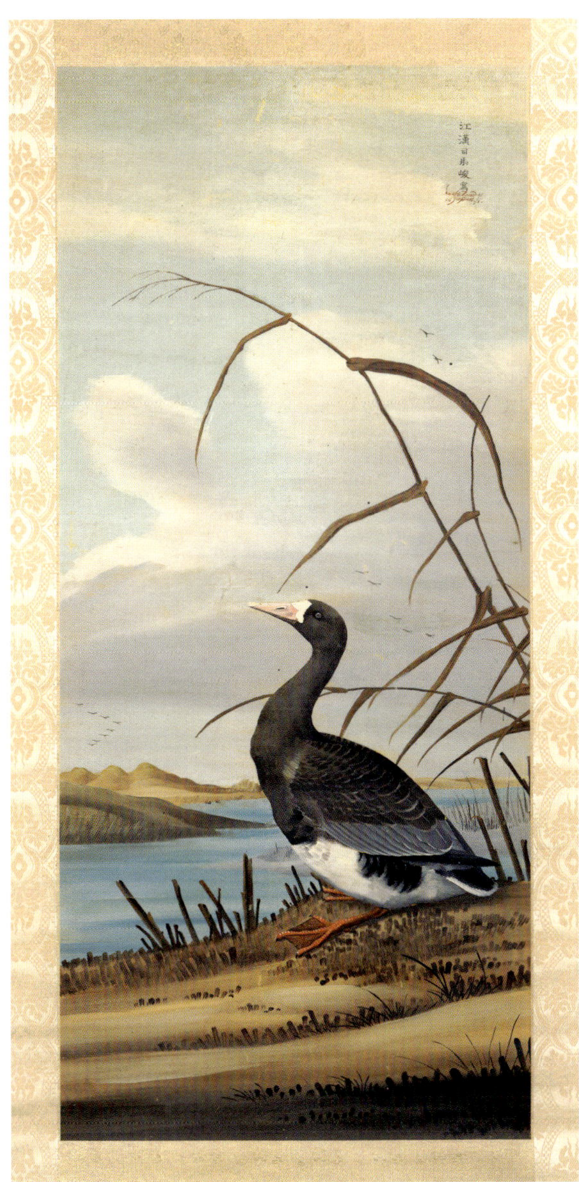

Goose

Shiba Kōkan (1747–1818)

Edo period, late 18th–early 19th century

The pairing of geese and reeds had been adopted by the Japanese from the Chinese by the late thirteenth century. Zen Buddhist masters had interpreted the theme as exemplifying monastic discipline, for the birds display precision in their flight and fidelity to the other members of their flock. Furthermore, the Japanese had an affection for compositions of birds and flowers in the course of the four seasons. In this image, the earthy palette is suggestive of autumn. Another painting by Shiba Kōkan, of a goose in a wintry landscape (now in a private collection), may originally have complemented the Boston scroll.

Despite its traditional subject matter, this composition—with its juxtaposition of the goose in the immediate foreground against a low horizon line—owes its inspiration to Dutch works of art. Kōkan also experimented here with a combination of Western and conventional Japanese pigments in an oil binder to create the effect of a European oil painting. For example, he used Prussian blue, an artificial colorant invented in Germany and introduced to Japan in the late eighteenth century, for the sky.

Hanging scroll; ink and color on silk
121.6 x 155.1 cm (23 1/4 x 61 1/16 in.)
William Sturgis Bigelow Collection 11.8121

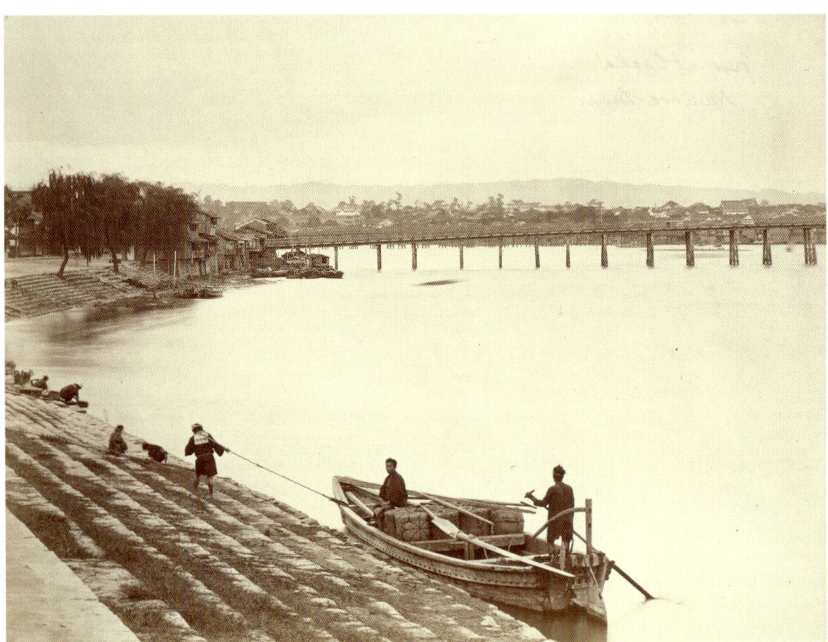

View of Osaka from the Yodo River
Ichida Sōta I (1843–1896)
Meiji era, about 1875

This luxury photographic print showing the Yodo River, which runs from Lake Biwa into Osaka Bay, encapsulates a fleeting moment in the history of the Western gaze on Japan. The first visitors to Japan during the 1850s, following the end of Japan's period of semi-seclusion, were diplomats, military men, traders, and missionaries. In time, improvements in security conditions and transport encouraged new visitors: men and women of leisure with a taste for exotic adventure, who began to arrive in the 1870s. Their desire for souvenirs, combined with some remaining restrictions on internal travel, created a market for photographs of places and people they had visited, as well as those they had not. It was not unusual for foreign visitors to go to a photographic studio and buy photographs, often packaged in an attractive lacquer album, even before setting out to see the country.

These photographs catered to Western consumers' preconceived notions of an untainted, preindustrial Japan. This taste extended to armchair travelers as well, and between the 1870s and 1900 or so, trade in photographs of Japan's landscape and people boomed. By the turn of the century, however, photographs were being overtaken by the new medium of the picture postcard, and the lifting of internal travel restrictions meant that people could actually visit all of the places they had previously experienced only through photographs.

Photograph; albumen print
22 x 27.5 cm (8⅝ x 10⅞ in.)
Gift of Jean S. and Frederic A. Sharf 2008.590

Excursion to View Cherry Blossoms by the Sumida River

Toyohara Chikanobu (1838–1912)

Meiji era, published December 27, 1887

The iron bridge in the background and the European fashions worn by the ladies make this print instantly recognizable as a work from the Meiji era. Opened in 1885, the Azuma Bridge appeared in many prints as a symbol of the new, modern Japan, sometimes combined with older national symbols such as cherry blossoms and Mount Fuji. The personages shown here are not explicitly identified, but viewers would understand that they represented the Meiji emperor (standing in the boat) and empress (wearing black) with their entourage. The imperial couple was presented as a model for the entire nation, with their modern, Westernized lifestyle that also incorporated traditional Japanese values, including an appreciation of the seasonal beauties of nature.

Scenes of elegantly dressed ladies and their male admirers enjoying cherry blossoms had been a staple of *ukiyo-e* woodblock prints during the Edo period. The printing business continued smoothly into the Meiji era, with many of the same artists and publishers, because traditional Japanese woodblock printing (often, as here, using synthetic aniline dyes) remained the most cost-effective method of full-color printing until the beginning of the twentieth century. Only then did Western printing methods (such as color lithography) supersede the woodblock process for commercial printing.

Woodblock print (*nishiki-e*); ink and color on paper
37 x 75.4 cm (14 9/16 x 29 11/16 in.)
Jean S. and Frederic A. Sharf Collection 2000.496a–c

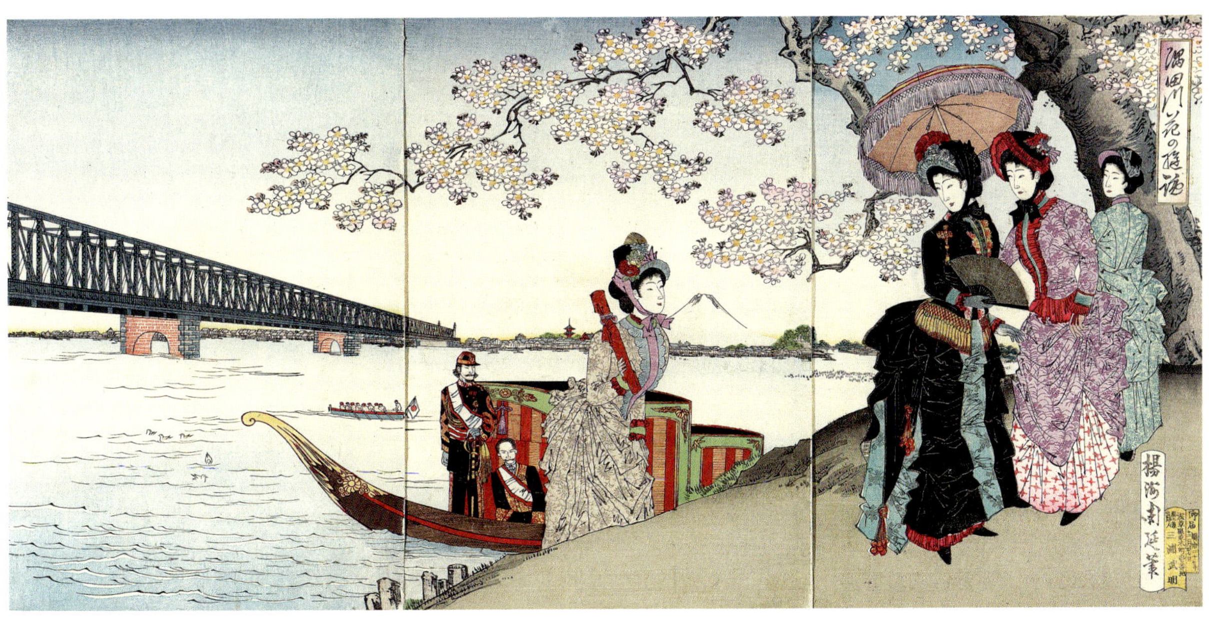

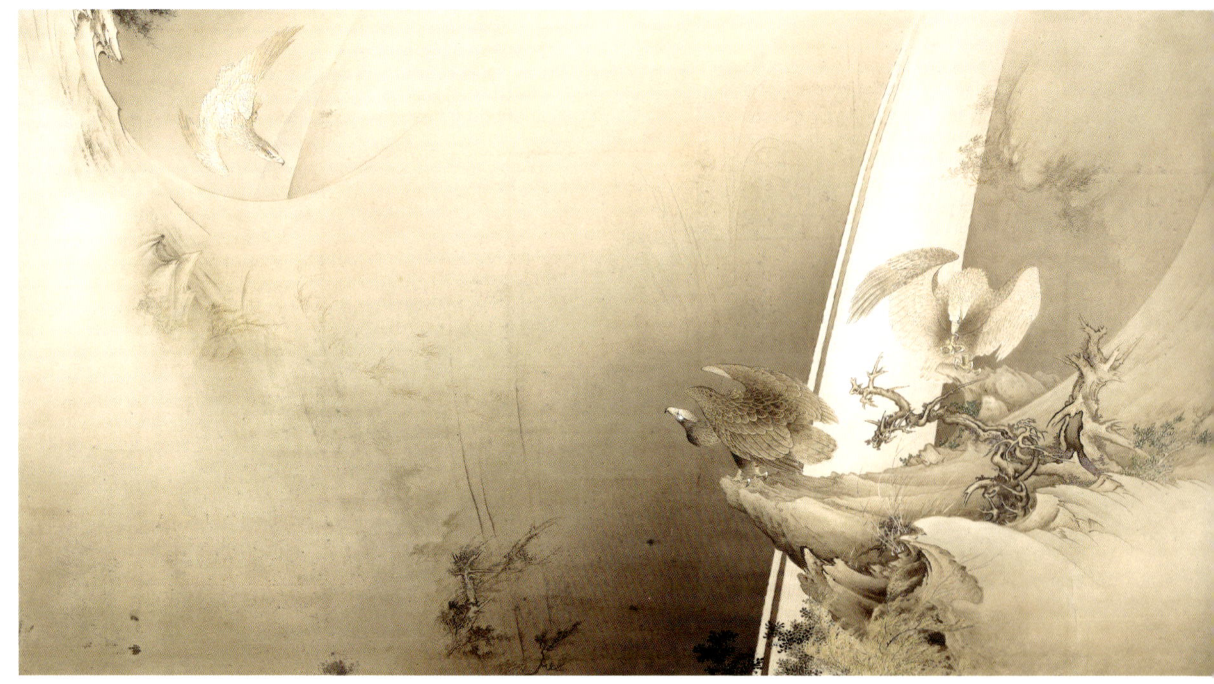

Hawks in a Ravine
Kano Hōgai (1828–1888)
Meiji era, about 1885–86

In this large-scale composition, Kano Hōgai exploited the dynamic brushwork typical of Kano-school painting—seen in the flat arc of the waterfall—but also incorporated Western techniques such as chiaroscuro to give the foreground rocks a sense of volume. This novel combination laid the foundations for a genre that has come to be known as *nihonga* (Japanese-style painting).

The son of a provincial official painter, Hōgai received his formal training in Edo, in the atelier of the conservative Kano school. In 1860 he joined his master in decorating the ceiling of Edo Castle, but with the fall of the Tokugawa shogunate, Hōgai lost his financial backing and was reduced to making a living by painting designs on export pottery and lacquer. His fortunes greatly improved in the 1880s when he was given a monthly stipend by two Bostonian collectors, Ernest Francisco Fenollosa and William Sturgis Bigelow. Fenollosa had denounced the Japanese preoccupation with Western-style oil paintings and advocated the revival of traditional Japanese art. Working together, Fenollosa and Hōgai shaped a new movement that created innovative works for the modern age by synthesizing Western techniques with those of ink painting.

Hōgai regularly exhibited at the Kangakai, a club organized by Fenollosa and Bigelow to encourage the appreciation of traditional Japanese painting. *Hawks in a Ravine* is thought to have been shown at the 1886 Kangakai exhibition.

Hanging scroll; ink and light color on paper
93.2 x 165.7 cm (36 11/16 x 65 1/4 in.)
William Sturgis Bigelow Collection 11.8740

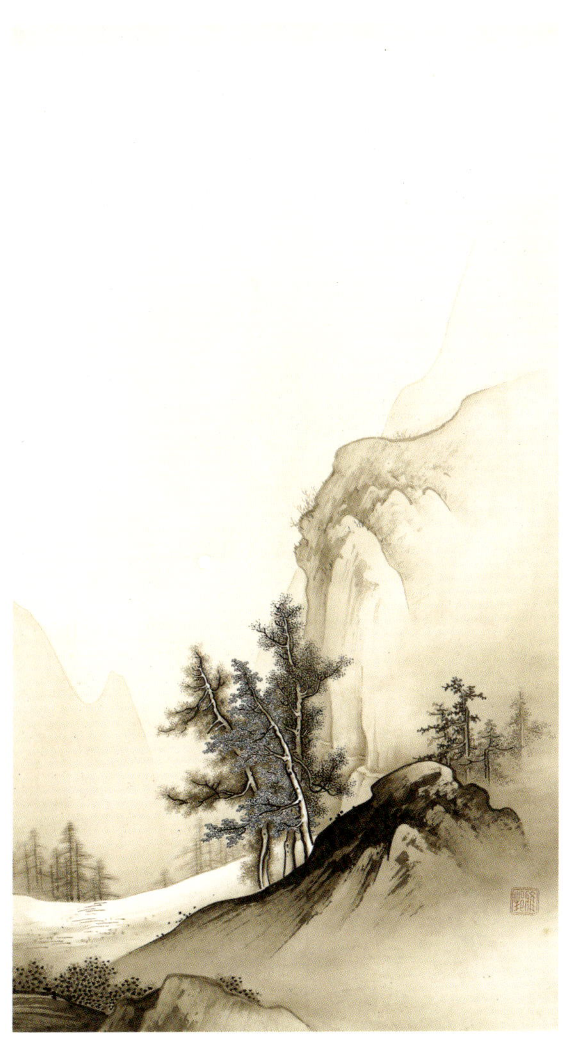

Landscape with Autumn Moon

Hashimoto Gahō (1835–1908)

Meiji era, about 1880s–90s

Hashimoto Gahō, like Kano Hōgai, strove to integrate Western methods of perspective and modeling with traditional subjects and media. In *Landscape with Autumn Moon*, he adopted the texture strokes of Kano-school painting for the definition of the foreground hillock. His handling of the moonlight reflected on the trunks and slope, however, reveals the influence of European techniques.

During the early Meiji era, when Japan sought to emulate Western culture and technology, Gahō struggled to support himself through regular commissions and resorted to painting fans produced for export. But the Bostonians Fenollosa and Bigelow, who also supported Hōgai, eventually granted Gahō a monthly stipend. In 1887 the Ministry of Education authorized the establishment of the Tokyo School of Fine Arts (now Tokyo National University of Fine Arts and Music). Kano Hōgai was appointed the head instructor, but with his untimely death in 1888, Gahō was charged with working out the practical means of executing paintings and instructing students according to the ideals outlined by Fenollosa and developed by his student Okakura Kakuzō. When Okakura was forced out as director of the school in 1898, Gahō supported him in founding the Japan Fine Arts Academy, which remains to this day the primary institution advocating painting with traditional materials.

Hanging scroll; ink on paper
86.7 x 47.2 cm (34 1/8 x 18 9/16 in.)
Source unknown 11.34893

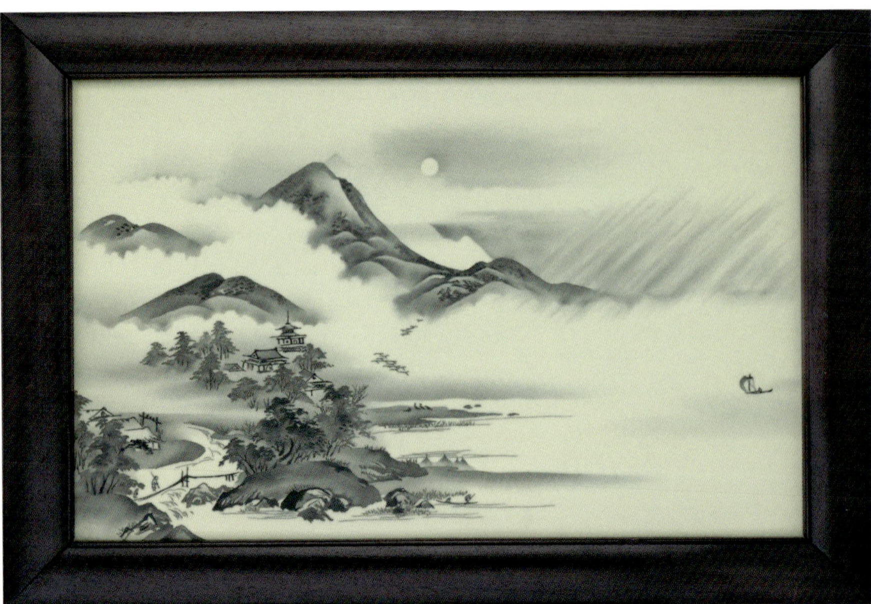

Plaque with design of the "Eight Views of the Xiao and Xiang Rivers"
Namikawa Sōsuke (1847–1910)
Meiji era, about 1893

This plaque uses the technique of cloisonné enameling to imitate the appearance of ink on paper. The surface was built up in many layers of colored glass paste, separated by thin metal ribbons fixed edgeways to a copper base. Each layer was fired in a kiln until it melted, and then the flawless, lustrous finish was brought out by a prolonged process of grinding and polishing.

Enameling has a long history in China, but it was not until the 1830s that the Japanese first succeeded in making crude imitations of Chinese enameled bowls and plates. Just sixty years later, Japanese cloisonné enamels had achieved global celebrity thanks to government patronage, foreign technical advice, and resourceful craft entrepreneurs such as Namikawa Sōsuke.

Namikawa pushed his craftsmen's techniques to the limit in an effort to emulate the best of traditional painting, in this case a landscape by the seventeenth-century Kano painter Naonobu. Namikawa was particularly celebrated both for his skill in rendering the metal-ribbon dividers almost invisible (sometimes, perhaps, even dispensing with them altogether) and for his subtle blending of colors through careful control of kiln temperatures. He was so pleased with this piece that he included it in a promotional brochure that he published in 1896.

Cloisonné enamels on copper, worked in silver-alloy wire, in the original hardwood frame
41.1 x 62 cm (16¼ x 24½ in.), excluding frame
Museum purchase with an anonymous gift and by exchange from a Gift of John T. Spaulding 2004.564

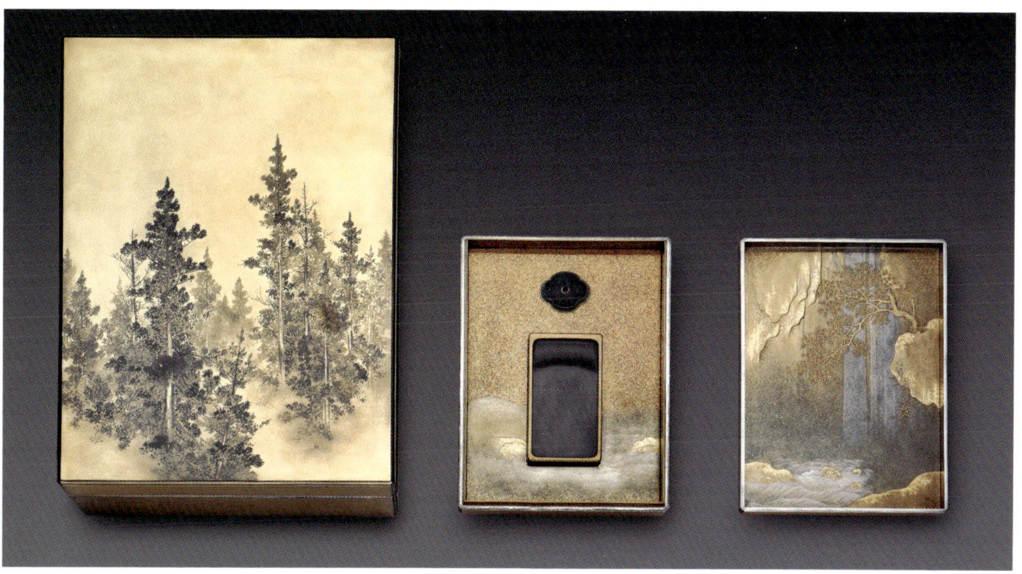

Document box and writing box with design of a cedar forest
Uematsu Hōbi (1872–1933)
Meiji era, about 1899

Although intended for display rather than actual use, the larger box in this set would traditionally have held writing paper, while the smaller box is fitted with an inkstone, used to grind solid ink with water poured from the metal waterdropper. The set was made for the Exposition Universelle held in Paris in 1900, for a separate section created by the organizers for "Craft Objects of Excellence," with both design and execution the responsibility of the maker. Uematsu Hōbi responded to this challenge by creating a lacquer masterpiece—his first recorded work—that combined two very distinct styles.

The insides of the lids are decorated mostly in traditional high- and low-relief lacquer. The outsides, in contrast, are executed in a demanding technique known as "polished-out picture" (*togidashi-e*) that had rarely, if ever, been attempted on such a large scale. Once he had completed the base coats of lacquer, Uematsu applied the atmospheric cedar forest design by sprinkling a mixture of silver and charcoal powder onto damp lacquer. He then applied lacquer to the entire surface and dusted on several layers of gold powder until the forest design disappeared. Finally, he polished the lid until the forest reappeared, flush with, or sometimes partially obscured by, the gold ground.

The forest landscape closely reflects the influence of new trends in contemporary ink painting, as seen in the work of Hashimoto Gahō.

Lacquered wood with silver rims
11.4 x 26.4 x 36.7 cm (4½ x 10⅜ x 14½ in.) and
4.3 x 17.2 x 23.3 cm (1¾ x 6¾ x 9⅛ in.)
Museum purchase with funds by exchange from the Charles Goddard Weld Collection, James Fund, a Gift of Yamanaka and Company, Boston, William Sturgis Bigelow Collection, Bequest of Mrs. Thomas O. Richardson, a Gift of Francis Gardner Curtis, a Gift of Mrs. Roger Cutler, a Gift of Mrs. Charles Goddard Weld, and a Gift of Misses Louisa W. and Marian R. Case 2006.1155–6

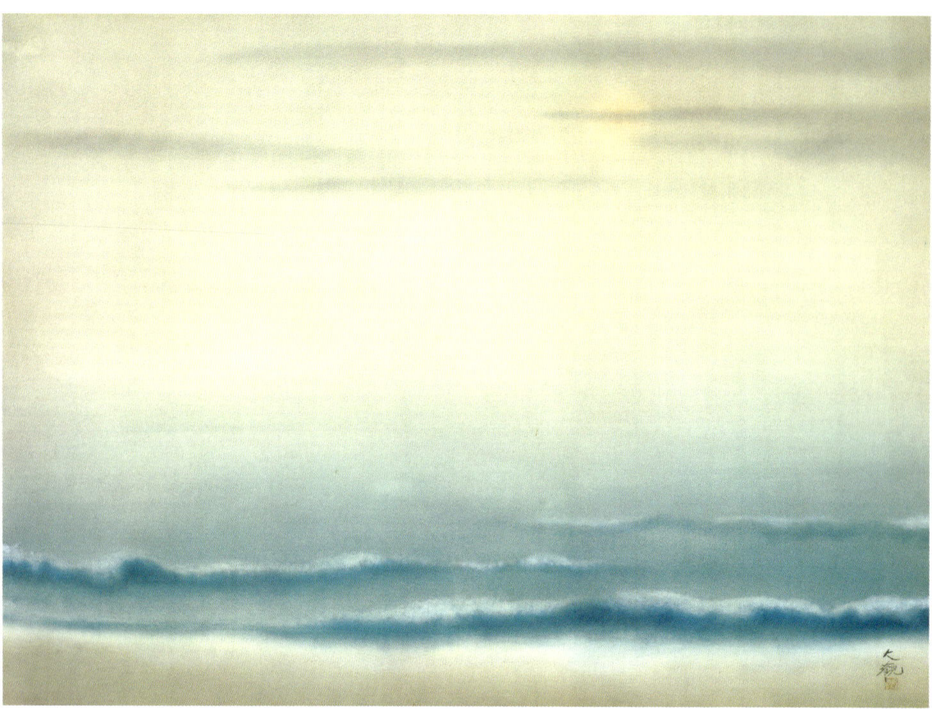

Waves in Moonlight
Yokoyama Taikan (1868–1958)
Meiji era, about 1904–5

This painting, by one of the most celebrated Japanese artists of the last century, represents a further stage in the endeavor to create a new art that would preserve the essence of Japanese tradition while infusing it with invigorating techniques from the West. Taikan here eschews the use of ink line, hailed by conservative artists as the defining element of Japanese painting, but exploits the intense colors of traditional pigments to evoke a new sense of atmosphere.

Waves in Moonlight was executed in Boston and exhibited at a show in Cambridge, Massachusetts, organized by Okakura Kakuzō shortly after he assumed his duties as advisor to the Museum of Fine Arts. He wrote in an accompanying pamphlet: "We claim that art must be national, that we shall be lost if cut away from our traditions, and, at the same time, we consider individuality to be the essence of vitality. We do not pretend to be ancient nor endeavor to be modern." Taikan interpreted these somewhat contradictory ideals by developing a painting manner known as "hazy style" (*mōrōtai*), of which this is an early example.

Boston critics responded favorably to the Cambridge exhibition, commenting on "the probity and purity of design . . . the utmost beauty of tone and atmosphere, and finally best of all, the imaginative impulse, which lifts naturalism above the commonplace plane of brutal realism and ennobles it."

Unmounted painting; ink and color on silk
48.8 x 64 cm (19 3/16 x 25 3/16 in.)
Gift of Mrs. Francis Gardner Curtis 41.499

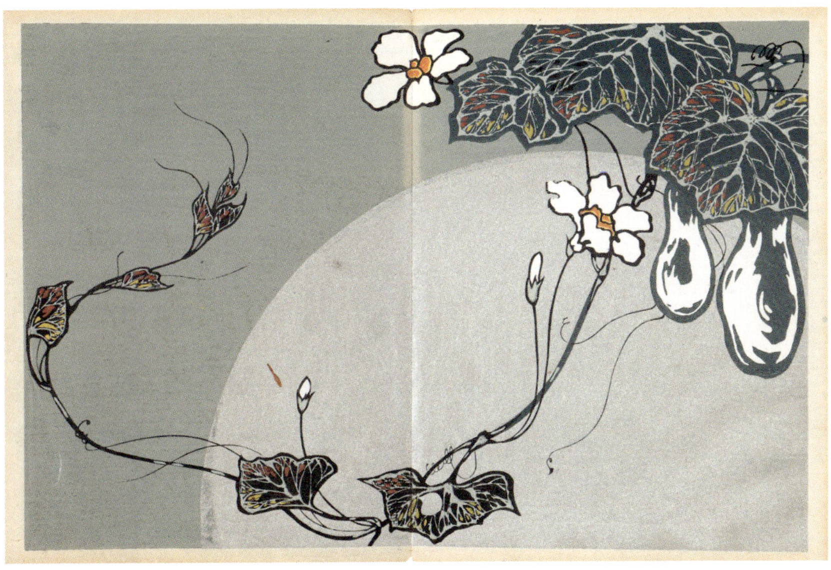

Patterns of Plants and Flowers from Nature
Furuya Kōrin (1875–1910)
Meiji era, published January 15, 1907

Although it depicts a time-honored Japanese subject, this gourd-vine-and-moon design strongly reflects the influence of Western Art Nouveau; the asymmetry and distinctive line typical of the Western style have often been linked, in turn, to European artists' exposure to Japanese art. Despite his debt to Art Nouveau, the designer of this book took the art-name Kōrin to emphasize his affinity for the native Rinpa style, initiated by Tawaraya Sōtatsu and the eponymous Ogata Kōrin in the seventeenth century. The book was published by the Unsōdō company, which was renowned for its continued use of traditional woodblock printing even when less-labor-intensive Western techniques, such as lithography and collotype, were being widely practiced in Japan.

In keeping with the literary nature of much Rinpa design, the gourd vine and moon are a reference to a chapter in *The Tale of Genji*, the great eleventh-century classic of courtly prose. Moonflowers are known in Japanese as "evening faces" (*yūgao*), a name given by the charismatic Prince Genji to a young lover with an exquisitely delicate constitution. Tragically, she dies on a moonlit night from the shock of encountering the jealous spirit of one of Genji's other lovers. Her presence is only hinted at here, imbuing the design with a melancholy that resonates with the subdued color scheme.

Woodblock printed book; ink and color on paper
with applied silver and gold
25.1 x 18.5 cm (9⅞ x 7¼ in.)
Gift of Arthur Vershbow 2001.864.1–2

1

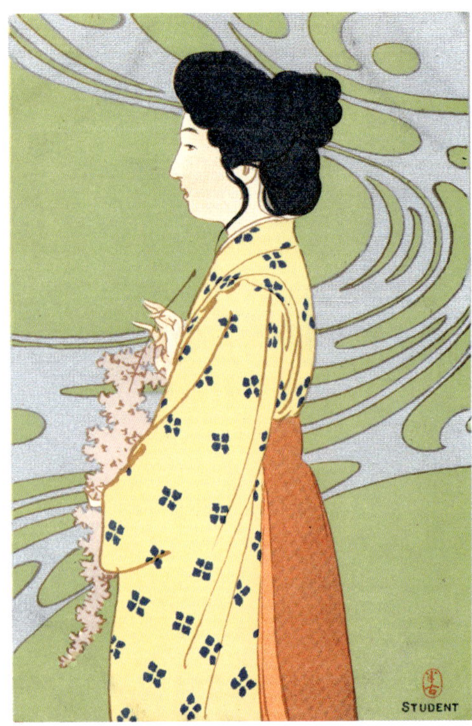

3

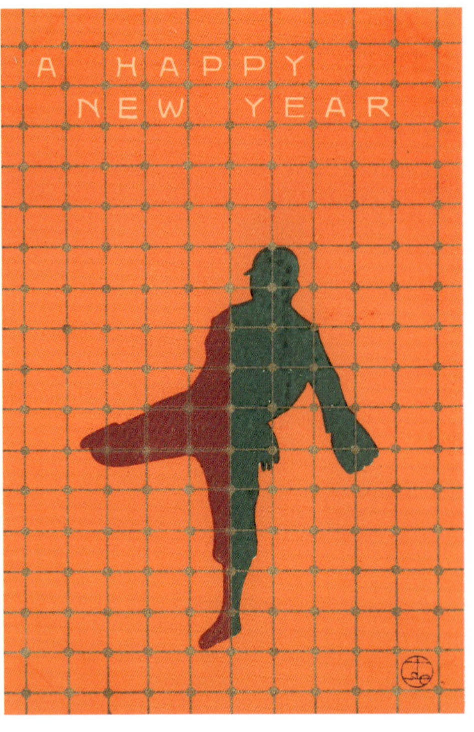

2

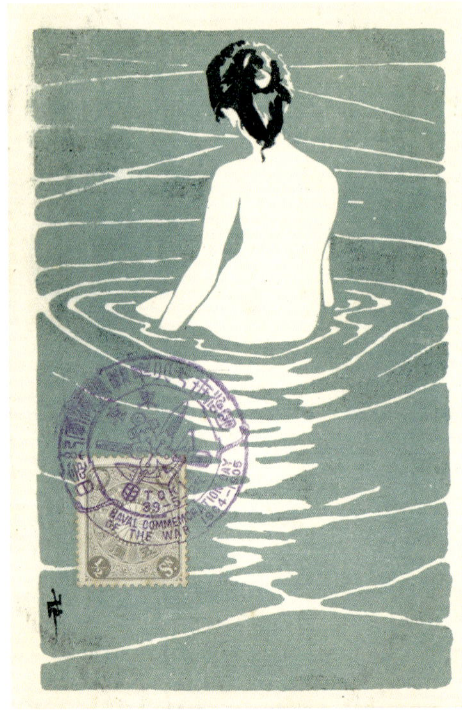

4

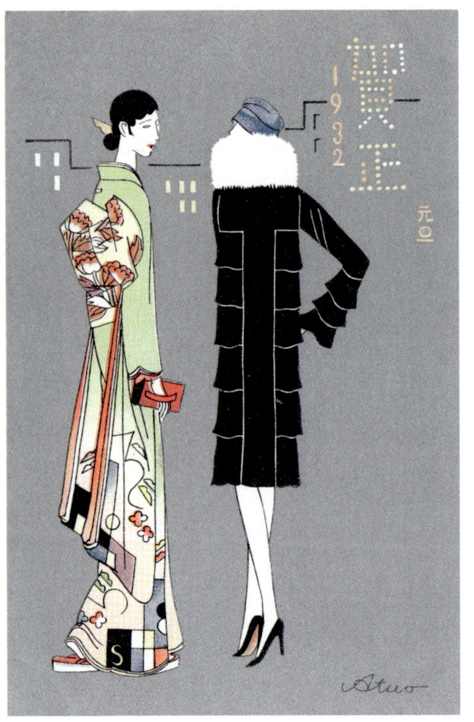

1 ***Student***
Kajita Hanko (1870–1917)
Meiji era, about 1905
Color lithograph; ink and metallic pigment, with embossed texture, on card stock
8.8 x 13.8 cm (3 7/16 x 5 7/16 in.)
Leonard A. Lauder Collection of Japanese Postcards
2002.965

2 ***Female Nude Seated in Water***
Ichijō Narumi (1877–1910)
Meiji era, 1906
Color lithograph; ink on card stock
8.8 x 13.8 cm (3 7/16 x 5 7/16 in.)
Leonard A. Lauder Collection of Japanese Postcards
2002.935

3 ***New Year's Card* from an unidentified series of baseball New Year's cards**
Takahashi Harumi (dates unknown)
Shōwa era, 1932
Color lithograph; ink and metallic pigment on coated card stock
8.8 x 13.8 cm (3 7/16 x 5 7/16 in.)
Leonard A. Lauder Collection of Japanese Postcards
2002.1217

4 ***New Year's Card: Women in Au Courant Fashion with Cityscape***
Atsuo (dates unknown)
Shōwa era, 1932
Color lithograph; ink and metallic pigment on coated card stock
8.8 x 13.8 cm (3 7/16 x 5 7/16 in.)
Leonard A. Lauder Collection of Japanese Postcards
2002.1474

During the early twentieth century, the postcard replaced the traditional woodblock print as the primary graphic art form in Japan. The first cards, introduced by the Japanese government in 1873 to emulate official Austro-Hungarian correspondence cards, were relatively simple. Following the decision by the Ministry of Communications in 1900 to relinquish its monopoly over postcard publication, many of the country's leading artists tried their hand at producing highly inventive and often lavish designs for the new format. By 1905 postcards enjoyed a boom, with hundreds of thousands of images produced. Popular magazines were devoted to the subject, and exhibitions of award-winning cards were organized throughout the country.

Postcard images dating from 1900 to 1940 capture a nation in transition. Produced when Japan was establishing itself as a major international power, following an unprecedented campaign of Westernization, some of the images reflect nostalgia for a bygone age. Many others, however, firmly embrace modernity by adopting European imagery and contemporary artistic styles, such as Art Nouveau and Art Deco. The most compelling designs combine elements of the different sensibilities of East and West. Thanks to the gift in 2002 of the Leonard A. Lauder Collection of Japanese Postcards, the MFA now possesses one of the world's largest institutional holdings of this intriguing art form.

Reclining Nude

Hashiguchi Goyō (1881–1921)

Taishō era, about 1916–20

As this exquisite drawing shows, Hashiguchi Goyō was thoroughly versed in Western techniques, having graduated at the top of his class in Western painting (*yōga*) from the prestigious Tokyo School of Fine Arts in 1905. He is better known, however, for his fourteen woodblock-print designs in the genre known as "new prints" (*shin hanga*), works that utilized the traditional block-cutting and printing methods of the old *ukiyo-e* woodblock prints in combination with a new, Westernized style.

Goyō's elegantly sensual depictions of beautiful women recall the work of *ukiyo-e* artists such as Kitagawa Utamaro. In this drawing, the sense of affectionate intimacy apparent in his graphic work is combined with a simmering eroticism that would not have been legally possible in a commercially published print. Many of Goyō's female models were geisha, professional musicians and entertainers who continued to wear traditional clothing and hairstyles even as other fashionable, affluent Japanese women were experimenting with Western dress.

Goyō's works are rare for several reasons: poor health limited his working capacity and resulted in his early death; high standards led him to spend much time on each work; and the great earthquake and fire that devastated Tokyo in 1923 destroyed massive numbers of works by Goyō and other *shin hanga* artists.

Sketch; graphite on paper
26.5 x 38 cm (10 7/16 x 14 15/16 in.)
Helen S. Coolidge Fund 1970.4

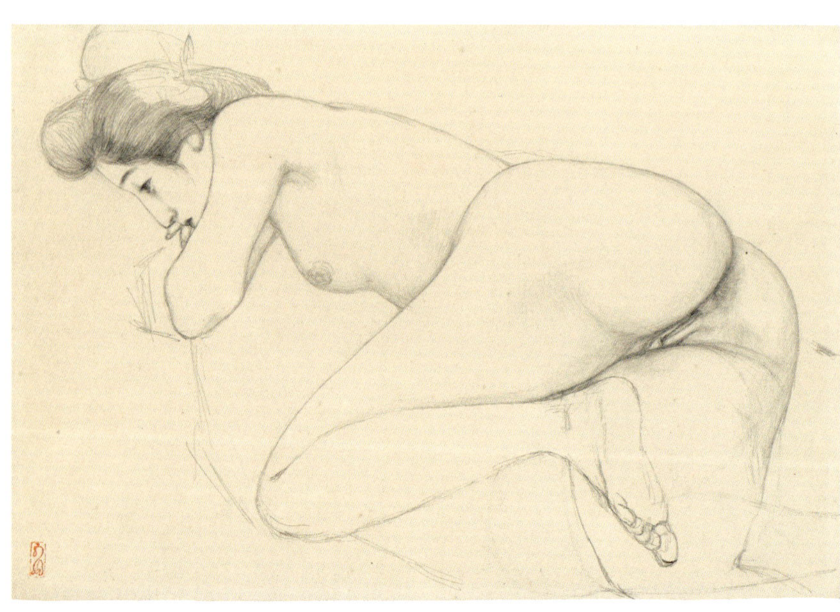

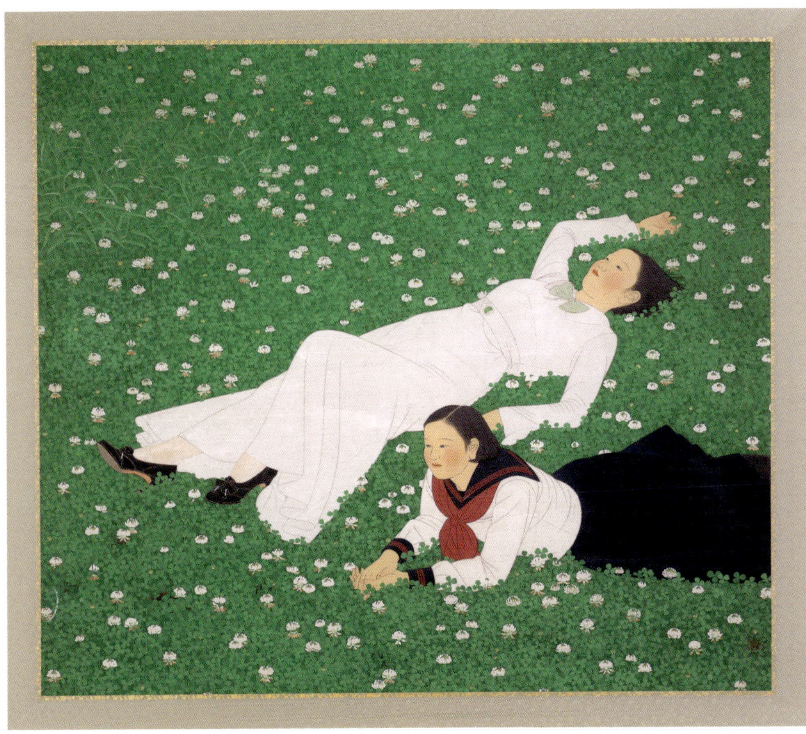

Clover

Tateishi Harumi (1908–1994)

Shōwa era, 1934

This monumental composition juxtaposes a pair of young ladies against a background of meticulously painted clover. The two modernly dressed women are seen frequently in Tateishi Harumi's works. The older of the two, who lies on her back with her arm outstretched, is thought to be the artist's younger sister. The younger lady, an adolescent wearing the sailor uniform of Japanese schoolgirls, remains unidentified.

The first decades of the twentieth century were marked by polarizing debates among factions of artists regarding the proper form that painting should take in describing a modernizing Japan. The primary opposition was between those who championed Western-style works (*yōga*), executed in European oil paints, and those who advocated Japanese-style compositions (*nihonga*), with their traditional mineral pigments and formats. As *Clover* suggests, however, several artists were able to synthesize the two styles.

Harumi himself was initially trained in Western-style oil painting, but later turned to a somewhat more traditional style under the guidance of the *nihonga* painter and printmaker Itō Shinsui. In this composition, Harumi employed European-style foreshortening and modeling of the figures while carefully building up layers of shell white and malachite—following Japanese painting conventions—to describe the field of clover.

Panel; ink and color on paper
180 x 199 cm (70⅞ x 78⅜ in.)
Keith McLeod Fund 2004.242

Poem No. 6: Image de la Mer

Onchi Kōshirō (1891–1955)

Shōwa era, 1948

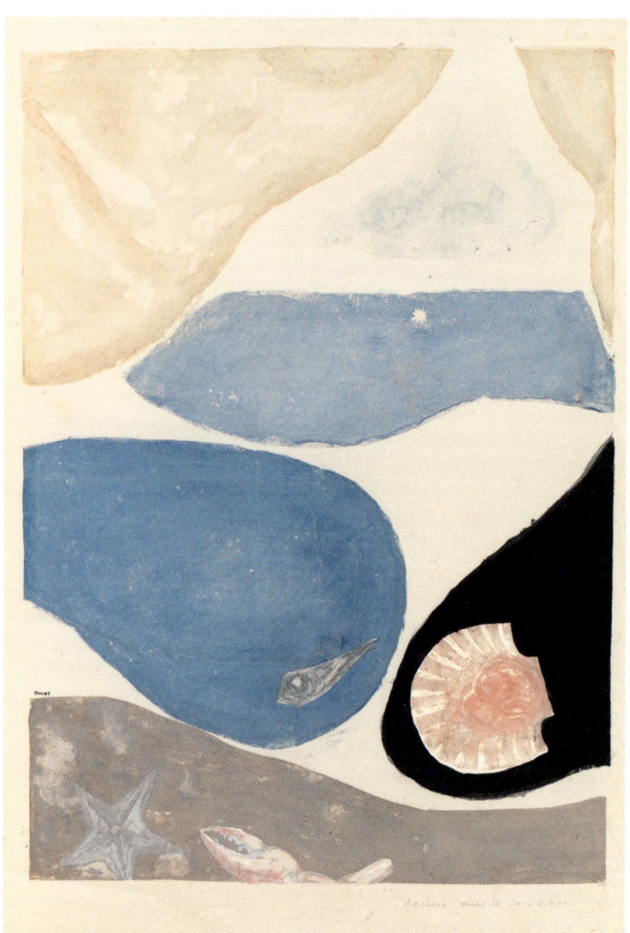

In this semiabstract work, images of a sea star, a crab claw, and a scallop shell containing a human fetus suggest that the ocean is the source of all life. Onchi Kōshirō, who often made the sea the subject of his prints and poems, is widely regarded as the founding father of the "creative print" (*sōsaku hanga*) in Japan. In traditional Japanese printmaking, the artist provided the design, but the block cutting and printing were carried out by specialist craftsmen. In creative prints, in contrast, the artist personally carries out every stage of the production process. Onchi viewed woodblock printing not as a convenient means of producing multiples but as a distinctive art form that owed its special character to the carving and printing processes. Sometimes he produced only one or (as with this image) two of a design. In addition to conventional wooden blocks, he also used natural objects or sheets of paint-soaked paper, as in this example.

Onchi was exposed to European abstraction early in his career, and for much of his life switched freely between figurative and abstract styles. During the years of increasingly oppressive militaristic government, however, he virtually abandoned his abstract work. Japan's defeat in 1945 stimulated a last flowering of Onchi's abstract style, when he used limpid, transparent colors and biomorphic forms to create lyrical, dreamlike effects.

Woodblock and paperblock print; ink and color on paper
78.6 x 55.1 cm (30 15/16 x 21 11/16 in.)
Asiatic Curator's Fund 59.478

Avanti

Shinoda Tōkō (born in 1913)

Shōwa era, 1984

The prints and paintings of Shinoda Tōkō apply the aesthetic principles of traditional ink brushwork to abstract compositions with timeless, universal appeal. In printmaking, the artist prefers lithography, because the process of drawing directly on the stone is similar to the calligraphic expression that is the fundamental basis of her art. Shinoda's works are primarily monochrome but often include a single note of brilliant color; the red streak in *Avanti*, added by hand, suggests the effect of a red seal on a piece of ink calligraphy.

Shinoda was trained from childhood in traditional calligraphy, initially by her father. She felt unhappily constrained, however, by the conservative adherence to the styles of past masters that she was expected to follow as a young artist. With the flowering of the Japanese avant-garde in the postwar period, she expanded her artistic repertoire in new directions, spending two years in New York City in the 1950s—the heyday of Abstract Expressionism—and developing her own distinctive style. Following a series of exhibitions in various countries, her work has become extremely popular with collectors both in Japan and abroad.

Lithograph; ink on paper, with hand coloring
53 x 71.5 cm ($20\frac{7}{8}$ x $28\frac{1}{8}$ in.)
Gift of Norman H. and Mary S. Tolman in honor of their daughters, Allison Tolman and Hilary Tolman Martineau
2006.1352

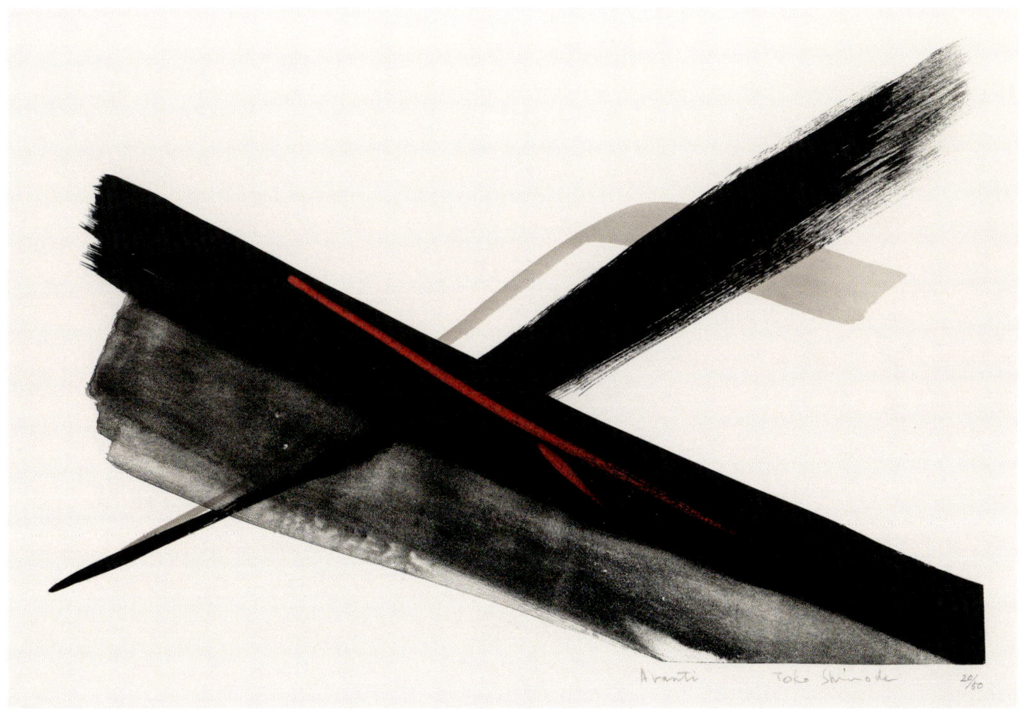

***Longevity* (*Kotobuki*) basket**

Iizuka Rōkansai (1890–1958)

Shōwa era, about 1935–45

Iizuka Rōkansai's *Longevity* basket was executed in the very demanding "bundled-weave" (*tabane-ami*) technique, which requires an extraordinary degree of skill in both splitting the bamboo and manipulating the width of the bundle at different points in the weave. Like many Tokyo baskets, it is finished with a deliberate coating of dust fixed with a layer of clear lacquer.

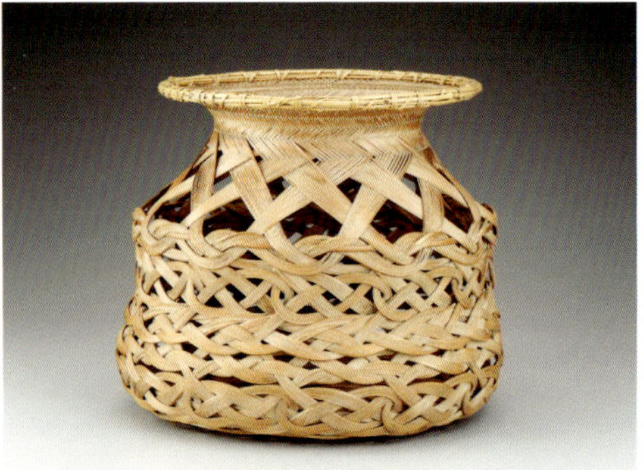

Although the Japanese have used bamboo for thousands of years, basketry did not emerge as a prestigious art form until the mid-1800s. Since then, Japan's bamboo artists have created a compelling artistic universe through careful selection and treatment of raw materials; intricate, contrasting woven patterns; inventive forms; and meticulous dyeing and finishing.

The first basket actually signed with its maker's name is thought to have been created in the 1870s. Like most high-quality pieces of the early period, it was made in the Kansai region (Kyoto, Osaka, Nara, and environs), where baskets were in demand as flower containers for tea ritual; these were at first based closely on Chinese models. In the second decade of the twentieth century, the Iizuka family established an art-basketry tradition in Tokyo. Thanks to the growth of a wealthy middle class and a progressive consumer society, during the 1920s Iizuka Rōkansai and his contemporaries quickly broke away from mainland styles and developed a uniquely Japanese basketry language, creating ever more challenging and expressive forms.

Madake and *negamaridake* bamboo, finished with dust and lacquer
H. 26 cm (H. 10¼ in.)
Keith McLeod Fund 2004.566a–b

Mountain River (Yamakawa)

Honda Shōryū (born in 1951)

Heisei era, 2005

This dramatically modeled, technically advanced, and outsized piece was crafted from fine stained bamboo strips woven in the twining (*nawame*) technique. Honda Shōryū (or Syōryū) is one of several contemporary Japanese bamboo artists who have gone even further than Iizuka Rōkansai, abandoning not only Chinese norms but also traditional functionality, preferring to create objects that are purely sculptural. He is also typical of artists of his generation in that he has sometimes been dogged by financial hardships and factional politicking, and is now sustained in large part by the enthusiasm of art lovers in the United States.

Shōryū first came to prominence in 1981 when he won an award at the Western Division of the Japan Traditional Craft Art Association. His career stalled thereafter, both because interest in bamboo art among Japanese collectors declined and because his work failed to secure acceptance at four Association exhibitions, the total necessary to achieve full membership in that exclusive group. Thanks to the patronage of the prominent American collector Lloyd Cotsen, Honda was eventually admitted to the rival Nitten exhibition, whose judges admired his revolutionary approach to basketry.

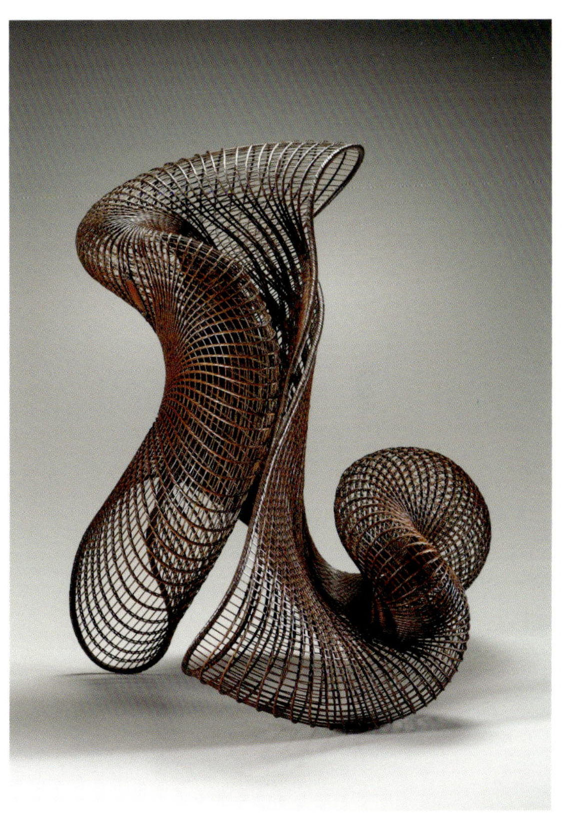

Madake bamboo
68.6 x 43.2 x 45.7 cm (27 x 17 x 18 in.)
Asiatic Deaccession Fund 2005.379

Meisen kimono

Meiji, Taishō, or early Shōwa era, first half of the 20th century

Meisen, as this kind of kimono is known, were the mark of city-dwelling, working Japanese women in the first half of the twentieth century. The bright colors and assertive design of this example reflect the influence of Art Deco, giving the garment a Western and very modern feel. Yet for all its decisive difference from the frugal samurai taste for small patterns and subdued colors of the previous era, the simple cut remains virtually identical, and the design is in fact a reworking of a traditional pattern.

Meisen are woven from relatively coarse silk obtained from defective cocoons, producing a strong, taffeta-like fabric. Large pictorial designs became possible owing to a new development in the traditional dyeing technique known as *kasuri*. Originally, warp threads had been bound by hand with binding threads and then resist-dyed to produce a pattern that emerged when woven. From about 1909, however, patterns were printed directly onto the warp and weft threads using stencils. Printing on both the warp and weft produced a sharper pattern, made more complex designs possible, and sped up production. Sold seasonally through the new department stores using attractive advertising campaigns, *meisen* were, for a period, the essence of chic.

Silk and rayon plain weave, warp and weft printed, with cotton plain-weave lining
133.4 x 116.8 cm (52½ x 46 in.)
Gift of John C. Weber 2004.76

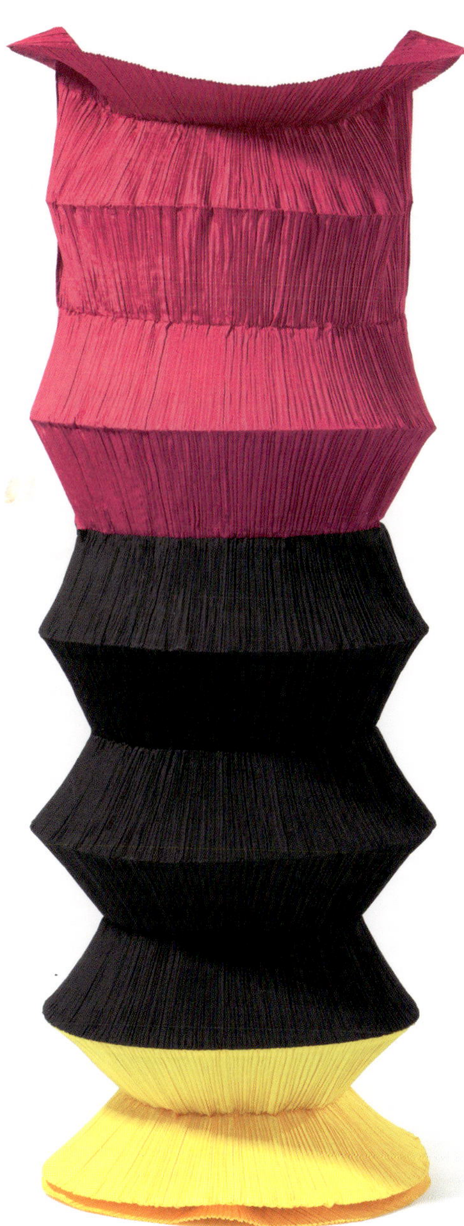

Flying Saucer dress

Miyake Issey (born in 1935)

Heisei era, 1994

Miyake Issey's *Flying Saucer* dress draws upon a long history of pleated clothing in the West, particularly the evening gowns of the Spanish couturier Mariano Fortuny. Yet Miyake's garment takes its shape from its own geometry rather than the body of the wearer; it resembles a Japanese lantern, which unfolds from a two- to a three-dimensional form. The elasticity of the fabric, though, allows the dress to respond to its wearer's movements.

Miyake's career has been described as "a metaphor for the recovery of Japan" following the country's defeat in World War II. Immediately after the war, Japan experienced a period of intense Americanization, but by 1970, when Miyake established his own design studio, the country was ready to forge a fresh cultural identity. Although addressing the specifics of his own career, Miyake could have spoken for the numerous architects, photographers, and graphic designers with whom he has collaborated when he stated, "My challenge as a clothing designer has been to create something different, not traditionally Japanese, not purely Western, but something that has the best of both: a new genre of clothing."

Heat-set polyester
Center back length: 111.8 cm (44 in.)
Gift of Miyake Issey 1998.239

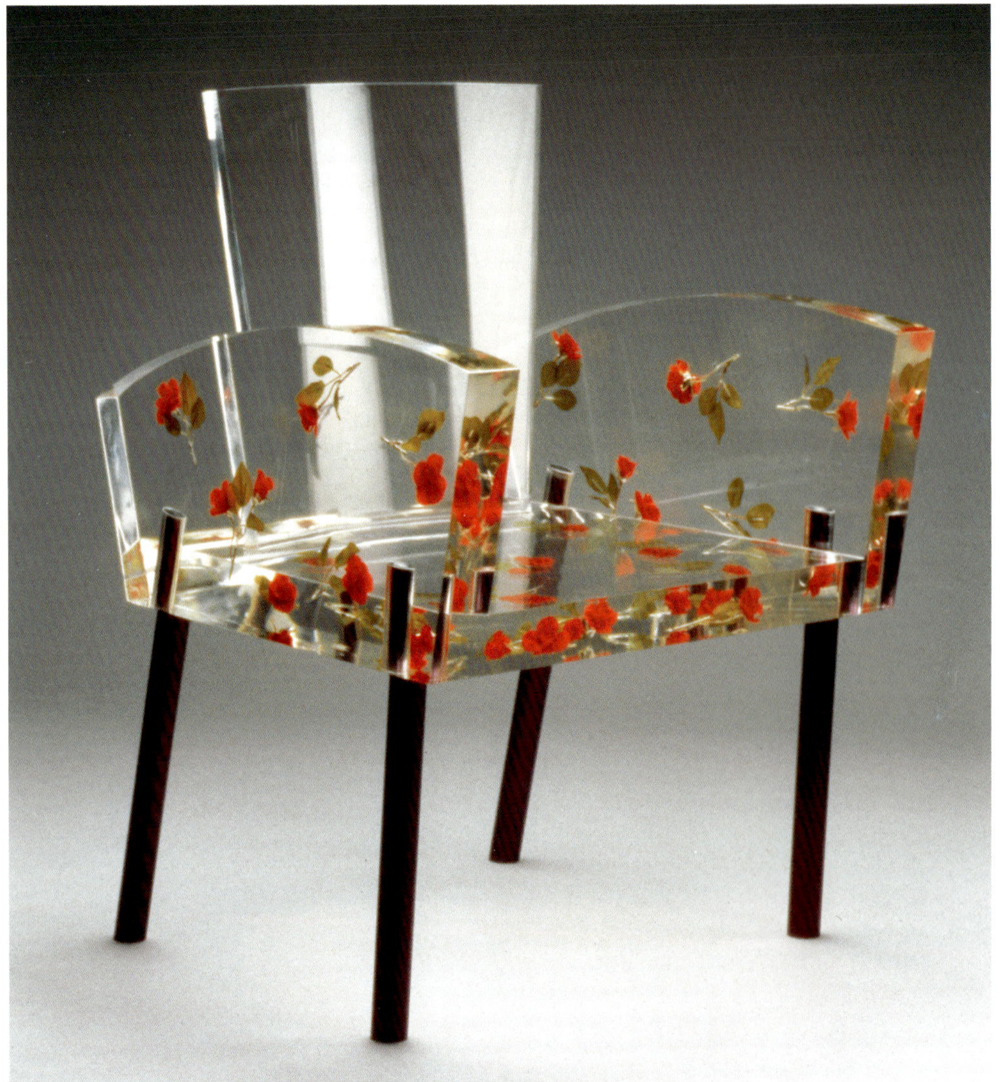

Miss Blanche

Kuramata Shirō (1934–1991)

Shōwa era, 1988

This chair is named for the tragic central character of Tennessee Williams's 1947 play *A Streetcar Named Desire*; the roses are a reference to the corsage worn by Vivien Leigh in the 1951 film version. It ingeniously encapsulates the nature of the protagonist: trapped by her sentimental notions, and in a state of panic induced by the realization that her youth and beauty are slipping through her fingers in a hard-edged world with which she is unable to cope.

Kuramata Shirō was best known for his pioneering interior designs, many of them produced for commercial venues such as Miyake Issey's boutiques. His training was initially in woodcraft and furniture construction, but he then studied Western design and, after a period working for department stores, struck out as an independent designer in the mid-1960s. Having experimented for a time with sculptures constructed from light, Kuramata was determined to produce objects that appeared free from the constraints of gravity and the impurity of visible structure. This resolve led him to work with industrial technologies and materials such as steel mesh, glass, and the transparent acrylic used in this chair, a work manufactured by the Kokuyo Company.

While Kuramata worked extensively in the Western idiom and later in life was involved with the Italian design movement Memphis, his Japanese roots are evident both in his minimalist aesthetic and in his fascination with the preservation of a transient moment, a perennial theme of classical Japanese culture.

Acrylic resin, silk, plastic, and aluminum
H. 90.2 cm (H. 35½ in.)
Maria Antoinette Evans Fund and Gift of Dr. John W. Elliot, by exchange and EDA Curator's Fund 1996.32

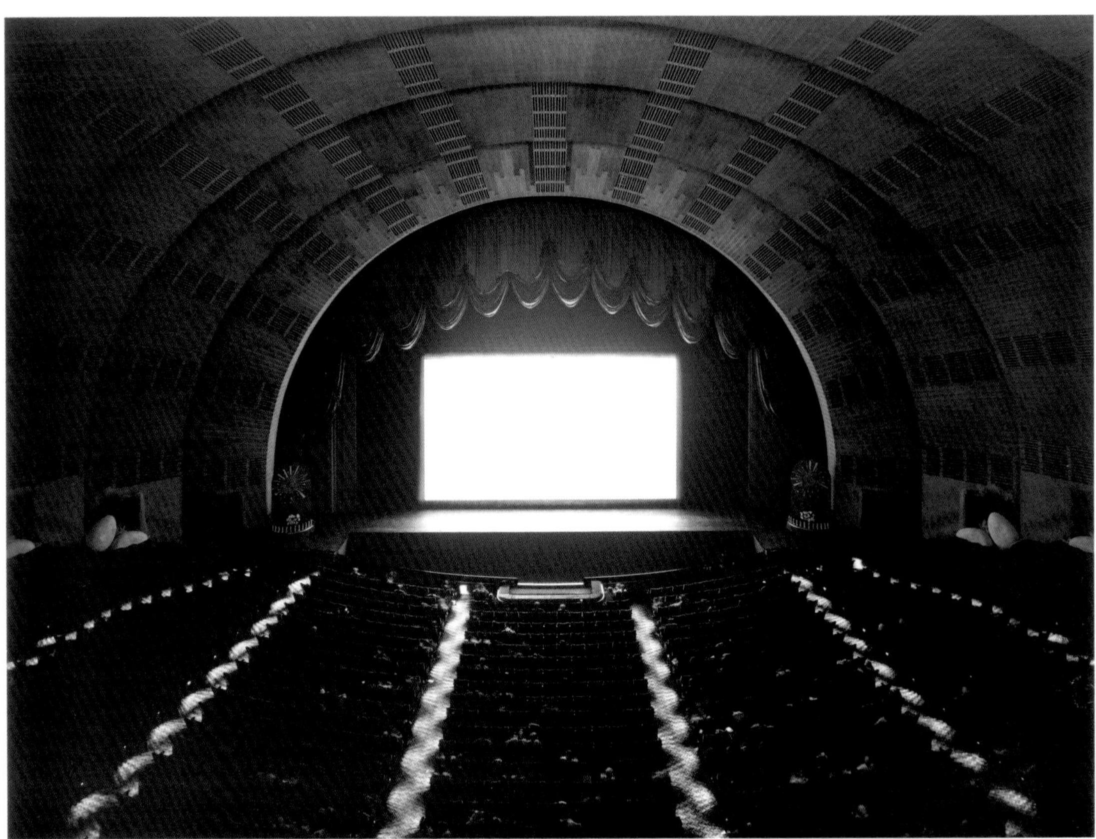

Radio City Music Hall, New York
Sugimoto Hiroshi (born in 1948)
Shōwa era, 1978

Since the 1970s, Sugimoto Hiroshi has explored the concept of time in a series of photographs of indoor and outdoor theaters, seascapes, dioramas, wax portraits, architecture, and mathematical forms. The idea of capturing the duration of a film with a still photograph inspired Sugimoto to create his now-famous movie-theater images. He realized that the long exposure time would result in a completely blank screen, but he heightened the visual interest of the pictures by concentrating on theaters that had inherently appealing architectural details. In this image, the projected film illuminates the Art Deco–style plaster and gold arches of the landmark building in Rockefeller Center, while the flickering of the aisle lights gives the illusion of twisted bands of energy.

Born in Tokyo, Sugimoto received his formal art training in California in the 1970s and then moved to New York, where he became aware of the ideas of Minimalism and Conceptualism. Now residing in both Japan and the United States, he has always tried to create images that are of international appeal, but his interest in process resonates with traditional Japanese aesthetic values.

Photograph; gelatin silver print
42.2 x 54.6 cm (16⅝ x 21½ in.)
Gift of Sylvan Barnet and William Burto in memory of Yasuhiro Iguchi 1992.472

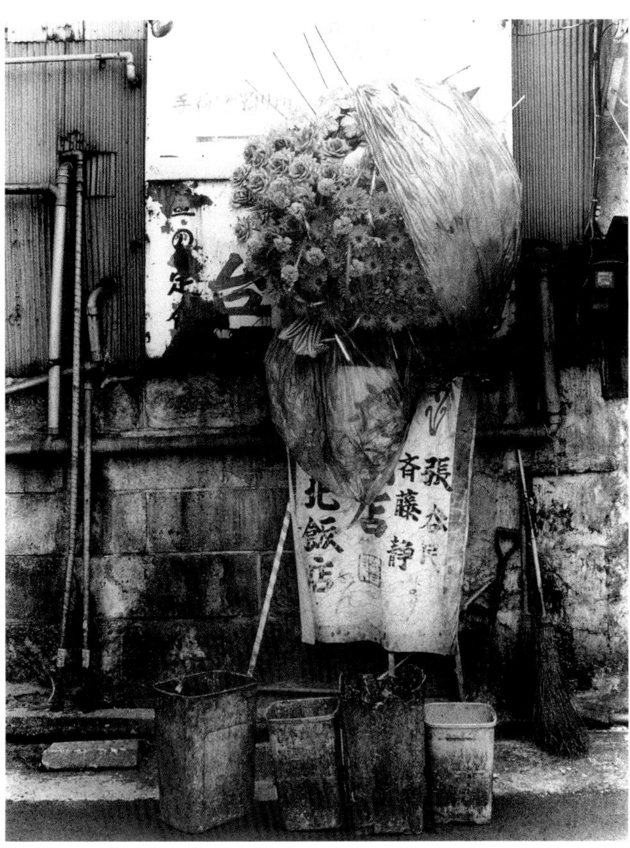

Store Opening Flowers for Hysteric Glamour, no. 4
Moriyama Daidō (born in 1938)
Heisei era, 1991

Store Opening Flowers is part of a 1993 project entitled *Daidō Hysteric*, commissioned by the avant-garde fashion company Hysteric Glamour. It shows a once-gaudy floral decoration, made to celebrate the opening of a new business, abandoned next to a row of trash cans. The gritty, at times almost raw style of the image is typical of the work of Moriyama Daidō, a photographer who came of age after the atomic bombings of Hiroshima and Nagasaki and the rapid Americanization of Japan.

Defining his own artistic voice in the 1950s, Moriyama eschewed the lyrical, carefully balanced photographs of more conventional contemporary European works. Instead he found inspiration in William Klein's prize-winning book *New York* (1956), which established a brash mode of capturing the stark realities of the city. Admiring Klein's intentional blurring of the camera's focus and deliberately grainy printing, Moriyama incorporated these techniques into his own seemingly impromptu images, which chronicle the transformation of Japan's urban landscape and the attendant disjunctions between tradition and modernity.

Photograph; gelatin silver print
43.2 x 55.9 cm (17 x 22 in.)
Horace W. Goldsmith Foundation Fund for Photography and Asiatic Deaccession Fund 2005.548

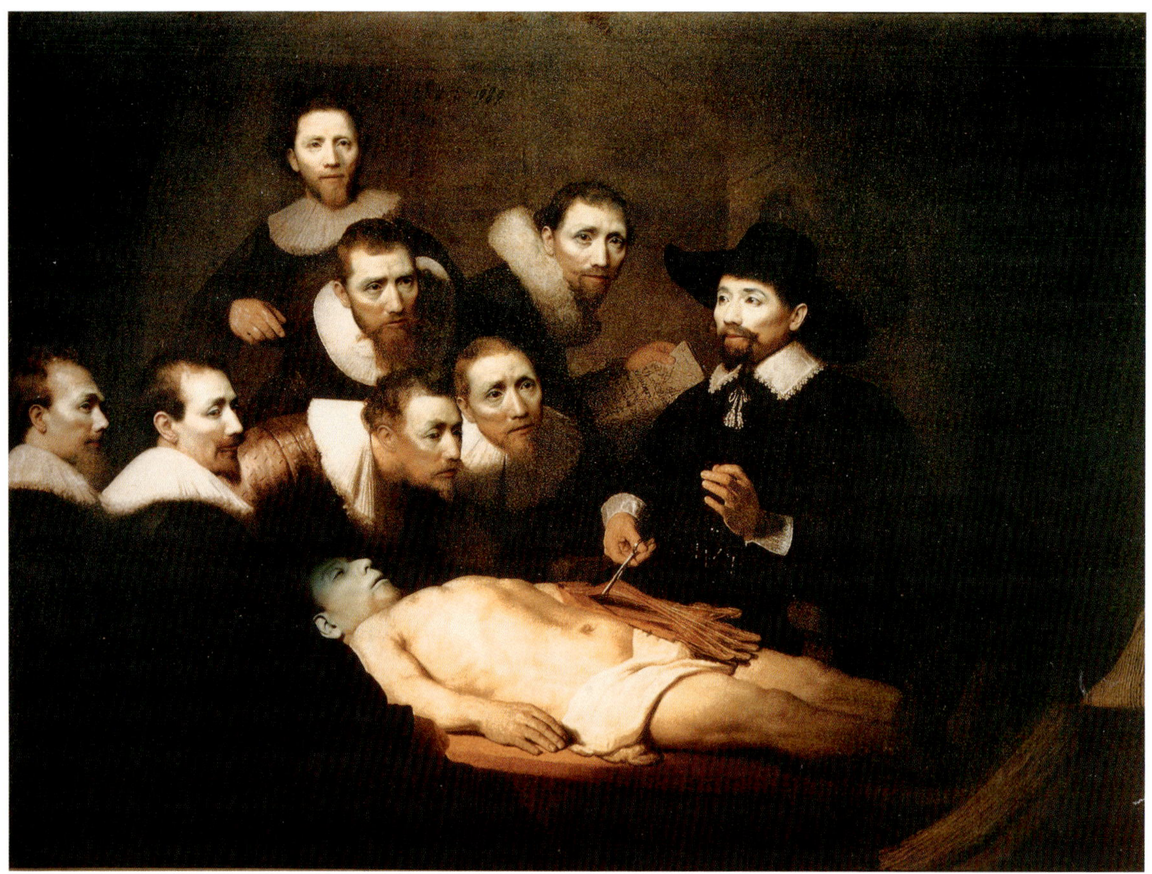

Portrait (Nine Faces)

Morimura Yasumasa (born in 1951)

Heisei era, 1989

Morimura Yasumasa came to global prominence in the late 1980s through his photographic manipulations of iconic Western paintings, including this same-size reworking—complete with gleaming frame—of Rembrandt's celebrated 1632 group portrait *The Anatomy Lesson of Dr. Nicolaes Tulp*. The original painting shows a varied group of strongly characterized individuals, but in Morimura's version all of the faces, both living and dead, are those of the artist himself. This almost vandalistic interpolation of a single set of alien Japanese features, in multiple, serves as a critique of the commodification and self-aggrandizement that characterized much Japanese art acquisition at a time of rampant consumerism, soaring asset values, and frequent financial scandals.

Morimura's mordant commentary, underlined by his choice of a group portrait whose bourgeois sitters vied (and paid) to be depicted, draws a sly contrast between the solid merchants of the Dutch Golden Age and the insecure nouveaux riches of Japan's short-lived boomtime. This and other self-interpolations by Morimura (including the *Mona Lisa* and works by Velázquez, Manet, and Duchamp) are also a comment on Japan's history since the start of the Meiji era, giving expression to a widely held perception that all attempts at "modernization" must inevitably result in a dangerous hybridity that can have disturbing consequences.

Photograph; chromogenic print and gilded frame

196.9 x 250.8 cm (77½ x 98¾ in.)

Ernest Wadsworth Longfellow Fund 1990.493

Metavoid 4

Akiyama Yō (born in 1953)

Heisei era, 2004

Akiyama Yō is a prominent pupil of Yagi Kazuo, the leader of a group that took the Kyoto ceramic world by storm in the late 1940s. Yagi taught a generation of artists to think deeply about the nature of clay and to challenge the dominance of traditional techniques without losing sight of the need for careful workmanship and skilled use of materials. In this piece, Akiyama subverted the normal use of the potter's wheel by throwing rings of clay, burning them on the inside with a blowtorch, and then turning them inside out so that their inner surfaces, cracked and distorted, appeared on the outside. Finally, he used wet clay to join them together and dressed the surfaces with a mixture of vinegar and iron filings before firing the entire piece in a gas kiln. This unusual treatment emphasizes the unfinished appearance of the piece, making it look as though it was dug from the ground after some violent, catastrophic geological event, rather than gradually shaped over the years.

Through the influence of Yagi Kazuo and other postwar leaders, and thanks to decades of steady economic growth, Japan has developed the contemporary world's most flourishing ceramic culture, with a global reach in terms of both artistic influence and penetration of the international art market.

Thrown, gas-burned, cut, folded, and slip-assembled clay
55.9 x 73 x 72.1 cm (22 x 28¾ x 28⅜ in.)
Gift of Alice and Halsey North 2004.2173

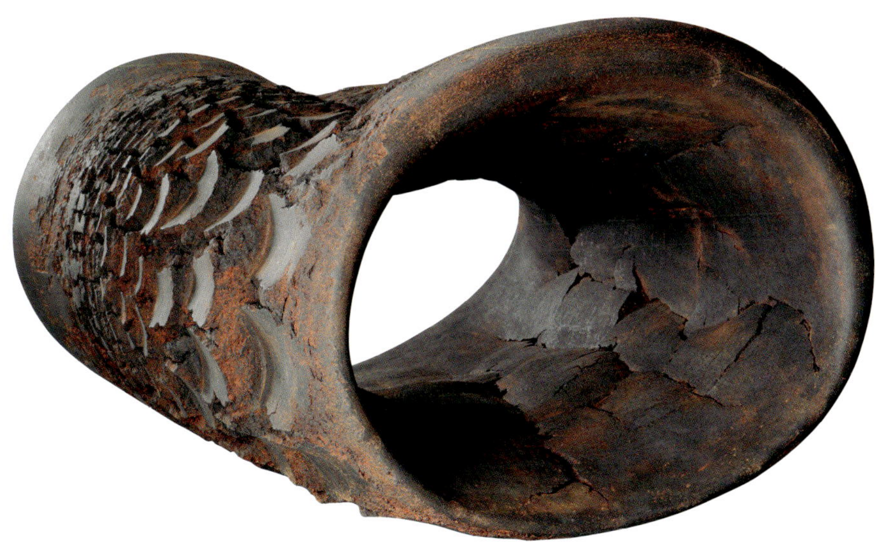

If the Double Helix Wakes Up . . .

Murakami Takashi (born in 1962)

Heisei era, 2002

Since 1992, Murakami Takashi's compositions have frequently included the two-eared figure of Mr. DOB, a cartoonlike character whose name originally developed from the abbreviation of a nonsensical Japanese phrase. Through the years, DOB has been transformed, sometimes appearing as an adorable icon and other times, as in *If the Double Helix Wakes Up . . .* , as a monstrous, fanged creature. The pulsating background of DNA strands in blues and yellows recalls Pop images that Murakami has long emulated; but Murakami, who trained as a traditional artist, has also pointed to the swirling, "super flat" forms of seventeenth-century Japanese painting as an important foundation for his work.

Although he was born more than fifteen years after the end of World War II, Murakami regards the atomic bombings of Hiroshima and Nagasaki as the defining events of his generation of Japanese and their successors. He argues that the subservient role the country was forced to assume under the Occupation and subsequent renewals of the U.S.-Japan Security Treaty has led to the infantalization of Japanese society. Japan's dependence on the West, he argues, has also manifested itself in an obsession with things *kawaii* (cute) and *otaku* (geek culture).

Three panels; acrylic on canvas mounted on wood
250.2 x 399.4 cm (98 1/2 x 157 1/4 in.)
Catherine and Paul Buttenwieser Fund 2002.108

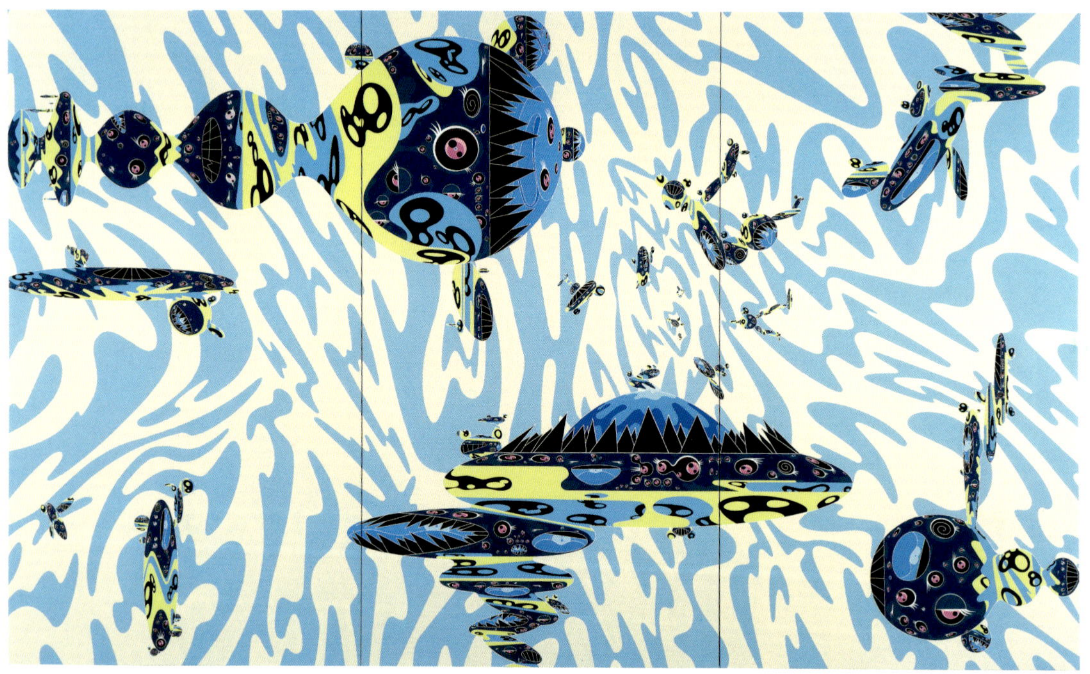

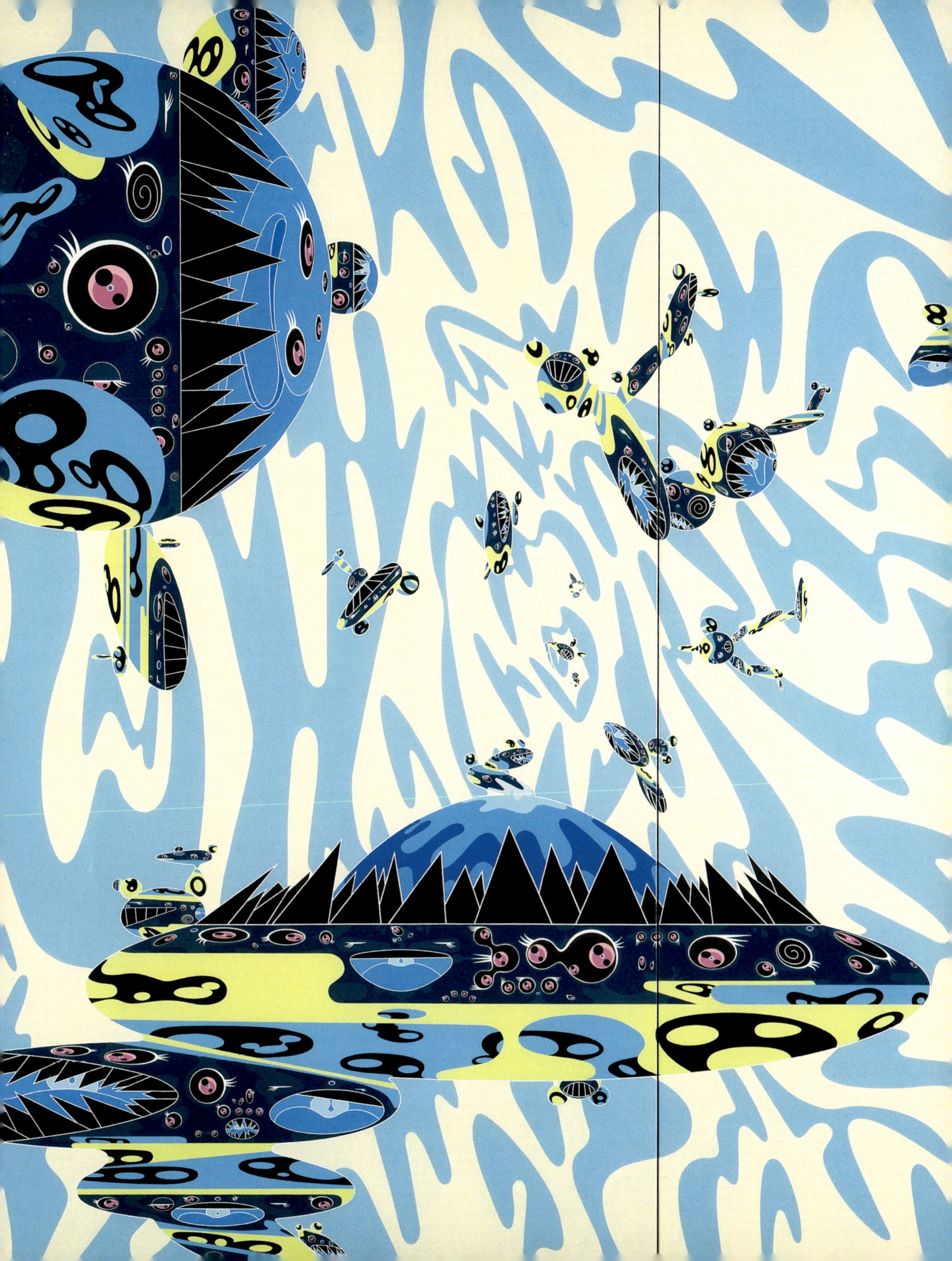

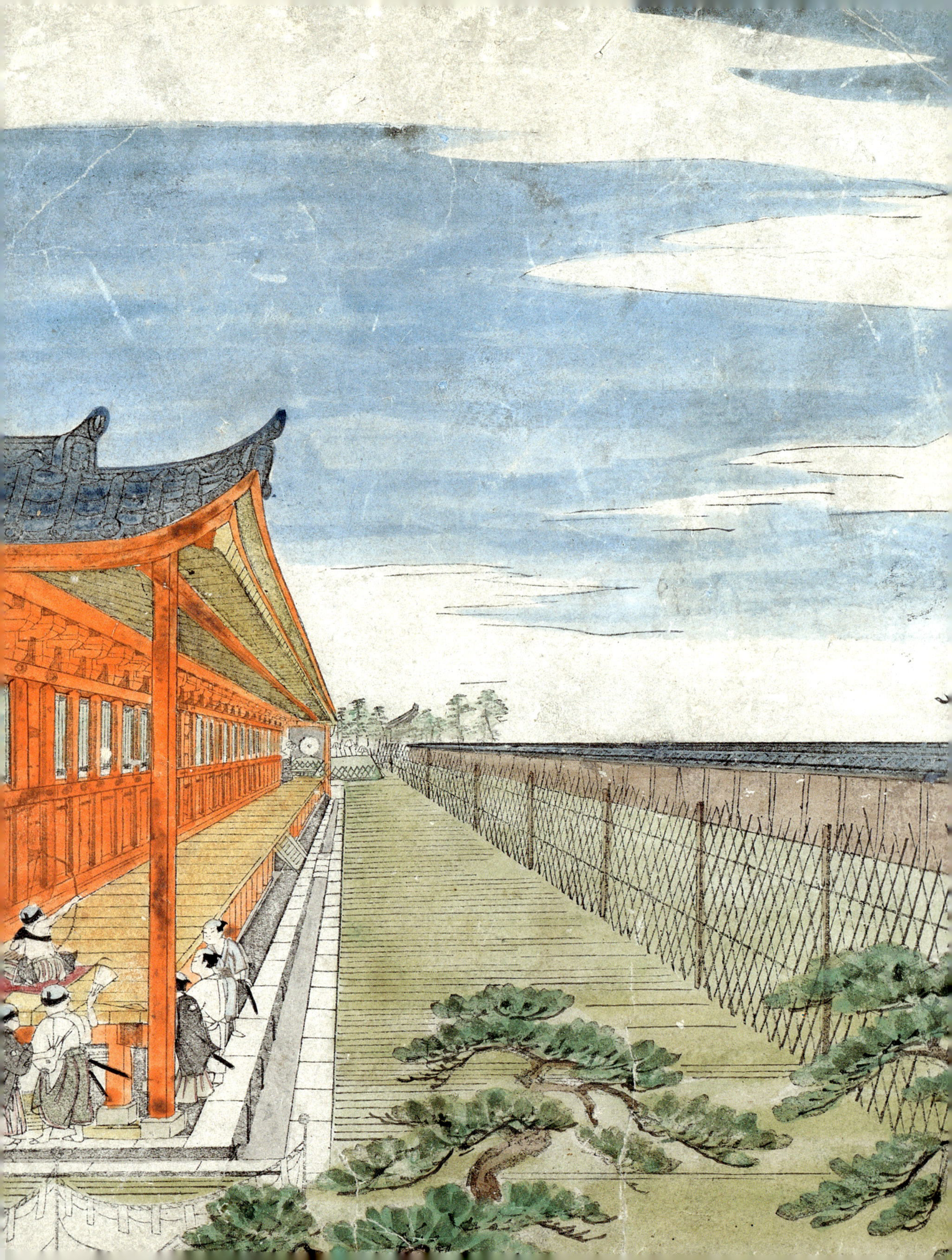

Timeline

Jōmon culture (about 8000–300 B.C.E.)

This hunting-and-gathering culture derives its name from its distinctive "cord-marked" pottery. About 1500 B.C.E., clay figurines (*dogū*) are produced in conjunction with shamanistic rites.

660 B.C.E According to Japanese mythology, Emperor Jimmu, the descendant of the Sun Goddess, ascends the throne.

Yayoi culture (about 300 B.C.E.–300 C.E.)

Rice cultivation, bronze and iron production, and the potter's wheel are introduced to Japan from the Asian continent. Characteristic of Yayoi works are weapons, mirrors, and bells (*dōtaku*), as well as smooth-surfaced utilitarian pottery.

Kofun period (about 300 C.E.–538 C.E.)

"Horse-riding" clans from the continent consolidate power and construct elaborate burial mounds, which are surrounded by clay cylinders (*haniwa*) in the shape of figures, animals, and houses. Among the tomb furnishings are bronze mirrors, swords, and items of personal adornment.

Asuka period (538–710)

Japan is transformed by the adoption of Chinese and Korean political, religious, and cultural institutions. The Yamato clan asserts political authority and the capital is moved from site to site, following the death of individual emperors, within the Asuka region (in central Honshu).

538/552 Traditional date for the introduction of Buddhism to Japan from the Korean kingdom of Baekje.

593 Prince Shōtoku assumes regency during the reign of Empress Suiko. He is said to have issued the Seventeen-Article Constitution, which centralized political authority under the imperial family.

about 607 Hōryū-ji, the earliest extant Buddhist temple in Japan, is established. The triad of Shaka (the Historical Buddha) and his attendants is the principal image. Fashioned from gilt bronze, it displays the linear treatment of body forms and drapery found in Chinese sculpture of the Northern and Southern Dynasties.

Nara period (710–794)

The Japanese enthusiastically embrace Chinese culture, including city planning and architecture, writing systems, and painting and sculptural styles. Buddhist temples flourish under the patronage of the imperial family and aristocratic clans.

710 Nara is established as the first permanent capital.

752 The Great Buddha (Daibutsu) is dedicated at Tōdai-ji, which is designated as the headquarters of a vast network of temples throughout the provinces.

784 The capital is moved to Nagaoka.

Heian period (794–1185)

In order to wrest power from the Buddhist temples in Nara, the imperial family moves the capital to Heian-kyō (present-day Kyoto). Following a break in official diplomatic ties with China, Japan adapts continental culture to its own native predilections. During the ninth century, the aristocratic Fujiwara family secures authority at court by serving as regents to successive emperors and ushers in an age known for its high aestheticism.

794 Heian-kyō becomes the capital of Japan.

806 The monk Kūkai returns from China with texts and objects that become the basis for Esoteric Buddhist ritual in Japan.

894 Japan discontinues official missions to China.

about 1000 Lady Murasaki writes *The Tale of Genji (Genji monogatari)*, the world's first novel.

1053 The temple Byōdō-in is constructed at the behest of Fujiwara no Yorimichi. The central image of Amida, Buddha of Infinite Light, by Jōchō becomes a model for sculpture produced throughout Japan in the eleventh and twelfth centuries.

1149 The sculpture *Dainichi, the Buddha of Infinite Illumination* (MFA) is dedicated, perpetuating the Jōchō style.

1159–60 The Taira and Minamoto warrior clans fight the Heiji Rebellion in support of rival factions of the court; the Taira prevail. The burning of the Sanjō Palace is the subject of the *Illustrated Scrolls of the Events of the Heiji Era* (MFA).

1180–85 The Taira and Minamoto fight the Genpei War over military control of Japan; this time, the Minamoto prevail. During the fighting, much of the ancient capital of Nara is destroyed by fire.

Kamakura period (1185–1333)

Although the emperor remains in Kyoto, the Minamoto family moves the seat of political power to Kamakura in eastern Japan. Warrior culture emphasizes a sparer, assertive aesthetic. With the arrival of Zen monks from China, interest in continental learning is renewed.

1189 Kaikei, one of the leading sculptors of the day, dedicates the image *Miroku, the Bodhisattva of the Future* (MFA) to the memories of his parents and teacher. Sculpture achieves a new naturalism under the Kei school.

1191 The Buddhist priest Eisai introduces Zen Buddhism to Japan.

1192 Minamoto no Yoritomo is appointed shogun, the official military leader of the country, by Emperor Go-Toba.

1269 Saichi's sculpture *Shō Kannon, the Bodhisattva of Compassion* (MFA) is dedicated.

1328 Kōshun's sculpture *Hachiman in the Guise of a Buddhist Monk* (MFA) is dedicated.

Nanbokuchō period (1333–1392)

Emperor Go-Daigo overthrows the Kamakura shogunate and tries to reassert the political authority of the imperial family, ushering in the period of the Northern and Southern Dynasties.

Muromachi period (1392–1568)

Members of the Ashikaga family assume the position of shogun and return the seat of political power to Kyoto. Enamored of Chinese culture, the elite import ink paintings and ceramics from the continent, which are then emulated by Japanese artists.

1397 Ashikaga Yoshimitsu builds the Golden Pavilion (Kinkaku) in the Kitayama district of Kyoto as part of his residential complex.

1483 Ashikaga Yoshimasa constructs the Silver Pavilion (Ginkaku) in the Higashiyama district of Kyoto as part of his residential complex. The Tōgudō, one of the adjacent buildings, contains the first room designed for tea ritual.

1543 Portuguese sailors make an accidental landing on Tanegashima. Contact with the West results in the importation of commodities such as woolens, firearms, and tobacco.

Momoyama period (1568–1615)

In the age of castle building, civil war engulfs Japan. Three successive warlords, Oda Nobunaga, Toyotomi Hideyoshi, and Tokugawa Ieyasu, attempt to unify the country.

1568 Oda Nobunaga seizes control of Kyoto.

1582 Nobunaga is assassinated and his general Toyotomi Hideyoshi assumes power.

1592–93 Hideyoshi unsuccessfully invades Korea.

1597–99 Hideyoshi invades Korea for a second time. Although his death ends the brutal campaign, Japanese soldiers return home with Korean potters, who will later develop the Japanese ceramics industry.

1600 Tokugawa Ieyasu emerges as the most powerful warlord following the Battle of Sekigahara.

1603 Ieyasu is appointed shogun and moves the seat of political authority to Edo (present-day Tokyo). The first performance of Kabuki theater is staged by itinerant female entertainers; later, only mature male actors will be allowed to perform.

Edo period (1615–1868)

The Tokugawa usher in an age of peace and prosperity. Castle towns—the largest of which is Edo—develop a sophisticated urban culture, and literacy becomes widespread.

1615 The Tokugawa defeat the remaining Toyotomi forces at Osaka Castle. Confucian-based regulations are promulgated to govern the behavior of all classes.

1627 *The Tale of the Soga Brothers* (MFA), a woodblock-printed illustrated book with movable-type text and hand-coloring, is published.

1639 The shogunate expels all Westerners from Japan, with the exception of the Dutch, who are permitted an outpost in Nagasaki harbor.

1657 The Meireki Fire destroys Edo, and the city is forced to rebuild.

1704 The woodblock print *Actor Tsutsui Kichijūrō in the Spear Dance* (MFA), attributed to Torii Kiyonobu I, is published.

1715 Torii Kiyomasu I's woodblock print *Actor Fujimura Handayū II as Ōiso no Tora* (MFA) is published.

1764 Sō Shiseki's hanging scroll *Willow, Flower, and Bird* (MFA) reflects the influence of Chinese compositions then available in the port of Nagasaki.

1765 The full-color woodblock print is developed.

1789 The luxury woodblock-printed book *Gifts of the Ebb Tide* (MFA), by Kitagawa Utamaro, is published.

1794 Tōshūsai Sharaku's woodblock print *Actors Sawamura Yodogorō II as Kawatsura Hōgen and Bandō Zenji as Oni no Sadobō* (MFA) is published.

1830 The woodblock print *Actors Onoe Kikugorō III as Shizuka Gozen and Nakamura Utaemon III as the Fox Tadanobu* (MFA), by the Osaka artist Ryūsai Shigeharu, is published.

1834 The literati artist Yamamoto Baiitsu completes his painting *Flowering Plum Tree* (MFA).

1854 Commodore Matthew Perry of the United States forces the Japanese government to reopen the country to trade.

Meiji era (1868–1912)

With the reestablishment of the emperor as the sole political authority, Japan embarks upon an unprecedented mission to modernize and Westernize the country.

1868 The new government is established under the leadership of Mutsuhito, the Meiji emperor.

1873 The Gregorian calendar replaces the lunar calendar system.

1887 Toyohara Chikanobu's woodblock print *Excursion to View Cherry Blossoms by the Sumida River* (MFA) documents the adoption of Western dress by the imperial family.

1889 The Tokyo School of Fine Arts (Tokyo Bijutsu Gakkō) is founded.

1894–95 The Sino-Japanese War is fought.

1904–5 The Russo-Japanese War is fought. Japan emerges as an international power after signing the Treaty of Portsmouth in 1905, concluding the war.

1906–7 Furuya Kōrin's woodblock-printed book *Patterns of Plants and Flowers from Nature* (MFA) and Ichijō Narumi's postcard *Female Nude Seated in Water* (MFA) reflect the influence of Art Nouveau.

Taishō era (1912–1926)

Seeking greater affluence and sophisticated cosmopolitanism, young people migrate to Japan's cities. Increasingly, the country becomes disillusioned by its relationship with the West.

1912 Toshihito, the Taishō emperor, ascends the throne.

1914–18 Japan joins the Allied forces in World War I.

1923 The Great Kantō Earthquake decimates the Tokyo-Yokohama region, forcing the cities to rebuild.

Shōwa era (1926–1989)

Japan seeks to expand its sphere of influence on the Asian continent, leading to World War II. Following the bombing of Hiroshima and Nagasaki and the Occupation by the Allied Forces, the country reexamines its past. The rebuilding of Japan leads to unparalleled economic growth.

1926 Hirohito, the Shōwa emperor, ascends the throne.

1934 Tateishi Harumi's *Clover* (MFA), a monumental painting that synthesizes Japanese and Western techniques, is exhibited at the Shin-Bunten exhibition sponsored by the Japanese Ministry of Education.

1937–45 Japan attacks China, eventually leading to World War II. Japan becomes an ally of the Axis powers.

1945 Hiroshima and Nagasaki are destroyed by nuclear bombs and Japan surrenders. The Allied Occupation begins.

1948 *Poem No. 6: Image de la Mer* (MFA) is produced by the "creative print" (*sōsaku hanga*) artist Onchi Kōshirō.

1952 The Allied Occupation ends.

1964 The Tokyo Olympics provide an opportunity for Japan to showcase its new economy. Tange Kenzō constructs the Olympic Stadium in Yoyogi, Tokyo.

1978 Photographer Sugimoto Hiroshi issues the gelatin silver print *Radio City Music Hall, New York* (MFA).

1984 Abstract artist Shinoda Tōkō produces the lithograph *Avanti*.

1988 Innovative designer Kuramata Shirō produces the chair *Miss Blanche* (MFA).

Heisei era (1989–present)

With the boom in technology, popular Japanese culture excites the international community. Japanese artists regularly exhibit their work throughout the world.

1989 Akihito, the Heisei emperor, ascends the throne.

Morimoto Yasumasa produces *Portrait (Nine Faces)* (MFA), his interpretation of Rembrandt's *The Anatomy Lesson of Dr. Nicolaes Tulp*.

1991 Moriyama Daidō issues the photograph *Store Opening Flowers* (MFA) in a project for Hysteric Glamour.

1994 Designer Miyake Issey presents the *Flying Saucer* dress (MFA) as part of his collection.

2002 Murakami Takashi completes the painting *If the Double Helix Wakes Up . . .* (MFA).

2004 Sculptor-ceramicist Akiyama Yō produces *Metavoid 4* (MFA).

2005 Honda Shōryū creates the basket *Mountain River (Yamakawa)* (MFA).

Further Reading

General

Akiyama, Terukazu. *Japanese Painting*. Geneva: Editions d'Art Albert Skira, 1961.

Coaldrake, William H. *Architecture and Authority in Japan*. London: Routledge, 1996.

Mason, Penelope E. *History of Japanese Art*. New York: Harry N. Abrams, 1993. 2nd ed., Upper Saddle River, NJ: Pearson/Prentice Hall, 2004.

Morse, Anne Nishimura, and Nobuo Tsuji, eds. *Japanese Art in the Museum of Fine Arts, Boston*. 2 vols. Boston: Museum of Fine Arts, Boston; Tokyo: Kōdansha, 1998.

Museum of Fine Arts, Boston. *Selected Masterpieces of Asian Art*. Boston: Museum of Fine Arts, Boston, 1992.

Paine, Robert Treat, and Alexander Soper. *Art and Architecture of Japan*. 3rd ed. New Haven, CT: Yale University Press, 1992.

Sharf, Frederic A. *Art of Collecting: The Spaulding Brothers and Their Legacy*. Boston: MFA Publications, 2007.

Varley, H. Paul. *Japanese Culture*. 4th ed. Honolulu: University of Hawai'i Press, 2000.

Art of the Temple

Addiss, Stephen. *The Art of Zen: Paintings and Calligraphy by Japanese Monks, 1600–1925*. New York: Harry N. Abrams, 1989.

Fontein, Jan, and Money L. Hickman. *Zen Painting and Calligraphy*. Exh. cat. Boston: Museum of Fine Arts, Boston, 1970.

Graham, Patricia J. *Faith and Power in Japanese Buddhist Art, 1600–2005*. Honolulu: University of Hawai'i Press, 2007.

Kageyama, Haruki. *The Arts of Shinto*. Translated and adapted by Christine Guth. New York: Weatherhill, 1973.

Morse, Anne Nishimura, and Samuel C. Morse. *Object as Insight: Japanese Buddhist Art and Ritual*. Exh. cat. Katonah, NY: Katonah Museum of Art, 1996.

Nishikawa, Kyōtarō, and Emily J. Sano. *The Great Age of Japanese Buddhist Sculpture, AD 600–1300*. Exh. cat. Fort Worth, TX: Kimbell Art Museum; New York: Japan Society, 1982.

Rosenfield, John M., and Elizabeth ten Grotenhuis. *Journey of the Three Jewels: Japanese Buddhist Paintings from Western Collections*. Exh. cat. New York: The Asia Society, 1979.

Saunders, E. Dale. *Mudrā: A Study of Symbolic Gestures in Japanese Buddhist Sculpture*. New York: Pantheon Books, 1960.

ten Grotenhuis, Elizabeth. *Japanese Mandalas: Representations of Sacred Geography*. Honolulu: University of Hawai'i Press, 1999.

Art of the Ruling Classes

Earle, Joe. *Lethal Elegance: The Art of Samurai Sword Fittings*. Boston: MFA Publications, 2004.

Hickman, Money, et al. *Japan's Golden Age: Momoyama*. Exh. cat. New Haven, CT: Yale University Press in association with Sun & Star 1996 and the Dallas Museum of Art, 1996.

McCullough, Helen Craig, trans. *The Tale of the Heike*. Stanford, CA: Stanford University Press, 1988.

Montreal Museum of Fine Arts. *The Japan of the Shoguns: The Tokugawa Collection*. Exh. cat. Montreal: Montreal Museum of Fine Arts, 1989.

Morris, Ivan I. *The World of the Shining Prince: Court Life in Ancient Japan*. New York: Kodansha International, 1994. First published 1964 by Oxford University Press and Alfred A. Knopf.

Murasaki Shikibu. *The Tale of Genji*. Translated by Royall Tyler. New York: Penguin Books, 2001.

Murase, Miyeko, ed. *Turning Point: Oribe and the Arts of Sixteenth-Century Japan*. Exh. cat. New Haven, CT: Yale University Press; New York: Metropolitan Museum of Art, 2003.

Museum of Fine Arts, Boston. *Courtly Splendor: Twelve Centuries of Treasures from Japan*. Boston: Museum of Fine Arts, Boston, 1990.

Shimizu, Yoshiaki, ed. *Japan: The Shaping of Daimyo Culture, 1185–1868*. Exh. cat. New York: G. Braziller; Washington, DC: National Gallery of Art, 1988.

Takeda, Sharon Sadako. *Miracles and Mischief: Noh and Kyōgen Theater in Japan*. In collaboration with Monica

Bethe. Exh. cat. Los Angeles: Los Angeles County Museum of Art, 2002.

Varley, H. Paul. *Warriors of Japan as Portrayed in the War Tales*. Honolulu: University of Hawai'i Press, 1994.

Varley, H. Paul, and Kumakura Isao, eds. *Tea in Japan: Essays on the History of Chanoyu*. Honolulu: University of Hawai'i Press, 1989.

Art of the Town

Clark, Timothy, Anne Nishimura Morse, Louise E. Virgin, and Allen Hockley. *The Dawn of the Floating World, 1650–1765: Early Ukiyo-e Treasures from the Museum of Fine Arts, Boston*. Exh. cat. London: Royal Academy of Arts, 2001.

Earle, Joe. *Netsuke: Fantasy and Reality in Japanese Miniature Sculpture*. Exh. cat. Boston: MFA Publications, 2001.

Elison, George, and Bardwell L. Smith, eds. *Warlords, Artists, and Commoners: Japan in the Sixteenth Century*. Honolulu: University of Hawai'i Press, 1981.

Guth, Christine. *Art of Edo Japan: The Artist and the City, 1615–1868*. New York: Harry N. Abrams, 1996.

Keyes, Roger S. Ehon: *The Artist and the Book in Japan*. Exh. cat. New York: New York Public Library; Seattle: University of Washington Press, 2006.

Kobayashi, Tadashi. *Ukiyo-e: An Introduction to Japanese Woodblock Prints*. Translated by Mark A. Harbison. Tokyo: Kodansha International, 1992.

Meech, Julia, and Jane Oliver, eds. *Designed for Pleasure: The World of Edo Japan in Prints and Paintings, 1680–1860*. Exh. cat. New York: Asia Society and Japanese Art Society of America; Seattle: University of Washington Press, 2008.

Morse, Anne Nishimura, ed. *Drama and Desire: Japanese Paintings from the Floating World, 1690–1850*. Exh. cat. Boston: MFA Publications, 2007.

Nagata, Seiji. Hokusai: *Genius of the Japanese Ukiyo-e*. Translated by John Bester. Tokyo: Kodansha, 1995.

Newland, Amy Reigle, ed. *The Hotei Encyclopedia of Japanese Woodblock Prints*. 2 vols. Amsterdam: Hotei Publishing, 2005.

Rosenfield, John M. *Extraordinary Persons: Works by Eccentric, Non-Conformist Japanese Artists of the Early Modern Era (1580–1868) in the Collection of Kimiko and John Powers*. In collaboration with Fumiko E. Cranston. Edited by Naomi Noble Richard. 3 vols. Cambridge, MA: Harvard University Art Museums, 1999.

Shirane, Haruo, ed. *Early Modern Japanese Literature: An Anthology, 1600–1900*. New York: Columbia University Press, 2002.

Singer, Robert T., et al. *Edo: Art in Japan, 1615–1868*. Exh. cat. Washington, DC: National Gallery of Art, 1998.

Japan and the Outside World

Brown, Kendall, Anne Nishimura Morse, and J. Thomas Rimer. *Art of the Japanese Postcard: The Leonard A. Lauder Collection at the Museum of Fine Arts, Boston*. Exh. cat. Boston: MFA Publications, 2004.

Conant, Ellen P. *Nihonga, Transcending the Past: Japanese-Style Painting, 1868–1968*. In collaboration with Steven D. Owyoung and J. Thomas Rimer. Exh. cat. New York: Weatherhill; St. Louis, MO: St. Louis Art Museum, 1995.

Dobson, Sebastian, Anne Nishimura Morse, and Frederic A. Sharf. *Art and Artifice: Japanese Photographs of the Meiji Era*. Exh. cat. Boston: MFA Publications, 2004.

Earle, Joe. *Splendors of Imperial Japan: Arts of the Meiji Period from the Khalili Collection*. Exh. cat. London: The Khalili Family Trust, 2002.

French, Calvin L., Tadashi Sugase, and Kiichi Usui. *Through Closed Doors: Western Influence on Japanese Art, 1639–1853*. Exh. cat. Kobe, Japan: Kobe City Museum of Namban Art; Rochester, MI: Meadow Brook Art Gallery, 1977.

Hiesinger, Kathryn B., and Felice Fischer. *Japanese Design: A Survey since 1950*. Exh. cat. Philadelphia: Philadelphia Museum of Art in association with Harry N. Abrams, 1994.

Keene, Donald, Anne Nishimura Morse, Frederic A. Sharf, and Louise E. Virgin. *Japan at the Dawn of the Modern Age: Woodblock Prints from the Meiji Era, 1868–1912*. Exh. cat. Boston: MFA Publications, 2001.

Munroe, Alexandra. *Japanese Art After 1945: Scream Against the Sky*. Exh. cat. New York: Harry N. Abrams, 1994.

Tucker, Anne Wilkes, et al. *The History of Japanese Photography*. Exh. cat. Edited and translated by John Junkerman. New Haven, CT: Yale University Press in association with the Museum of Fine Arts, Houston, 2003.

Figure Illustrations

Unless otherwise noted, all objects are in the collection of the Museum of Fine Arts, Boston.

fig. 1, p. 12
Detail of *Woman Looking at Herself in a Mirror*, 11.7424 (see p. 172)

fig. 2, p. 14
La Japonaise (Camille Monet in Japanese Costume)
Claude Monet (French, 1840–1926)
1876
Oil on canvas
1951 Purchase Fund 56.147

fig. 3, p. 15
Interior of a Bathhouse
Torii Kiyonaga (1752–1815)
Edo period, about 1787
Woodblock print (*nishiki-e*); ink and color on paper
William Sturgis Bigelow Collection
30.46–7

fig. 4, p. 16
Photograph of Morse, Okakura, Fenollosa, and Bigelow, 1882, Japan

fig. 5, p. 17
Transcendent Attacking a Whirlwind
Soga Shōhaku (1730–1781)
Edo period, about 1764
Six-panel folding screen; ink and light gold on paper
Fenollosa-Weld Collection 11.4510

fig. 6, p. 20
Fireflies at Ochanomizu
Kobayashi Kiyochika (1847–1915)
Meiji era, about 1880
Woodblock print (*nishiki-e*); ink and color on paper
William Sturgis Bigelow Collection
11.26605

fig. 7, p. 21
The Fine Arts Museum and the Shōjō Fountain at the Second National Industrial Exposition in Ueno Park
Utagawa Hiroshige III (1842–1894)
Meiji era, 1881
Woodblock print (*nishiki-e*); ink and color on paper
Jean S. and Frederic A. Sharf Collection
2000.508a–c

fig. 8, p. 21
Jar
Muromachi period, 15th century
Shigaraki ware; stoneware with natural ash glaze
Morse Collection. Museum purchase with funds donated by contribution
92.3509

fig. 9, p. 23
Dragon and Snake
Katsushika Hokusai (1760–1849)
Edo period, about 1804–18
Painting for a paper lantern; ink and light color on paper
William Sturgis Bigelow Collection
11.9113

fig. 10, p. 30
Detail of *The Death of the Historical Buddha*, 11.4221 (see pp. 72–73)

fig. 11, p. 32
Main Image Hall (Great Buddha Hall) at Tōdai-ji, Nara, originally constructed in 752, last rebuilt in 1962
Photo courtesy of Tōdai-ji

fig. 12, p. 33
Detail of *The Transformation of Māra's Arrows and the Temptation by Māra's Daughters* (see p. 77)

fig. 13, p. 34
Detail of *Bodhisattva*, 12.128 (see p. 39)

fig. 14, p. 37
Detail of ritual banner with decoration of Sanskrit characters, 1972.857 (see p. 79)

fig. 15, p. 86
Detail of *A Tale of Brief Slumbers (Utatane sōshi)*, 11.9456 (see pp. 112–13)

fig. 16, p. 86
Detail of *Night Attack on the Sanjō Palace*, 11.4000 (see pp. 94–95)

fig. 17, p. 87
Detail of *The Picture Contest*, from *The Tale of Genji* (*Genji monogatari*), 11.7131 (see p. 114)

fig. 18, p. 90
Himeji Castle (built 1601–18) seen from the north
Photo courtesy of Kōdansha Ltd. and Himeji City

fig. 19, p. 91
Detail of poem from the *Anthology of Ancient and Modern Poems* (*Kokin-shū*) with design of wisteria (see p. 115)

fig. 20, p. 97
Detail of *Night Attack on the Sanjō Palace*, 11.4000 (see pp. 94–95)

fig. 21, p. 99
Detail of *Night Attack on the Sanjō Palace*, 11.4000 (see pp. 94–95)

fig. 22, p. 133
Observance of the Obon Festival, from *Famous Places in Kyoto in the Twelve Months*
Yokoyama Kakei (1816–1864)
Edo period, 1858
Section of a handscroll; ink, color, and gold on silk
William Sturgis Bigelow Collection 22.432

fig. 23, p. 134
Detail of *Scenes from the Pleasure Quarters of Kyoto*, 06.286 (see pp. 140–41)

fig. 24, p. 135
Colors of the Triple Dawn (*Saishiki mitsu no asa*)
Torii Kiyonaga (1752–1815)
Edo period, 1787
Woodblock printed book; ink and color on paper
Nellie P. Carter Collection. Bequest of Nellie Parney Carter 34.395

fig. 25, p. 138
Detail of *Scenes from the Nakamura Kabuki Theater and the Yoshiwara Pleasure Quarter*, 79.468 (see pp. 156–57)

fig. 26, p. 189
Alternate view of *Minister Kibi's Trip to China*, 32.131 (see p. 194)

fig. 27, p. 190
Detail of *European King and Members of His Court*, 11.4312 (see p. 195)

fig. 28, p. 191
Detail of *Excursion to View Cherry Blossoms by the Sumida River*, 2000.496a–c (see p. 205)

fig. 29, p. 192
Detail of *Tearoom*
Saeki Shunkō (1909–1942)
Shōwa era, 1936
Ink, color, and silver on paper
Charles H. Bayley Picture and Painting Fund and Museum purchase with funds donated anonymously 2007.815

Index

Page numbers in italics indicate illustrations.